Virgin
rock
yearbook
93/94

1215

Virgin Rock Yearboot pic by Stephen Sweet

Virgin rock yearbook 93/94

1215

edited by tony horkins

Virgin

First published in Great Britain in 1993 by
Virgin Books
an imprint of Virgin Publishing Ltd
332 Ladbroke Grove
London W10 5AH

A catalogue record for this book is available from the
British Library

ISBN 0 86369 767 4

**Produced by The Cooling Brown Partnership,
Hampton, Middlesex for Virgin Publishing Ltd**

Editor: Tony Horkins
Art Direction: Mark Norton at 4i
Design: Sue Rawkins
Assistant Editor: Chris Roberts
Editorial Manager: James Harrison
Picture Research: Hannah Platten
Computer page make-up: Mick Goodrum
Production: Rupert Wheeler
Colour reproduction: Wellmak Ltd, Hong Kong

Printed and bound in Great Britain by Bath Colour
Books, Glasgow

Contributors:
The Year In Review: Nick Duerden, Tom Doyle,
Chris Roberts and Tony Horkins
On The Record/Critics' A-Z: Tom Doyle
Off The Record: Graeme Kay and Nicola Martin
Listings: Zane
Acts of the year/Genres/Misc: Phil Alexander,
Lloyd Bradley, Glyn Brown, David Davies, Chas de
Whalley, David Hutcheon, Cliff Jones, Paul Lester,
Caitlin Moran, Sylvia Patterson, Mal Peachey, Chris
Roberts, Roger St Pierre, Martin Townsend, Paul
Trynka, Jon Wilde and Simon Williams

UK chart information © CIN, from data supplied by Gallup
US charts supplied by Billboard © BPI Communications

Picture Credits: Record labels
A & M Records
Arista
Atlantic
Carlton
Chrysalis
Circa Records
Columbia
Eastwest
EMI Records
Epic
Fiction
Greensleeves Records
Maverick
Motown
Nude
Polygram Video
Polydor
RCA
Reprise
Rykodisc Europe
SBK Records
Silvertone Records
Sire
Uk Records
Virgin Records
Vision Video Ltd
Warner Bros
Warner Home Video
WEA
Wild Card

Picture Credits: Photographers
Alexa Dalby
Andrew MacPherson
Anton Corbijn
Christophe Kutner
David Scheinmann
Eddie Monsoon
Fin Costello
James Fry
Jean Baptiste Mondino
Joel Bernstein
John Swannell
Jon Mided
Kevin Davies
Kevin Westenberg
Kristine Larsen
Lawrence Watson
Lorenzo Agius
Lynn Goldsmith
Mark Borthwick
Matt Anker
Melodie McDaniel
Michael Aalsmand
Patrick Demarchelier
Paul Tyagi
Pete Cronin
Peter Gabriel
Peter Gravelle
Peter Stone
Phil Knott
Phil Ward
Preston
Richard James
Richard Lohr
Roger Hilton
Steve Double
Steve Pyke
Tom Sheehan
Watal Asanuma
Yudi Elizondo

contents

● **Compiling a volume like the Rock Yearbook is clearly a time of intense activity, but I think we can beat that this year – anyone involved in Virgin 1215 will testify that nothing they have ever done was as exhausting, challenging or rewarding as creating a brand new national commercial rock station.**

From the moment in April that Richard Branson handed over to Richard Skinner, we have been on air 24 hours a day, seven days a week, broadcasting the music that millions of rock fans have been waiting for all their lives. And they are listening to us in ever-increasing numbers, which means that there will be more exhausting, challenging and satisfying years to come, as we ensure that the 'much more music' station goes from strength to strength.

And it's much more new music too, because while classic album music has its place, such tracks as *What's Up* by 4 Non Blondes and *Runaway Train* by Soul Asylum sit proudly at the top of the most-played list covering our first months on air. That surprised a few people, I'm pleased to say.

So it's entirely appropriate that we should be associated with the Virgin Rock Yearbook 93/94. This is a one-stop guide to a whole year of music, compiled with the kind of informed attitude that we know serious rock music lovers appreciate – it's what we do ourselves, after all.

In these 192 pages you will find a complete month-by-month review of 52 weeks of intense activity in the music business, with a featured album and live act for each month, plus news, quotes, key dates and off-the-wall snippets.

Ten acts of the year are profiled in depth – from kd lang to U2 to Arrested Development – along with a look at what's been happening in every major music genre. There's a critics' A-Z of the major releases of the year; reviews of significant books, films, videos and fanzines; complete UK and US chart listings for every week between September 1992 and August 1993, concentrating – as we do at the station – on the album charts. There are special feature pieces from Virgin 1215 presenters, as well as a reference section with contacts and addresses for the UK music industry. This is a Yearbook that's crisp, that's detailed, and has a very definite edge.

It's good to see the Virgin Rock Yearbook back; the proofs have been essential reading in our offices for the last few weeks. Enjoy it – and keep listening.

by **David Campbell,** *Chief Executive* of **Virgin 1215**

The heart of the machine

Virgin 1215 has one of the most sophisticated radio studios in the world. *Joint programme director* **John Revell** looks at the huge benefits that this studio brings to the whole station.

" ... A paperless, but not a people-less, studio."

Setting a completely brand new radio station in motion – from scratch, in around four months – was extraordinary, exhilarating and exhausting. Something that I insisted on from day one was that the new station would have the very best in studio technology. Yes, to be more efficient and to create a unique sound, but also to let the presenters concentrate on what they're best at – presenting.

Anyone who's worked in radio knows the chaos that usually reigns supreme in the studio: endless pieces of paper falling off the desk, albums in the wrong sleeve, faded marker boards with a playlist from somewhere in the late 60s, logging sheets lying like guano on the floor. A recipe for mayhem.

The system we settled on for Virgin 1215 aims to cut out the hassle and the headaches. At the heart of the system is the brand new RCS Master Control computer into which feed our Selector music programming computer and also our traffic (commercials) scheduling computer.

As well as enabling us to create Virgin 1215's unique music policy, Selector also takes care of most of the mundane logging of PRS royalty payments. Initially, there was some reluctance from the presenters when it came to using this state of the art system, but after a couple of months their confidence grew and I think if I decided to take it away they would probably never speak to me again (on second thoughts!). The most important thing to remember about this new technology is that it's only a tool, it doesn't dictate what we do on air, and is really only as good as the people who use it.

The Selector hooks up to Master Control, a truly fantastic piece of kit, which is the real brains of the set-up and integrates virtually every part of our operation: displaying the complete running order, controlling the hard disk that contains all the commercials, jingles and sweepers (those 'coming next' type pieces) as well as our current playlist tracks, and displaying scripts and background information for the presenters. And it takes on a few chores like working out all the invoices for ads, which of course we'd love to do, but we're gracious enough to leave up to Master Control.

What does all this mean in the studio? Well, if you walk into the main studio (on air 24 hours a day, but just knock first) overlooking the gardens in Golden Square, the main impression is one of light and space. We were very keen to create a pleasant working environment for the jocks. Most studios tend to be situated in the middle of a building with no natural daylight. The presenters get a great view and facing them are three main monitors: the one on the left shows them the running order, which is entered in advance, and gives them all the timings they need as well as telling them what they need to be looking for next.

The hard disk automatically runs the playlist tracks, but for the rest of the music all they have to do is turn round to the Wall of Sound behind, where we rack over 1500 CDs, each in a CD cart which can be slammed straight into the machine.

Ahead of them is the linker monitor which flashes up any scripts or information the presenters need, while over on the right is a cart wall and a screen linked up to a hot key pad so that they can get instant access to jingles and sweepers. Because everything is digital there's no need to rewind anything – it's always instantaneously available – and there's an additional feature that allows the presenter to preview the intro, hook or outro of a track while still broadcasting the track in real time.

Everything runs off Master Control. We were the first station in the UK to use it (others have now realised the immense benefits) and we were certainly only the second station in the world to install the system. The first, a Paris station, trust it so much that everyone can go home at 8.30 and leave it in command over night, merrily playing away all night. At 1215, we still prefer to keep a hefty human involvement. A paperless, but not a people-less, studio.

When anyone comes to look round the set-up they are universally knocked out, but inevitably ask, "What happens if it screws up?" Without touching wood, I'd say the system is pretty well bomb-proof – we have two identical back-up systems running in tandem with the main computer. If by any slim chance all three should fail, then we have a complete extra back-up of everything on digicart 3½ inch computer disks.

As a final failsafe if we're doing outside broadcasts like the Breakfast Shows from Toronto and Sydney, we have one of the presenters back in London mirroring every move the guys overseas are making, again just in case. In reality the quality on these OBs is exceptional, since we use an ISDN system that sends the broadcast digitally down a phone line. Not only does it sound great, but it costs about one tenth of a satellite link and whereas if a satellite link goes down it can be very difficult to hook up again, if the phone line goes down you just call back. We use the same ISDN system for live events – like the U2 gig in August – for the same reasons: it's good, it's stable and it's incredibly cost-effective.

The signal created in our studios or received from outside is then treated in what looks like a small cupboard of electronics just outside the studios (which is basically what it is) where we compress the sound, beef it up and send it down a land line to a transmitter in Crystal Palace, whack it up 30,000 miles to a satellite and beam it back down to transmitters all round the nation.

And that's how Virgin 1215 reaches you.

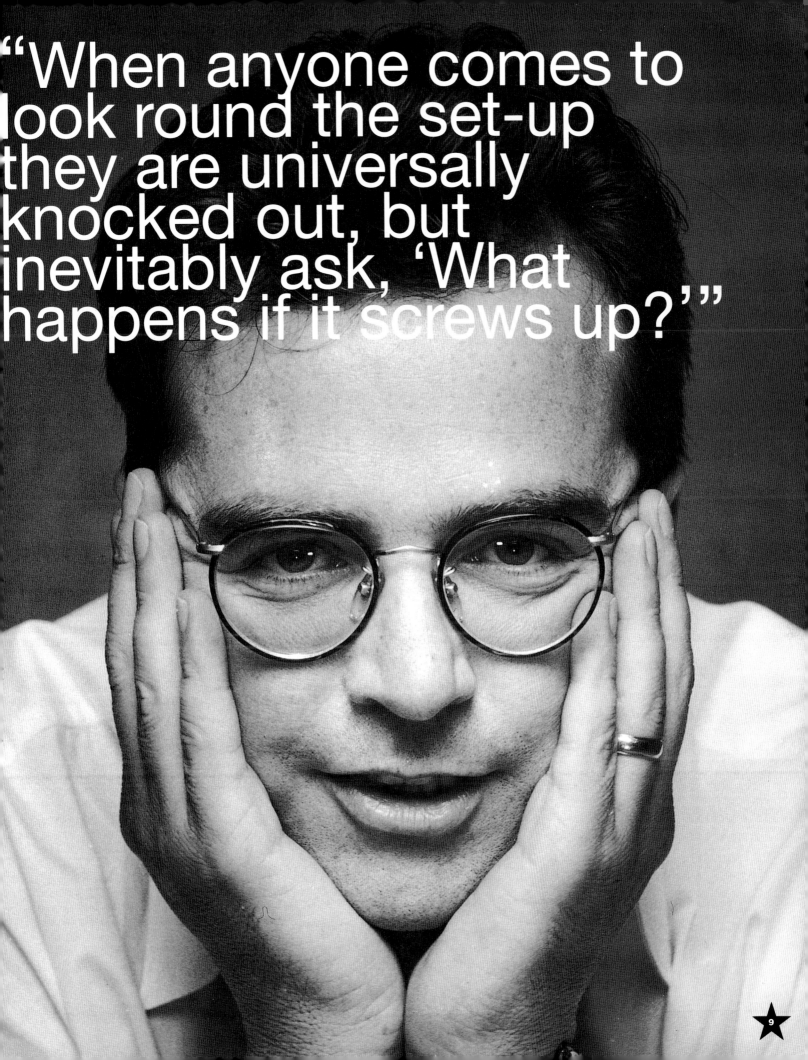

"When anyone comes to look round the set-up they are universally knocked out, but inevitably ask, 'What happens if it screws up?'"

September

Peter Gabriel
Us

Four years in the making, Peter Gabriel's sixth 'proper' solo album – Us – was the result of collaboration with over 100 musicians (13 of whom didn't even appear on the final product). A deeply personal album, much of Us was inspired by Gabriel's therapy, undertaken to cope with two failed relationships as he went in search of – as Vox put it tastefully – "the bastard within".

"After years of theatrical artifice in Genesis, followed by a solo career characterised by introspective musings on political and philosophical matters, with *Us* Peter Gabriel turns his attention to more personal matters. There's a gentleness to Gabriel's approach which serves his songs well, and which lends his combinative approach towards world music a sense of respectful universality." **The Independent**

"...disregard all suggestions that this is an 'adult' album, designed for sensitive, musicologically correct, vaguely troubled fortysomethings. *Us* is, first and foremost, start to finish, a truly wonderful blast." **Q**

"The *Us* of the title is not just the obvious Us, the world community that Gabriel has espoused for a decade now. It's also the Us of the personal relationship, although anyone expecting a sordid kiss 'n' tell autobiography will be disappointed." **NME**

"Richly diverse, and intensely personal, *Us* is an album that broods, celebrates and embraces at once. As a 60-minute whole, it is a stunning album of great cohesion... An important milestone." **Music Week**

"Peter Gabriel's carefully-measured articulate work reflects the man himself. Rarely autobiographical, he prefers to work inside other characters in order to express extreme emotions. Kate Bush clearly influences *Us,* as it seems PG has picked up on some of KB's vaguely hippy themes of self-discovery and communication." **Vox**

"Cynics may complain that the idea of trawling the world for colourfully authentic musical effects is hardly new. The beauty of *Us,* though, lies in its freedom from any whiff of gimmickry..." **The Sunday Times**

"Musically it's his most complete record – a cleverly constructed strata of sound palpitating with world music influences from bagpipes to talking drums. And while its songs were generated by the collapse of two long-term romances and subsequent therapy, *Us* avoids mawkish introspection for emotional honesty." **The Observer**

"Lyrically, it's an extremely intimate album with Gabriel plumbing his own soul to such depths that it would be embarrassing if it weren't so beautifully expressed and obviously genuine." **Today**

"...a cycle of songs in which a middle-aged man tries to come to terms with himself..." **The Daily Telegraph**

snippets

Manchester plays host to a five-day music seminar named 'In The City', and featuring the likes of The Auteurs, Band New Heavies (right), Ozric Tentacles, Milltown Brothers, The Frank & Walters, Suede and even Bananarama, performing at venues around the city.

In the States, controversial rapper **Ice-T** announces details of his own talk show, "Ice-TV". The show is to feature clips from black exploitation films from the 70s such as Shaft, which will be followed by discussions about black issues.

An extremely rare stereo version of the **Bob Dylan** album *Freewheelin'* is discovered in a thrift shop, purchased for $2 and subsequently auctioned for $12,000.

The Grateful Dead cancel their tour when it is announced that Jerry Garcia has contracted a disease of the lungs. A spokesman for the band says, "30 years of smoking Camel Straights will leave their mark".

Three ex-members of 80s supergroup **Japan**, Steve Jansen, Mick Karn and Richard Barbieri, are briefly reunited to provide the backing on the first British tour of One Little Indian hopefuls No-Man.

Trouble flares at Manchester's Dry Bar (once part of the Factory empire) when raiders brandishing machetes, rifles and sawn-off shotguns make off with more than £10,000 in cash during an after-hours raid.

Jackie Edwards, reggae singer and composer of The Spencer Davis Group's *Keep On Running*, dies in Jamaica aged 52.

CD supergroups **Genesis, Simply Red** and **Dire Straits** launch a campaign to boycott the new DCC format, complaining that the major record companies are ripping them off with a lower royalty rate than usual, owing to development costs.

Bill Clinton announces that he's a massive U2 fan and talks to them during a live radio phone-in in the States. A spokesman for U2 says: "The group were very surprised by Mr Clinton's knowledge of their early work. His favourite LP is *The Joshua Tree*. It's nice to know they have fans in such high places."

Metallica's bass-player Jason Newstead verbally attacks Guns N' Roses when the group walk off stage in Montreal after only 35 minutes. "It's hard to understand Guns N' Roses' antics," said Newstead, "because we rely not so much on behaviour, as going out there and doing a good show."

Astonishing everyone (especially U2 and Simply Red, one imagines), Primal Scream win the 1992 Mercury Music Prize of £20,000 for their Screamadelica album. A statement from Creation Records read: "Primal Scream are to music what George Best was to football. Beautiful, sexy, talented, dangerous and currently the best rock 'n' roll band in the country. Screamadelica was undoubtedly the best LP of the last 12 months – it deserved to win."

1
The Frank And Walters release *This Is Not A Song*, their first official Top 40 hit, on Go! Discs Records.

★

The Birthday Party reform for the finale of a Nick Cave gig at London's Town & Country Club, performing classics from the band's repertoire, including *Nick The Stripper* and *Dead Joe*.

★

Seven years after it first charted, The Smiths' classic single *How Soon Is Now?* is re-released by WEA REcords.

5
Suede play a low-key London gig for fan-club members only at the tiny White Horse Venue in Hampstead.

7
Pop Will Eat Itself release *The Looks Or The Lifestyle* on RCA Records. It is their last official release for the label because they are unceremoniously dumped only months later.

★

Boss Drum by The Shamen is released on One Little Indian Records and goes on to become a number one album.

★

Sugar, the new band from former Husker Du frontman Bob Mould, release their debut album *Copper Blue* on Creation.

★

REM issue a statement that their next album, *Automatic For The People*, will not "divorce the band from their teenybopper fans" as reported in the previous week's NME.

★

The Town & Country announce the opening of a new venue in Leeds.

★

The The re-release their first-ever single, *Cold Spell Ahead*, on Some Bizarre Records. The record was originally deleted after a run of 2,000.

★

The Manic Street Preachers release their version of *Suicide Is Painless* (Theme From MASH), originally recorded for the NME Ruby Trax compilation. It goes on to become their first Top 10 hit.

★

Ice-T's thrash-metal outfit, Body Count, release their debut album on WEA Records.

13
London-based alternative radio station XFM begins its second four-week trial period. Guests include Carter, Suede, Jason Donovan, Vic N' Bob and Sean Hughes.

14
Moose release their second album, *XYZ*, on Hut Records. They are subsequently dropped from the label when the American distributors refuse to release the record in the States.

★

Sinead O'Conner releases *Am I Not Your Girl?*, her album of big band standards and show-stoppers.

★

Suede mark the release of their second single on Nude, *Metal Mickey*, with their debut "TOTP" appearance the following week.

★

Public Enemy issue their *Greatest Misses* LP on Def Jam, a compilation of new tracks and remixes.

★

Prince releases the *Symbol* album on Paisley Park. The closing track, *The Sacrifice Of Victor*, hints at the small one's new moniker with the lines "When I reach my destination/That's when I'll know/That's when my name will be Victor/Amen".

While recording in New York, Sinead O'Connor takes time out to help at Manhattan's Sine Cafe by cleaning tables. She causes further empuzzlement and controversy with the sleeve of her Success Has Made A Failure Of Our Home single, which features a photograph of murdered Guatemalan street child Carmona Lopez. The Sun's Piers Morgan calls it "the most tasteless record sleeve of the year". Chrysalis Records release a statement saying, "There is nothing remotely tasteless about the sleeve. It shows a street child who was beaten by four Guatemalan police officers in 1990 and later died of his injuries." Morgan retaliates with a statement saying, "I suspect that Ms O'Connor's motive for using the photo might have something to do with the sales of her last two singles."

LIVE!

The 1992 Reading Festival

proves to be a bit of a washout. Perhaps it is the Lord Vince Power (the promoter who lost the festival this year only to win it back in 93) performing an almighty rain dance, but the 40,000 crowd present end up soaked. The Manic Street Preachers cause controversy when Nick Wire's smashed bass is thrown into the audience but hits a security guard instead. The hit of the weekend are, of course, Nirvana. "The Seattle superstars played a storming set," said the NME, perhaps unaware of the pun.

photo: LF

snippets

Mental Icelandic rockers **The Sugarcubes** announce they're to split. A spokesman for the band told the press, "They came together when they were very young and over the years have done their own things, musically and in other areas of the media. They've grown apart professionally, although they're obviously still very close personally."

● *Legendary boozy ex-football-player George Best appears in the video for The Farm's version of* Don't You Want Me. *It is a momentous occasion for the world of rock.*

The annual MTV Awards saw conflict between Nirvana and Guns N' Roses. Firstly Courtney Love confronted Axl Rose about some comments he'd made about her on stage in Florida. Then, during Nirvana's set, Chris Novoselic said "Hello, Axl" and was met straight afterwards by an angry Rose (plus, suspiciously, a TV crew) demanding to know what the bass-player meant by the remark.

Shabba Ranks is accused of rape by one of the girls who takes part in his *Trailer Loads Gals* video. A statement from his record company says, "He has been accused four times of rape and cleared every time. It's probably got a lot to do with the fact that his album's gone platinum. He's a very rich man."

snippets

A **Disposable Heroes Of Hiphoprisy** fan is arrested skateboarding in Sheffield wearing one of the group's T-shirts featuring the words "I can express more emotions than laughter, anger and Let's Fuck."

● **The Black Crowes'** Chris Robinson is charged with assault after he puts his foot on the shoulder of a security guard allegedly harassing a fan at the group's Washington DC concert.

The Shamen hit back against allegations that their *Ebeneezer Goode* number one hit is about, woo, drugs. A statement issued from their record company says, "The only references to drugs in the song are 'salmon', which means cigarettes and 'Veras', as in Vera Lynns, which is rhyming slang for gins not skins."

Gay Rights Organisation Outrage! reacts angrily against Buju Banton's Boom Bye Bye single, which they claim "explicitly celebrates the murder of gay men and lesbians". The offending lyrics include: "Woman edge up on another an a lay down in a bed/Hug up one another an a rub down leg/Send for the 'matic and the Uzi instead/Shoot them batty boy come let we shoot them".

Top Heavenly Records artists, **Flowered Up, St Etienne** and **The Rockingbirds**, team up to record an EP of Right Said Fred songs (entitled The Fred EP) for the benefit of The Terrence Higgins Trust.

At a time when **Madonna** is becoming increasingly obsessed with her 'bits', her latest movie, Body Of Evidence, is given a NC-17 rating (the equivalent of an 'X' in the old days) by the Motion Picture Association Of America, thus ensuring that what remains of her teenybop audience have no legal access to the film.

While recording in Hamburg, **Depeche Mode** give an impromptu performance around the hotel bar's piano of three songs from their *Songs Of Faith And Devotion* album, as well as pissed-up renditions of tunes by Elvis, Mott The Hoople and Gloria Gaynor.

Bono causes confusion in New York by being driven through Times Square wearing a silver stetson and accompanied by Wynona Ryder and a dog wearing sunglasses.

Brian May and **Roger Taylor** present HIV-positive US basketball player Magic Johnson with a cheque for $300,000 – proceeds from the re-release of *Bohemian Rhapsody* – to be put to good use as part of the tall one's AIDS research foundation.

14

A demonstration is held outside EMI Records by thousands of anti-racism Morrissey fans protesting against his use of right-wing imagery at the Madstock gig in Finsbury Park. A statement by the protesters reads: "We want Morrissey to issue a statement clearly opposing racism and supporting black and white unity against racists and against the Europe-wide fascist movement." Morrissey responds by saying, "If I'm racist, then the Pope is female – and the Pope isn't female".

21

Happy Mondays' 'difficult' last album, ...Yes Please, is released to mixed reviews. It is also the last album to be released on Factory Records. (RIP)

★

The reformed Television release their first album for 14 years on EMI Records.

★

Twelve years after his death, Island Records release a CD box set retrospective of Bob Marley's best work, entitled *Songs Of Freedom*.

★

David Bowie signs a long-term solo deal with BMG Records and the BMG-linked Savage label in the States. He had been without a solo deal since *Never Let Me Down*, his last album for EMI.

★

Parlophone rockers Radiohead release their second single, *Creep*. It doesn't make the charts, but is nevertheless heavily featured among the critics' choice lists of singles at the close of the year.

★

Lemonheads release *Confetti* from their *It's A Shame About Ray* album, following up their first British hit, Simon & Garfunkel's *Mrs Robinson*.

26

The date planned for a massive rave held on the hallowed turf of Wembley Stadium and featuring The Orb, Opus 3 and Xpansions. The show is aborted due to council pressures.

28

EMF release their second album, *Stigma*, on Parlophone Records, the follow-up to their highly successful 91 debut, *Schubert Dip*.

★

An anti-Nazi album entitled *Never Again!*, featuring the likes of The Shamen, Flowered Up and Pop Will Eat Itself, is released.

★

The Pet Shop Boys issue the video of their 1991 World Tour, entitled 'Performance', filmed over three nights at Birmingham NEC.

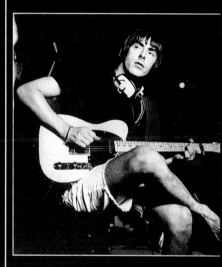

Paul Weller releases *Above The Clouds*, the third single from his eponymously-titled debut solo album on Go! Discs Records.

★

The Orb release their *Assassin* single on Big Life Records, their last single for the label before they contest their deal.

29

Prince's fan club, The Dream Nation, hold the Annual UK Prince convention in Norwich. Prince doesn't attend.

great expectations

October

"Archer's voice has the sad prettiness of Phoebe Snow... she rocks out in the decorous but natural manner of Paul McCartney."

Tasmin Archer
Great Expectations

Listing her influences as Squeeze and Costello, 29-year-old Bradford lass Tasmin Archer was as surprised as anyone when her odd Dickensian dress-style and strong soulful tones captured the imagination of the public and took her debut single, Sleeping Satellite, *to number one. The resulting LP,* Great Expectations, *did not disappoint...*

"...she has evolved a songwriting style sublimely oblivious to such revolutionary developments as rave culture and grunge. The songs here are solid verse-chorus-middle eight jobs in time-honoured Pop Craftsmanship fashion, produced with mainstream solidity and apparently directed at the heart of the US pop charts."
The Guardian

"Impressive debut from an aspiring singer who graces bubbly pop, yet in pursuit of mass appeal is not afraid to let the odd socio-political commentary filter through. As a result, there's much to admire here."
Daily Express

"Tasmin is that rare beast, a black woman who plays rock and pop in a music world where black women usually have to be disco divas or nothing. Only Joan Armatrading and Tracy Chapman have cracked this market to date. Tasmin is rockier than both." **Today**

"None of these songs panders to the dancing-queen or soft-soul archetypes, though there's more genuine soul in

Archer's voice than any of the legions of Paulas and Whitneys and Mariahs churned out by the American music industry."
The Independent

"Archer's debut album will challenge the strongest will. *Great Expectations* is great driving music that doesn't overstretch its muscles." **Time Out**

"Making number one with your first single is a dream debut that invites disappointment to follow. Fortunately, *Great Expectations* indicates that *Sleeping Satellite* is no fluke. Its other 10 tracks are similarly built around sturdy choruses..." **The Observer**

"She's got Belinda Carlisle's cheekbones and her streamlined sense of melody, she sings of loving God and heaven like Amy Grant, and she's made an LP of carefully concocted MOR ballads..." **Select**

"Archer's voice has the sad prettiness of Phoebe Snow... she rocks out in the decorous but natural manner of Paul McCartney. A strong start." **Q**

"*Great Expectations,* her debut album, finds Ms Archer powering her way through a set of predominantly balladic tracks but, while her voice is pleasant to listen to, the songs themselves are something of a disappointment." **Cosmopolitan**

"...armed with effortlessly hummable melodies and cracking good pop hooks. As a pop machine, *Great Expectations* is built to perfection..." **City Limits**

"Tasmin's something of a vocal find. It's when she lets rip with the ballads that she really shines." **NME**

snippets

U2 invite the White House telephone operators to their gig in Columbia, South Carolina, by way of thanks for being good-humoured when Bono telephoned them nightly in an attempt to talk to the President from the stage of their Zoo TV tour, offering them free use of the band's private jet. George Bush finally reacts to the nightly calls in a speech in which he says, "I have nothing against U2. But the next time we face a foreign policy crisis, I will work with John Major and Boris Yeltsin. And Bill Clinton can consult Boy George."

After months of rumour and gossip, Nirvana's **Kurt Cobain** admits to using heroin, calling it a "little habit", in which he dabbled "once or twice a year". The Nirvana singer was prescribed Methadone pills after developing a stomach disorder during de-tox. Speaking to The LA Times after the birth of his and Courtney Love's daughter Frances, Cobain said, "I can't tell you how much my attitude has changed since we've got Frances. Holding my baby is the best drug in the world. I don't want my daughter to grow up with people telling her that her parents were junkies."

Five hundred Irish **Carter The Unstoppable Sex Machine** fans sign a petition condemning the group for missing out Northern Ireland and Eire from their forthcoming tour. A spokesman says, "We were hoping to play some December dates in the north and the republic, but hadn't been able to find large enough venues available."

A cancer-stricken Frank Zappa cancels some European dates to return to the US for treatment. He tells the European press, "I was in bad shape, but I'm better now."

Roger Daltry begins work on a film about The Who's former wild man drummer Keith Moon, commenting: "He was the funniest, most outrageous, kindest and most selfish person I've ever met in my life."

EMF deny rumours that they plan to split after manic keyboard-player Derry Brownson is quoted in the Daily Mirror saying, "We may not be around much longer. We've never looked on EMF as a career. If we carry on too long, there's a danger we'll end up like every other useless, boring band in the charts." An EMI spokesman hastily claims, "Derry's quote was taken out of context – the interview from which that quote was lifted was a very light-hearted affair."

1
U2's The Edge and Adam Clayton are interviewed on London's alternative radio station, XFM.

3
Inspiral Carpets release their third album, *Revenge Of The Goldfish*, on Mute Records.

★

Body Count are vetoed as support act to Guns N' Roses by promoters who consider them "an inappropriate act".

5
In the midst of reunion rumours, Virgin Records release a digitally-remastered compilation of The Sex Pistols' best-known tracks, *Kiss This*.

★

Nine Inch Nails issue their six-track Broken mini-album on Island Records.

★

John Lennon's Academy Award for the *Let It Be* album is auctioned for $100,000 in New York.

★

Avenue by St Etienne is released on Heavenly Records as a taster for their second album, *So Tough*.

★

Verve release *Gravity Grave* on Hut Records. It becomes their third independent singles chart number one.

★

Stereo MC's release *Connected*, their third and breakthrough album, on Gee St/Island Records.

★

Bob Geldof's *The Happy Club* album is released on Vertigo Records. It does not go on to rival *Dark Side Of The Moon* sales-wise.

9
The Ramones issue *Poison Heart*, the first single from their 577th album, *Mondo Bizzarro*.

★

Belly release the *Gepetto* EP on 4AD records, and announce that they've parted company with bassist Fred Abong.

10
Guns N' Roses guitarist Slash marries model Renee Saran in Los Angeles.

★

Happy Mondays' final tour kicks off at Leicester De Montfort Hall.

12
In the light of Bob Mould's re-emergence with Sugar, WEA Records re-release Husker Du's albums, *Candy Apple Grey* and *Warehouse Songs And Stories*.

★

A critically-lauded Talking Heads greatest hits retrospective entitled *Sand In The Vaseline* is released by EMI Records.

★

The stomping Abba classic, *Voulez Vous* is reissued by Polydor Records.

17
The Bob Dylan tribute concert is screened by Channel 4.

19
Julian Cope releases *Jehovahkill*, his fourth and final album for Island Records.

★

Debut album by demented Cork indie trio The Frank & Walters, entitled *Trains, Boats & Planes* is released on Go! Discs Records.

snippets

REM's **Mike Mills** announces that the band will not tour the *Automatic For The People* album but plan to tour after a new album in 93, by which time they will not have performed live (apart from acoustic performances) for three albums. Meanwhile, Peter Buck speaks out against rumours that Michael Stipe has AIDS. "Michael is the healthiest person I know," he says. "We've all been tested. We have insurance at the level we're at."

Original Sex Pistols bass-player Glen Matlock threatens to sue the band over a promo clip for a re-released Anarchy In The UK in which shots of him appear alongside ones of Sid Vicious. John Lydon comments: "People and their egos! I should have pressed the erase button!"

● The stage collapses at a **They Might Be Giants** show in Milwaukee only minutes after singer John Flansburg urges their fans to "ignore all the fire laws and go ahead and polka".

American trainer company LA Gear attempt to sue Michael Jackson for a mind-boggling $46 million. They claim that Jackson actually refused to wear their trainers when appearing in a commercial for the company!

A Bob Dylan tribute concert at Madison Square Garden featuring the likes of Stevie Wonder, Eric Clapton and Neil Young becomes a controversial event when Sinead O'Connor is booed off the stage two weeks after tearing up a photograph of the Pope on US coast-to-coast TV show "Saturday Night Live". Scheduled to perform Dylan's *I Believe In You,* she is jeered by the angry audience until she launches into a fierce acapella rendition of Bob Marley's *War*. Minutes later she is led from the stage, sobbing and being "comforted" by Kris Kristofferson. "Nothing prepared for 'Boo!'" screamed the NME headline, while Q plumped for "Sinead – provocative or petulant: discuss".

Photo: LFI

Shaun Ryder admits that Happy Mondays are considering a two-year break after their forthcoming tour. "I'm really proud of how everybody in our band are friends and still get on," he says cynically. "To keep that, I'm quite willing to split the band after this tour for two years and let us all get out and try different things." So-called 'insiders' claim the singer feels the rest of the band are suffering from "ego problems".

The highly-important, successful and talented **Roger Waters** attacks Madonna in an American magazine. "She's made all these rotten records," he fumes, "and she's this awful, ugly, dull person who – by virtue of the fact that she's completely fearless and shameless and blatant and cheap and bad – has become successful."

Tina Turner announces plans to film the story of her life from her Nutbush cotton field days to her successful comeback in 1984. Whitney Houston is rumoured to be up for the role, although Turner is allegedly not particularly keen on the idea.

Robert Smith tells a Sunday newspaper that he plans to split The Cure after their current world tour. "I know I've said before that I was going to pack it in," he says, "but that was usually out of frustration and anger. This time it's not like that."

Mick Jones denies that The Clash are to reform, despite multi-million dollar incentives from American promoters for the group to tour the States.

In a rebellious moment, **Bruce Springsteen's** MTV Unplugged set becomes exactly the opposite when the grizzly rocker whacks his electric guitar into an amp and performs a Plugged set instead.

nippets

The Temptations' former lead singer Eddie Kendricks dies of cancer in Birmingham, Alabama, aged 52. He was most famous for his soaring falsetto voice on hits such as My Girl and The Way You Do The Things You Do.

My Bloody Valentine, dropped from the Creation roster due to their massive recording budgets, fall on their feet and are signed to Island Records for a "hefty sum".

Pearl Jam perform a free concert in Seattle's Magnusson Park in an attempt to encourage young people to vote. The concert costs them $100,000 and they are joined on stage by Chris Novoselic and Dave Grohl of Nirvana.

▲ The lovely Whitfield Crane of 'top' American rockers Ugly Kid Joe silences hecklers at Cambridge Corn Exchange by waving his dick at them.

Julian Cope issues an advert for his *Fear Love This Place* which features a rant against Guns N' Roses, who he calls "homophobics in puff gear". He runs into further problems when the workers at the plant pressing up his *Jehovahkill* album refuse to work on the album due to its title.

Two people are stabbed at an Ozzy Osbourne concert in Oklahoma City after he goads the audience for not being **"crazy enough"**.

Brian Wilson claims that he's into getting back together with the rest of The Beach Boys. "I've been thinking about rejoining," he admits. "I've written a couple of new songs... I'm excited. We all feel that we have something really great to put out on the market."

Boy George's dance label, More Protein, is dropped by Virgin Records after a string of minor hits and flops from the likes of E-Zee Posse, Eve Gallagher and MC Kinky. A statement from Virgin says, "The company has spent 18 months undergoing a rationalisation process and it's regrettable that we've had to part company with More Protein. However, we still retain Boy George as a solo artist."

19
Pipping Mick Jagger's next solo effort to the post, Keith Richards' surprisingly interesting *Main Offender* is released by Virgin Records.

★

In the midst of controversy surrounding her Sex book, Madonna's *Erotica* album slips into the shops virtually unnoticed. As things which shift by the bucketload go.

21
Sinead O'Connor announces her "retirement" from the music business following her appearance at the Bob Dylan tribute concert (see Snippets). In a statement she claims: "What I learnt was that there is no longer any point in trying to use music as a means of communicating with people."

23

Jesus And Mary Chain kick off a 24-date American Rollercoaster tour accompanied by Curve and Spiritualized.

24
Brian May announces plans on Radio One to issue previously unreleased Queen tracks recorded before Freddie Mercury's death.

26
Three years on from her highly successful debut album, *Raw Like Sushi*, Neneh Cherry releases the follow-up, *Home Brew*, which features *Trout*, a duet with Michael Stipe.

★

Bruce Springsteen begins the final leg of his American tour in Denver.

★

The Shamen release the *Boss Drum* single, the follow-up to their controversial *Ebeneezer Goode* number one.

★

Faith No More release *Everything's Ruined* from their *Angel Dust* album on London Records.

31
The Farm, Erasure and Billy Bragg join Arthur Scargill on a demonstration in London organised by the Lesbian And Gay Rights Coalition.

★

The Orb perform the final date of their 'The Orb Experience 1992' tour at Manchester Academy.

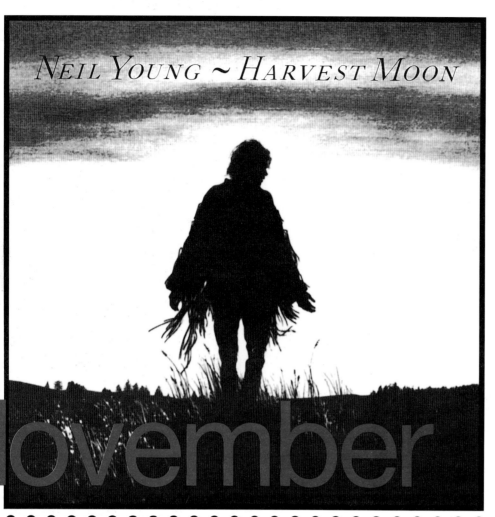

NEIL YOUNG ~ HARVEST MOON

November

"... a beautifully melodic and resonant set of songs about life, love and longevity.'

back pages of his own life with nostalgia and regret. Lyrically, the album focuses wistfully on lost opportunities, lost love, lost friends and, in the greater scheme of things, the lost environment." **Melody Maker**

"On the cover of *Harvest Moon,* Young's scarecrow silhouette stands against a prairi sky. The record inside may be the best worl he's ever done, but you never know. He's still got a long way to go." **Vox**

"He seems to have exorcised the demons in his soul that have driven him to all manne of daring challenges in the meantime, chugging along with the ol' acoustic blissfully recreating the mood of searching melancholia that originally established him as a crucial force way back when." **Rock World**

"After his awesome, four-album, electric, amp-damage sequence of *Eldorado, Freedom, Ragged Glory* and *Weld,* it's quite a trip back to the woods, but *Harvest Moon* is at times a beautiful record." **Select**

"*Harvest Moon* is stately and sedate, tracking the travails of elemental love, mostly. Straying from the purely personal, Young rues the innate bellicosity of man, and the sullied purity of natural beauty. Quite quietly, *Harvest Moon* is solid gold recast, with molten repose." **The List**

"He'll have his day again, will Neil. Bless him and his unstinting faith in sideburns." **City Limits**

Neil Young
Harvest Moon

After four albums of raw, howling feedback, Neil Young re-assembled the musical cast of his 1972 country classic, Harvest, *to record a sister album 20 years on. Echoing the spirit of the original,* Harvest Moon *took the scenes of love and lament to new heights...*

"Nostalgia is often the last resort of scoundrels but *Harvest Moon* is ultimately not content to be *Harvest 2,* even as it re-affirms and re-examines Young the naive romantic, still dreaming after all these years." **Q**

"Just like Godfather II, this effort is even better than the original. *Harvest Moon* has none of the awful strings that blighted *Harvest,* it boasts a stronger collection of songs and a much prettier cover." **The Daily Telegraph**

"*Harvest Moon* may not prove to be one of Young's benchmark albums, but it's a beautifully melodic and resonant set of songs about life, love and longevity. *Harvest* had a sparse, self-pitying quality, where the new one is lush and generous of spirit..." **The Guardian**

"Despite the many deliberate self-references, *Harvest Moon* is not so much a sister to *Harvest* as *Harvest* grown up and re-examining itself, poring over its youthful hopes and impulses, neither nostalgic nor grown especially bitter." **NME**

"An older, wiser and frequently woeful individual, Neil Young flicks through the

snippets

The singer of Satanic American group **Deicide** receives death threats from UK animal rights groups following his ill-advised confession that he tortures animals. It does nothing to deter him and he retaliates by saying, "Tell them to bring their fucking furry friends with 'em, the bigger the better, and we can really have some fun. Satan lives."

Boyz II Men's single *End Of The Road* becomes only the third single in 30 years to spend more than ten weeks at the top of the US charts, surpassing previous chart-topping efforts by Elvis Presley and The Ink Spots.

London group **Soho** claim to be the subjects of an MI5 investigation following the release of a track called *Claire's Kitchen* which alleges an affair between the Prime Minister and a Downing Street caterer. The group claim that their premises have been broken into and thoroughly searched and that their phone has been tapped.

Elton John announces his contribution of over £500,000 in personal donations and royalties to AIDS charities. It is the same month he attempts to sue American magazine Hard Copy over a story in which they claimed he had moved to Atlanta in order to be near an AIDS hospital. A week later he announces a $39 million deal with Time-Warner.

Ronnie Bond, former drummer with The Troggs, dies in Winchester of an alcohol-related illness, aged 40. He still hadn't got that drum roll right. Drummers? I shit 'em.

▲ In the midst of split rumours, **Happy Mondays** cancel their entire European tour due to it coinciding with the birth of guitarist Mark Day's first child. Pundits who put it down to Shaun Ryder's legendary drug intake are told, "Shaun hasn't touched drugs on this tour, neither on or off stage".

A New York pressure group called The Sinead Brigade tear up photos of the Pope outside the city's St Patrick's Cathedral, many of them wearing Sinead masks and carrying "The Pope Must Apologise, Not Sinead" placards.

2

Bon Jovi release their *Keep The Faith* album on Phonogram. A Jesus Jones remix of the title track is rejected on the grounds that it sounds too techno.

★

Irish agit-rockers Therapy? put out their first major label album, *Nurse*, on A&M Records, and enjoy mammoth success.

★

Blondie's classic *Eat To The Beat* album is re-released by Chrysalis Records.

★

Bob Dylan releases his acoustic 'comeback' album, *Good As I Been To You*, on Columbia Records.

★

Chrysalis Records issues *The Terry Hall Collection*, a compilation of the singer's work with The Specials, The Fun Boy Three and The Colourfield.

★

Mancunian technoheads 808 State release their third album, *Gorgeous*, on ZTT Records.

★

Neil Young returns with the near-classic *Harvest Moon*, the follow-up to 1972's definitely classic *Harvest*.

★

What will turn out to be the last-ever Happy Mondays single, *Sunshine & Love*, is the final release on Factory Records. It flops.

★

Pink Floyd release a retrospective box set, *Shine On*, on EMI Records.

★

Del Amitri make a bid for the charts with their *When You Were Young* single.

3

Atlantic Soul Machine release their debut LP, *Coast To Coast*, a mix of covers and classic soul greats, that spawns the turntable hit, *What's Wrong With Me*.

9

Guns N' Roses issue *Yesterdays*, one of the umpteen singles from their *Use Your Illusion* double album set.

★

The Manic Street Preachers release *Little Baby Nothing*, their duet with ex-porn star Traci Lords. True to form, it sucks.

snippets

● **James Brown** gives a speech to students in Oakland, California advising them to stay in school. "The worst killer in the world is ignorance," he said. "With all the successes I've had, I've been broke four times because of ignorance. There's nothing can take the place of knowledge."

The Fall leave Fontana Records after a three-year relationship. A statement on behalf of the label reads: "Both parties felt the relationship had gone as far as it could – but we wish them every success in the future."

After months of offers and negotiation, **Suede** re-sign to indie Nude Records, which is now licensed through Sony.

Julian Cope is dropped by Island Records who reckon him, at 34 years of age, to be too old and uncommercial. A spokesman for Cope tells the NME, "It's ironic that he should be released [from his contract] at a time when he's at his creative peak and his work is more popular than ever. I wonder whether the same view would apply if Neil Young or Van Morrison came knocking at the door."

A £250,000 statue to commemorate Freddie Mercury is proposed to be built in Holland Park.

U2's live *Zoo TV* special is broadcast from Dublin with cameo appearances from William Burroughs and Bill Clinton. The group themselves appear in the audience of "The Gay Byrne Show" watching a group of U2 impersonators covertly miming *Who's Gonna Ride Your Wild Horses?* The cathode-ray spectacular draws a confused response for its eclectic and perverse barrage of light and sound, but many see it as one giant leap for rock'n'roll.

The end of an era is signalled when Factory Records goes bust with debts of over £2 million. The label had been in existence for 14 years and was the home of New Order, Joy Division, Durutti Column and Happy Mondays among many, many others.

snippets

George Michael enters into a legal battle to free him from his contract with Sony Records, believing his contract to be financially inadequate and restrictive.

Simon Gallup of The Cure collapses in the middle of the band's European tour, allegedly after contracting pleurisy, and is replaced by ex-Associates bass-player Roberto Soave.

● **Axl Rose** is found guilty of misdemeanour and given two years probation following a riot at a Guns N' Roses gig in St Louis, Missouri. He is also ordered to donate $50,000 to St Louis child abuse charities.

Nine Inch Nails' video for the track *Happiness In Slavery* is banned by The British Board Of Film Classifications. This may have been due to scenes of American performance artist Bob Flanagan piercing his hands and chest with sharp objects and supposedly severing his own genitals.

Rapper Marky Mark is sued by an American man who claims the star repeatedly kicked him in the face and broke his jaw while another man held him down.

Kurt Cobain's liner notes for the Nirvana compilation album Incesticide *are leaked, and contain a section where he writes: "Last year a girl was raped by two wasters of sperm and eggs while they sang the lyrics to our song* Polly. *I have a hard time carrying on knowing there are plankton like that in our audience."*

Rita Marley is cleared of fraud, although she admits forging her dead husband's signature on documents transferring funds to her and her family. Bob Marley died in 1981 without making a will.

The Beach Boys' **Mike Love** begins legal proceedings against Brian Wilson claiming that he undermined his involvement in the group's biggest hits in his autobiography Wouldn't It Be Nice? – My Own Story.

Beverley Craven bemuses the rock world by announcing that her forthcoming tour will be sponsored by Tampax, provoking jokes about 'Beverley Craven Unplugged' and suchlike.

The original line-up of **Black Sabbath** is reunited for a show at Costa Mesa, California, the first time the group had performed together since Live Aid. Ozzy Osbourne gets so excited that he moons at the audience during Iron Man.

Mark Chapman, John Lennon's murderer, begins writing his autobiography, tentatively titled Let Me Take You Down.

The Shamen, Happy Mondays and **Jesus And Mary Chain** are amongst the groups adding their support for Charter 88, a campaign against the violation of human rights in this country, including police pressure on New Age travellers.

► **L7's Donita Sparks shocks viewers of Channel 4's "The Word" by dropping her jeans during a performance of the group's hit Pretend We're Dead and performing the climax of the song almost naked. A spokesman for the programme claims: "I suppose you could call it artistic expression."**

9

Madness put out their live version of Jimmy Cliff's *The Harder They Come*, recorded at their Madstock Finsbury Park gigs.

★

Swiss dance nutters Yello issue a compilation of their finest moments, *Essential Yello*, on Phonogram.

★

American art-rockers Pere Ubu issue their tenth album, *The Story Of My Life*, on Phonogram Records.

★

Techno-fiends The Prodigy release their debut album, *Out Of Space*, on XL Recordings.

★

Glum shoe-gazers Ride release a compilation of outtakes and B-sides called *Smile* on Creation Records.

★

Brian Eno releases his second album of the year, *The Shutov Assembly*, an ambient collection.

16

Mick Jagger releases his third (and subsequently mostly successful) solo album, *Wandering Spirit*, on East/West.

★

Otis Redding's classic *Dock Of The Bay* hit is reissued by East/West Records.

★

Prefab Sprout release *I Remember That*, lifted from their *Life Of Surprises* compilation album.

23

Phorever People by The Shamen, the fourth single from the group's number one album *Boss Drum*, is released.

★

Ruby Trax, the NME's 40th anniversary LP which features 40 groups' renditions of number one hits, goes on sale in the shops having previously only been available on mail order.

29

Sinead O'Connor appears at the International Concert For Human Rights at London's Royal Festival Hall, her third appearance since she announced her "retirement".

30

Nirvana release *In Bloom*, the fourth single from their *Nevermind* LP.

★

Suzanne Vega issues *Blood Makes Noise* from her *99F* album on A&M Records.

December

Nirvana
Incesticide

With all quiet on the Nirvana front, this collection of B-sides, sessions and demos was apparently released to combat bootleggers cashing in on the band's phenomenal success. It also provided a thirst-quenching stop-gap for fans feverishly awaiting the follow- up to Nevermind…

"**Thankfully, it reveals that Nirvana were not the kind of band who squandered their apprenticeship cranking out homely Troggs and Dave Clark Five cover versions.**"

"In joining up the dots on the periphery of Nirvana's early work, *Incesticide* provides some exciting moments and a fascinating insight into what makes the band tick." **Q**

"The *Incesticide* material is a clear-eyed look back at their underground origins, with drums and guitars ablaze and few concessions to radio-friendliness." **The Guardian**

"Here's where Nirvana slowed down and swelled up and spilled out in dramatic slow motion, found the appalled, lurching shape of *Smells Like Teen Spirit,* and became the monsters they are today. The rest is history." **Melody Maker**

"*Incesticide:* A title so indicative of Nirvana's humility, while at the same time bringing home their guilt and self-disgust at this retrospective exercise." **NME**

"Nirvana force together the power of heavy metal, the subversive attitudes of punk and the melodies of pop, forming a critical mass that when detonated made this humble Seattle trio into the rock phenomenon of the early 90s. No other band today mixes pleasure and pain better than this." **Vox**

"Thankfully, it reveals that Nirvana were not the kind of band who squandered their apprenticeship cranking out homely Troggs and Dave Clark Five cover versions. Indeed, much of this compilation offers the kind of rudimentary metal angst that you might expect from the band who finally hit paydirt with *Nevermind.*" **Rock CD**

"…Still, that's 'slackers' for you: too lazy to deliver another album and, judging by much of this material, they can hardly be bothered to write a complete song either, settling instead for incessant repetition of one line where two might do." **The Independent**

"If you've lived in a large soundproof hanger for the last year, get out and buy this album, strap yourself in, turn on and be prepared to be converted." **Indiecator**

"Here's the festering fury, the blocked idealism, the dysfunctional hopefulness and grey bleakness of Washington skies that fuels it all. There ain't much that's patently pop about it, really." **Kerrang!**

▶ **Peace Together,** a campaign aimed at benefitting young people in Northern Ireland, is launched, with the likes of The Shamen, The Orb and Sinead O'Connor eager to participate. A single and a series of live events is planned with a host of stars.

Mark Chapman, the man who shot Lennon, has a fan club! Or so a recent biography of the killer suggests. Open days for members, however, have yet to take place.

U2 announce dates for their summer 93 Zooropa tour. More than 165,000 tickets are sold in a single day. MacPhisto, Bono's latest alter ego, becomes increasingly delirious.

After much speculation, **The Happy Mondays** fall into disarray, claiming "ego problems" as a major factor, and announce a "two year holiday for the band". In other words, Happy Mondays split.

Manic Street Preachers' bassist Nicky Wire continued to make controversy the very centre of his life following his remarks at the band's Kilburn National show. He told fans, "I hope Michael Stipe goes the same way as Freddie Mercury", in reference to Stipe's Aids rumour. This statement, being far from politically correct, fails to win the band many new friends.

REM's ever-enigmatic singer, Michael Stipe, is rumoured to be suffering from Aids due to his increasingly gaunt appearance and his reluctance to tour. A spokesperson shrugged off such rumours saying, "some journalist putting two and two together and getting five". So there.

Gloria Estefan turns down a $5 million sponsorship deal for her next tour from an un-named soft drinks company. It was, she claims, "only money".

PJ Harvey fly to Minneapolis to work on their second album, *Rid Of Me*, with seminal hardcore producer, Steve Albini. The successor to *Dry* is due for April 93 release.

December**Diary**

1

REM have another single from their *Automatic For The People* LP in the chart. This time it's *Man On The Moon.*

★

Ice Cube is in action again, making big noises with his *The Preditor* album.

5

Whitney Houston's rendition of Dolly Parton's *I Will Always Love You*, the theme song from the film The Bodyguard, in which she stars alongside Kevin Costner, reaches Number One and stays there for what seems like an eternity.

6

Arrested Development, new age, laid back hippie rappers from Atlanta, Georgia, ascend to Sensation Of The Moment as their single, *Everyday People*, continues to climb the chart. A one-off date at the London Astoria becomes very much An Event.

7

Morrissey releases a new single, *Certain People I Know.*

Neil Young releases *Harvest Moon*, an album that sends everyone into universal hyperbole, with Vox Magazine suggesting, "this record may be the best work he has ever done."

★

Tasmin Archer, still flushed with success after her Number One single, *Sleeping Satellite*, releases her debut album, *Great Expectations*. The title comes from the novel by Charles Dickens.

★

Madness, continuing to milk their reunion for all it's worth, issue *Madstock*, a live album from their triumphant Finsbury Park shows, complete with 30,000 fans on full – and unpaid – backing vocals.

12

Suede's Brett Anderson adorns the cover of Melody Maker – again! – with Lesley from Silverfish smearing lipstick

across his mouth. Inside, they contribute to a frank sex debate.

13

The Lemonheads, Boston's finest melodic 'grunge' band led by 'sex kitten' Evan Dando, see their cover of Simon and Garfunkel's *Mrs Robinson* cruise into the charts, giving Dando his first ever hit. The single coincides with the release of The Graduate (the single was originally the film's theme tune) on video.

14

Abba re-release *Thank You For The Music* with a track called *Happy New Year* on the flip side. How apt.

★

House Of Pain, American Irish rappers who caused a sensation with *Jump Around* earlier this year, release their first album, *Fine Malt Lyrics.*

★

Bob Dylan surprises all by releasing an album of cover versions called *Good As I Been To You*. Vox magazine, fairly enamoured with this item, was moved to comment, "… sounding weary at journey's end, but enriched, invigorated by the past, and ready to face a new beginning."

★

The 70s revival gains momentum when Denim, fronted by Laurence from mid-80s outfit Felt, release their debut album, *Back In Denim*, a homage to everything great about the flare-festooned decade.

snippets

The B-52s have been forced to cancel their UK tour due to family illness. The tour, their biggest ever in this country, is immediately re-scheduled for February.

REM's *Automatic For The People* tops the critics' end-of-year poll for albums, while Suede, entirely predictably, top the singles poll with either *The Drowners* or *Metal Mickey*, depending which magazine you read.

Sinead O'Connor sells her Californian mansion and donates the proceeds to the starving Somalians.

George Michael announces that he intends to write and produce forthcoming albums for rock 'n' soul glitterati, including Aretha Franklin, Elton John, Brian Ferry and Stevie Wonder. The project is to be recorded under the name **Trojan Souls.**

L I V E !

The Sundays break their apparent vow of silence by touring in support of their recently released second album, *Blind*. They are greeted with unending reverence and devotion: "Swooning and sighing through the best of both albums, tonight is a golden hour of The Sundays, reaffirming the unfashionable quality of subtlety, melody, poetry and grace," remarks Melody Maker, while NME is moved to comment of the band some call the Indie Fleetwood Mac, "David Gavurin's guitar seems to be on first-name terms with melody. Even his crescendos seem musical, and the effects pedals sometime give those suspended notes a hint of stately grace."

photo: LFI

Nick Cave and Shane MacGowan duet on Louis Armstrong's *What A Wonderful World*. The festive season's greatest drunken chorus.

Morrissey goes on tour, selling out every venue in triumphant fashion. As tickets for his Alexandra Palace show in London sell out in mere minutes, he announces an extra low-key show at the Astoria.

Pop Will Eat Itself are dropped from RCA Records despite enjoying their most successful period to date. Their most recent album, The Looks Or The Lifestyle, debuted at Number 15 and their last nine singles were all consecutive Top 40 hits.

Evan Dando, *leader of The Lemonheads, issues a statement of apology to the press in response to the controversy following his lunchtime solo show at Ronnie Scotts last month. The gig was so heavily attended by various music biz types that an estimated 500 fans were locked out and angry.*

snippets

The Town And Country Club,

London's most revered concert venue, receives notice that it is to close on March 24 next year. This prompts mass outcry from the music business and public alike who all lobby for its survival.

William Shatner, Captain Kirk from "Star Trek" no less, has a record released by the increasingly maverick Creation label. The album features a host of cover versions, including his own idiosyncratic renditions of Lucy In The Sky With Diamonds and Mr Tambourine Man. It does not become a big seller.

Ice T wins the latest of endless legal battles over his hyper-controversial Cop Killer track, this time in New Zealand. The Body Count album, on which the track appears, was previously banned from sale under anti-obscenity legislation.

Helmet, the grunge act who signed a record deal worth £1.2 million, were dealt a blow when their drummer, John Stanier, was seriously injured when the band's tour bus crashed. He was rushed to hospital suffering chest and abdominal injuries and broken ribs.

Ride and **The Charlatans** announce plans of a co-headlining tour to take place early next year under the banner 'Day Tripper'.

Altern 8, the Top Ten rave band identifiable only by their face masks, announce that by early next year, their mission will have been achieved and they will split.

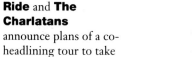

14

The song may remain the same, but Chris Rea becomes increasingly inventive with his album titles. His latest work masquarades under the unlikely name of *God's Great Banana Skin*.

★

The Farm, bad luck baggy merchants from Liverpool, finally manage a successful headline date in London after their proposed show a month before on Friday the 13th ended in disaster.

★

The Auteurs, headed by the aloof and deeply cynical Luke Haines, release their debut single, *Showgirl*. Poetic, profound and unmistakably English in tone, they are immediately hailed The New Suede. Haines, displeased at this assumption, sulks.

15

Nirvana, never out of the news, are strongly rumoured to be appearing at next year's Brit Awards. (It never happens.)

★

Kate Bush, probably the nation's favourite female singer/songwriter, is rumoured to be planning to tour sometime next year. If it goes ahead, it will be her first ever tour. This news comes shortly after the revelations that a certain Purple One has expressed interest in working with her.

★

St Etienne, reputedly the latter-day Blondie, play a one-off Christmas extravaganza at London's SW1 club under the enticing promise of a 'Night Of Fear'.

16

Jason Donovan releases *As Time Goes By* from the West End Musical, Joseph, clearly aiming for that festive Number One. He wasn't banking on Whitney's film-backed smash, however.

★

Izzy Stradlin, former Guns N' Roses guitarist, throws his support act, The Wildhearts, off his UK tour claiming a personal disagreement with member Ginger, dating back several years.

★

James play a semi-acoustic tour of the UK in an attempt to get back to their roots and quash those 'the new Simple Minds' accusations.

17

Blur, arrogant pop upstarts who apparently killed baggy last year, play a Christmas show at London's Hibernian Club to a less than half full crowd. They leave clutching a bag of Suede records promising to go away and re-invent themselves. Allegedly.

19

Nirvana's Kurt Cobain adorns the cover of Melody Maker sucking on a dummy and holding baby daughter, Frances Bean, in his arms. His T-shirt reads 'Grunge Is Dead', and inside he plays the happy father to the full.

★

Suede's Brett Anderson graces the NME's Xmas issue, dressed rather inexplicably as Sid Vicious.

21

The future of fore-running Riot Grrrls, Babes In Toyland, is thrown into doubt, as rumours of a split abound.

25

Christmas! Whitney at Number One. Still…

29

Frank and Walters, Cork's deliriously happy three-piece, release a new single from their *Planes Boats And Trains* album. *After All* is their third single.

★

Sultans Of Ping FC, mad Irish pranksters, release *U Talk 2 Much* from their forthcoming debut album.

★

The The release their first single in eons. *Dogs Of Lust* marks their return with a swagger.

31

Year ends with Suede seemingly the most important band in music today.

January

DUSK

"Coming on like a post-Thatcher John Lennon, Matt Johnson's tales of emotional violence and social disintegration still cut to the bone."

The The
Dusk

Ending a near four-year silence, Matt Johnson returns in typically morose fashion with an album that delves into the underbelly of a metropolis in all its seedy glory. Johnny Marr's guitar work pushed the record to the tip of perfection, with the critics decreeing the record his finest hour...

"Here is a man almost demanding ridicule, proffering a beaker of piss, begging you to snatch it away. It's all too easy to ignore his occasional habit of turning out excellent records." **Melody Maker**

"It can be a struggle at first, as Johnson never lets up from his blacker-than-black world-view. But *Dusk* is a rich and hugely rewarding experience which draws you to its cold bosom again and again." **NME**

"...Very nearly the best The The album yet. On it, without drastically diluting his celebrated world-view of grim despair and bleak, bleak foreboding, Johnson achieves just the right balance between pop and death, a good tune and the end of the world." **Time Out**

"As a songwriter, Johnson has long had a morbid fascination with the underside of contemporary life, and it is the vivid way in which he details this often sorry and sordid world-view that is his particular gift." **The Observer**

"It's raw and angry, often cracking into aggravated bluesy distortion, yet gentle and sparse. The ten tracks float into existence like poisonous smoke from a damaged reactor, hanging around your head like unwanted breath." **Select**

"Despite *Dusk's* monumental miserabilism, its aspirations to importance which crash under a weight of stock urban nightmare imagery and chronic over-acting, it is a very enjoyable record indeed." **Q**

"The overall impression is still one of po-faced miserabilism, rampant, but far more stylishly presented than anything since The The's 1984 masterpiece, *Soul Mining.*" **The Sunday Times**

"*Dusk,* the new album by The The, is so depressing and morbid that I almost feel socially irresponsible in recommending it." **The Daily Telegraph**

"With *Dusk,* The The reveals itself as a band in full command of its gifts at the very beginning of collective musical discovery." **Rolling Stone**

"Coming on like a post-Thatcher John Lennon, Matt Johnson's tales of emotional violence and social disintegration still cut to the bone." **I-D**

"Make the most of it; this may be the closest The The ever get to a pop record." **Sky Magazine**

snippets

Faith No More heighten suspicions that they've gone ever-so-slightly loopy by releasing a cover version of The Commodores' *Easy*. More bizarre still, the record is accepted en masse as being really rather good and goes Top 3.

Hole, the Seattle-based band fronted by the volatile Courtney Love, wife of Nirvana's Kurt Cobain, release a new single, *Beautiful Son*. The sleeve photograph, picturing a pubescent blond-haired boy, is believed to be a pre-teen Kurt. Kurt 'n' Courtney, however, admit to nothing.

The Charlatans' keyboard player, Robert Collins, is arrested and charged with robbery and possession of a firearm. If found guilty he faces a five-year prison sentence, which would inconvenience the band's future not a little.

Nirvana and the increasingly infamous **Courtney Love** (this decade's Yoko Ono?) are enraged about the prospect of an unauthorized biography about Kurt's band. The authors, Britt Collins and Victoria Clarke, and Mr and Mrs Cobain become arch enemies.

Marky Mark, brother of New Kids' Donny and owner of disturbingly large pectorals, faces a charge of assault after he and his bodyguard are alleged to have broken a man's jaw during "an incident" in Boston.

> **Albert King, legendary blues man, dies this month, aged 69. Wayne Jackson, a member of his backing band, says, "The world music scene has lost a real innovator and a real gentleman".**

Frank Black, previously Black Francis, leader of The Pixies, announces the Boston band's split. "From the ashes of The Pixies, rises something else," he said; a roundabout way of saying that he intends to go solo.

● **Courtney Love** (this decade's Esther Ofarim?) is suing Cedars-Sinai Medical Centre in Los Angeles, the hospital where she gave birth to Frances Bean, for allegedly releasing records which revealed that she was treated for heroin addiction during her pregnancy.

Steve Albini, fresh from his production work on the new PJ Harvey record, is to produce Nirvana's follow-up to *Nevermind*, despite his previous strenuous denial. The first he heard about it, he says, was when he read it in the British music press.

Alice In Chains, hard rocking US outfit also tagged with that ubiquitous 'grunge' label, play their first UK tour.

Simply Red cancel their three Birmingham NEC shows when singer Mick Hucknall falls foul of the flu.

The Cult, those enduring, consummate Goths, re-release their classic single *She Sells Sanctuary* to help plug their forthcoming Greatest Hits package.

"I'm sure J and Kurt and I don't know what we're saying..." Sugar's Bob Mould on the difficulties of people like himself, Dinosaur Jr's J Mascis and Nirvana's Kurt Cobain being mythically elevated to the so-called Godfathers Of Grunge.

2
Melody Maker re-visit their first Suede front cover back in March 92 with another of Brett and Co, this time proclaiming their status as The Best New Band In Britain - officially. Readers' polls in every other music magazine confirm this without question.

★

New music show, The Beat, hosted by eternal teenager Gary Crowley, begins on the ITV network at some time after midnight. Guests encompass everyone from The Shamen to Radiohead to Deacon Blue.

4
Ice-T appears in Vox showing off his frighteningly large collection of guns, his greatest love in life – seemingly. "I like to appear vulnerable," he says, somewhat improbably.

5
Apache Indian, Anglo-Asia's first ragga star, finally becomes a mainstream success after years as an underground artist. Duetting with Maxi Priest on *Fe Real* gives him his first top 40 placing.

6
David Bowie has lost over £2.5 million in royalties to an Italian mafia-linked bootleg fraud, who copy and sell his material through loopholes in Italy's copyright laws.

8
Womad folds with debts of £300,000.

9
Andrew Ridgley joins former partner George Michael in preparing to sue Sony Music for underpaid royalties to the tune of £958,000, while George is also after unpaid monies from Faith, amounting to £386,000.

10
Sugar's *Copper Blue* album sits proudly at Number One in the Indie Charts.

11
Ian McNabb, once the singer with 80s combo The Icicle Works, releases his debut single, *If Love Was Like Guitars*.

★

Sister Sledge revive their career effortlessly by re-visiting *We Are Family*. Oddly enough, it sounds as much of a classic as ever.

★

Bon Jovi and Cher release singles today, but they both sound so similar in style and tone that no one can tell them apart.

★

The Wedding Present release *Hit Parade 2*, the second instalment of their hit-a-month run, featuring the last six singles released between July and December last year.

★

Jonathan King, media mogul, releases his album *Anticloning* to a feverishly expectant audience. It sells not at all like hot cakes.

13
Axl Rose, fined $33,000 for his part in the St Louis stadium riot in 1991, finally pays up, not once but twice. "If it's going to a good cause, that's great. We've already given millions to charity, so this is peanuts," he says.

16
Dinosaur Jr, hailed as (one of the many) Godfathers of Grunge, release a new album, *Where You Been?* Critics hail singer-songwriter J Mascis a star as he appears on "The Clothes Show" talking about, ahem, Grunge Fashion.

snippets

"I think we both realised that it was becoming a bit painful to work together and that we didn't need to put each other through that misery."
Annie Lennox on why Eurythmics disbanded.

Radiohead, rapidly becoming everyone's second favourite New Band (due in no small way to their single *Creep* which becomes something of an anthem), play a low-key free gig at London's ULU and it becomes the most talked-about show in an otherwise quiet month. "To watch Radiohead perform in 1993 is to watch a rare and magical thing. The psychotic adulation [*Creep*] elicits from this sweaty morass of converts is validation enough," gushes Melody Maker. Three months later, the magazine makes them cover stars.

photo: LFI

Outrage!, the campaigning gay rights group, sends a copy of the Senseless Things' recent single, Homophobic Asshole, to its current "Top Ten Homophobes". They include the likes of Axl Rose, Buju Banton, John Major, Garry Bushell and Pope John Paul II. Each will receive a copy of the record and a compliment slip saying, "Promising You A Queer 1993".

ROSKO SPEAKS!
"American music has reached a point of frustration! Rap got to rappy, metal got to grungy and no one understands ragga!!! This is a statement that reflects the majority not the music special interest groups. The backlash has been "New Country" a fusion of pop/rock/and hillbilly. For the first time, radio stations are playing more new country than top 40 or rock etc. This of course will not last as nothing lasts forever, but fuses in to a new form of something else. This is the music for 93, love it, or leave it."

snippets

▶ **Wilson Phillips,** bimboesque girl three-piece whose members include Brian Wilson offspring, are rumoured to have split up after their album *Shadows And Light* flopped and their entire US tour was cancelled due to poor ticket sales. Their record company, EMI, however, hotly deny this.

Paul McCartney has signed a £100 million deal with Capitol-EMI which will see him snug until the end of his career.

The Beatles announce that they are working together for the first time in 22 years. The remaining three members will collaborate on a documentary about the group, entitled The Long And Winding Road.

Putting Our House In Order, a fund-raising project aiming to increase awareness for the homeless in the UK, is launched. Bands from every field (rock, dance, indie etc) will collaborate on the Rolling Stones' *Gimme Shelter*.

Dizzy Gillespie, all-time jazz legend, dies of cancer this month. As well as his contributions to music, he was a life-long campaigner against racism.

Perry Farrell, former singer with Jane's Addiction until he split the band last year, announces that his new project will go under the name of Porno For Pyros. An album is expected shortly.

"There's a fine line between 'Come and look at me, I'm God' and 'Come and look at me, I'll entertain you and make you feel like fucking your girlfriend.'" Depeche Mode's **Dave Gahan** *muses on the power of fame.*

"We went to the Vatican. We saw the Pope and asked him if we could do a gig in St Peter's Square. He said he thought it was a great idea but, unfortunately, there's a decree dating back 2,000 years forbidding rock bands playing there." The Frank and Walters telling yet more fibs.

January Diary

16
REM play a secret gig at the 40 Watt Club in their hometown of Athens, Georgia, for Greenpeace.

★

Genesis release a very long live album called *The Way We Walk Vol II: The Longs,* meaning that no such thing as a three-minute pop single will appear here. It doesn't.

★

Sheffield plays host to the cream of today's musical crop, including Lemonheads, Stereo MCs and Senseless Things, in a week of live music, press and promotion, with Radio One broadcasting live from there each night.

18
Duran Duran release their comeback single, *Ordinary World.* It goes on to become a US Number One.

★

Nick Berry, "Eastenders" Wicksy, puts his, er, unique vocals down on record once more. His conviction slightly outweighs his talent.

★

Johnny Marr and Chrissie Hynde feature on the launch album by Moodswings, a project headed by Billy Bragg producer, Grant Showbiz.

21
Les Negresses Vertes' lead singer Helno is found dead in Paris today. He died of a heroin overdose.

23
Jamiroquai, a new name in updated 70s funk, plays the Town and Country Club in what seems like an ambitious venue for such a new name. The place, however, sells out.

★

Julian Cope releases *Rite,* an instrumental meditation album on his own Ma-Gog label. Mail-order release only, he stresses that this isn't a proper Julian Cope album??

25
Belly, fronted by Tanya Donelly, ex of Boston band Throwing Muses, release their debut album to massive critical acclaim. "*Star* has the same perfection, power and woozy logic of a fairy tale, simultaneously cosy and scary," proclaims Melody Maker.

★

Jesus Jones release their third album, *Perverse,* the second greatest rock album of the 90s so far – according to their leader Mike Edwards, at any rate. Who pipped 'em to the post, says he? The Young Gods, apparently.

★

Mick Jagger releases a brand new solo single called *Sweet Thing.* Melody Maker offer this snippet of advice: "Leave it out, grandad".

26
Inordinately angry LA outfit, Rage Against The Machine, storm into London and play a ferocious gig at the Camden Underworld that leaves people quaking in their boots at their bone-shaking conviction.

★

The Screaming Trees, another heavily touted American band, arrive in the UK for their first European tour.

27
REM's Michael Stipe teams up with film director Oliver Stone for a new movie about political life in America.

31
Nordoff-Robbins Music Therapy Rock And Pop Memorabilia Auction takes place at London's Oxford Circus HMV Store. A plethora of rock rarities are donated by stars to help raise money for children with physical disabilities.

★

Whitney Houston still at Number One...

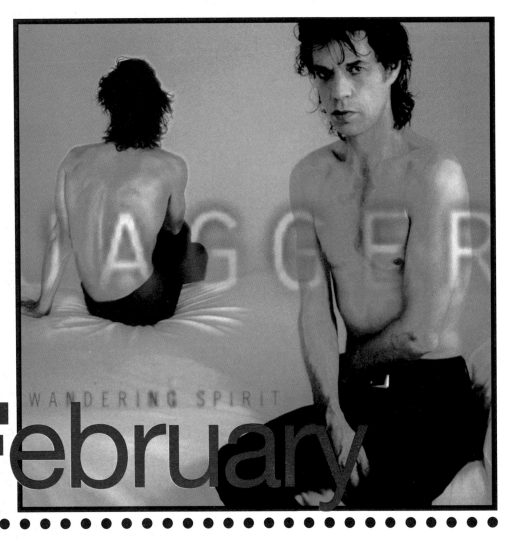

February

"... you have to remind yourself that we are in the company of a man deep into middle-age who has been cranking it out for four decades now."

Mick Jagger
Wandering Spirit

Having pressed the pause button on the Stones for the time being, Mick Jagger decided to have another shot at this solo lark. Wandering Spirit marked his third time out alone and another chance to discover if there is life without Keef...

"*Wandering Spirit* may never approach the glory of his early 70s heyday but, by golly, it has a damned good go. All in all, a worthy redress of balance." **Select**

"...Reaffirms Jagger's supreme vitality as a performer. His high, harsh tone and his outlandishly slack verbal mannerisms have been imitated time without number yet still remain utterly distinctive." **The Times**

"Despite welcome glimpses of the old Jagger wit, the lesson of *Wandering Spirit* is the same one he failed to heed on his previous two solo albums: you have nothing to prove, so relax." **Q**

"...Offers a generous menu and a few mouth-watering courses. It's not a banquet, but then beggars can't really be choosers when it comes to Mick Jagger, Stone alone." **Vox**

"You shrug your shoulders and reckon that whatever it was he once had has gone and was probably all down to Keef, chemistry and chemicals, anyway. Yet elsewhere, Jagger is firmly in control, well sussed about what works best for him." **NME**

"What a fine, fine album. The main part of the glory, must without a doubt, go to rock's Groovy Grandad." **Melody Maker**

"There is something vampiric about the way he has rejuvenated himself with fresh musical blood. The Jagger voice is as gnarled and guttural as it should be." **The Independent**

"...Sounds more like a Rolling Stones record than the group's own recent product, cleverly exploiting their legacy to emerge sounding rather like a successor to 1972's *Exile On Main Street.*" **The Observer**

"*Wandering Spirit* is much better than its predecessors might have led you to expect. Rick Rubin's flat, hard production and Jagger's purposeful vocals interact persuasively." **The Guardian**

"Jagger swaggers through this storming set with such gleeful abandon that you have to remind yourself that we are in the company of a man deep into middle-age who has been cranking it out for four decades now." **Rock CD**

"It hooks you in immediately, and like the man himself is lean, mean and muscular." **Today**

snippets

Henry Rollins puts his hardcore band on hold as he takes to the road for a series of spoken word gigs. No frills, no jokes, no punch lines, he plays the down-to-earth raconteur to perfection. "He's just a guy, sure, but a fun guy to spend an evening with," said Melody Maker.

Morrissey and Prince plan to meet in Los Angeles with a view to collaborating on a single in the near future.

Ruby Trax, the NME's highly-acclaimed charity compilation album, raises over £250,000 for The Spastic Society.

Paul Weller is being sued by former Jam members Rick Buckler and Bruce Foxton. They claim they are owed up to £200,000 in unpaid video, merchandising and publishing royalties which have accumulated since the band split 11 years ago.

"If we are all convinced that the original spirit, enthusiasm and spontaneity is still there, we'll reform." John Cale musing on whether the **Velvet Underground** will get it together again. They do.

Fela Kuti, the Nigerian singer-superstar, faces a possible death sentence after being arrested and charged with "conspiracy and murder".

The Saw Doctors, Ireland's natural successors to the currently stuttering Pogues, become one of the very few bands today capable of selling out tour after tour without hit singles. They play throughout February and seemingly everybody goes to see them.

● **Prince buys a nightclub in Los Angeles. The Vertigo Club, with a capacity of 1,200, will act as a sister club to his Glam Slam club in Minneapolis.**

The Primitives, carbonated 80s pop band fronted by the very blonde Tracy Tracy, split up. A spokesperson is quoted as saying, "I think they just couldn't see any way forward."

▼ **Billy Idol,** everlasting punk 'icon', denies stories that he technically died last month after collapsing outside a nightclub in LA. It was alleged that his life was saved by paramedics after he had been seen "swigging vodka and smoking marijuana" shortly before his collapse.

The Jim Rose Circus Sideshow hits the UK and creates endless controversy over their act(s). A sneak preview on "The Word" highlights their love for hanging heavy objects from unlikely body parts and a profound ability to regurgitate an amalgamation of ketchup, chocolate sauce and Pepto Bismol. Urgh.

1

U2 are spotted at Windmill Lane studios in Dublin where they are recording new tracks for a possible EP release in the near future.

★

Fish, one-time Marillion mainman, has a new album out called *Songs From The Mirror*. It's not a two-way thing.

★

Sultans Of Ping FC release their debut album, *Casual Sex In The Cineplex*, to a fairly general critical mauling. Cries of "novelty!" can be heard.

5

Stereo MC's play The Town and Country Club. The excitable crowd swear that rapper Rob Birch is the new Messiah.

★

Polygram Records plan to revive the recently deceased Factory Records within the next ten days.

6

The Wedding Present headline the NME-organised *Lost In Music* Seminar at The Town and Country Club, a day of music and chat about how to succeed in the music biz.

8

The Lemonheads see their last album, *Lovey*, re-released as Evan Dando's star continues to rise.

★

Julian Cope raises over £2,500 for anti-fur campaigners Lynx through the raffle of his Cosmic Ass-Hole microphone stand, over his sell-out four-night run at the Town and Country Club.

★

The Tragically Hip, reputedly Canada's answer to REM, release their third album, *Fully Complete*.

★

Belly's debut album, *Star*, goes straight into the chart at Number Two. 4AD, their record label, effuse pride.

Ice-T is dropped from his record label Time Warner after the controversy surrounding his *Body Count* album; specifically the track *Cop Killer*. US rap bible The Source commented, "No one is safe in rap now…"

Jamiroquai, fresh from signing an eight-album deal with Sony, releases club favourite, *When You Gonna Learn*.

★

Lenny Kravitz, retro rocker extraordinaire, releases a new single, *Are You Gonna Go My Way*, today. It's also the title of his forthcoming album.

★

Bob Dylan touches down at the Labbatt's Apollo for the first of three nights.

★

Rage Against The Machine's eponymous debut album is released to tumultuous rapture.

12

Billy Bragg plays a low key London gig with the much-revered rasta poet Linton Kwesi Johnson.

13

Henry Rollins describes Rage Against The Machine as, "The most happening band in the USA!" This earns them countless credibility points.

15

Michael Penn, singing brother of actor Sean, releases his second album, having reaped considerable stateside success with his first two years earlier.

snippets

The Auteurs debut album, *New Wave*, comes out and endless column inches are devoted to the band. "On the evidence of this stunning debut," says Melody Maker, "they sound like they are here to stay." Singer Luke Haines, however, still doesn't learn how to smile.

Rage Against The Machine appear on "The Word", airing their new single, *Killing In The Name*, which features the line, "Fuck you, I won't do what you tell me," repeated over and over. The show is deluged with complaints.

Van Morrison is joined on stage at the Dublin Point this month by Bono, Bob Dylan, Elvis Costello, Chrissie Hynde, Stevie Winwood and Kris Kristofferson for a version of Dylan's It's All Over Now, Baby Blue.

Belly take to the road on the crest of mega-fame as *Star,* their first LP, soars towards the top of the charts, and singer Tanya can't quite stop smiling. "Belly encapsulate our desires and enraptured us all. Someone to die for? Probably," beams NME. "Relish Belly for what they are – an increasingly and justly popular part-time delight," proclaims Melody Maker, while Select is smitten with Gail the bassist: "She stalks around the stage wielding her huge bass like a pitchfork, her hair slamming back and forth with the beat."

Ice-T and Ice Cube are set to join forces to launch a range of fashion wear. Strange, but true. T wants to create a, "Gap for would-be urban guerillas". Each item will carry a gun logo.

● *Rump, obscure Sub Pop band, are set to release a single attacking "Beverly Hills 90210" star, Shannon Doherty, who plays pouting, smirking Brenda in the series.*

Nirvana's Chris Novoselic is planning a spoken word gig in London in aid of charity, possibly for Bosnian children. **"A good time is guaranteed,"** guaranteed a spokesman.

"The Late Show" has a No Nirvana Special, featuring the cream of American rockery and excluding its most famous exponent (hence the title). Bands included are Sonic Youth, Pearl Jam, Screaming Trees and Belly.

photo: LFI

snippets

"Make no mistake, Alice In Chains are the real deal. Real kill-yourself music." Melody Maker nominate a Next Big Thing.

Bill Grundy, the TV presenter made infamous after his on-screen clash with The Sex Pistols, died aged 69. After "that incident" in 1976, he rarely worked in television again.

Michael Jackson appears in front of a worldwide audience of countless millions as a special guest on Oprah Winfrey's show. In the hour-long show, he attempts to put paid to the many rumours that surround him. The world coos.

circumstances in Birmingham. He was just 24.

● **Kylie Minogue signs to the groovy deConstruction label and promises brand spanking new material by the autumn.**

Zodiac Mindwarp, enduring 80s maverick, almost dies from a massive brain haemorrhage. "It was like my head exploded. I woke up covered in blood and snot," he said. He promised to curb his excessive drinking habits in the future.

Spiral Tribe, underground rave merchants, appear in court charged with public order offences arising from their Castle Morton rave last May. If convicted, they could face jail sentences.

Huggy Bear, leaders of 93s Riot Grrrl movement, appear on "The Word"'s

Valentine's Day special. After a segment on two self-confessed "bimbos", the Huggies scream abuse at presenter Terry Christian and are chucked out of the studio.

Happy Mondays, after intense speculation, finally confirm their split in the face of a potential £1.7 million deal with EMI. The parting is far from pleasant.

Musical Youth's Patrick Waite is found dead in mysterious

15

Elvis Costello teams up with The Brodsky Quartet for an album of quasi-classical music. Vox Magazine, for one, gives it the thumbs down.

★

Depeche Mode's latest bid for world domination comes in the form of a brand new single, *I Feel You,* out today.

★

Right Said Fred feature on this year's ghastly Comic Relief single, *Stick It Out.*

18

Therapy?, Belfast's thrash metal post-punk outfit, play a midnight show at London's Camden Palace.

20

Dinosaur Jr begin their UK noise-fest tour with the similarly adored Come and Bettie Serveert in support. The amps are turned up to 11 each night.

22

Suede release their third single, *Animal Nitrate,* as a taster for their debut album, which should hit the shops in a month.

Bryan Ferry returns after an inordinately long silence with a cover version of *I Put A Spell On You.*

★

Simply Red play the first of three sold-out nights at

Birmingham's NEC as part of their biggest tour to date.

★

Living Colour, pioneering black rock act, release their third album, *Stain.*

★

kd lang, country diva who recently embraced pop, re-releases her *Constant Craving* single.

★

St Etienne release their second LP, *So Tough,* today. It, apparently, "takes your mind on a non-stop, quasi-erotic journey through the places of beauty and horror in this world and other worlds."

East 17, 1993's Teen Pin Ups With Attitude, unleash their first album, *Walthamstow.* Their manager, Tom Watkins, also guided Bros and the Pet Shop Boys to megastardom.

24

BBC2 show Neil Young live in concert. Grown men cry.

25

Belly play London's ULU and sell it out in a matter of hours, making them Very Hot Property. A Town and Country Club date for two weeks later is quickly arranged to appease fans.

27

Take That sit pretty in the singles chart with *Why Can't I Wake Up With You?* They make Bros seem just a distant memory.

★

Factory Records remains dormant despite rumours earlier in the month that hinted Polygram were poised to step in.

"From funk-rock to Hendrix soul, the glam icon expands his retro-pop lexicon."

March
•••••• • • • • • • • • • • • •

Lenny Kravitz
Are You Gonna Go My Way

He may be Joe Public's favourite retro rocker, but few artists grate on the critics' collective nerves the way Lenny Kravitz does. As he becomes more and more successful, so the diatribes become more acute. The two (Kravitz-vs-Critics) live in perfect disharmony…

"Third time around and Lenny Kravitz is still shagging an elegantly dressed corpse. Fashionably crumpled, worn in the right places, but utterly empty." **NME**

"As a solo artist, he's big on attitude and woefully short on new ideas, hippy revival or not." **Vox**

"His great strengths remain: meticulous creative mimicry, a gift for pleasing melody and innate good taste, but there's little here he hasn't done better." **Q**

"[It's] by no means a bad record, but it's a peculiarly joyless affair. Maybe it's all those paisley shirts giving him a headache." **Select**

"Here, his well-documented obsession with glories from the past again serves to stifle rather than inspire his undoubted talents." **Time Out**

"There is the familiar mix of hard rocking struts and tender ballads written in the image of the usual heroes… Kravitz may be stuck in a groove, but his timing is good." **The Times**

"Anybody complaining that 'they don't write songs like they used to', will find Lenny writing songs exactly like they used to. He's got the past sewn up, but what else can he do?" **The Guardian**

"Kravitz is yet to squeeze past his influences with a style of his own, but

snippets

Polly Harvey is interviewed in the Evening Standard magazine claiming that her imminent material will be even more abrasive than previous work. "Like, just how much more horrible, nasty and unpleasant can I make all this...?" she grins.

The Rainbow in Finsbury Park is set to re-open as a music venue in May after 12 years. The venue is set to be refurbished at a cost of £500,000.

Shaun Ryder claims he is so broke after the Mondays' split that he is given two months to pay a £650 court fine for drunk driving.

meanwhile his musical equivalent of Antiques Made To Order is a pleasurable diversion."
The Daily Telegraph

"Is it a bird, is it a plane, is it Jimi Hendrix? No, it's Lenny Kravitz and adequacy will always be his problem." **Hot Press**

"At its best, this latest work skilfully negotiates a truce between the 60s and the 90s without sounding remotely compromised." **Rock CD**

"From funk-rock to Hendrix soul, the glam icon expands his retro-pop lexicon." **I-D**

Radio One inadvertently play the uncensored version of Rage Against The Machine's *Killing In The Name* on the chart run-down. Listeners are bombarded with four-letter words and reach for the phones to complain en masse. Like, don't they have lives??

The Undertones' intended reunion tour has been scrapped by singer Feargal Sharkey. The band was offered £250,000 to play six British shows, and all but Sharkey jumped at the chance. The singer is now far too busy as an A&R man at Polydor.

Ice-T's *Home Invasion* album comes out on Rhythm Syndicate Records, after being dropped by Time Warner over the *Cop Killer* furore.

Wendy James, ex of Transvision Vamp, returns with her first solo album. Nothing too bizarre about that, until it is revealed that the entire songsheet was donated to her by one Elvis Costello.

Select magazine stick Brett from Suede on the cover against a backdrop of a Union Jack proclaiming, "Yanks go home!" Inside, they celebrate the alleged return of proud Brit pop.

1
Spin Doctors, riding high in the American Top Ten, release *Little Miss Can't Be Wrong.*

★

The High, baggy pop merchants of 1989 – a sort of sub-Stone Roses – finally return with a new single. No one notices so their 15 minutes appear to be up.

★

Tom Waits sees his classic *Heartattack And Vine* single re-released as it is used to plug the latest Levi's ad on TV with Screamin' Jay Hawkins on vocals. Waits is not entirely pleased.

4
Shabba Ranks, the world Number One ragga star, has had a scheduled appearance on America's "The Tonight Show" pulled because of his homophobic remarks recently made on "The Word".

8
That Petrol Emotion, the band who invented indie-dance back in 1987, release *Detonate My Dreams* on their own Koogat label.

★

Blast First, the label which brought Sonic Youth, Dinosaur Jr and Big Black to the world before folding in 1989, plans to re-launch.

★

Frank Black's much-anticipated solo album hits the record stands.

★

Duran Duran come back with a new album. Much to everyone's surprise – even the band – people buy it.

★

The Cranberries, lilting Irish four-piece oft compared to the Sundays, finally release their inaugural album after months of delay.

9
Blaggers ITA, anti-fascist ska-activists, sign to EMI.

★

Paul Weller embarks on a short British tour, taking time out from rehearsals for his second solo album.

10
Vince Power, owner of the Mean Fiddler group, announces his intentions to buy the Town and Country Club, increasing his London venue tally to seven.

12

Paul Young teams up with his old backing band The Q Tips for a trip down memory lane at selected venues.

13
The Shamen take their Progeny Tour on the road and proceed to blow people's minds. Like, wow.

★

The music weeklies finally embrace the 'crusty move-ment' properly as Back To The Planet and Ozric Tentacles adorn Melody Maker's cover. Inside, they discover exactly What Is A Crusty.

★

2 Unlimited, Belgian pop rap duo, top the singles chart with *No Limit.* The poetic and inspired line "techno techno techno techno" becomes a national punchline.

★

Lenny Kravitz proves that the critics know nothing at all whatsoever as he watches his latest album cruise into Number One ahead of the latest Sting album. He swings his flares with pride.

LIVE!

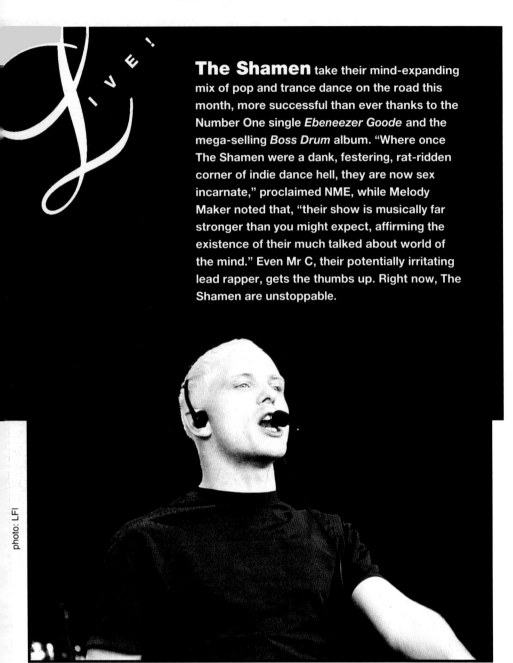

photo: LFI

The Shamen take their mind-expanding mix of pop and trance dance on the road this month, more successful than ever thanks to the Number One single *Ebeneezer Goode* and the mega-selling *Boss Drum* album. "Where once The Shamen were a dank, festering, rat-ridden corner of indie dance hell, they are now sex incarnate," proclaimed NME, while Melody Maker noted that, "their show is musically far stronger than you might expect, affirming the existence of their much talked about world of the mind." Even Mr C, their potentially irritating lead rapper, gets the thumbs up. Right now, The Shamen are unstoppable.

"It would be tragic if the band just plummeted. I'd have to go off and be a star in a completely different way." Brett Anderson on the completely unthinkable.

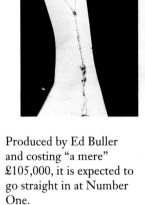

Shakin' Stevens has to pay £500,000 in legal costs over royalties owed to his former band The Sunsets. "We were all mates and Shaky betrayed us," said the drummer.

Michael Jackson's current album, *Dangerous*, is rumoured to be something of a flop, despite selling 15 million copies – peanuts compared to the sales of *Bad* and *Thriller*.

Suede's debut album is finally scheduled for a March 29 release.

Produced by Ed Buller and costing "a mere" £105,000, it is expected to go straight in at Number One.

"Morrissey made it uncomfortable to eat meat in his presence. We moved on to fish, but then he said, 'Fish have feelings too…'" Ex-Smiths bass guitarist **Andy O'Rourke** *on the vagaries of being a carnivore in His company.*

"I'm very sim___. I'm just happy to p___ and sing for p___le." Lemonheads' Evan ___do on the meaning of life, the universe, and everything.

snippets

Mick Hucknall of Simply Red has set up a production company to discover new talent in the record industry.

XFM, London's only indie radio station currently bidding for a full licence, announces details of a profile-heightening gig to take place at Finsbury Park in June. The Cure will headline.

"Doesn't it just make you want to take the silly old fuckwit outside and shoot him?" Melody Maker reviews the new Sting album.

London's Town and Country Club watches its final days tick away as its closure date of March 24 looms. The honour of final ever T&C gig goes to Van Morrison.

Depeche Mode's new album, *Songs Of Faith And Devotion*, enters the charts at Number One in its first week of release.

Daisy Chainsaw, punk pop one-hit wonders responsible for the manic *Love Your Money*, part company with their somewhat unpredictable singer Katie Jane Garside.

Pop Will Eat Itself, recently dropped by RCA

in the face of major success, turn down offers from EMI and Epic and instead sign to minuscule indie label, Infectious.

Rolf Harris soars into the Top Ten with his decidedly unique adaptation of the Led Zep classic, *Stairway To Heaven*. Were he dead, Robert Plant would turn in his grave.

The Stone Roses, 1989's Suede, apparently now have enough tracks recorded for that elusive second album. A single is expected in early summer, though no one holds their breath.

"Maybe I'm just not cut out for being in a band..." Ex-Pixies singer **Frank Black,** on the eve of the release of his solo LP.

- - - - - - - - - - - - - -

The Radio One Top 40 Show is aired peppered with mistakes after a mix-up by chart compilers Gallup. Twenty of the Top 40 placings were inaccurate.

★

Ride and The Charlatans play their two Day Tripper shows in Brighton and Blackpool to rapturous applause.

15
Run DMC, true rap pioneers, return with a new single, *Down With The King*.

★

Van Morrison releases a *Best Of*, volume II.

★

"I've had so many bad reviews that I wouldn't be able to make another record if I took them seriously." Mick Jagger as the reviews for his third LP pour in.

16
London's ULU plays host to a week of benefit gigs in aid of the Gimme Shelter charity. Kingmaker, New Model Army and Thousand Yard Stare appear.

20
Dinosaur Jr's leader, J Mascis, announces a sabbatical from the band as he attempts to recover from tendonitis, a form of RSI.

★

Huggy Bear, those Riot Grrrl activists, become the latest sensation to scorch the music weeklies. It becomes impossible to ignore them.

★

American Music Club issue their Mercury album. Select says, "Eitzel pens another classic".

★

Harry Connick Jr releases an album called *Eleven*, which was recorded back in 1978 when, coincidentally enough, this generation's Frank Sinatra was 11.

★

Brett Anderson and David Bowie meet and are interviewed for the NME, Brett beside himself at meeting his hero.

22
Sonic Youth, the band who reputedly discovered Nirvana, have a new single out, entitled *Sugar Kane*.

★

The Fall release their first single since being "relinquished" from their deal with Fontana Records. *Glam Racket* allegedly pokes sly fun at Suede, suggesting that Mark E Smith is as cantankerous as ever.

★

The Cranes, Portsmouth's arch Goths, release *Adrift*, their first single since touring the world with The Cure. Robert Smith's influence is omnipresent.

26
Hole, the Seattle band fronted by Courtney Love, grace "The Word" premiering their new single, *Beautiful Son*.

29
Belly re-release their *Gepetto* single with a particularly giddy rendition of Tom Jones' *It's Not Unusual* on the B-side.

★

Suede's album finally arrives. The hammered-into-submission nation takes a deep breath and swamps the record shops in an attempt to purchase a copy. It becomes the fastest selling debut since Frankie Goes To Hollywood's.

April

Depeche Mode
Songs Of Faith And Devotion

Released at the end of last month and totally dominating the charts' upper echelons throughout April, Depeche Mode truly come of age with this, their tenth album. Regal, saintly, and so high it kisses the sky, it makes their birthplace of Essex seem unnervingly close to heaven…

"By avoiding the disco sex-song option, the Mode reveal how much room for musical manoeuvre is afforded by the sex/sin format. Depeche Mode sound like God!" **Q**

"…is another fine record, which should ensure their status until the mid 90s." **Vox**

"Depeche Mode are much too interesting to avoid now that they are grown up. [This] is a very fine record indeed." **NME**

"Cruel people think the new-look tattooed Dave Gahan looks like [Ministry's] Al Jourgensen played by Mr Bean, but [this LP], as rich and rank as a pop record can be, will shut them up." **Select**

"Never just a synthesizer group, they are synthesizers, expert magpies with a striking gift for genre digestion and populist mimicry." **Melody Maker**

"This latest album shows that they have eclipsed their most recent achievements and hauled themselves onto a new plateau where there is no competition. These are songs to celebrate." **Rock CD**

"The great strength of Depeche Mode, and on this album more than ever, is their ability to use new sounds and technology yet sustain the old virtues of song, melody and harmony." **Today**

"This astonishing, powerful album is Depeche Mode's tenth, and kills any residual notions of them being a 'synth-pop' act stone dead. This is a masterpiece." **The Guardian**

"A dark, moody affair. A huge album with longevity." **Music Week**

"Depeche Mode excel themselves once more with this storming leather-clad rocker. It's big." **I-D**

"… they have eclipsed their most recent achievements and hauled themselves onto a new plateau where there is no competition."

snippets

Paul Calf becomes the music industry's favourite comedian, overtaking Newman and Baddiel. His drunken performances on Jonathan Ross's "Saturday Zoo" are watched by all. 'Bag o' shite' becomes the country's latest catchphrase.

Happy Mondays look set to re-emerge, still fronted by Shaun Ryder, but with a new line-up behind him, including ex-Smiths guitarist Craig Gannon.

Jah Wobble, old PIL bassist and, incidentally, one-time tube driver, signs a long-term contract with Island Records.

Shabba Ranks is still paying for his misjudged anti-gay comments on "The Word" last month as his appearance on "Top Of The Pops" is marred by gay rights activists.

▼ **Bruce Springsteen** is the latest in a long line to release an MTV *Unplugged* album. The suitably understated record is lapped up by Broooce fans.

Hole and **Huggy Bear** play a hyper-publicized female-only gig at London's Subterania. Despite the pre-show coverage it receives, the venue is only a third full.

The Lemonheads return to these shores as giants. Their national tour is stuffed to bursting with willing brides, only too happy to take singer Evan Dando's hand in marriage.

REM are understood to have finished writing the follow-up LP to *Automatic For The People*. An end of year release date is suggested.

● Metallica continue to tour the Far East despite riots at a show during which two people are believed to have died, with 51 injured.

"Nothing pisses the gods off more than a reluctant messiah, you know."
Terence Trent D'Arby
on, er, himself.

1
Shaggy, sudden pop-ragga megastar, is at Number One with the irresistible *Oh Carolina*, a feat which commences the official Summer Of Ragga.

4
Suede at Number One in the album charts. But of course…

5
New Order return after a four-year silence with their first single for London Records after Factory's demise. *Regret* is the name it goes under.

★

Back To The Planet release *Teenage Turtles* in which they blame the cartoon characters for just about everything. Quite right too.

★

Sugar, fronted by ex-Husker Du man Bob Mould, release their second album in less than a year. Critics declare him God. Just for a change.

★

World Party, eco-rockers led by Karl Wallinger, finally release their long-awaited new single *Is It Like Today*. It's described as "the history of the world in a pop song".

★

Madonna flirts her way back into the Top Ten with her not-so-classic version of the classic *Fever*.

★

The The have a new single *Slow Emotion Replay* out today.

★

REM release their fourth single, *Everybody Hurts*, from their *Automatic For The People* LP.

★

Aerosmith run into trouble with London Transport over the promotional poster for their album, *Get A Grip*. The poster features the LP cover art of a cow's udder with one pierced teat and the band's logo branded on its hind quarters.

10
Blur continue to plot their re-invention by graffiti-ing *Modern Life Is Rubbish* anywhere reachable. The NME, by a stunning coincidence, are on hand to capture this raw anarchy on film.

★

As David Bowie's umpteenth album, *Black Tie White Noise,* is poised for release, the Melody Maker admits it's "intermittently very good".

12
Sub Sub, Mancunian dance act, burst into blooming life with *Ain't No Love*. Critics proclaim it one of the dance records of the year.

★

The Bluebells, rejuvenated by a current Volkswagen TV ad, are Number One stars with *Young At Heart*. Talk of an 80s revival ensues. The 90s revival? Oh, that's next week.

13
The Orb, ambient purveyors par excellence commence a brief tour of the country, via – most probably – outer space.

★

Frank Black unleashes his Beach Boys-penned *Hang On To Your Ego* single.

The Lemonheads, all of a sudden, are everywhere. Everyone loves the Lemonheads, everyone loves tilt-necked Evan Dando. As he sweeps across the nation this month, NME tries to see through his guise before shrugging helplessly, "True, his dopey image is controlled, contrived and rather over-emphasised – there is a sharp, quick-witted guy shielded by dumb shyness in there somewhere – but there seems little point in dropping the facade now." Melody Maker: "Sometimes it appears so easy that I'm convinced there must be a recipe book where Evan gets all his songs." Suddenly, Evan up there is heaven down here.

"Posturing Robert Plant was dodgy enough when I first did it. Now it's ridiculous!" Robert Plant, the sensible fortysomething in 1993.

snippets

Suede's London Kilburn National gig on April 8 is pulled with only hours to go due to a technical hitch at the venue. Approximately 3,000 fans are locked out, distraught and not entirely happy with the situation.

Holly Johnson, one-time front man of 80s legends Frankie Goes To Hollywood, announces that he is HIV Positive.

The Orb are seeking a new home after their breakdown with soon-to-be former label, Big Life Records.

● **U2** take legal action against the Performing Rights Society, claiming they are owed millions of pounds in royalties from European live shows.

Raw Soup, a new yoof music TV show, is launched on the ITV network. Did someone say teething troubles?

photo: LFI

"The tide's going out and I'm marooned on this beach and I'm watching this kid from Nirvana eating ice cream." World Party's Karl Wallinger in a world of his own. Allegedly.

snippets

James Brown appears in a rare interview in the NME. "When I went to jail I slept for three months. I was tired," he says.

....

To launch Virgin Radio, **Richard Branson** undertakes a helithon, flying by helicopter from Edinburgh to London via five other British cities, reporting live to the station throughout the day after its 12.15 Manchester lift-off.

....

"I feel very similar to a lot of men – I don't feel particularly different to them. What's the problem?" **Polly Jean Harvey,** *23, female.*

....

New Order and **Sinead O'Connor** plan to co-headline the Peace Together show in Dublin next month. Sinead says she will crawl over broken glass to perform. Erm, now read on.

Shane MacGowan, the former Pogue, looks set to sign to Creation despite being wooed by ZTT Records. Since his departure from The Pogues in 1991, he has kept a deliberately low profile.

....

Madonna has meetings with ABC Television with a view to producing a mini series on the already legendary singer's early life.

"We never thought Everything But The Girl would stick around – if we had, maybe we would have chosen a better name." Ben Watt, the man behind the girl.

"I write about a certain kind of woman, those who make young men in the neighbourhood resort to crime." Ice Cube on justifying song titles like *A Bitch Is A Bitch.*

16
Aztec Camera announce details of a new single called *Dream Sweet Dreams.*

18
Back To The Planet's gig, at London's Brixton Fridge, does not attract ticket touts. Why? Crusties have no money!

19
Mega City Four, the original transit-core gigging band, bound back with their *Iron Sky* single.

★

Blur skid back on to the pop scene with their new single *For Tomorrow.*

★

London's Town and Country Club re-opens under the new name of The Forum. Check out those shiny new bars…

★

World Party's third album, *Bang,* explodes onto the scene. Ho ho.

★

Pop Will Eat Itself release *Weird's Bar & Grill,* a full-length live album celebrating some of their favourite gigs.

24
PJ Harvey grabs a snoozing chicken in her arms for an NME cover opportunity.

26
Maria McKee, the flame in Lone Justice, returns with new material, headed by the single *I'm Gonna Soothe You.*

★

Kingmaker, pretenders to the indie crown, release their (chartbound) *Ten Years Asleep* EP.

★

The Fall, legendary Mancunian grumps, release *The Infotainment Scan,* their 17th album. Phew.

★

Porno For Pyros, Perry Farrell's new band after Jane's Addiction, unleash their eponymously-titled first album.

★

The Farm play a one-off gig for charity at Liverpool Philharmonic Hall, with a 70-piece orchestra and choir backing them.

★

Morrissey has his first live video, *Live In Dallas,* out today.

27
Michelle Shocked, US folk hero, brings her Arkansas Traveller Show to London.

29
Van Halen hit Wembley Arena as part of their European tour.

30
Virgin Radio launched in Manchester at the Virgin Megastore at 12.15pm by Richard Branson. The first music is a specially recorded verstion of *Born To Be Wild* by INXS.

DONALD FAGEN · KAMAKIRIAD

May

"Fagen's albums ease you into a womb-cosy dreamstate... a wave of nostalgic bliss, they conjure an unreachably sexy place, a romantic vale of calm..."

"A remarkable piece of work, and one which does entirely without rock 'n' roll. This is American 'speculative fiction' as a hi-speed soundtrack to your alienated life. It'll make you want to eat mud." **Time Out**

"The kind of portrait that could only be painted by a youthful sci-fi enthusiast and jazz buff turned sourpuss pop cynic. Grown up album of the year, so far." **The Independent**

"*The Nightfly* was a monstrously hard act to follow, but incredibly Fagen has pulled it off. I don't know when he is planning to release his third solo album, but when he does I will be first in line, pension book in hand." **The Daily Telegraph**

"… a monument to the intellectual and technical ingenuity of a bygone age. Superlative in sound but bereft of feel, it is an immaculate irrelevance." **The Times**

"Fagen fans have had to wait 11 years for the follow-up to *The Nightfly,* and they won' be disappointed by this sweet, funky, effortlessly cool concoction." **Today**

"I'd play the whole album on a flight because it's brilliant. And it stands up to the ravages of time." 10cc's Eric Stewart in **Rock World**

"Old Steely Dan fans are waxing lyrical and insisting that it has been well worth the 11-year wait. Anyone else may be inclined to dismiss it as a strange, meandering and ultimately very boring exercise in self-indulgence." **Daily Express**

Donald Fagen
Kamakiriad

It took 11 years for former Steely Dan frontman Donald Fagen to follow up the hugely successful Nightfly, *an enormous period not lost on the album's many critics. Writing for the Telegraph, Tony Parsons reckoned he'd be ready with his pension book for the follow-up, but not everyone agreed...*

"The sole problem is that *Kamakiriad* is a concept album. It's about driving a car through a future landscape and the things that happen along the way. Boring old sci-fi. How passé. Plenty of majesty but no mystery at all." **NME**

"Exquisite rather than lush, the music is not only sensually brilliant but exactly catches the subtle paradoxes of Fagen's dreamworld. As suggestively scenic and addictively repeatable as the best road movie, *Kamakiriad* amply justifies a very long wait." **Q**

"Most great records jolt you into responding, Fagen's albums ease you into a womb-cosy dreamstate. Like a wave of nostalgic bliss, they conjure up an unreachably sexy place, a romantic vale of calm. That Fagen manages to achieve this with an effortless-seeming, though actually meticulous, craft is miraculous." **Melody Maker**

"Steely Dan fans – the bad news is, you died. The good news is, you woke up in heaven. *Kamakiriad* is beyond the twilight zone." **Vox**

ting denies a rift
etween Kayapo Indian
nief Raoni in a press
atement. "There is no
ft... and I am still a
ember of the Rain Forest
oundation. Someone
ynically used my name to
ttack the Indians. Whose
de are you on?"

• • • • • • • • • • • • • • • • • •

ormer **Housemartins**
rummer Hugh Whittaker
s sentenced to six years in
rison after a series of
ttacks on his ex-business
artner. "I lost all normal
egard you would feel for a
uman being. I lost that
egard, this mutual thing,"
e said when questioned
bout attacking James
Iewitt with an axe.

Morrissey returns with a live album recorded in Paris, Beethoven was Deaf, to mixed opinion. "Beethoven was indeed deaf, and halfway through this record, how I envied him." said the Melody Maker. "There is a nightmarish spectre

lurking in the grooves of a once great man who's decided to turn up at parties dressed up as a jingoistic thug and talk to men in suits about marketing ploys," reckoned NME, while Vox thought "this recording seems no more vital than Gary Moore's new live album or Wet Wet Wet's". Mozzer did find a friend at Rock CD, however: "Something suspiciously close to a masterpiece," he said.

"I know how to ride, it's no big deal." Guns N' Roses guitarist Gilby Clarke before breaking his arm during a charity motorcycle race. He was temporarily replaced by former Roses guitarist Izzy Stradlin.

ig Star, the legendary
JS guitar group fronted by
Alex Chilton, re-form for
JS dates. "Alex's voice
oars from falsetto to
God," reckons Melody
Maker.

• • • • • • • • • • • • • • • • • •

▶ **Eric Clapton wins an armful of heavy metal at the Grammy Awards Stateside. Awards were ...er, awarded for his Unplugged LP, his Tears In Heaven soundtrack song and the new acoustic version of Layla, winner in the Best Rock Song category.**

May**Diary**

1
Utah Saints release their third single, *Believe In Me*. This time the sampling gurus 'borrow' a little material from Human League's Phil Oakey and Crown Heights Affair.

4
Spin Doctors choose *Two Princes* as the second single from *Pocket Full Of Kryptonite*... few predict its subsequent mega-success.

5
Rumours abound that Prince has "quit the music business" halfway through an American tour. He's said to want to concentrate on "live theatre, interactive media and motion pictures". Warners prepare to take solace in their library of over 500 unreleased Prince tracks…

6
A church service for guitarist Mick Ronson, who died on April 29 from cancer of the liver, is held in London. Famed for his seminal work with David Bowie, Ronson had also worked with everyone from Bob Dylan to Morrissey.

9
Bono unveils his new on-stage persona, 'MacPhisto', to 45,000 U2 fans in Rotterdam. In white face, gold lamé suit and cartoon devil horns, Bono's decadent "Last rock star" is described by sources close to the band as "Quentin Crisp on acid".

★

Verve release *Blue* on multi formats, with the 10-inch version featuring a piece of blank verse written and recited by singer Richard Ashcroft.

10
Mega City Four release their new album *Magic Bullets*, and announce the appropriate full-scale UK tour.

★

Seattle's The Posies release their *Frosting On The Beater* album

on Geffen. It's produced by Don Fleming and variously described as "all the best bits of every other record" and "a treat and a half".

12
Iggy Pop signs to Virgin Records and announces his first UK dates in three years.

13
Four years after the release of *Technique*, New Order return with *Republic* on London, their first LP since the demise of Factory Records.

14
Charlatans keyboard player Rob Collins pleaded not guilty and elected to trial by jury on charges relating to a firearms incident.

15
Believe, Lenny Kravitz's second single from his *Are You Gonna Go My Way* LP, is released.

17
Aztec Camera release their fifth album, *Dreamland*, produced by Roddy Frame and Ryuichi Sakamoto.

★

Anthrax's new album, *Sound Of White Noise*, released on Elektra, is produced by Dave Jerden of Jane's Addiction/Alice In Chains fame.

snippets

George Michael's *Five Alive* EP gets to Number One, his live version of Queens' *Somebody To Love* doing the business. Recorded at last year's Freddie Mercury Tribute gig, *Somebody* wasn't the bestubbled-one's first choice. "Actually, the first thing I wanted to do was *Under Pressure*," he said. "But Roger Taylor said Annie Lennox had already taken it ..."

Nirvana fall out with producer Steve Albini over the making of their *Nevermind* follow-up. "Until we have the songs recorded the way we want them, Nirvana will not release this record," reckoned the band's Kurt Cobain. And Albini? "I finished my work in February and I've been talking about it almost daily ever since. I'm quite tired of talking about it."

After two years without a sniff of on-stage activity, The Mission unveil the new line-up for a projected tour. Mish mainman Wayne Hussey and drummer Mick Brown are joined by former Spear of Destiny guitarist Mark Gemini-Thwaite, former Pretenders/Primitives bassist Andy Hobson and keyboardist Rik Carter. Meanwhile, original Mish bassman Craig Adams finds a gig with Hussey's former partner Andrew Eldrich in the Sisters of Mercy.

PJ Harvey burned across the UK like a forest fire, her star in the ascendant and the critics queuing up to lionize the abrasive young woman. Of her Nottingham Rock City show, The Observer wrote: "Her performance was so uninhibited as to suggest that *Rid Of Me* was a cathartic scream, a dark unburdening of which she is now relieved," while Lime Lizard ventured: "The current PJ Harvey live experience is an immense, towering achievement." NME plumped for: "Imagine a gold platform heel stamping into your face forever." Of her Bristol University show, MM went so far as to say: "Polly's insights are so much more wicked and accurate than any of the contrived cheap thrills Suede get so lauded for." Polly good show!

▲ **Pop Will Eat Itself** tell their fans not to buy their soon-to-be-released singles compilation LP after a row with their record company, RCA. "If people have to buy it then they should wait two or three weeks until it's in the bargain bins, or steal it," reckoned singer Clint.

Paul Oakenfold is announced as guest DJ on U2's *Zooropa* dates and reveals to the Melody Maker his approach for the forthcoming four-month jaunt. "I don't think I'll do anything particularly different," he says. "I'll play across the board music, just good music that creates a happy, positive atmosphere before the band go on stage."

"Marc Bolan is an important part of Hackney history and culture," says Councillor Andy Buttress, as T Rex fans launch a campaign to erect a memorial outside Hackney Town Hall, in the 70s star's Stoke Newington birthplace. *"We support the move to commemorate his significant contribution to rock music."*

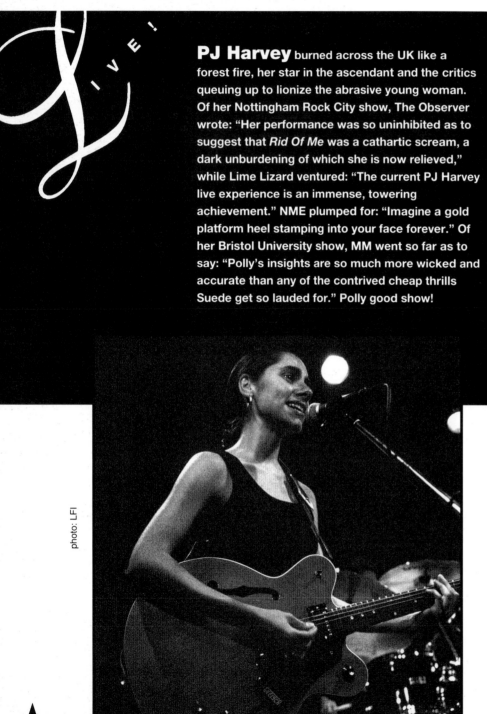

photo: LFI

snippets

Bob Dylan confirms his headline appearance at London's Finsbury Park Fleadh festival. It's Bob's first UK wind-in-the-hair extravaganza since 1984, when he played with Santana at Wembley Stadium.

Despite 12 singles chart hits in a year, The Wedding Present part company with a peripatetic RCA Records. "We've never felt as comfortable with the new regime as with the one that signed us in 1988," admits David Gedge, "most of which has now disappeared."

Ice-T is bravely snubbed by Madame Tussauds! Acolytes of Ice approach the wax museum's management to hint that the rapper is ready and willing to model, but the idea is vetoed. "People don't ask us for a model of themselves," opines a spokeswoman for the tourist attraction. "*We* ask *them.*"

▼ **Right Said Fred** face legal action over their Number One smash *Deeply Dippy*. Singer/songwriter Jim Penfold issues a High Court writ, alleging that the chord sequence and opening chorus were his own creations in 1987. The Fred decline to comment, but a spokeswoman says, "The boys are aware of what's going on."

Jim Jarmusch's new film, **Coffee And Cigarettes**, is premiered at the Cannes Film Festival. A 12-minute short from a series of same, it stars Tom Waits and Iggy Pop! "I was very fortunate to work with two musicians/performers who seem to represent the opposite ends of the rock'n'roll spectrum, but who've been a strong inspiration for my own work and life," says Jarmusch.

One-time **House Of Love** guitarist **Terry Bickers** leaves Levitation after an emotionally fraught Tufnell Park Dome show on May 14. "Levitation are a lost cause as far as I can tell," he harangues the audience. "We've completely lost it, haven't we? Haven't we?" The rest of the band describe this as "a great surprise". Perhaps wisely, Bickers concludes, "This is the last time you'll see me for a bit."

● The former Hammersmith Odeon, just getting used to the moniker Hammersmith Apollo, finds itself re-named again as The Labatt's Apollo Hammersmith. A thorough external facelift is promised.

Former Whirlwind singer and guitarist Nigel Dixon dies after a long battle with cancer. Whirlwind were best known for their live stints with Blondie, Motorhead and Ian Dury and their Chiswick label releases. After they split, Dixon accompanied former Clash bassist Paul Simenon to El Paso, returning to the UK to front Simenon's Havana 3AM.

17
Megadeth's new single, *Sweating Bullets*, is backed by a "gristle mix" of their previous hit *Symphony Of Destruction* by Nine Inch Nails leader Trent Reznor. "True psychotic genius," brags bassist Dave Ellefson.

★

Oklahoma's "goofy and inspired" Radial Spangle release their Mercury Rev-produced debut album *Ice Cream Headache* on Mint Industries. "People will talk about it until they die", claims an enthusiastic MM.

19
Jellyfish, now down to a duo, follow up their enormously successful debut LP with the release of *Spilt Milk*.

★

Turning their debut eponymous LP into a virtual greatest hits, Suede release *So Young*, single number four.

20
Tasmin Archer releases *Lords Of The New Church* from her *Great Expectations* LP.

21
Kingmaker thrill the student fraternity by unleashing their second album *Sleepwalking* on Chrysalis, and announcing an extensive tour.

★

Manchester's pop-punk legends The Buzzcocks release their first new studio album for 13 years. *Trade Test Transmission* is greeted as a rip-roaring success.

22
Morrissey and Siouxsie Sioux enter discussions regarding a musical collaboration. According to a spokesman the liaison looks "pretty likely".

23
Former Pogue, Shane MacGowan, signs to WEA's ZTT label. The world awaits his first "more rock orientated" recordings, even though his collaboration with former Thin Lizzy and Motorhead guitarist Brian Robertson was said to have proved unsuccessful.

24
The Waterboys' first LP in three years, *Dream Harder*, released on Geffen.

★

Lisa Stansfield releases *In All The Right Places* – a soul ballad from the Indecent Proposal soundtrack.

★

Arrested Development continue to, well, develop, as their first video compilation, *Eyes As Hard As A Million Tombstones*, emerges.

★

Alice In Chains release the *Angry Chair* single on Columbia as they record tracks for Arnold Schwarzenegger's Last Action Hero.

25
Bizarre kidnapping rumours circulate concerning Fishbone. According to reports from Los Angeles, guitarist Kendall Jones walked out on the band to join a religious cult, then bassist Norwood Fisher led a kidnap bid to retrieve him! As the band fly into Britain for live dates, both are expected to show, with or without bibles…

28
Former Sugarcubes singer Bjork demonstrates her unique vocal styling on her first solo single, *Human Behaviour*, a hit for One Little Indian.

29
The heavy metal press announce the cancellation of the Donington Monsters Of Rock festival. It's only the second time it's been cancelled in its 12-year history; the 1989 show was cancelled after two fans died in a crush in 1988. Promoters in 1993, Aimcarve, felt they couldn't assemble a bill which matched the standards of other bills.

30
Guns N' Roses add another date at the Milton Keynes Bowl after selling out May 29. "The cheers of 50,000 never sounded so empty," reckoned the MM.

THE WATERBOYS
DREAM HARDER

June

"Dream Harder is a psyche-altering explosion of spiritual fireworks. Mike Scott has done this. It's so brilliant to have him back."

The Waterboys

Dream Harder

Mike Scott, the man who is The Waterboys, used to be Scottish. But then, with 1985's This Is The Sea, he became a bona fide Irishman. These days, however, he's become a consummate Noo Yawker, and among bizarrely mixed reviews his latest opus is said by some to be a paean to his beloved Big Apple...

"New York stinks. The roads are a mess, the atmosphere's poisonous, the people are rude and you are likely to get killed. It seems to have done Mike Scott a power of good." **Select**

"Here Mike Scott just sounds lost in New York, adrift in a dodgy sequel subtitled Room To Roam Alone. *Dream Harder*? Must Try Harder." **Vox**

"...Wears a gigantic grin that begs forgiveness for its more hysterical moments and bombastic guitar barrages. In the process, he's made a unique record that veers maniacally from the lovable to the laughable." **Q**

"*Dream Harder* is a psyche-altering explosion of spiritual fireworks. Mike Scott has done this. It's so brilliant to have him back." **Melody Maker**

"*Dream Harder* is some party. You've got to accept the premise that Mike Scott has some kind of a vision, and allow him to tell you about it." **NME**

"... is blighted by ethereal tosh about corn circles, Pan, Glastonbury and the like. But the man who wrote *The Whole Of The Moon* is obviously capable of great things and [this] has some spectacular moments." **The Daily Telegraph**

"For all its New Yorkised production sheen, the new album is still Scott-as-hippie-gypsy." **The Guardian**

"With its loud drum sound, inflexible rhythms and soaring electric guitar solos, it's plainly designed to reflect the greater noise and faster pace of life in the urban jungle." **The Times**

"One of modern music's saints who will always prove to be one of its necessary evils." **Time Out**

"He can't decide whether he should return to his old Dylan-influenced ranting or go along with the neo-hippy zeitgeist, which you might have thought would have difficulty co-existing." **The Independent**

"Scott's enthusiasm for thundering tunes and offbeat themes is infectious." **The Observer**

snippets

Terence Trent D'Arby returns from the abyss that is pop star obscurity, by gracing the front cover of Q Magazine butt naked. Anything to plug his new *Symphony Or Damn* album.

Simply Red's album *Stars* is on its way to becoming the UK's biggest ever seller, now registering over 3¼ million sales. Only Jacko's *Bad* has sold more.

U2's Adam Clayton and supermodel Naomi Campbell are seen out and about, setting the tabloids' tongues a-wagging. Is marriage in the offing...?

The Saw Doctors' keyboardist Tony Lambert wins a whopping £850,000 on the Irish National Lottery. He instantly becomes Britain's most hated man. Something to do with jealousy.

Tom Waits is suing his former manager for allowing his *Heartattack And Vine* track to be used in the current Levi's TV ad.

Teenage Fanclub bounce back into the fray with a new EP entitled, simply, *Radio*. "I think it was Spin Magazine that said our album was the best record made by white people in the last 10 years."

"**M**y weird masterplan hasn't changed. I want to be the heaviest, meanest, rocking-est ... all those things. It has nothing to do with Nirvana." Smashing Pumpkins' Billy Corgan re-asserts his masterplan as their new single, Cherub Rock, comes out.

What absolute bollocks!" they tell Rock CD.

Select magazine attempt to breathe new life into the 80s with an eight page – !! – revival feature focusing on the decade's finer moments. Like, er, Spandau Ballet. ▼

"I don't like fiction that much. You don't have to read them all the way through..." The not entirely well-read **Billy Idol.**

"The shit that goes in the charts! Shit! Fuck Rick Astley! Fuckin' white frauds!" **Jamiroquai's** Jay Kay voicing a slight disapproval at 'youth' music.

Bjork, Icelandic pop princess, releases one of the year's most eagerly anticipated albums in Debut. It's immediately hailed as something of a classic.

The Peace Together concert in Belfast scheduled to take place at the end of last month was dramatically called off at the last minute after headliner Peter Gabriel pulled out.

4
Blur begin a national tour on the back of their vaguely warmly-received second album, *Modern Life Is Rubbish*. Their stage set includes a cooker, fridge, and settee.

5
The Peace Together concert in Dublin falls to pieces as Sinead O'Connor, almost mimicking Peter Gabriel's actions at the Belfast show last week, fails to appear, leaving only New Order to save the day.

★

The The play a rare live date at London's Brixton Academy.

7
Senseless Things, spiritual sons of indie stalwarts Mega City Four, have the whole of their Postcard label back catalogue released on one album, entitled *Postcard CV*.

★

Janet Jackson tops the UK and US album charts with her latest meisterwerk, *janet*.

8
Maria McKee tours the country playing to rapturous crowds. When she doesn't return for a second encore at her London date, the otherwise most polite crowd show their discontent by booing and throwing plastic beer glasses at the stage.

9
Harry Connick Jr graces the Albert Hall with his elegant, debonair presence.

11
Slowdive and Cranes, shoegazing and goth semi-stars respectively, begin a double-headed tour to see if anyone can remember them from 1991.

★

Suede play their debut US show in Los Angeles. A local paper is moved to comment that they are "on the verge of something really big".

★

Therapy? play their biggest headlining date at London's Forum. It's something of a success all round.

13
Gabrielle (who?) makes chart history as her first ever single, *Dreams*, debuts at Number Two, the highest debut placing ever for a brand new female artist.

14
Guns N' Roses release two live videos, delightfully emblazoned *Makin' Fucking Videos, Parts I and II*.

★

Terence Trent D'Arby teams up with delicate UK soul diva Des'ree for his new sort-of-hit single, *Delicate*.

★

Fishbone have a new album called – deep breath now – *Give A Monkey A Brain And He'll Swear He's The Center Of The Universe*.

16
Brian May, former Queen guitarist and beau of ex-Eastenders' Anita Dobson, embarks on his first solo UK tour.

LIVE!

Maria McKee has the kind of boundless energy that, bottled and sold, would make you a fortune. As her second solo album receives glowing praise, she plays a series of dates that confirm just why she's considered so cherishable. "Maria McKee is the best live performer I know. Tonight her heart beats wild and free, and there was still something in reserve. Of course, she has yet to reach her volcano but this was a Vesuvius of a show," bespoke Melody Maker, while NME agreed that "Maria McKee is simply awesome".

photo: LFI

snippets

Dire Straits' **Mark Knopfler** receives an honorary music degree from Newcastle University. "It's a great honour," he beams, quietly.

Ozric Tentacles unleash their sixth album, *Jurassic Shift*, this month. Initial quantities of the long player come with the sleeve made out of hemp. Smokin'!

● **Henry Rollins** teams up with **Sonic Youth's** Thurston Moore and **Nirvana's** Chris Novoselic to record a version of Elvis Presley's *Love Me Tender* for a new movie set in Los Angeles.

"Motherfuckers!" **Metallica's** James Hetfield tentatively greets his German audience. Politeness is not uppermost in this man's vocabulary.

Morrissey announces plans to retire after his next couple of albums, but tempts pundits by saying that he may team up with his former Smiths partner Johnny Marr before he bows out.

After **Sinead O'Connor's** shock non-appearance at Dublin's Peace Together concert, she takes out an £18,000 advert in the Irish Times, explaining via a 104-line poem her reasons for pulling out.

The Velvet Underground reform and go out on the road, all aged 50 if they're a day. "At first you can't help laughing," notes NME. Others prefer to sob authentically.

The Pet Shop Boys amble back into view with a new single, *Can You Forgive Her*, and some very large cone-shaped hats. They still look as morose as ever.

XFM's Great Xpectations concert at London's Finsbury Park lights up the metropolis as **The Cure, Carter USM, Sugar** and many more play to 30,000 indie fans. Backstage, however, it is FMB – stars of the unintentionally hilarious Channel 4 rockumentary " The Next Big Thing" – who are mobbed by adoring fans.

Prince heightens rumours that his brain cells have gone AWOL by announcing to a bemused world that he has changed his name to whatever you may have decided to call the symbol on the cover of his last LP.

snippets

"It pisses me off when people call me cute, when people say I giggle, and that I'm coy ..." The not-in-any-way cute, giggly or coy Tanya Donelly of Belly.

U2 sign a six-album deal with their record company Island to the tune of somewhere in the ballpark of £150 million. That's rich.

"Suede? Turgid. It's not even David Bowie again. You get rid of Morrissey, he moves to America, you wake up in the morning and there's Brett Anderson." The Cure's **Robert Smith**. *Diplomatic? Him?*

16

Jennifer Lynch, daughter of director daddy David, teams up with clog-wearing crusty merchants New Model Army to direct their latest video. Surely it cannot be funnier than *Boxing Helena*?

★

Kate Bush enlists Prince, Eric Clapton and Jeff Beck to work on her forthcoming LP *The Red Shoes*. The record is expected later this year.

17

Nirvana's Kurt Cobain links up with legendary US author William S Burroughs for an American single, a 12-minute thing called *The Priest They Called Him*.

19

UB40 hit the Number One spot with their rendition of Elvis' *(I Can't Help) Falling In Love With You*. It features in the new imminent Sharon Stone vehicle, *Sliver*.

21

Sinead O'Connor teams up with country legend Willie Nelson for a cover of the Peter Gabriel/Kate Bush classic *Don't Give Up*.

★

Manic Street Preachers, punk revivalists, contradict everything they've ever said by releasing a second album, *Gold Against The Soul*. Their initial manifesto was to release just one album, watch it sell 16 million copies, then split up. Time for Plan B.

★

Billy Idol limps back into the spotlight with his *Cyberpunk* album. The critics savage it with glee.

★

Kinky Machine, would-be indie sex gods who sound disarmingly like The Sweet, release their debut album today.

★

Fishbone, the US ska/funk/rock hybrid, face legal action as guitarist Norwood Fisher is taken to court facing charges of the

attempted kidnapping of Kendall Jones, Fishbone's former axe hero who quit the band after his bizarre religious conversion.

22

Jimmy Barnes, Aussie rocker with muscles just everywhere, hits Glasgow, touting his aggressive pub rock.

25

Glastonbury!

26

The Orb become further embroiled in legal action with their record label Big Life in an attempt to break free from their contract.

★

Stereo MC's adorn the Melody Maker cover as they storm across Europe as special guests of U2.

28

Julian Cope releases his second mail-order LP of the year. This one assumes the title *The Skellington Chronicles*.

★

Manic Street Preachers pre-empt their July tour with a secret gig at London's Marquee Club. It's sweaty.

★

Deborah Harry returns with a brand new solo single, *I Can See Clearly*. An album follows next month.

★

Glastonbury eases to a close after three very full, very intense, very spaced-out days, man.

29

Barenaked Ladies, Canadian sensations who sound like The Housemartins on helium, start to sell out every gig they play, starting tonight.

July

U2
Zooropa

U2 get weirder still. It's official. Bono has now become MacPhisto, complete with devil's horns and satanic cackle. And Zooropa, their sixth LP, is their wildest outing to date. Nothing like a U2 album 'should' be, this twists and turns in a curiously melancholy experimental mode and – generally, at least – is welcomed in reverential tones…

"Ten years ago, hell, five years ago, U2 were the last group you'd have bet on to pull off a record like this. U2 have finally hit upon some fundamental truths and then gone and made a good record about them." **Melody Maker**

"Pounding techno rhythms and processed sounds abound. U2 should be leading the way – assuming they have anything left to say." **NME**

"They never used to make records like this. In 93 they've gone one further: their first truly weird album. U2 are totally out of their heads and *Zooropa* is one big sexy question mark." **Select**

"*Zooropa* juggles many balls. It's all over the place… and Eno's appliance of science results in an airier, looser sound altogether." **Vox**

J2 ZOOROPA

"Zooropa has boldly sent U2's music spiralling into another dimension. It is clever stuff. If U2 get any bigger they will burst."

"The band's obsession with the bubble of modern technology and adspeak is hardly as cutting edge as they think, but their willingness to experiment has paid off handsomely."
The Observer

"Although it's unlikely to win them new fans, *Zooropa* proves that the world's biggest rock band is flexible enough to move with the times."
The Guardian

"A trip. A rollercoaster ride. A delve into the imagination. Ten tracks and it's very, very good. The most bizarrely cool thing they've done yet." **Rock CD**

"At its best, *Zooropa* is sky-funk, music from a band who, permanently or temporarily, have renounced the old folkways for new airwaves to declare that white men, they speak with digital tongue." **Hot Press**

"*Zooropa* has boldly sent U2's music spiralling into another dimension. It is clever stuff. If U2 get any bigger they will burst." **The Times**

"The world's biggest band takes a cybernetic joyride on its newest album, an outgrowth of the *Achtung Baby* aesthetic."
Billboard

"*Zooropa* is no easy listen. It broods and sulks, ducks and weaves, unwilling – or unable – to be pinned down."
Scotland on Sunday

snippets

The KLF, Britain's most inspired and inventive rave act who recently quit the music business, now seem set to return under a new guise, The K Foundation after, apparently, "five years of research" that has taken them on deep space safari via pop stardom.

Happy Mondays' former singer Shaun Ryder records a duet with Stella from Manchester's space-pop outfit **Intastella.**

▲ **Manic Street Preachers,** currently on a UK tour, are performing nightly renditions of the Mondays' classic *Wrote For Luck.*

Huggy Bear are rumoured to be on the verge of splitting up over, it is claimed, "boyfriend problems". Many struggle manfully to restrain their chuckles.

July**Diary**

1
Madonna announces details of her forthcoming Girlie Show tour this autumn. A date at Wembley Stadium on September 25 sells out in an hour.

3
Barbra Streisand, fresh from escorting Nescafé man Andre Agassi to Wimbledon every day (well, at least up till the quarter-finals), makes a rare chart appearance with her new album *Back To Broadway.*

4
Smashing Pumpkins play an ultra-rare acoustic show at London's Raymond's Revue Bar, better known as a strip joint.

5
U2's sixth album, *Zooropa,* hits the shops, and, naturally, Number One.
★
Sugar play Brixton Academy in London.

8
Sinead O'Connor pulls out of a stage adaptation of Shakespeare's Hamlet in Dublin, just a week before curtain rises. Do we see a pattern emerging here?

10
Blaggers ITA are thrown off the Manic Street Preachers tour after band member Matty is accused of assaulting a Melody Maker journalist after a show.
★
Take That's new single *Pray* tiptoes in at Number One within a week of release. The biggest teen sensation since Bros. Unarguably. These things are important, right?

Kurt Cobain is arrested at home in Seattle for assaulting wifey Courtney Love after an argument over guns in the house. Allegedly, of course.

11
Neil Young headlines Finsbury Park for a storming live set, supported by Pearl Jam, James, Teenage Fanclub and Four Non Blondes.
★
Vanessa Paradis, diminutive French starlet, plays her first ever London date to a hall packed with men and… well, more men.
★
Maxi Priest and Shaggy play the Brixton Academy as the Summer Of Ragga continues.

12
Suede play an Aids benefit gig at London's Clapham Grand. The show is filmed for posterity, directed by Derek Jarman. Special guests on the night include Chrissie Hynde and Siouxsie Sioux.

14
REM's singer Michael Stipe appears naked in an art film, Drink Deep, showing at London's ICA as part of a film package entitled Naked City, which also includes interviews with Lydia Lunch and Henry Rollins.

15
INXS play London's Forum as part of their so-called Pub Tour of 1993, a chance for them to get back to their roots and meet their fans.

16
Bjorn Again, Australia's Abba copyists, continue their seemingly relentless loop-tour of the country, now well into its second year of sold-out gigs.
★
Steven Spielberg's Jurassic Park – the film of the summer, if not the millennium – comes out today and, suddenly, nothing else in the entire world matters.

snippets

"Everything here is a bit old and a bit sickly. It's got that John Hurt vibe. Everything in London has cancer, ha ha!" **Bjork** on settling into a new city.

Neil Young is that rarest of commodities: an aging rock star for whom undying respect just continues to grow. He never makes a comeback because he never goes away. Neil Young is always there, somewhere. UK appearances this month prompt possibly rabid hyperbole from critics everywhere in a rare moment of total unison. "We leave drained, uplifted, reassured, with a warm glow suffusing our souls, smiles creasing our faces. An astonishing affirmation of one man's art," glowed Melody Maker. "Even now, at 48, there is not another guitarist to rival the sheer physicality of his work," remarked NME. It must be nice to be Neil Young.

The Red Hot Chili Peppers place an ad in LA Weekly, seeking a replacement for departed guitarist Arik Marshall. The half page ad was illustrated by bassist Flea's dinky daughter Clara.

● *The entire* **Joy Division** *and* **New Order** *back catalogue is re-released to endless re-appraisals of the band they're calling England's finest.*

Freaky Realistic, day-glo pop persons, slim to a two-piece after singer Justin has a rehearsal studio bust-up with rapper Michael and needs hospital treatment. Michael immediately hot-foots it back home to Dallas.

All About Eve, hippy revivalists with long flowing skirts and sequins, have finally split up, bored with descriptions such as this.

"They're the real deal." Bono on current credible support act **Stereo MC's.**

The Proclaimers, Scotland's acoustic duo, have a shock hit in America with their four-year-old UK hit *I'm Gonna Be (500 Miles)*, after it features in the Johnny Depp movie Benny and Joon.

The inaugural **Phoenix Festival takes place in Stratford on Avon over three days from 16th July. The event is marred by police clashing with travellers. Twenty-one people are treated for minor wounds and a security guard is stabbed.**

▲ **Prince** has changed his name yet again, the second time in a month. No longer the symbol from his LP cover, he now wants to be known as Victor, and plans to release two greatest hits packages in the autumn under his new moniker.

PJ Harvey's drummer Rob Ellis quits the band. He is believed to be fed up with the constant touring over the last six months.

"The main thing in life is to eat food and have somewhere to bury your bone…" Faith No More's bearded **Jim Martin** *on the finer things in life.*

"Rubber trousers are great. I sweat loads in them, and they make a sound when I move. A wet sound." **Polly Harvey,** wearer of rubber trousers. Special occasions only.

Select magazine carries a feature entitled Married To The Mob in which they interview pop stars' husbands, wives and partners. It reads suspiciously like Hello! magazine.

Paul McGuinness, manager of **U2,** pays £15,000 in a charity auction for Bono to play a game of chess with Russian world chess champion Gary Kasparov.

The Clash are at the centre of exaggerated rumours that they are about to reform. Any day now. Perhaps. Apparently they were offered £50 million to get back together again. A sufficiently tempting figure…?

Meatloaf has an album launch party bash to attend – his own. *Bat Out Of Hell II* doesn't come out till the autumn, but this doesn't stop him dressing up as a wolf and telling everyone that the record will sell millions upon its release. Probably.

"Naked City", yet another music yoof TV show, hits Channel 4 on Friday nights hosted by new media starlet **Caitlin Moran.**

"Do you know where I can buy some weird kind of jockstrap?" Debbie Harry on, er… oh, don't ask.

Prince (or is that Victor?), **Lenny Kravitz, St Etienne** and **Primal Scream** have all written tracks for **Kylie Minogue's** new album due in September. Pete Waterman, it can now be confirmed, has nothing to do with the project.

Siouxsie Sioux and **Morrissey** have recorded a duet together. Due for release soon, the record, its contents and style are as yet shrouded in mystery.

Johnny Rogan, author **of Morrissey And Marr: The Severed Alliance – the book which incensed the former Smiths singer so much that he issued some kind of fatwah on the author – promises yet more revelations about the band's early days. Morrissey scowls further still.**

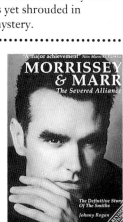

'A major achievement' *New Musical Express*

MORRISSEY & MARR
The Severed Alliance

The Definitive Story Of The Smiths
Johnny Rogan

JulyDiary

16
Guns N' Roses are raided by drugs squad officers just hours before they are due on stage in front of 70,000 fans in Argentina. Nothing is found and the gig goes ahead.

17
Jim Rose, leader of The Circus Sideshow, is rushed to an Amsterdam hospital after eating one too many light bulbs in a day. As you do. Their UK tour is set back at least a week.

★

Faith No More headline the Phoenix Festival amid increasing whispers that they are soon to be no more.

18
Jamiroquai's launch album, *Emergency On Planet Earth,* hurtles straight in at Number One.

19
The Peace Together Charity releases a compilation album in the sincere hope it sells after the near-disasters of the live shows and the lack of interest afforded the single a month earlier.

★

Smashing Pumpkins release their second album *Siamese Dream.* "It'll be hard for anyone to top this one," says Select.

★

The Waterboys release their new single *Glastonbury Song,* a good three weeks after the festival of the same name. Not the best of marketing strategies?

20
Nick Heyward, he of sensible-pullovered 80s popsters Haircut 100, attempts to return to the limelight with a small London show. An EP is to follow. So far, the intended 80s revival is stalling unspectacularly.

House Of Pain return to these shores fresh from seeing their *Jump Around* single finally do the business over here, clomping all over Brixton with support acts, Cypress Hill and Funkdoobiest.

23
Stiff Little Fingers set Wolverhampton alight (well, not quite) at the start of a mini revival tour.

24
Nirvana have recruited former Goodbye Mr McKenzie guitarist 'Big' John Duncan to expand their line-up to a four-piece for an intended tour this autumn.

★

Kurt Cobain glares ominously from the cover of the NME. Inside Courtney explains away Kurt's recent arrest while Nirvana's profoundly anticipated next album, *In Utero,* plays in the background.

26
Sweet Relief, a benefit album for maverick country singer Victoria Williams, who is suffering from multiple sclerosis, comes out featuring contributions from The Lemonheads, Matthew Sweet, The Waterboys and many more.

★

Iggy Pop, still very much alive and kicking after all these years, starts a UK tour in Wolverhampton.

★

Take That's squelchingly exciting debut tour arrives for three heady nights at Wembley Arena. Teenage riot!

29
Elton John auctions his entire private record collection. All proceeds go to Aids charities.

31
Depeche Mode play their only UK show at London's Crystal Palace. Support comes from Sisters Of Mercy, fronted by Dracula's nephew Andrew Eldrich.

August

"One moment dark and melancholy, the next sparkling with a killer pop melody and a jangling guitar ..."

The Breeders
Last Splash

When Pod introduced the idea of The Breeders in 1990, Kim Deal was a member of The Pixies and Tanya Donelly was taking time out from Throwing Muses. Three years on and Tanya is into her Belly while The Pixies are no more, and Kim the catalyst steers the helm of The Breeders. Last Splash made waves, but it wasn't a unanimous winner with the critics...

"A rickety whole at the best of times, this record comes out meandering when it thinks it's being experimental. Directionless rambles stumble into one ear and out the other." **Select**

"*The Last Splash* is wilfully abstract. Kim Deal loves cut-up lyrics that wriggle to make no sense. Each song includes a phrase that'll keep you awake, but they tend to start nowhere and end nowhere else." **Melody Maker**

"What feels like hours of sub-grunge noodlings and wearisome apathetic vocalising – not a hint of Pixies wit or eccentricity... this disappointing showing..." **Q**

"There are classic pop moments here which easily equal any Pixies peak... The Breeders have bounced back from a personal crisis and made an effortlessly classy album." **Vox**

"It's a frustrating album, inasmuch as the peaks are considerable but fleeting, and the troughs aren't really troughs at all, just mere hollows that break the momentum...

Perhaps this still fledgling group still need to find their feet and attain the confidence where they don't feel obliged to impress so much. Or maybe we just expected too much." **NME**

"*Last Splash* is an album that impresses on its own terms without relying on the memory of The Pixies. One moment dark and melancholy, the next sparkling with a killer pop melody and a jangling guitar, The Breeders swap moods with a reassuring disregard for musical barriers and blinkered tastes. A weirdly exhilarating record." **Metal CD**

"This is another great Breeders album. *Last Splash*: hell of a splash, it's got everywhere. Let's wallow... Compared to the relative grace and delivery of *Pod*, this is raucous, lunatic, eight-cars-with-no-tyres-in-the-driveway family-next-door." **Lime Lizard**

snippets

A plot to assassinate **Ice-T** and **Ice Cube** is uncovered by the FBI, following the firebombing of the offices of the National Association for the Advancement of Colored People in Tacoma, Washington. Ice-T's manager calmly decides: "Basically these guys are just fucked-up youths. There are loads of these pinheads in America. A lot of them have black people on their hitlist."

Whitney Houston sues The New York Post for 60 million dollars, after they allege she was taken to hospital following an overdose of diet pills. The paper prints a full retraction, but Whitney persists.

August's biggest pop story came when news broke of Michael Jackson's alleged relationship with 13-year-old Jordan Chandler. Jackson's two homes in California were raided by police investigating claims that Chandler had been molested by Jackson, with the tabloids covering the allegations in lurid detail after receiving a leaked nine-page report from the Los Angeles Department of Children's Services. In it, Chandler described how his and Jackson's relationship grew from a chance meeting to one involving masturbation and oral sex. Jackson was on tour in Bangkok at the time of the allegations, but was soon cancelling many performances due to reported ill health. Guilty or not guilty, the most powerful figure in show business looked unlikely to ever fully recover from the front-page, worldwide story.

▼ **Paula Abdul** wins in court Stateside, denying claims that her voice was "enhanced" by uncredited backing vocalist Yvette Marine on the multi-million-selling *Forever Your Girl* album. She weeps with joy and relief.

Nostalgic satellite channel **UK Gold** reveal that reruns of 70s "Top Of The Pops" are their biggest draw. (An exemplary 1977 edition includes Smokey Robinson, Baccara and The Sex Pistols.) At the same time the current programme quivers under the threat of the BBC axe.

Pet Shop Boys take to wearing very pointy hats. A nation giggles, but the boys determinedly plan the release of their *Very* album for Sept 20th.

Arguments go on in the aftermath of the riot that occurred at the Phoenix Festival. Many claim security guards used excessive force to quell disturbances. Promoter Vince Power strenuously denies this: "We've got an impeccable record."

In Swansea, **Manic Street Preachers** are booed offstage and bassist Nicky Wire is rushed to hospital with concussion after being hit by a bottle. "Well done, you brainless wankers!" shouts singer James Bradfield. The Manics admit they are not overly beloved in their homeland. "Tom Jones doesn't get this grief!" they plead.

MTV announce they're going to court to change the rules on the amount of money they have to pay to screen pop videos. They're demanding a return of all monies paid to VPL, the company that bills MTV for the use, since 1987.

August**Diary**

1

Melody Maker prints an exclusive track-by-track preview of the new Nirvana album, *In Utero*, while NME boasts a Kurt Cobain interview. Produced by Steve Albini, the record is scheduled for September 13 and includes titles such as *Heart-Shaped Box* (the first single), *Frances Farmer Will Have Her Revenge On Seattle*, and *I Hate Myself And I Want To Die*.

2

U2's *Zooropa*, reckoned to be the year's fastest-selling album, shifts over 200,000 in its first week of release despite the "notoriously slow summer market". Further cheering news – more singles and albums are being sold than at the same time last year.

★

The Mercury Music Prize shortlist features the expected press darlings - Suede, PJ Harvey, Stereo MCs and The Auteurs, plus New Order, Sting, Apache Indian, Dina Carroll and others. Suede's album is installed as 2-1 favourite to lift the trophy.

★

The Pogues' first single for three years, *Tuesday Morning*, is written by Spider Stacy and released by Warners.

★

David Sylvian and Robert Fripp collaborate on the album *The First Day* , and Jane Siberry re-emerges with *When I Was A Boy*.

★

New rap messiahs Cypress Hill unleash the Black Sunday album to rave reviews.

7

Zooropa makes it to Britain, and Glasgow Celtic Park leaves the critics divided from "No you fools, no" to "U2 are up there and out there right now". Tens upon tens of thousands don't see any problem.

8

James announce details of their Brian Eno-produced album *Laid*, which is set for September release. "It's very naked, big and vulnerable," says Tim Booth.

9

Sugar release a limited edition seven-inch featuring *Tilted* and *JC Auto*, from the Beaster album.

★

A live album from Nick Cave And The Bad Seeds, *Live Seeds*, is set for September 6 release on Mute. It ranges from *The Mercy Seat* to *Tupelo*.

11

The first of U2's four Wembley Stadium shows witnesses a guest appearance by, of all people, Salman Rushdie. "I'm not afraid of you," he tells Bono/MacFisto. "Real devils don't wear horns."

12

Cocteau Twins are back! Their first album on Polygram is to be *Four-Calendar Café* on Sept 27th, and a single, *Evangeline*, will precede it. Rumours abound that Elizabeth Fraser has written intelligible lyrics.

snippets

● New Order's **Bernard Sumner** denies sticky rumours that the band are to split after a "farewell" Reading appearance. "We haven't talked about splitting at all," he says. August 22 sees an ITV documentary on the Manchester mavericks. New Order's Bernard Sumner is recruited by former Stone Roses manager Gareth Evans to produce a single by Lee Sharpe, Manchester United's latest football star. It's Bernard's second footie-related music project: New Order's *World In Motion* was the England squad's theme song for the last world cup.

Dave Lee Travis, the well-loved much-respected etc DJ, often known as "the Hairy Monster", sometime motor-racing enthusiast and Page Three photographer, stuns the airwaves, announcing live on Radio One that he is quitting the BBC after 26 years' service. "Changes are being made here which go against my principles and I just cannot go along with them," he snarls. The BBC retaliate by sacking him.

LIVE!

In her first headline show as a solo artist, former Sugarcubes singer **Bjork** warmed the hearts of punters and critics alike at London's Forum. "It's not often an artist makes you forget the smokiness, humidity and general misery of your surroundings. Bjork's debut London show deserves every superlative in the Thesaurus," reckoned The Guardian. "Bjork melted every heart in the house, just as we knew she would. She was transparent, translucent, transcendent. And very, very special," said the starstruck Melody Maker. NME, on the other hand, reserved final judgement for the next time: "This was a brave coming-of-age bash, so hiccups were inevitable. The citizens of her magic kingdom may leave disappointed, but most will keep the faith."

"I have absolutely no respect for the English people," we find **Kurt Cobain** saying *'allegedly' in* Michael Azerrad's *book* Come As You Are. *"They make me sick."* Kurt's *comment on the quote? "This is a joke. I obviously do not hate all English people... my only intolerance is for intolerance."*

▶ Banana's skinned: in an announcement that rocked the music industry, **Bananarama** were dropped by their record label of 11 years, London, for failing to get their last two albums in the top 20.

The ubiquitous **Suede** plan a new single for October release. It may well be *Still Life*, an acoustic ballad premiered at Glastonbury. There will also be a live video, filmed largely at their Brixton Academy show, before the year's end.

snippets

The latest rumours about rumours about rumours about **The Stone Roses** suggest they may be planning two huge shows in Glasgow and Manchester. "They're not looking for normal venues," it is announced. Is this the start of the 90s revival?

▶ If it is, then naturally **The KLF** will be around. Full-page ads in the dailies, placed by 'The K Foundation', urge readers to "Abandon all art now". "We honestly don't know what all this is leading up to," sighs their publicist.

"I have given this decision two years of thought," says **Natalie Merchant** upon disbanding 10,000 Maniacs after 12 years. "No irrational or explosive events brought it about – only a desire for change and a need for growth. This is a natural passage for which I've prepared." Yes, but has she been reading The Bjork Guide To Solo Success?

"What's my name?" hollers, er, let's call him Prince for now, during his mega live shows. Nobody's quite sure of the correct answer. Nevertheless the unforgettable whatsisname has a new single, Peach, and a flock of greatest hits packages ready for release.

Talking of **Aerosmith**, they dump Megadeth as opening act on their Stateside 'Get A Grip'

tour for being sulky. "They weren't happy and we don't want to tour with anyone who isn't having a good time," say the rock'n'roll survivors, beaming with joie de vivre.

Yet more dissention in the Mac ranks: **Stevie Nicks** takes her flowing dresses elsewhere, leaving Fleetwood Mac originals Mick Fleetwood and Christine McVie to be joined by guitarist Dave

Mason (formerly of Traffic), Bekka Bramlett and her husband Delaney.

Guns N' Roses are blamed for the death of Jason Bryant, a 20-year-old Australian fan who is alleged to have hanged himself while listening to the Roses track Estranged. "I believe this band is inciting kids to do this," claimed the boy's mother.

September promises to be a month and a half. As well as the numerous aforementioned, new albums hit the shops from a variety of big-name sources. Kate Bush promises *The Red Shoes*, with guest appearances from Eric Clapton, Jeff Beck, Lenny Henry and that bloke who used to be called Prince, while The Cure release yet another live album, imaginatively titled *Show*. Paul Weller gives us *Wild Wood*, Squeeze offer *Some Fantastic Place*, and Teenage Fanclub come up with *Thirteen*. Still hungry? October should see *Construction for the Modern Idiot* by The Wonder Stuff, *Hat Full Of Stars* from Cyndi Lauper, and *Come On Feel The Lemonheads* by, yes, The Lemonheads. And we aren't forgetting some highly visible Beatles re-issues, new efforts by The Stone Roses (allegedly), Crowded House, and Belinda Carlisle. Oh and did we tell you about the second Take That album...? (That's enough now – Ed.)

13

Shaun Ryder and Intastella secure a deal with new label Planet 3 for their *Can You Fly Like You Mean It* single. Back from the dead??

17

Iggy Pop plays London. London loses. Release of Iggy's *American Caesar* album marches closer.

23

Levellers release their second album, following hot on the heels of an incomprehensible rambling diatribe against the music press in Melody Maker.

★

Sisters Of Mercy grant us a compilation album of greatest hits called *A Slight Case Of Overbombing*. There's also a video compilation and a typically understated new single, *Under The Gun*.

★

Curve return with a new EP, *Blackerthreetracker*, and have their second album *Cuckoo* set for September.

★

Back To The Planet release the *Daydream* single and continue their seemingly endless tour of Britain.

★

As if all this wasn't too much, Carter USM give us the *Lean On Me, I Won't Fall Over* single and threaten the Post Historic Monsters album for September 6.

24

The Boo Radleys' *Giant Steps LP* collects moist-panting steamy reviews across the board.

27

Van Morrison headlines this year's WOMAD festival at St Austell Cornwall Coliseum.

★

It's that Reading Festival time of year. The Friday headliners include Porno For Pyros, Rage Against The Machine and Ned's Atomic Dustbin.

28

While Saturday night means The The, Siouxsie And The Banshees, Therapy? and Ozric Tentacles.

★

Unless you're at Dublin RDS, where the U2 Zooropa show is set for the biggest worldwide audience for a live radio broadcast of all time. That's: of all time.

★

Or at WOMAD. Day two, and James headline.

29

If it's Sunday you must be healing that archetypal Reading hangover with New Order, Dinosaur Jr, Lemonheads and a specially-reformed Big Star.

★

Or at WOMAD listening to Peter Gabriel doing his headlining thang.

30

The Breeders, enjoying their first singles chart success with the *Cannonball* EP, release the *Last Splash* album on 4AD.

★

A new Big Star album, after all these years. *Live At Missouri University 4/25/93* features Alex Chilton and Jody Stephens with a little help from The Posies, and includes the late Chris Bell's *I Am The Cosmos* as well as a cover of T Rex's *Baby Strange*!

★

Oh my golly, it's that Nirvana single. Finally.

Hey! Let's get unplugged

As if the idea had never occurred to anyone in a million years, every musician half worthy of the name is rushing to ditch their amps, banish the backline and just be at one with their instruments. Commercially a good career move, aesthetically sound, but hardly revolutionary, as **Richard Skinner** recalls.

You'd be forgiven for thinking that MTV have recently re-invented authentic music. In the last couple of years it's been getting increasingly difficult to move without stumbling over yet another Unplugged release rising up the album or video charts, or another squad of electro–techno–freaks desperately retuning a battered old six-string to prove that they still know the chords to *House of the Rising Sun.* Things are almost reaching the point where you start sympathizing with Bruce Springsteen and plugging the whole bloody lot back in!

As we all know, there's nothing new under the sun, just different ways of marketing it. And the Unplugged 'phenomenon' is no exception. Acoustic live sessions first cropped up on radio back in the 70s – and probably before – when local radio stations and the BBC would record special sessions which then might well find their way into the marketplace as B sides or 'additional tracks'. And even as far back as 1972 Carole King and James Taylor (then being touted as the leaders of the New Rock!) played simple acoustic piano and guitar sets for BBC TV. You see, it's all been done before!

So what's happened to make it so appealing in the early 1990s? One obvious answer is that an acoustic version of a track we have all known and loved and listened to endlessly in its electric version is seen in a different and occasionally wondrous light, given a whole new set of colours and shades, and a new lease of life. For example, Clapton's Unplugged version of *Layla* is an extraordinary piece of music. You know where its starting point is but the whole piece takes on a completely unexpected mood and takes you by surprise.

Another theory is that the rise and rise of Unplugged sessions is part of the anti-sampling backlash – a reaction against the perceived 80s feeling that the role of the musicmaker was to be but a jackdaw selecting fragments of glittering gems, and mixing it all into something very occasionally greater than the sum of its parts.

All the old fogeys who'd never got beyond second billing at the Nag's Head would stare into the bottom of a pint of Theakston's and mutter something about "These young kids don't know what music's all about".

Well, some of the young kids who are at the cutting edge are also proving pretty adept at showing just what they can do without a battery of samplers, sequencers and synths: Arrested Development are very much a case in point. That said, an acoustic session can put the fear of God up a band who really don't know what they're doing live (no names, no lawsuits). That's when it definitely sorts the chaff from the other stuff.

Although it's probably wrong to suggest that playing acoustically is better than any

other way, I believe the beauty of this kind of session is that the performance is stripped right back to basics, leaving the songwriter and performer unprotected, unable to hide behind a wall of sound or any effects boxes and echo chambers, so that you can hear just what gave them their edge in the first place. In my BBC days I once sat down with Paul McCartney between a couple of live sessions and he just played two or three songs on his acoustic guitar; the power of his voice and the guitar was extraordinary and intimate.

From the start of Virgin 1215 we brought artists into the studios to create acoustic sets. Our Golden Square studio was the venue for Everything But the Girl (appropriate, given their own Acoustic release). They produced a set that was so polished, so precise, so damn perfect that nobody who was listening in could believe that we hadn't taken the whole set directly off their CD. But I can assure you – I was there, enjoying every moment – that Ben and Tracey just stood up and played, live, with grace under pressure.

In fact, Studio One was built as part of our commitment to putting live music on air, but limited to small, controllable groups – the studio is not some vast soulless hangar of a recording studio, just an intimate room where the effect is like a close-knit chamber group performing.

Tasmin Archer was our first guest – since then we've welcomed Robert Plant, Marc Cohn, Maria McKee, Bruce Hornsby and Squeeze, amongst others, to come and prove their worth. Often the session provides a welcome chance for the musicians to relax. Bruce Hornsby was working on a new album at the time he came into the Virgin 1215 studio and was moving into a much bluesier mode, perhaps as a result of his new role as a Grateful Dead sideman – he used the session almost like a master class as he ran through everything from boogie woogie to jazz fusion.

Robert Plant was so pleased with the versions of some old Moby Grape numbers that he put together for us that they now form part of his live set. Anyone who saw the Guns N' Roses and U2 gigs in the last year or so will know how effective the change in pace and mood can be in mid-concert, especially when the band drops down from a stadium-scale extravaganza to four guys on a small stage having fun.

We've had record companies approaching us for the use of the acoustic sessions on releases – my ambition somewhere down the line, if we can sort the rights clearances out, would be to release the very best of the 1215 sessions on a single CD. I'll dream on awhile.

After MTV's success in marketing the whole idea (and even MTV have been running acoustic sets for ten years), what was a radio programming device has become a TV/video staple, and a useful means of expanding (and extending) a musician's career. Unplugged might sometimes feel like a fad, but my instinct is that it's got a lot more legs yet. Even if that means another wave of musicians looking just a little bit smug that they still know how to play, that's no bad thing. Long may it last.

"I once sat down with Paul McCartney between a couple of live sessions and he just played two or three songs on his acoustic guitar; the power of his voice and the guitar was extraordinary and intimate."

Is this the vinyl curtain?

Bludgeoned by the onslaught of digital formats, its lustrous appeal is fast making vinyl a collectors' item. One-time analogue addict **Tommy Vance** spins some thoughts.

They used to call us vinyl junkies. But that was back in the days when records were records, when there were only singles and albums and a format was something you wiped your feet on at the front door after a hard night out at the local palais.

And, sure enough, there was something junkie-like about the way we used to covet and crave those latest chart releases on shiny black vinyl with their bright pop art labels. The thrill and expectation as we slipped them out of their sleeves, followed by the rush of pure pleasure as the needle dropped into the groove for the very first time on the new Stones single or Led Zep album. That was what made life really exciting back in the 60s and 70s.

But that was then and this is now. And the romance of record collecting is sadly a thing of the past. I'm not saying that the music was any better back then, because there are still great records made today that push the pleasure buttons. Such is the wonder of rock'n'roll. And the reason I personally believe it will never f...f...fade away.

I, however, find it hard to get worked up in quite the same way over a little silver CD and those terrible jewel cases that they've designed so badly. Don't you miss the joy and delight of holding a Roger Dean gatefold album sleeve in your hands? I know I do.

As a fan of good music, though, I don't mourn vinyl. CD was inevitable. And I would never dream of knocking it. When the technology is there, and it does a better job than anything you've got already – without the skips and scratches of an archaic electromechanical system first developed over a hundred years ago – then you've got to use it, haven't you? There's absolutely no doubt in my mind that the sounds they get onto a CD these days are simply the best. Even if years of listening to Black Sabbath and Metallica at immense volume on headphones for the Friday Rock Show has left me a little deaf!

I'm not surprised in the slightest when the latest figures put out by the BPI tell me that well over half the albums sold in this country in the last 12 months were on CD. Especially as it appears like only 35% of homes in the UK own a CD player. But my guess is that there's a true rock fan living in each one. And they've all been turned on by the beauties of CD sound just the way I have.

Digital formats have certainly taken over the broadcasting business lock, stock and barrel. We never play vinyl on Virgin 1215, for example, although I'm sure they still do on some One FM shows. And I'm not even sure that Virgin has a turntable in the building.

Occasionally, of course, we'll decide to programme an oldie that isn't already available on some compilation CD in the station library. But then we'll have it digitally copied. Not onto DAT or any of those other digital non-starters like DCC or MiniDisc. We go straight to one of the super new RCS floppy disks which you simply slot into a computer.

So all we Virgin jocks waved goodbye to the revived 45 long ago! And I've got rid of all my vinyl too. I had nearly 14,000 albums. They took up a whole room. Because I've got just about everything I'll probably ever want to hear at home or in the car on CD, I just knew I'd probably only go rummaging amongst the old 33s maybe once or twice a year at the most. So I sold them all to a dealer.

But just because CD has carried all before it, vinyl hasn't vanished off the scene totally. It's down but it's by no means out. And some people do a roaring trade in it. That's because there are still analogue addicts out there who mainline on vinyl and hit the specialist shops. Only now they buy second hand, at second hand prices, scratches and all. And if they find something particularly rare, in good nick and in its original sleeve, they'll happily hand over fistfuls of fivers to bag it.

As for those who can't get a regular fix in their home town, they buy off the street at one of those record fairs that seem to spring up everywhere nowadays. Or else they get their stuff through the post, recorded delivery courtesy of the mail order pages of magazines like Record Collector or Vox's Record Hunter. So if the thought of life without needles and turntables gives you the shivers, then you know where to go to kill the craving.

As for me, I've managed to kick the habit. I'm not a vinyl junkie any more, and I have no regrets. Sometimes, though, when I pick up an old LP cover and slip my fingers into the cardboard, a lump comes to the throat or elsewhere. But you've got to live in the present, haven't you? And look to the future. Rather than get all nostalgic, I can't wait for the day when great music will come to me on a chip just like my kid's computer game.

It'll still be rock'n'roll alright. And I just know I'll like it!

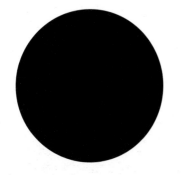

"Sometimes, though, when I pick up an old LP cover and slip my fingers into the cardboard, a lump comes to the throat or elsewhere."

"There's absolutely no doubt in my mind that the sounds they get onto a CD these days are simply the best."

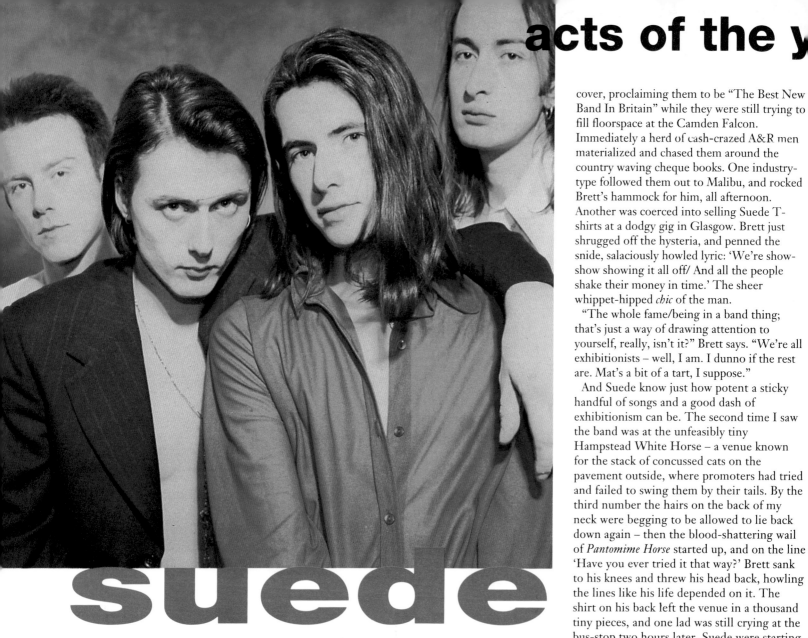

suede

"A thousand articles tried to carve up the appeal of the band – they're the new Smiths, the new Sex Pistols, the new Beatles. No… they're the first Suede."

★ It must be an odd feeling – knowing that nearly every warm-blooded mammal in the Western Hemisphere would willingly shag you until you squeaked. Sex and songwriting machines Brett Anderson and Bernard Butler could, feasibly, have spent September 92 to August 93 flat on their backs; every sordid whim being attended to by a brace of love-swamped Pop Kids and a clutch of hyperventilating journalists. Instead, they released three wonderstruck singles, toured until their fringes were sodden with sweat, released the instantly notorious *Suede* album, and scared the socks off a hundred ligging music industry types at The Brit Awards. And Brett *still* had the energy to slap his arse with

his microphone like a jockey whipping a horse to victory.

Let's climb into our spangly moonboots and warp back to the beginning of Suede's journey up Rock's Sticky Highway To Hell. It's September 92. It's raining out. The skinny boy-queen Brett is prowling the "Top of the Pops" stage, the thinnest and laciest of blouses lashed to his body with sweat. *Metal Mickey* is putting everything else in the Top 20 to shame. Mat, the bass-player, still has a very horrid haircut.

The last few months have been a blur – four skinny, Mother's Pride-white boys came shivering out of the dingy suburbs, and scooped a laudatory Melody Maker front

cover, proclaiming them to be "The Best New Band In Britain" while they were still trying to fill floorspace at the Camden Falcon. Immediately a herd of cash-crazed A&R men materialized and chased them around the country waving cheque books. One industry-type followed them out to Malibu, and rocked Brett's hammock for him, all afternoon. Another was coerced into selling Suede T-shirts at a dodgy gig in Glasgow. Brett just shrugged off the hysteria, and penned the snide, salaciously howled lyric: 'We're show-show showing it all off/ And all the people shake their money in time.' The sheer whippet-hipped *chic* of the man.

"The whole fame/being in a band thing; that's just a way of drawing attention to yourself, really, isn't it?" Brett says. "We're all exhibitionists – well, I am. I dunno if the rest are. Mat's a bit of a tart, I suppose."

And Suede know just how potent a sticky handful of songs and a good dash of exhibitionism can be. The second time I saw the band was at the unfeasibly tiny Hampstead White Horse – a venue known for the stack of concussed cats on the pavement outside, where promoters had tried and failed to swing them by their tails. By the third number the hairs on the back of my neck were begging to be allowed to lie back down again – then the blood-shattering wail of *Pantomime Horse* started up, and on the line 'Have you ever tried it that way?' Brett sank to his knees and threw his head back, howling the lines like his life depended on it. The shirt on his back left the venue in a thousand tiny pieces, and one lad was still crying at the bus-stop two hours later. Suede were starting to matter in a big way.

At the end of April 92, Suede finally put their names to a contract with the specially formed Nude Records, causing broken hearts amongst A&R men the world over, and released their debut single, *The Drowners*, which topped the Independent Charts. Morrissey wandered along to a gig and was spotted jotting down the lyrics to *Drowners* B-side, *My Insatiable One*. Strangers stopped each other on the streets, and commented that lyrics like 'On the highwire, dressed in a leotard, there wobbles one hell of a retard,' and 'On the escalator, we shit paracetamol,' were almost too eclectically brilliant to have on a debut release.

In September – after *Metal Mickey* had skipped up merrily to Number 17 in the charts, and given the British Pop Scene a pinch on the arse – a hysteria-sodden, sold-out tour followed. The heavyweight papers started running articles on Suede – or rather, the *hype* around Suede. The music industry was so demoralized that the idea of a genuinely talented, loquacious, bastard goodlooking band seemed too improbable. It *had* to be hype, didn't it? April 93, and *Animal Nitrate* was stomping around at Number 7 in the charts; blood on its hands and a painfully bright glitter in its eye. Nine months earlier, Brett had stated that one of his ambitions was to have a song about perverted sex in the Top Ten. *Nitrate*'s lyrics run 'So in your council home he broke all your bones/ And now you're taking it time after time… what does it take to turn you on, now you're over 21?' Big chocolate biscuit for career-fulfilment due *there*, I think.

And now Suede were a genuine, screaming teenagers, Top Ten, Smash Hits pop band, recording a debut album that doubters and devotees alike were gagging to slap on their turntables, the rumour-mongers charged in and started handing out leaflets. Bernard and Brett were at each other's throats, Brett had an expensive sniffing habit, the album sounded appalling, Mat was addicted to tea, Simon was a Christian… in the midst of all this furore, Simon quietly announced he was gay, in order, he said, "to get laid," and Suede received an invite to play The Brit Awards, even though they hadn't been nominated in any category. A nation huddled round their TVs, fruitcake in one hand, cocoa in the other, and waited for four washed up junkies to formally end their careers.

Bernard swaggered on stage, took off his coat, picked up his guitar, and the band launched into a screamingly leather-clad

lurch-and-destroy performance of *Animal Nitrate*. Brett threw his microphone around like the thing was giving off electric shocks, and Bernard was just a stomping blur of peacock blue silk shirt and unfeasibly girly hair. They stalked off stage with Bernard's guitar propped up against the amp, shrieking feedback to a boggle-eyed audience, and advance orders for the album doubled the next day.

Now the rumour-mongers had been proved wrong, it was time for the analysts, intellectuals and theorists to wade in. A thousand articles tried to carve up the appeal of the band – they're the new Smiths, the new Sex Pistols, the new Beatles. No… they're the first Suede. Ah, but the lyrics – Brett wants to be a girl, wants to be a boy-girl, wants to be taken over, wants to dominate, wants to be loved, he's the living embodiment of the Stone Roses' petulant 'I wanna be adored' demand. No… Brett writes stories, which might be about him, might be about someone else. Ah, well then, Suede are so fragile that the pressure of recording the album will ruin them. Ahem…

Suede the LP came out in May 93, and went straight in at Number One, no messing, big pouty kiss from the judge. The week before, WH Smith recorded a rush on thesauruses bought by frothing music journalists. In the first week of release, *Suede* was selling four times as many copies as the Number Two

album; it went gold in the first week, and Radio One's Simon Bates introduced the next single from the album, *So Young*, as a "great single from the ever marvellous Suede." Suede's press officers moved to a bigger building, and the doubters admitted that Suede may have done well in Britain, but America would greet them with nonchalantly cocked guns and the drawled enquiry: "You ain't from around these parts, are you, boys?"

Suede packed their glittery blouses and teabags, and swanned off to the States in June 93. America is impossibly huge, but miraculously Suede seem to have won over 80 percent of that sprawling nation already. The press had done their homework and read the British reviews, and so knew which references to constantly harp on about, which adjectives to weld onto a paragraph, and exactly *how* many times they could ask Brett if Suede were the new Smiths before being briskly yet cheerfully told to shove off.

But will the next year be as revelatory? Will the band be able to continue fire-walking with mass adulation, and the always-looming and inevitable backlash? Of course they will. They are Suede. They are Insatiable.

CAITLIN MORAN

"We're all exhibitionists – well, I am. I dunno if the rest are. Mat's a bit of a tart, I suppose."

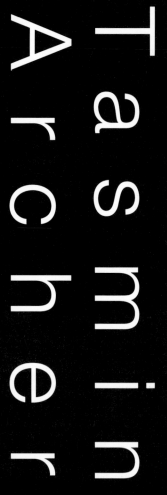

Tasmin Archer

" ... a 29-year-old black girl, born and bred in Bradford, West Yorkshire, torn, musically, between a love of Judy Garland and an aching to be Elvis Costello."

★ In 1992/93, it would have taken a rich imagination indeed to have conjured up a more unlikely pop star than Tasmin Archer.

The image would be unforgettable: a 29-year-old black girl, born and bred in Bradford, West Yorkshire, torn, musically, between a love of Judy Garland and an aching to be Elvis Costello, and presenting herself to the world in an ankle-length charcoal great-coat and workman's boots.

The revelation that her first single, *Sleeping Satellite*, was about the failure of humanity to capitalize on the Apollo moon-shots should have surprised no-one. For although her first album would be entitled *Great Expectations* – hence the Dickensian image – the rule with Tasmin Archer was going to be: expect the unexpected.

Yet within six weeks of its release as her debut single, in September 92, *Satellite* had locked into a triumphant orbit at number one in the charts. It would subsequently reach the same position in five other countries, and enter the Top 10 in a further 12.

Tasmin Archer had arrived – whoever she might be…. As it transpired, like Sade and Carmel before her, Tasmin Archer was actually the name of a group, as well as the singer. Co-writers and chief players on all the material were an affable duo soon to be

dubbed The Two Johns – keyboard-player John Beck and former chemical engineer, and long-time boyfriend of Tasmin's, John Hughes.

Tasmin herself was a real enigma. The daughter of Jamaican parents who'd come to Britain in the 1950s looking, vainly, for decent work – "there wasn't a right lot going for them" – she had day-dreamed of musical stardom all through school.

"Singing was an escape for me," she says in a Yorkshire accent that signals blunt, unashamed honesty. "It was a way in which I could get away from the life that was actually reality for me, because though we weren't totally, *totally* poor, we couldn't afford to go on holidays and things like that."

Her home was always full of music – her mum's Jim Reeves and Brook Benton records; her brother's Public Image and Morrissey singles. In the privacy of her own room, she listened to everything from Elvis Costello – whose attacking singing style she admired – to The Carpenters and Judy Garland, "who could always get a tear out of you."

Leaving school she took the only work she could find – sewing the pockets on trousers in a factory. It was poorly-paid, and the workshop, which eventually went out of business, so badly lit that Archer's sight was weakened and she had to wear glasses.

But she'd always been able to draw an audience in the school playground for her singing, and she carried on performing in the evenings, backing up bands in pubs and clubs before meeting one Phillip Edwards, a local musician and sound engineer. She sang, briefly, with his group, Dignity, but was sacked after a year, ostensibly because her voice didn't blend with the other girl singer's.

The memory still hurts. "I was devastated," she says, "I was crying. I thought my world had caved in."

A fortnight later, though, Edwards was on the 'phone telling her about a studio he was opening in Bradford's Little Germany. Would she like to come down and help out? Having just been made redundant from the factory, Tasmin leapt at the chance, and though her studio duties also involved sweeping the floor and cleaning the toilets, she got the chance to sing with a number of the local bands that used the place.

She was also introduced to John Beck and, after some ups and downs between herself and Beck, to John Hughes, who became the third song-making partner and a distinct calming influence on the trio.

Tasmin fell in love.

"He's got such a logical and peaceful attitude to things," she says. "He helped me push my voice and not hide it." The three 'jammed' in

"I can't stand stereotypes, particularly black ones."

the time-honoured tradition, with Tasmin – who plays no instrument other than her voice – acting as 'musical editor'.

In a one-off lapse of taste, they played gigs as The Archers, and even considered covering the programme's theme tune, but they also, during 1987, wrote *Sleeping Satellite*, and a whole slew of songs which, some three years later, would result in a publishing deal with Virgin, and in 1991, a record deal with EMI.

Their first album was completed by the end of 1991, the title *Great Expectations* taken from Tasmin's favourite Dickens book.

"I related to Pip, the hero, because he's got ambition," explained Tasmin, "but when he achieves that he's confused because he's rejected his background to get there. The only way for him to cope is to remember who he is and where he came from."

It would take another year – during which Tasmin would form and test her live band – before EMI's incoming managing director, Jean-François Cecillon, would make the group a priority act. Then the pressures of overnight stardom would test just how well Tasmin herself could cope.

In the event, as *Sleeping Satellite* rose to number one, the novice star found all the attention, "absolutely terrifying".

"I expected it to be like the films, like fantasy" said Tasmin " – no worries and no-one asking you awkward questions. But I soon found the real world isn't like that. You have to learn to suffer for your art."

Archer's harsh initiation into the fame game was all the more intensive because she was a black girl singing straight pop – and because the single itself was scarcely a run-of-the-mill, 'I love you love' ditty.

The Two Johns had been influenced by a magazine article about the moon shots: now they found their song was once again whipping up serious-minded radio debates about the real purposes of the 1960s' space race. As for Tasmin, she was facing race questions of a different kind, based on the usual, stereotypical assumptions that black singers should always make dance music.

"Being black isn't an issue for me," she told one interviewer, "I don't think about it until I look in the mirror. Some people may not like our sound but then that's their problem."

Finding herself the only black face at a London gig by heavy metal stars Thunder, she admitted to being more offended by a black security guard who wanted to know why she was listening to such "crap" music. "I can't stand stereotypes," said Tasmin, "particularly black ones."

She was determined not to be another pop stereotype, either, waiting a full four months to issue the follow-up to *Satellite* – "why hype people?" – and then choosing a song, *In Your Care*, about an even less cosily commercial

subject: that of child abuse.

Released in February 1993 – by which time Tasmin had scooped the award for Best Newcomer at The Brits – the single cruised into the Top 20, generating much-needed funds for the charity ChildLine.

"I wasn't abused as a child, but I can imagine situations where you are abused mentally by older people in positions of responsibility, especially at school," explained Tasmin, sensibly widening the abuse debate.

At the end of February, Tasmin Archer took to the road for her first, headlining tour, although on previous outings she'd provided sturdy support for everyone from Curtis Stigers to Squeeze and The Eagles' Glenn Frey. A month later she was in America, laying the ground-work for the May US release of *Great Expectations*. The work-load was beginning to seem a little easier, but still there was no sign of an inflated ego – or any question that Tasmin Archer, 'the pop star', would now be re-locating to Los Angeles – or even South of the Watford Gap.

"I'm comfortable with the North," she said. "Everyone in the South seems to have a place to go, things to do – even the tramps! In Yorkshire they're a bit slower in their approach, a bit more British if you like."

But an album that had sold 100,000 copies in three weeks, and the success in May of a third single, *Lords Of The New Church*, meant she was able to think about offering her parents a bit of much-needed support.

"The money might not make a difference to them," she conceded, "but maybe it will. It'll make a difference in that they'll get to do things that they couldn't do before."

Certainly Tasmin herself was suddenly enjoying life to the full. The girl who'd only ever been to Blackpool, "or on a school trip or something", found herself back in America, during June and July, playing seven major showcase concerts in cities like New York, Chicago and LA, and appearing on the prestigious Arsenio Hall TV show.

On her return, she immediately began writing for a second album, and making plans for the August release of a fourth single, *Arienne*.

If Tasmin has made plenty of unpredictable moves to get this far, she's unlikely to take an easier route during 1994.

"Really the last album was quite safe and tame as far as I'm concerned," she says. "It's the next album that's going to contain a few surprises."

MARTIN TOWNSEND

U2

"The former preachers of pomp
have discovered irony and glitz in a
fit of sardonic hyper-activity."

★ U2 refuse to stagnate. Their constant restless self-reinvention, flavoured with wit, parody and a new sense of glamour, has been one of the most cheering and endearing spectacles in recent rock's itching and confused tapestry. Whereas the 80s saw them changing from fresh young iconoclasts to something worryingly similar to a flatulent dinosaur, they've embraced 90s technology and culture with a hop, a skip and a vengeance. By simultaneously sending up their blustery rock'n'roll heritage and sending out matchlessly grand records and electric visionary live shows, they've placed themselves firmly on the plateau of pop messiahdom they always so avidly aspired to. Now they are never less than interesting and often more than heroic.

The last year has seen a relentlessly high scattergun profile, a gargantuan and radical European tour, the almost accidentally panoramic *Zooropa* album, a Vogue cover and even a tabloid-trembling showbiz marriage. Oh, and a multi-million pound six-album worldwide deal. The new improved U2 have been pretty much *in excelsis*.

Since the superb *Achtung Baby* brought the Dublin foursome back to critical and popular acclaim at the tail end of 91, the Zoo TV and Zooropa tours have spread the word and rifled off an array of bewildering images. The former preachers of pomp have discovered irony and glitz in a fit of sardonic hyper-activity. Bono, in wrap-around bug-eye shades and shiny leather suit, became The Fly, only breaking character to break up the rhythm. "There were reports of egomania", he said, "and I just decided to become everything they said I was. Might as well. The truth is you are many people at the same time; you don't have to choose." The Edge described Bono as "a nice bunch of guys".

The scale and ambition of a show are vast, utilizing enough power through four generators (and 1,200 tonnes of equipment) to run approximately two thousand homes. Under the stage, a mini TV station is set up, capable of broadcasting and receiving live transmissions. Along with Trabant cars, video monitors litter the stage and walls – Bono holds the channel-changer.

"Never in the history of rock'n'roll touring has so much bullshit been produced for so many by so few", he quipped, though he could also talk a good *rationale*. "Zoo TV came from a moment when, like everyone, I was watching the Gulf War with a remote control in my hand and watching human lives being mutilated live on CNN; then you could switch to a soap opera or a sneakers ad. I remember one of the bomber pilots came back after a sortie to turn Iraq into a car park, and when asked what it felt like, he said: "It's all very realistic." I really understood surrealism after that... we have phone sex lines instead of real sex, we train fighter pilots in video arcades. I understood how Picasso couldn't paint human faces after the war."

U2, after playing to their weaknesses for too long, had started playing to their strengths. They embraced the ridiculous OTT aspects of rock'n'roll performance in order to highlight the chaos of the "real" world. Bono took to making phone calls from the stage – the more memorable included ordering ten thousand pizzas for the city of Detroit and persistent badgering of leading politicians. A certain presidential candidate, one Bill Clinton, responded by calling the band on a live radio programme. Subsequently he met the band, who hassled him over the Irish visa system before concluding he was "pretty cool... now we'll be on his back for the next four years."

Just as they played with televisual images, U2 revelled in twisting their own. "Let's play with it and distort it and manipulate it and lose ourselves in the process of it. And let's write about losing ourselves in the process of it, because that's what's happening to everybody else on a smaller scale anyway." Throughout the year the band took delight in relaying masses of misinformation. Perhaps the supreme post-modern irony came as they achieved more crossover exposure than ever when, in May, bassist Adam Clayton announced his engagement to 'supermodel' Naomi Campbell. The more gossipy sections of the media rubbed their hands with glee – perhaps the 'serious, righteous' U2 were a fun thing to have around after all.

In February, U2 had won the Grammy for Best Rock Vocal for *Achtung Baby*, and in March they dominated the Rolling Stone readers poll to an embarrassing extent, winning every major category, even 'Sexiest Male Artist'. But Bono was in modest mode. On learning that The Edge had come runner-up to Eric Clapton as 'Best Guitarist', the singer sighed: "You see, people are getting it the wrong way around. I'm a good singer, he is a *great* guitar player. He is so far ahead of the posse. While everyone else is imitating, he's creative."

Also in March, U2 sued the Performing Rights Society in an action welcomed by other leading bands, claiming the organization had inadequately accounted the £140 million it annually collects. By June the group tapped a happier financial spring, renewing their contract with Island/Phonogram in a deal rumoured to be one of the biggest in music business history.

From March to May the band had been dabbling experimentally and workaholically in the studio in Dublin. Originally mooted as a spontaneous EP, *Zooropa* eventually extended to an album and emerged in July to unanimous praise. Far more than a mere adjunct to *Achtung Baby*, it found The Edge, Flood and Brian Eno combining as producers to choreograph a nervy, compellingly neurotic record, reminiscent of such disparate strands as Bowie's *Station To Station* and The Stones' *Tattoo You*.

"Never in the history of rock'n'roll touring has so much bullshit been produced for so many by so few"

Critics sucked in their breath and acclaimed its lack of overt commercialism, but anyone listening to *Zooropa* more than twice found themselves humming such melancholy croons as *Far Away, So Close* (written for the new Wim Wenders movie) in the wee small hours. The title track crystallized U2's obsession with the times' bombardment of meaningless adspeak and platitudes, and *Babyface* proved they could still knock off a pop nugget without blinking. Bono stretched his falsetto, The Edge intoned *Numb* with onomatopoeiac joy, and *Some Days Are Better Than Others* pushed their wry humour to the fore. The album ended with *The Wanderer*, a song written for and sung by Country & Western legend Johnny Cash.

"He arrived in Dublin and I wrote a song for him the same day," said Bono. "It's Johnny Cash goes to the moon. People asked how we got him to do it, but Johnny Cash has been to the moon many times. It's one of the best things that we've ever recorded, and I'm not even on it." It has to be said there are those of us who'd strongly disagree, for all the most flattering reasons.

Meanwhile the Zooropa 93 tour had blitzed 30 European cities from May through to August, culminating in eight British dates and three rousing homecoming shows in Cork and Dublin. Bono continued to adopt increasingly loopy stage personas. He was sighted early on as 'MacPhisto, the last rock star', in white face, gold lame, and cartoon devil horns, lovingly described as "Quentin Crisp on acid". The video imagery was equally controversial, everything from Nazi propaganda documentaries to huge papier-mâché caricatures of the band members being thrown into the boiling pot.

U2 have evolved rapidly and dazzlingly, both surrendering to contemporary over-stimulation and taking it on at its own game. They are possibly alone in keeping the phrase 'classic rock'n'roll band' viable and vivid. By losing themselves in the maelstrom of modern life, they're winning.

CHRIS ROBERTS

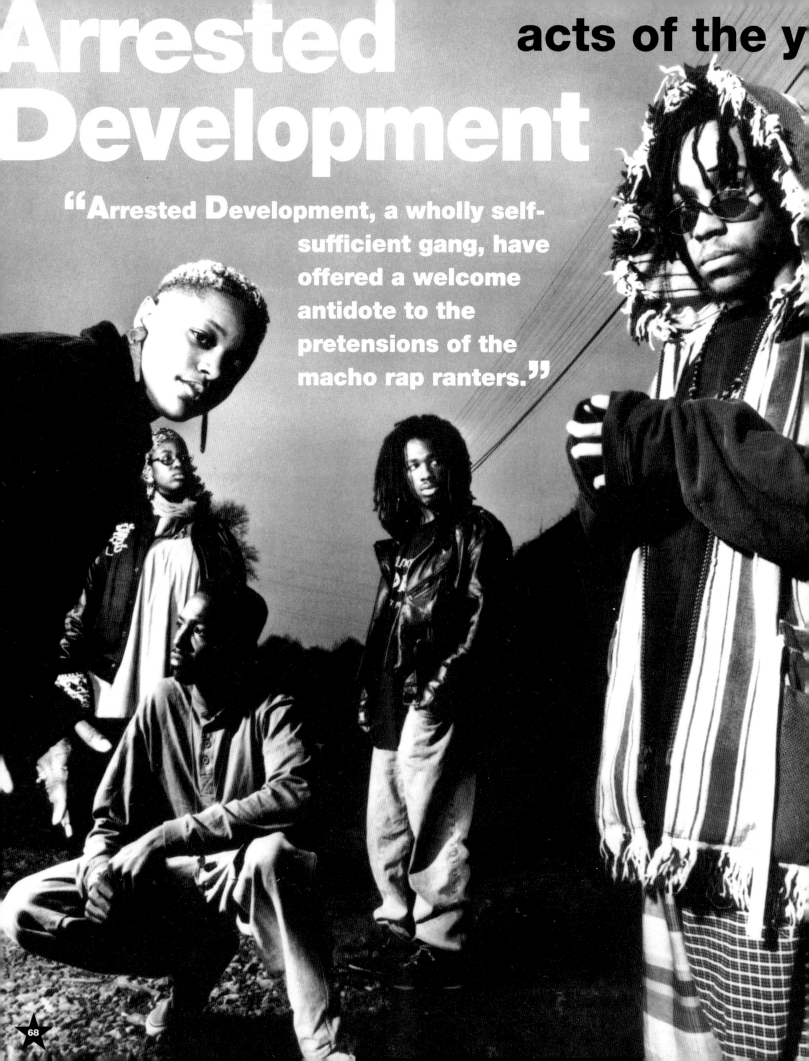

Arrested Development

"**Arrested Development**, a wholly self-sufficient gang, have offered a welcome antidote to the pretensions of the macho rap ranters."

★ In the last 12 months, Arrested Development have pushed themselves to the forefront of the so-called alternative rap movement along with Disposable Heroes Of Hiphoprisy and DC Basehead. As last year's debut album, *3 Years 5 Months and 2 Days in the Life of…* demonstrated, this tight-knit six-member group are the most original voice to emerge in hip-hop for several years. The title of their groundbreaking debut refers to the time that lapsed between the formation of the group and the eventual signing of their recording agreement with Chrysalis.

Describing their work as rejuvenating music, life music or southern-fried-cultural-folk-ethnic-rap-funk, they have also been dubbed the world's first rural rap group. This is in no small part due to their base – the country fringes of Atlanta, Georgia, the birthplace of Martin Luther King and Coca-Cola. Symbolically, on *3 Years 5 Months…*, sampled sounds of birds and chickens dominated rather than the regulation car horns and guns of rap tradition, emphasizing their carefully measured distance from the time-honoured anger of urban rap packs.

As Speech, the elected leader of this self-styled democratic dictatorship, has commented: "Describing us as agrarian rappers is a little wide of the mark because we don't actually live on farms and milk cows all day or whatever. But, when you go to my house, you're gonna pass fields with horses, farms, grass and trees. When you look out of my back window, you're gonna see a forest. That's how we live and, to some extent, our music is always going to be a product of our environment. It would be dishonest for us to come across as typical gangster rappers. That's not our thing. We've passed through that already. We started off bragging and cussing but our viewpoints changed and we started to evolve in a different direction. Sooner or later, it became what we now call life music. Three years, five months and two days of life music."

Leading the charge of the reconstituted hip-hop nation into the middle of the 80s and the tail-end of the millennium, Arrested Development, a wholly self-sufficient gang, have offered a welcome antidote to the pretensions of the macho rap ranters, placing their emphasis firmly on a positive awareness of their environment. With the lyrical preoccupations ranging from teenage pregnancy to homelessness, from the abuse of power within the black Baptist church to the insidious evil of video games, they have succeeded in redefining the rap agenda. The first mixed-sex rap act since Funky Four + 1 in the 90s, their ideology is strictly non-sexist, non-racist, pro-family values. They might yearn for revolution although, as they note on the song *Mama's Always On Stage*: 'Can't be a revolution without women/can't be a revolution without children.'

Released in late summer 92, *3 Years 5 Months…* built slowly and finally went through the roof with the Top 10 success of *Tennessee* on both sides of the Atlantic. By the end of that year, the album featured prominently in most major music paper polls. Occupying a broad church of voices and styles, it immediately cut a wide swathe through the rap mainstream. Offering a delirious scramble of jazz, classical, reggae, soul and country, *3 Years 5 Months…* negotiated a fertile space somewhere between the cataclysmic eco-rap of The Jungle Brothers and the uncompromising agit-rap of Disposable Heroes. They might have lacked the street-smart credentials, but they appeared to redefine rap as a means of paying back 20 years worth of radical black music on fast forward, without the self-conscious slang obscurity, knowing hollers to their posse and strident proselytizing.

Incredible as it might seem, Arrested Development are probably the first Southern-styled act to polevault to major league status since Georgia's soul balladeer Peabo Bryson struck gold in 1982 with the shag-along classic *Tonight I Celebrate My Love*. Along with spiritual freedom, African self-determination and free-range hen farming, high on their agenda is their attempt to rehabilitate the image and pride of the American South.

"I think the South has never really been looked at as anything progressive," Speech remarked last year. "But, y'know, people don't understand. James Brown came outta the South and he influenced people from everywhere, especially the rap industry. Even so, the South has never been promoted as a place of joy, a good place for people. Most black people in America originated from the South and Arrested Development are trying to promote it as a place that people need to go back home to."

Over the course of the last 12 months, their curve has veered upwards with a furious momentum. There have been a string of international hit singles: *Tennessee* (an open letter to God); *People Everyday* (a funky-reggae rewrite of Sly Stone's *Everyday People*, and *Mr Wendal* (harrowing, hypnotic musical odyssey through American slumland). There's been enough trophies and awards to fill all their mantlepieces several times over, including a virtual clean sweep at the MTV Awards. They were asked by Spike Lee to record *Revolution* for the closing credits of his celebrated *Malcolm X* movie. Then, to cap it all, there has been the recent release of their *Unplugged* album, a 67-minute low-key jamboree that included innovative alternative versions of eight tracks from their debut.

Not least, there has been their live performances that have received some of the most metaphor-gushing raves seen in a camel's age. These 'celebrations' invariably provide a frenzied fusion of modern African dance, rabid street theatre, synchronized quartet rapping and communal provocation; with bales of hay, washing lines and live chickens as optional extras. Integrated in all senses of the word.

The recent departure of vocalist Dionne Farris has heightened speculation whether Arrested Development can repeat the phenomenal success of the last 12 months. Already, the irrepressible Speech is preparing to raise the ante.

"Everyone's saying that we can never top *3 Years And Five Months…*, but we've already left that behind. 1994 is a whole new chapter. Arrested Development are moving on. I see us making music for years and years to come, all of it straight from our souls. The only way to do it is by being true to ourselves. How will it affect people? Who knows. We didn't know how these albums would affect people and their success won't influence the way we make the next one."

"The biggest enemy is complacency. Success leads to complacency. But Arrested Development will not be distracted from their true purpose. If people loved these albums because they came straight from the soul, then they'll love the next one too. It's coming from the same place, only this time it'll go deeper and wider. Nothing can stop us now."

JON WILDE

"I see us making music for years and years to come, all of it straight from our souls."

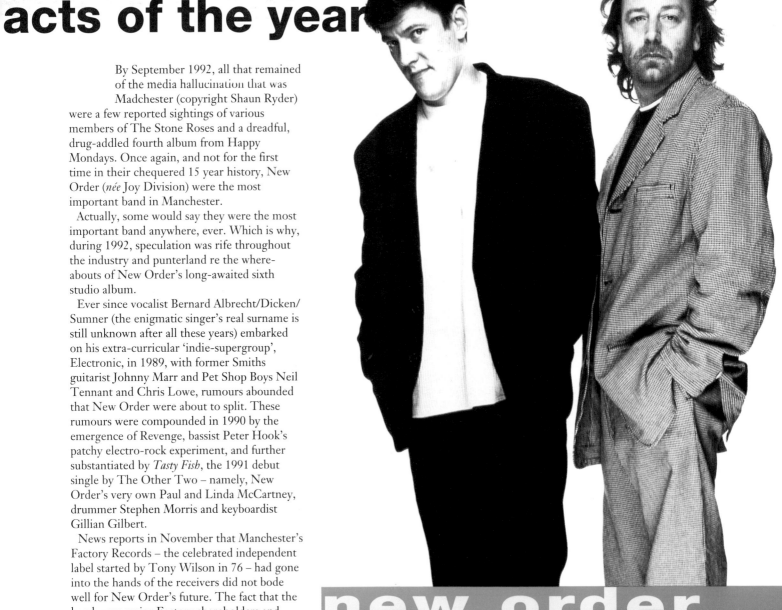

new order

By September 1992, all that remained of the media hallucination that was Madchester (copyright Shaun Ryder) were a few reported sightings of various members of The Stone Roses and a dreadful, drug-addled fourth album from Happy Mondays. Once again, and not for the first time in their chequered 15 year history, New Order (*née* Joy Division) were the most important band in Manchester.

Actually, some would say they were the most important band anywhere, ever. Which is why, during 1992, speculation was rife throughout the industry and punterland re the where-abouts of New Order's long-awaited sixth studio album.

Ever since vocalist Bernard Albrecht/Dicken/Sumner (the enigmatic singer's real surname is still unknown after all these years) embarked on his extra-curricular 'indie-supergroup', Electronic, in 1989, with former Smiths guitarist Johnny Marr and Pet Shop Boys Neil Tennant and Chris Lowe, rumours abounded that New Order were about to split. These rumours were compounded in 1990 by the emergence of Revenge, bassist Peter Hook's patchy electro-rock experiment, and further substantiated by *Tasty Fish*, the 1991 debut single by The Other Two – namely, New Order's very own Paul and Linda McCartney, drummer Stephen Morris and keyboardist Gillian Gilbert.

News reports in November that Manchester's Factory Records – the celebrated independent label started by Tony Wilson in 76 – had gone into the hands of the receivers did not bode well for New Order's future. The fact that the band were major Factory shareholders and looked set to lose large sums of cash with the label's demise hardly helped matters, either.

Then, of course, there was The Hacienda, the (in)famous club that first opened in 1982, one into which New Order had consistently ploughed vast quantities of money. An Ecstasy-fuelled death and a series of gun-related incidents that reflected Manchester's increasingly violent gang warfare situation did little to improve The Hacienda's reputation; nor its mounting debts and cashflow problems.

So it was that the club and the label with which New Order had always been associated – both operations, like the band themselves, infused with the triple spirits of wayward innovation, fierce intransigence and wilful Northern independence – were coming apart at the seams. The financial and, indeed, human cost of all this chaos was considerable. As The Face put it in April 1993, "The fall of the house of Factory… left a car crash of broken careers, huge personal debt, a string of broken promises and some confused and bitter people in its wreckage."

Despite it all, The Hacienda, unlike Factory, managed to survive this period of disorder virtually intact. As did New Order themselves, who, contrary to public expectation, appeared in the news pages of the British music press in early 93 with stories of impending new material.

Yet, not surprisingly, the Fac-ups and the fracas of the previous Winter of Discontent had no small effect on the members of New Order. This certainly explains why the first New Order articles of 93 were centred around New Order's depressed, even (quietly) devastated reaction to Factory's collapse.

"Factory going down was sad, really," Bernard Sumner told one journalist earlier this year. "Because no matter what people say about Tony Wilson and about Factory, basically their ideals were very sound. It was just businesswise they didn't have a clue, which is what made me angry."

Peter Hook, too, was in a philosophical mood after The Crash. "The whole thing about Factory was it was such a huge part of our lives," he said. "We've still got the best out of it, though, like our history. And there's still The Hacienda and Dry (the Hac's bar-annex, located up the road from the club). So although we've lost a lot, we've not lost everything."

Stephen Morris was less sad than furious. "Who's gonna work with him (Tony Wilson) again?" asked the drummer, solemnly and rhetorically, in one article. "We're not. No way, not after what we've been through." Morris' partner was equally disturbed. "It's definitely not the same as it was before," said Gillian, overcome with post-Factory tristesse. "Now it's a lot more fragmented. That whole Factory fiasco (is) hanging over our heads."

Regret, New Order's 21st single and their first since *World In Motion* – the World Cup football anthem recorded with the England soccer squad that reached Number One in summer 1990 – was released in April this year to much acclaim. *Regret* not only marked the

> "For a band who singlehandedly came up with the idea of setting human suffering and existential doubt to the monumental pulse of disco, New Order surpassed their own dazzling achievements."

different record to 89's *Technique*. For a band who singlehandedly came up with the idea of setting human suffering and existential doubt to the monumental pulse of disco, New Order surpassed their own dazzling achievements on *Republic*, its gleaming surfaces covering a multitude of oblique references to the pain and panic of the Factory calamity. Like all their records, this was dance music to think, even cry to; dance music for people who don't necessarily like dancing.

However, *Republic* was not, as many had anticipated, New Order's response to the techno advances made by the likes of Orbital and Spooky. Like David Bowie before them, New Order are able to assimilate as if by magic whatever musical tendencies happen to be in vogue at any given moment, using them for their own ends. *Republic* does feature state-of-the-art technology and glacial dance rhythms, but they are just part of the bigger New Order sound-picture: Stephen Morris's precision-engineered machine-beats, Gillian Gilbert's simply affecting synth-patterns, Peter Hook's maudlin bass motifs and Bernard Sumner's exquisitely fragile vocals.

Notwithstanding critical ambivalence, *Republic* was an unqualified commercial smash, entering the charts at Number One in May and spawning two further hit singles in July (the mellifluously moody *Ruined In A Day*) and August (the deceptively upbeat *World*), the first revamped by renowned reggae rhythm section Sly & Robbie, the second restructured by top London DJ Paul Oakenfold.

To complete a successful though decidedly stormy 12 months, New Order headlined the last day of the Reading Festival at the end of August, while, just a few weeks earlier, they had their entire Factory back catalogue re-released by London. From the icy majesty of Joy Division's *Unknown Pleasures* and *Closer* LP masterpieces (initially released in, respectively, 1979 and 1980) to *Technique*, here was possibly the most highly-regarded oeuvre of the last two decades, and proof, as if it were needed, that New Order are one of the most emotionally and physically rewarding bands on the planet.

Astonishingly, after 15 years (surely theirs is one of the longest, and most consistently pleasing, careers in the history of pop) *Republic* suggests the best is yet to come. Only a recent news report in Melody Maker about New Order's imminent fragmentation into three (Electronic, Revenge and The Other Two) has implied otherwise. We can only hope that such unfounded stories, at least while New Order are this inspired, don't come true.

start of the band's relationship with their new record company, London Records, it also seemed to speak of the turmoil of the preceding months in its lyrics. 'I would like a place I could call my own/Have a conversation on the telephone/Wake up every day, that would be a start/I would not complain of my wounded heart… I was upset, you see, almost all the time…' went the typically downbeat words, which Bernard Sumner sang with dolorous intent.

The music itself was marvellous, a New Order-ish blend of melancholy and euphoria, the guitars gently slashing out a gorgeous riff against a heavenly and mournful melody. *Regret* reached Number Four in the charts, aided somewhat by a bizarre "Top Of The Pops" performance which saw the band beamed live via satellite from the Venice Beach set of "Baywatch" (the US TV soap based in Los Angeles) to the Beeb's rather less exotic studios in Elstree. The televisual image of

these four definitively thin, pale and interesting northerners surrounded by swarms of bronzed babes and tanned hunks was surreal in the extreme.

But then, New Order have made a career out of confusing and confounding audiences, out of not doing The Right Thing.

From their cryptic, information-free, Peter Saville-designed record sleeves to their and Factory's policy of No Advertising to their joyous post-Joy Division experiments with dance, New Order have a casual, almost innate ability to baffle and perplex.

This New Order did in no uncertain terms with *Republic*, their debut album for London, released in May, this time to extremely mixed reactions. The monthlies – Select, Vox and Q Magazine – thought it paled in comparison to the group's previous work, whereas the NME and Melody Maker reckoned it was their finest effort to date.

Unarguably, *Republic* was a completely

PAUL LESTER

REM

"REM do not have shaved heads, tattooed testicles, film star wives, uncontrollable egos or Messianic pretensions. What they do have is an unrivalled grasp of what makes a song resonate."

★ When the news broke that REM's 1991 album, *Out Of Time*, hit Number One in America, singer Michael Stipe celebrated not by flinging furniture out of hotel windows, nor by fornicating with a harem of under-age groupies. He celebrated by walking his three mixed-breed pups at a creek near his home in Athens, Georgia before proceeding to the city hall to attend a meeting about the historic preservation of some local buildings. This might seem like fairly untypical rock star behaviour, but then REM are no typical rock band.

Launched in 1981 by a stunning independent single, *Radio Free Europe*, REM's rise has been profoundly unobtrusive by normal rock'n'roll standards. Through the 80s, they shifted almost imperceptibly from the relative obscurity of America's alternative college radio scene to thunderous international acclaim.

From the jangly garage rock of 1983's

Murmur to 1987's rather grungy *Document*, each of their albums sold a little better than its predecessor. Then, with 1988's *Green*, their first Warners release and their thankfully short-lived flirtation with arena-sized rock, REM began their ascent through the commercial roof. "I'm thrilled and terrified that this album has been so warmly received," Stipe said at the time. "This album establishes REM as real fossil fuel. We're solid, we have a pretty good bone structure. I feel pretty primed but that doesn't mean that my knees are going to hold out. But at least I know that, if I die tomorrow, my voice will be there on record and no one could do anything about it."

1991's obsessional, bittersweet *Out Of Time* was arguably their first masterpiece and it made them global superstars overnight. Their ability to innovate within a relatively limited combination of musical elements without losing their distinctive voice had always been the most surprising and satisfying thing about each REM album. Even so, *Out Of Time* was nothing short of a revelation, offering the most poignant and contagious melodies heard since the heyday of The Beach Boys; and the most stimulating rock permutations heard since the rise of the New York New Wave.

"Suddenly I realized that we were part of pop culture," Stipe said at the time. "And I didn't mind at all. I have a feeling that as a media figure or a singer, I have a lot more to offer than a lot of what goes down. Especially in America. Everything is so facile and ridiculous. We're pretty much a living surrealist novel. The whole continent breathes weirdness. Not that I'm the voice of rationality, but I'm excited that people are getting excited about us."

With their 1992 album, *Automatic For The People*, REM were surely aware that they only had to equal the might of *Out Of Time* to consolidate their position among rock's premier elite. As it turned out, *Automatic* polevaulted them to the front of the queue. Suddenly, media pundits from here to Timbuktoo were hailing them and U2 as the world's greatest rock'n'roll bands. Not since the days of The Beatles and The Stones 25 years earlier had critical opinion been in such complete accord with public taste.

Automatic was surely, unarguably, their most powerful and beautiful record to date. More downbeat than its predecessor and less instantly inaccessible, it found them near enough perfecting their marriage of emotive melodies and imagistic lyricism, the kind that continues to keep the pop psychologists busier than bees in a treacle pot.

"With this album, I consciously tried to make things clearer," Stipe slyly remarked. "But, at the same time, I never thought it was important for people to understand what I was singing about. I think music is beyond rational thinking."

From the elegiac *Man On The Moon*, through the brainteasing *The Sidewinder Sleeps Tonight*, to the sexually suggestive *Star Me Kitten*, *Automatic* took the melancholy feel of their recent work and distilled it into the kind of aching sorrow that one never expects to find outside Nick Drake, Scott Walker and early Jackson Browne records. Never had REM sounded so luxuriant or so ruminative; the whole record might best be described as a treasure hunt where the treasure is time and the hiding place the past. Living up to their billing as the intelligent face of 90s rock, they insist on crafting songs in such a way that the listener is transported to emotional territories where he/she doesn't know how to react. This is most evident in a song like *Monty Got A Raw Deal*, which has variously been described as "an epitaph for the post-60s generation," and, "a song about chronic emotional dependency." In other words, a basic work of genius.

"Everything with REM is circuitous. It weaves in and out of itself and you always come back to where you started and start all over again."

Thus, in the last 12 months, REM made the biggest artistic advance of their 13 year history and demonstrated that public acceptance does not necessarily mean that one has to be defined by that success. At a guess, REM's art is based, like all the best art, on a condition of fundamental boredom. In effect, REM have defined themselves in terms of what they reject: rock'n'roll cliché, big tent crowd-pleasing, vacant posturing, false/forced intimacy, cut-price sincerity, routine, stupidity, obviousness. Like all the best rock'n'roll bands, REM are a law unto themselves.

"I think our entire mode of operation is cyclical," Stipe says. "The music, and even the way that I talk, may seem like it's constantly chasing its tail, but not in an unmotivated or bad way. Everything with REM is circuitous. It weaves in and out of itself and you always come back to where you started and start all over again. That's a great way to follow. It's hypnotizing; it's a music that draws you in, if you're there to be drawn in."

Perhaps the most remarkable element of REM's success is its democratic pull. Everyone, it seems, has a good word for them: teenagers, parents, pensioners, critics, students, milkmen, policemen. This is not so far-fetched. After the release of *Automatic*, REM were voted Top Pop Act by the Metropolitan Police Gazette. Commented its editor, Detective Sergeant Philpot: "REM pulled two-thirds of the vote, which was a surprise because I've never heard of them. However, my wife tells me that they write good toe-tapping tunes and meaningful lyrics. That probably explains the breadth of their appeal. They're welcome to pop into any police station in Britain for a nice cup of tea and a fig roll or two."

Virtually alone among the modern rock fraternity, REM have become hugely successful, have continued their assault on perfection, whilst maintaining their dignity.

REM do not have shaved heads, tattooed testicles, film star wives, uncontrollable egos or Messianic pretensions. What they do have is an unrivalled grasp of what makes a song resonate; a way with words; impeccable taste in everything apart from shoes; a marvellous sense of ambiguity; an equally marvellous sense of timing; insatiable artistic curiosity.

In 1992, just after the release of *Automatic For The People*, an American psychic prophesied that REM would soon break up. "Alternative music is going to fall by the wayside," he said. "There will be internal problems within the band with everybody wanting to do their own thing and not being successful." Rumours of the band's imminent demise were heightened when Michael Stipe announced plans to record a solo album that would include cover versions of Gang Of Four's *Paralysed*, Pylon's *Gravity*, 10,000 Maniacs' *Hey Jack Kerouac* and Steppenwolf's *Magic Carpet Ride*.

However, as Stipe assured the readers of Rolling Stone: "We have a pact to keep going until the end of the millennium. Then we'll break up. That way, we'll hopefully avoid being one of those dumb bands who keep going, not realizing how bad they are. So we've got eight years left. It doesn't seem likely that in that time we'll make our own version of *Chicago X1V*. I can't see that happening. I think the stuff we're doing now challenges in energy and emotion and feeling anything we've ever done."

Over the course of eight albums, but especially their last two, REM have joined the select pantheon of bands (The Rolling Stones, MC5, T Rex, Television, The Smiths) who have changed the rock metabolism for the better. After 12 years, they still seem like the band least likely to walk on stage with cucumbers down their trousers.
May Heaven reward them.

JON WILDE

kd lang

"By mid-93, she became the pop world's first honest lesbian icon, a diva by whom the world is intrigued and to whom it is almost in thrall."

★ "My idea of beauty is change and intrigue," kd lang has said; and those two qualities could easily be seen as the ones that combined to project her to the heights of success where she now resides. This was lang's year, as much for the fact that she seemed to discover herself as that she was discovered. As late as the start of 1992, she was a torch and twang country singer of indeterminate sexuality. By the end of that year, following the major crossover success of her faultless and inspired fifth LP, *Ingénue*, and the declaration of her lesbian status, she was hailed as a ground-breaking talent of epic proportions; by mid-93, she became the pop world's first honest lesbian icon, a diva by whom the world is intrigued and to whom it is almost in thrall.

Bob Dylan wants to write with her, magazines vie to snap the androgynous planes of her face and chatter about the sexy hipness of sapphism, and Madonna sighs of her, "Elvis is alive – and she's beautiful." lang, for her part, maintains her sharply articulate cool while admitting how much she digs it all. It's been not just a momentous year for the singer on a personal level, but one in which she altered the sociology of the pop pantheon almost single-handed.

Though it seems to have happened almost overnight, lang's success has taken, in the

normal way, almost ten years to achieve. Born Katherine Dawn Lang (she prefers the lower case rendering because "it's generic and, unlike Cherry Bomb, it's a name, not a sexuality") in the small Canadian town of Consort, this farmer's daughter had become a skilled pianist and guitarist by adolescence and, at the age of ten, had already sent some songs to her then favourite country singer, Ann Murray, who declined to reply. After high school, lang studied music at Alberta's Red Deer College, and then drifted into perform-ance art; her coup was performing the first heart transplant involving a plastic heart, a show in a gallery basement which lasted 12 hours. "We made the heart and arteries out of carrots and pickled beets. It was really just self-exploration, where I learned about spontaneity, concentration, understanding the movement of creativity."

After a series of jobs including truck-driving, lang grew absorbed with country music. Although its reactionary ethic would eventually make country a demanding mistress, it seemed at the time her natural home. "I rejected country at first," says lang; "and then I began to understand that it was white American blues." In addition, lang admits she was becoming more romantic about her background. She played Patsy Cline in a local dramatic production, 'Country

Chorale', and "I realized that that's where I came from – I knew about people like Tammy Wynette, like Loretta Lynn. Also, I liked the kitschness of it." A statement that points up lang's ever-present irony, something that could easily have helped draw her to what is arguably the corniest of musical styles. Nevertheless, although her idol, Cline, produced hits which were the epitome of the sugary Nashville sound that was the hallmark of 60s country, Cline's songs were also soul ballads, and Cline's reputation as a feisty woman in a genre that expected its females to be submissive had its own appeal. lang dubbed her band The Reclines, a genuflection in Patsy's direction.

The hokey notion of country sat a little awkwardly on lang, at the start, and she spoofed it for all she was worth, with brushcut hair, no make-up and a gingham dress festooned with plastic farm animals. Her first outing, *A Truly Western Experience*, brought her to the attention of Sire records boss Seymour Stein: "The glossy picture made her look like Buddy Holly in drag, but I fell in love with the record."

Signed to Sire, lang's next album, the Dave Edmunds-produced *Angel With A Lariat*, drew accolades (Rolling Stone voted her 'Female Vocalist of the Year'), but it also drew snarls from diehard country fans, antagonized by her

... *"and I think there's a little bit of Trini in all of us"*

haircut and ambiguous sexual stance. On top of which, lang was a vegetarian. As a kid, her pets were "two cats, an alligator and a chimp. When I was about four, we had to shoot the chimp because it went crazy. I was very upset. Maybe that's why I'm an animal rights activist now."

Whatever caused it, lang spearheaded a campaign around this time called *Meat Stinks*. "If you knew how meat was made," she announced on frequent TV spots, "you'd lose your lunch." In Alberta, where Consort is but a tiny settlement, hate mail was dispatched and lang's records boycotted. "In that community," she says, "meat is how they make their dollar. But I can't see that eating meat is ultimately a good thing. And the truth is, they weren't playing my records, anyway."

Never mind. The kudos and notice she'd achieved hooked lang a duet with Roy Orbison, and in 1987 they shared a Grammy for Best Country Collaboration on *Cryin'*, a Top Ten hit in the UK when re-released last year. In 1988, she began her breakthrough into the wider music-buying audience with the lushly sensual *Shadowland* and, at the last time, ditched the Aunt Sally outfits and the fringed cowboy chaps. Forsaking rhinestone glitz and tack, she honed her look and grew her hair into a come-on cowlick that drooped waywardly in her eyes. She stopped acting like a mannish woman and became a feminine man. It was dangerously erogenous.

Shadowland appealed to country consumers partly due to the presence of such stalwarts as The Jordanaires, Brenda Lee and Loretta Lynn, and schmaltzy tracks like Chris Isaak's *Western Stars* perfectly exemplified the self-explanatory 'torch and twang' style; lang used the phrase as the title for her next album. This was mostly self-composed with the help of instrumentalist Ben Mink, and it earned her grudging accolades from even the biggest country bigots. It was, in a sense, to be her swansong to that genre. lang says now, "The Saturn Return [the disruptive movement of that planet back into one's astrological sign], which you go through from 28 to 31, had a profound affect on my work, and it inspired me to switch from country music. Everything was – still is – in turmoil. I love country music, but it was like a lover I'd outgrown and it was time to move on." The May 1992 appearance of *Ingénue* marked a radical departure for the singer. Far from country, Country & Western or that strange colt "new country", it was lang's first all-original album. It is a product of a new maturity and an inspiration that lang believes stems from falling in love "overwhelmingly, for the first time", and "relinquishing control". The music is couched in arrangements influenced both by her love of Eastern European folk as well as by North African tempos, and co-songwriter Mink's

Hasidic Jewish heritage.

Although the album trod water uneasily for a month or two, its broad appeal and the undeniable strength and beauty of the singles taken from it swiftly lead to major honours. In February 1993, lang was nominated for a Brit award for Best International Newcomer and on 24 February she won the Best Female Vocal (Pop) Grammy for the sprightly single *Constant Craving*. The lyrics of the album, lang's biggest-selling LP so far (platinum in the States and gold in the UK), hint at deep soul-mining, at once resonant with longing and radiant with joy.

It's a heady combination, and one that has resulted in near-hysteria when she appears live. It has long been lang's kick to tease about her sexual predilections, opening gigs with sly innuendo; and so, when she appeared last May at London's (now Labatt's) Hammersmith Apollo, she repeated the formula for old time's sake, though everyone knew the score. "There has been a lot of speculation in the press, and I think now's the time to come out," she announced to thunderous stomping and applause. "Yes – I am a Trini Lopez fan." Coyly: "And I think there's a little bit of Trini in all of us." The gig proceeded, to raucous cries of "Get yer kit off!" from the two-thirds female audience, to which the singer

responded with a shameless display of flirting.

Then there were the notorious snaps in August 93's Vanity Fair, depicting a pinstriped lang swooning in the equally enraptured arms of supermodel Cindy Crawford, who appears to be shaving her. Frank, funny and provocative, the photographs blow sky-high any stereotypical view of the butch, be-booted and boiler-suited lesbian. In response to questions, lang has said, "I know I'm a dyke role model, but being gay is just one thing that I am – it's not my main concern. Art transcends that. I've felt an incredible intimacy with my audiences since I came out. They're making an anti-homophobic statement by being there; but personally, I'm not political at all." Nevertheless, lang has been instrumental in making female androgyny de rigueur in a wholly new way.

The fact is that it's not solely lesbians but *everyone* who currently seems to find lang attractive, which may be because of her sheer bravery as well as her talent. While her star continues to rise, lang remains steady. "My goal now is to stay creative and have a career of longevity and history. It boils down to that."

GLYN BROWN

"Gabriel has manoeuvred himself onto the cutting edge. He's a man for whom innovation is not only a passion but a credo."

★ Far from being one of rock's comfortable middle-aged dinosaurs, peddling a glorious past and occasionally chucking together a celebrity-strewn collection of nostalgic tat to pay the bills, Peter Gabriel has manoeuvred himself onto the cutting edge. He's a man for whom innovation is not only a passion but a credo.

In a year that saw the release of his long awaited follow-up to 1986's acclaimed album *So*, Peter Gabriel has achieved more than most artists do in a lifetime. Those who berate him for taking six years to get around to recording another album (his record company for one) should take a quick glance at the man's impressive list of extra musicular activities and reconsider.

Us (released September 92, highest chart position Number Two) is possibly the most

accomplished of Gabriel's six solo albums to date. A trip through his own troubled psyche, highlighting the intense feelings of love and loss that arose during the breakdown of his marriage to wife Jill and his turbulent relationship with Rosanna Arquette, *Us* is deeply introspective and, on the face of it, wilfully uncommercial. It still sold a healthy three million copies and rising.

The lack of hit potential has made little difference, as *Us*, even in its bleakness, seems to have struck a universal chord with his fans. Through tracks like *Blood Of Eden* and the passionate *Come Talk To Me*, the "angel and devil" nature of Gabriel's psyche is revealed. "There's a lot of relationship stuff in there," he claimed on its release. "All the emotions and ideas you have going on inside you that give rise to the confusion inevitably form a large part of what *Us* is about."

He freely admits that his own five-year programme of therapy helped him come to terms with the 'destructive bastard' aspect of his character. "I was in therapy for years trying to work out why I was behaving the way I did, why things couldn't last, and I think it helped me acknowledge the monster in me."

Working again with world musicians, a trend he began on *So*, the influences on *Us* are as diverse culturally as you'd expect. It is, however, the simple stripped down songs like *Washing The Water* and *Blood Of Eden* where Gabriel is at his best, proving once and for all that he's transcended any one style or mode of delivery.

So saw Gabriel setting new standards in video production and state of the art graphic techniques (*Sledgehammer* and *Big Time* in particular) and the videos for *Us* continued that tradition, eagerly awaited by both the industry and MTV kids alike. The video for the second single, *Steam*, the album's only real attempt at commercial pop (released 12 October 92, highest chart position Number Ten) was a slice of pure optical titillation, Gabriel's image distorted and manipulated into various weird and wonderful guises including the front of a steamtrain and a bodybuilding hunk. The video, directed by Stephen Johnson, featured state of the art

digital effects and is rumoured to have cost well into seven figures.

It was, however, the strange video for *Digging In The Dirt*, a song dealing with the therapy that followed his marriage break-up in 1986, that provided the most bizarre incident of the last year. Gabriel, always keen to suffer for his art, was filmed while a league of snails slimed their way over his body. One of these was a giant African breed called the Radula whose teeth-like incisors became lodged in Gabriel's face. Leech-like, it had to be removed forcibly, leaving 40 incisor marks in his skin. This love of video and graphic techniques found novel and revolutionary outlets on Gabriel's Secret World tour, which began in April in Stockholm.

A fan of PC power, he has used desk top publishing systems to launch The Box Magazine. Not a fanzine, but a quarterly forum for like-minded folk, it's a colourful, well produced, glossy affair under Gabriel's editorial direction. Like Black Ice and Mondo 2000 it is essentially dedicated to the emerging technologies, although the various diverse interests of Mr Gabriel are also dealt with, from cybersex and virtual reality to the ozone layer and graphology! (The Box is available by subscription only from The Box, PO Box 35, Bath Avon BA1 1YJ.)

Amongst his fellow believers in a technological future are Brian Eno and Laurie Anderson, with whom he is collaborating on a world first, The Real World Experience Park. With the granting of a 16-acre site in Barcelona and the blessing of Spanish Prime Minster Felipe González earlier this year, its realization has come an important step closer. Gabriel describes the experience park as "an obsession", a subterranean theme park to be hidden under a tranquil landscape where artists, film makers, programmers, writers, musicians and performers can come together to create an interactive experience for the senses. Eno describes the project as a "great new art form exploring the relationship between man and culture, culture and nature and man and nature."

Not renowned for his ability to stand the rigours of lengthy tours, Gabriel has nevertheless managed to wow 'em night after night across Europe and the US on his Secret World tour. He promised something special and delivered it. The set, designed by French Canadian opera designer Robert Lepage, is a visual circus of symbolic delights, with platforms and gantries where Gabriel popped up throughout the show in various guises and costumes. The overall effect was to take the rock concert away from pure performance and into the realms of theatre.

He pulled out of a peace concert in Ireland, blaming the fact that there were no Irish bands on the bill as promised. He thought the net result of an all-English roster was patronizing. The planned appearance with *chanteuse* Sinead O' Connor further fuelled rumours that he was romantically involved with the singer. The tabloid press laid seige to his home in Wiltshire as speculation reached fever pitch.

There was also a memorable appearance at this year's Brits awards where he received an award for best producer for the *Us* album. He gave those awaiting his arrival for the UK dates of the tour a brief taster of what was in store. Complete with false muscled gropesuit, his ultra camp version of the hit single *Steam* was, along with Suede, the highlight of the show.

While 'charidee' fatigue has definitely set in elsewhere in Rockland, Gabriel's deep-rooted commitment to human rights issues remains ongoing.

A man for whom risk appears to be a chief motivating force, the "angel Gabriel" (as some have dubbed him) seems more than willing to put his royalties where his mouth is, much to the dismay of his accountant.

WOMAD, an organization he helped found,

once again hit financial trouble this year. Just as he bailed them out in 1982 with a one-off reunion of his former group Genesis, this year he stumped up the cash to clear debts arising from the ambitious staging of the WOMAD festivals of last year. "I couldn't just watch them disappear after all they've achieved," said Gabriel. For the first time he headlined this year's WOMAD festivals in Cornwall and Bath, ensuring capacity crowds and a good taking at the gate to aid the coffers of the pioneering world music events. His general

love of World Music acts continued with the release of albums on the Real World label which he helped found. Amongst last year's CDs was *Plus From Us*, a collection of music by the artists who appeared on and influenced the making of *US*, including Eno, Shankar and William Orbit. He also staged an exhibition at the London Contemporary Art Fair of the works commissioned for the sleeve of the album.

At the end of a truly hectic year, Peter Gabriel's music has become the most conventional thing he does. *Us*, while not as commercially successful as *So* and twice as costly to make, has bestowed on Gabriel the enviable status of being both middle-aged and for mass consumption, yet universally credible. It seems his long-adhered-to maxim that "the fringes of what I do today will become the centre of what I do tomorrow" continues to pay big dividends.

CLIFF JONES

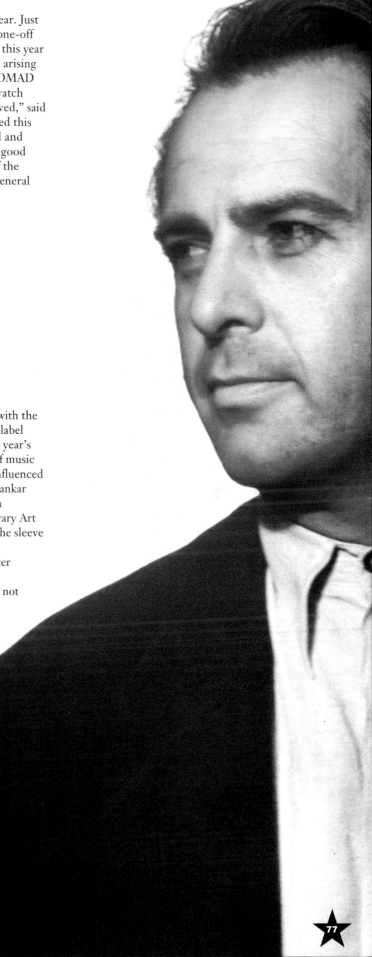

belly

> "Belly's debut recording filtered into the national psyche with all the euphoric highs and desperate lows befitting the experience of being out of one's mind."

⭐ In the summer of 92 Tanya Donelly said she'd be highly chuffed if she made a record that could be "a genuine substitute for heroin. That would be making a real contribution!"

And, by Jove, she'd already done it! Belly's debut recording, the *Slow Dust* EP, filtered into the national psyche with all the euphoric highs and desperate lows befitting the experience of being out of one's mind on the ill-advised killer sedative. Belly, however, would never leave you dead, just shimmering with the soporific tingles of knowing that you'd really, *really* felt something. And that's pretty much what Belly are all about: nightmares lit from below with fairy-lights, a gothic cavalcade round the plaintive emotions of Patti Smith, The Cocteau Twins,

Sinead O'Connor and The Cure. Except sweeter, which probably means even *more* deadly.

All the elements, then, of Tanya's favourite reading matter in the whole world ever: Grimm's Fairy Tales – with all the small children lost in fabulous everglades being stuffed in ovens by warty old women that that implies. Tanya has always had a deep obsession with the underworld, the ethereal and the surreal and an imagination like hers needs its outlet. Until two years ago she'd only half-found one. She was co-founder of Rhode Island's Throwing Muses with her half-sister Kristin Hersh in 1986. She was on the fiddle, as it were, as she couldn't have sung out-front to save herself: "I could barely *talk* in 1986," she remembers.

It took the subsequent side-kick collaboration with Kim Deal and The Breeders before, at the end of 1991, she decided: "I'm getting old, I wanna do this! I thought 'Enough strong women in my life! I wanna be the strong woman now…'"

Belly began as Tanya, brothers Tom and Chris Gorman (film production assistant/ graphic designing surfer chums) and ex-

Throwing Muses bassist Fred Abong. They first came to Britain in the summer of 92 with the aforementioned *Slow Dust* EP and many pronouncements on what a magical word "Belly" was. It had always been Tanya's favourite – "so womby, earthy, womanly, beer belly-ey!" She told us of the folks who'd changed her life: The Flying Burrito Brothers, Billie Holiday, Ennio Morricone, Janis Joplin, the Rolling Stones, Mary Margaret O'Hara, Neil Young, Woody Guthrie and Jesus Christ (as in *Superstar*, the motion picture soundtrack). She was ephemeral, miniature, ludicrously sensitive and sported indie-pop's most gigantic winning grin *ever*.

The nation, quite rightly, went "hurrah!" in very large measures indeed. The *Gepetto* EP followed to even more silvery plaudits about gossamer goblins on the rings of Saturn and the like, and in January the better part of the Western hemisphere exploded in the populist magnificence of the *Feed The Tree* EP (followed, moments later, by the debut *Star* LP). *Feed The Tree* went to a criminal 32 in the soaraway singles charts while *Star* gleaned justice at Number Two in the album charts. The only persons, it seemed, not delighted

"Wounded nerds everywhere are attracted to us. But I'd rather attract them than people who want to look up my skirt."

with the placing were the big-wigs down at Paul McCartney's office in Soho Square, London. *Star* had eclipsed, amongst others, Paul McCartney's super new LP. They phoned up 4AD and demanded to know "how they did it".

"When I heard they'd called," wobbled Tanya, "I threw up." Paul McCartney had been her all-time childhood hero, she'd had an "unhealthy, obsessive" crush on old Wacky Thumbs Aloft and it was he who'd first inspired her to start her own band. Throwing up, meanwhile, has formed a mainstay of the Donelly psyche; ever since she started school, in fact, whereupon every day of her formative years she vomited on her school room desk.

"I had one of the most unpleasantly awkward adolescences on the planet," she recalls, "I thought I was the ugliest girl alive. Kristin was my only friend pretty much and I didn't have any kind of relationship with a male until I'd left high school."

And so she vomited. Things were so bad the teachers used to move her desk away from the other kids "because I was starting a puke chain. I was a… total geek."

Tanya has now found some semblance of stability, doubtless due to the confidence that artistic success can induce. *Star* centres around the turning point in her life: "I was completely, physically revamping my life. New band, new relationship, new situation."

You'd have to search deeply for the metaphors of change, however; the Nashville-recorded *Star* is a lyrical creep-show: a woman kills herself and her baby in front of her husband (*Fool Moon, Empty Heart*), a heroin addict is raped (*Dusted*), an adulterous Chinese woman has a dog strapped to her back until it decomposes (*Slow Dog*)… even the sublime jollity of the breakthrough *Feed The Tree* has the hallmark Donelly spook-factor. In the American mid-west, tradition once deemed that members of a family buried their dead by a single tree, fertilizing the roots with the de-composing body. Yum!??

"So the song *says*…" smiles Tanya, "basically, respect my ass and be there until I die, which is a lot to ask, really." She just can't help herself. Tanya knows full well she sounds like a nutter at times and that's fine by her.

"Fairy tales have come naturally to me since I was little," she notes, "that's the way I think, that's the way I talk. Anyway, I don't believe that pop music should be literal. And I find obsessive love songs more interesting. I don't think I've ever heard a healthy love song that I've liked because I don't think love is necessarily healthy. Love's… creepy."

Such incandescence, of course, has brought her legions of fans of the suicidal bedroom moper variety: "Wounded nerds everywhere are attracted to us. But I'd rather attract them than people who want to look up my skirt."

The flimsy indie blubbers, of course, were not so content with the addition to Belly in spring 93, of Gail Greenwood from hardcore punksters, Boneyard. "Scary heavy metal chick from hell!!" they howled as Gail stormed the national stages with legs akimbo and hair a-flail; she was Slash in a mini-skirt and the kids were bamboozled. Gail, however, was pivotal to the new-found live confidence Tanya had been looking for and it worked, even when Gail called audiences "wankers" because she thought it was an ironic compliment. Americans eh? Gail had been sent a tape of *Stars*, loved it, but had reservations about her contribution.

"I said, number one, I'm much older than you guys, I'm 33, I'm a sea hag," she hoots. "Number two, I have a life, 'cos I'm teaching. And number three, I have an obnoxious stage presence."*Just* what Tanya wanted. "Enjoy yourself", she said, "and we will, too."

Thus, Belly had it all; they were tough, spooky and good-looking. And this got right up the nose of the so-called Riot Grrl movement who accused Tanya of exploiting her immense good-lookingness and her fabulous teeth etc etc. Their argument seemed to centre around the belly of Tanya herself.

Cut-off tops? Gender traitor!

"I don't consider it to be particularly sexy!" fumes Tanya, "I don't go on stage in my bra and I never would. I'm not interested in exposing my body. The worst treachery is attacking another woman. If they're pissed off, be pissed off with men who hit women, who kill women. Do something about that."

As for the male journalists slavering on about her cutesy laugh and dental majesty…

"It pisses me off when people call me cute, when people say I giggle – it's a load of bullshit! When I giggle, that's a fucking involuntary muscle spasm, I've no control over that. That's something that's been projected by particular men on to me. I'm just not a very sad person, I'm a happy person."

As she should be. Tanya's future now looks glistening. She and Tom Gorman are working on Belly's second LP, and Tanya will be spending time with her fiance Chick Graning from avant-garde rockers Anastasia Screamed, who sang backing vocals on *Star*. The two of them might even consider recording a country LP together.

"We wanna do one!" she howls, "Our voices do sound good together, too. Mr Gravel and Miss Priss." Or she may take up Tom Jones' recent offer to write some songs for him – Belly have performed a "gritty" rendition of Tom's *It's Not Unusual* across the entire planet throughout the year. Other than that she's still searching for the ultimate in security: to give everything up for the good of others.

"I'm an ambitious person," she ponders, "but not very focused. I'd like to get to the point where I'm empowered enough to do something that'll serve the needs of someone other than myself, like volunteer work. I mean, there's definitely mornings when I wake up and think 'what kind of a fucking job is this? Who is it helping?'"

She thinks she'll get there. After all, it is written, fittingly, in the stars. A friend of her mum reads tarot cards and this year told Tanya that in her late 30s/early 40s she would finally realize her ultimate ambition.

"She told me I'd do something…" states Tanya in her oblique, confidently magical way, "that would feed my soul."

SYLVIA PATTERSON

79

BLACK CROWES

"Trendy by virtue of their espousal by the likes of Guns N' Roses, the Black Crowes have won their stature by sheer hard work."

★ Unreconstituted, traditional rock'n'roll. That's the cause The Black Crowes espouse. Where rock music has become more and more glossy and marketing-led, this Atlanta band records in small studios and promotes their records the hard way: on the road. Nearly four years ago The Black Crowes, led by the sibling nucleus of Chris Robinson on vocals and Rich Robinson on guitar, won a surprise hit record with their debut LP, *Shake Your Money Maker*.

That's if surprise is the right word for an album that took a whole year of constant touring before peaking at Number Four in the US charts. In the summer of 92 The Black Crowes followed up with *The Southern Harmony And Musical Companion*, cementing their status as one of the universe's premier rock attractions. Admirably unconsidered, this follow-up retained all the boozy Faces-inspired sloppiness of their debut, but stretched out to embrace the out-and-out guitar freakery of new member Marc Ford, while maintaining the rootsy three chord traditional songwriting skills that had helped the first album win its exalted status.

According to Chris, the first album "was like when you have sex with someone and you're the only person who has an orgasm. This second album is like when you have sex and you both come at once. The second time it's a little sexier and a little bolder."

Since that point in the middle of 1992, it's really been more of the same. As they did with their first album, the Black Crowes set out to promote *The Southern Harmony And Musical Companion* in exactly the same labour-intensive way as its predecessor, playing seemingly every venue in the United States, from city stadia to obscure clubs. Trendy by virtue of their espousal by the likes of Guns N' Roses, the Black Crowes have won their stature by sheer hard work.

Chris and Rich Robinson were seemingly born into a career in rock music. Their father, Stan, enjoyed a hit single with *Boom-A-Dip-*

Dip in the rock'n'roll boom of the late 50s, while mother Nancy had a career as a Nashville Country and Western singer behind her. The brothers made their debut in a punk band, Mr Crowes' Garden, in 1984. Having recruited bassist Johnny Colt, guitarist Jeff Cease and drummer Steve Gorman in 1988, the newly-named Black Crowes signed to the Def American label in 1989. Their debut album was produced by George Drakoulias, ex-A&R man who had decided to move with the band when his previous employers refused his advice to sign them.

The Robinson brothers share songwriting duties, 26-year-old Chris providing the words while younger brother Rich, 24, writes the melodies, usually in open guitar tunings learned from Ry Cooder and Led Zeppelin records. As personalities they're noticeably distinct, Chris lanky and talkative, while his brother remains comparatively restrained. Both brothers take a workmanlike pride in the speed with which they followed-up on their debut album. "We had a week off," says Chris. This is our main chance. If I take a break now, I'm a pussy." Rich: "All the time we were on tour with the first album we spent 22 months racking our brains, thinking Jesus, what do we do with our second album? Then we got home and did the whole thing in about eight days. We had the studio booked for about three weeks, then our mom had a heart attack so we had to work around that. But in the week before it happened we wrote eight new songs – we had a whole album's worth of stuff we wrote on tour that we threw away. There's only two songs on the album that we've had for a while."

According to Chris: "Those songs on the last album… we played them to no-one, like in clubs with nobody there at all. Then we played them to thousands. So the new songs were written with a different mindset. It's heavier. I wanted to put a sticker on the album. It would say 'contains no apathy', 'cause that's what we're up against in this jaded age where

If Chris and Rich have a hangup about videos, it's one that's amply compensated for by their gluttony for sheer hard touring, which has filled the year since the release of *Southern Harmony*… From small American venues, to European festivals, they haven't stopped. In fact Chris reckons they've gained an even bigger appetite for this particular form of hard graft since the departure of original guitarist Jeff Cease early in 1992. Cease's disappearance was originally described in the manner of a Vietnam movie: "You go out there for two years, and not everybody makes it back." A year on, Chris Robinson is more blunt:

"That was just a nice way of saying the guy can't play. To tell the truth, we all resented the fact we had to back him up. On the new album Rich didn't have to write all the solos. With Jeff there was never that freedom – he was like an albatross around our necks. What Marc does speaks for itself. Like, they tried to get him to join Guns N' Roses, but that guy doesn't have to play behind anyone."

Ford's move was probably a wise one. While Guns N' Roses retain their status as a world-class attraction, the Crowes are coming up fast. At a time when the world is returning to the spiritual values of the late 60s and early 70s, they're even beginning to look distinctly contemporary, rendering irrelevant the descriptions of them as Faces or Stones clones. Understandably, that accusation, according to Rich, "pisses us the fuck off", but Rich's love of the vintage Ron Wood and Keith Richards sound does admittedly extend to the recent commissioning of a British Zemaitis guitar as used by Ron 'n' Keef.

Pointing out that his own musical forebears lifted more than a riff or two from the likes of Chuck Berry or Willie Dixon, he comments that "it's better to borrow from rich English guys than to steal from poor black guys."

More importantly, where bands like the Rolling Stones have come to view rock music as a part-time activity, for the Crowes it's their whole life. They mean it all, from the 'free us – no narcs' and marijuana flags they unravel on stage, to the extended guitar solos last seen in the days of the Allman Brothers. For a stadium-status band, they're about as far away from the corporate side of rock music as it's possible to get.

Chris: "I know that the industry is never going to change. They're businessmen, man, they're not fans. And people who live that way, their opinion about what I do doesn't matter as much as people who think that rock'n'roll is a language for young people to keep it together."

"Our music is not polite, it doesn't fit nicely into any category, it's not what any of those despicable marketing people from the record companies want. And that's what's good about it."

PAUL TRYNKA

everybody's seen and done it all already. Well, I refuse to let it affect me.

"There's like this whole thing of how your next record has got to sell more than the last one, you've gotta buy a bigger car, you've got to record a bigger video. So who gives a shit? Just give me one record that makes me cry, or one record that makes my backbone go funny. All we need is good bands that just get up there and play."

Which is obviously what the Black Crowes set out to do, despite the obligatory modern concessions of the video age. "Everything is seen as a marketing tool, man. I mean, that's ludicrous to me. But if all I have to do is make a couple of videos a year, that's not too bad. At least I don't have to get on my knees and spit the cum out like some whore."

"it's better to borrow [riffs] from rich English guys than to steal from poor black guys."

Leaders of the package

Thousands flocked to the huge Lollapalooza events across the States last year, given the chance to catch an eclectic array of bands sharing the bill as part of a nationwide tour. But the package tour itself dates back to the frisky 50s, as

Nick Abbot

reveals.

Variety truly being the spice of life, it's easy to understand the continued popularity of the package tour. Here's the chance to see not just one, but several acts on the same stage, though in reality what you get is a series of sound bites, a sort of live in-concert version of your favourite compilation album.

Natural successors to the variety shows of the music hall era, package tours really got off the ground in the 1950s. In those days, American DJ Alan Freed – the man often credited with having sparked off the whole rock 'n' roll revolution – would contract two or three big name stars along with half a dozen aspiring unknowns for a couple of weeks, pack them into an old bus and embark on a whirlwind tour of the American theatre circuit.

True to legend, the pay would usually be derisory – with even the big names never quite sure they would get their dues at the end of it all – and the pace was gruelling. Each act might only get to perform two or three numbers, but there would usually be an afternoon matinee and two evening shows, followed by a through-the-night drive to the next dot on the map.

Promoters on Black America's 'chittlin' circuit' of one-night-stands were quick to get in on the act, and astute R&B stars like Johnny Otis, Ray Charles and Ike and Tina Turner quickly realised they could earn far better money if they could offer a complete evening's entertainment.

The ever-astute James Brown turned the concept into an art form, using not only other, lesser, singers but dancers, comics and other performers too – all of them charged with the job of pumping up the atmosphere to the point where Hank Ballard, himself a successful artist thanks to his million-selling original of *The Twist*, would bound on stage and proclaim: "It's showtime, ladies and gentlemen. He's the King of the brand new heavy heavy funk ... Mr Superbad ... the hardest working man in show business ... Soul Brother Number One ... Mr Jaaaaaames Brown!"

Pop package tours became the norm in the UK too. Larry Parnes – the infamous 'Parnes, Shillings And Pence' of music business folklore – packaged up his stable of artists, with stereotyped names like Rory Storm, Billy Fury and Marty Wilde. Meanwhile, the wide-eyed young Beatles got their chance to share billings with legends like Little Richard and Sam Cooke, whose music they had been listening to so avidly for years, often on rare imported singles.

The promoters were firmly in charge. Put on a single star turn with just one other act in support and the artists can wield quite a lot of negotiating power, but on a package? Well, even the biggest of names was just one star among several on the bill. If an act started throwing its weight around, asked for more money, a better dressing room, or maybe a couple of days' rest from the endless grind, it was easy to sack them and bring in a replacement. This happened to The Drifters when they were dismissed en-bloc for 'unprofessional behaviour' and another younger, more eager group on the same bill was pushed up the listings to replace them, in the process changing name from The Crowns to ... The Drifters!

At Harlem's legendary Apollo Theatre, they took things even further, holding an amateur night when a seemingly endless succession of hopeful (or indeed hopeless) talents would take the stage and brave the wrath or earn the approval of the toughest audience in the world – with no-hopers being pelted with soggy missiles and literally hooked offstage by a merciless individual lurking in the wings.

A variation on the theme was the single-label package tour – Motown's 'Motortown Revue', headlining acts like the Supremes, The Four Tops, Marvin Gaye and Stevie Wonder; and the Memphis sound 'Stax Volt Revue', with Booker T & The MGs plus the Mar-Keys horn section providing the gutbucket Southern raunch that distinguished the work of Sam and Dave, Carla Thomas, Eddie Floyd and, of course, the late Otis Redding.

As the 60s pop explosion gathered momentum and flowered into the rock revolution, the bigger packages outgrew the likes of the Liverpool Empire, the Paris Olympia and the Brooklyn Paramount and the era of the great outdoor package concerts began – often presenting for a full day, or several days, a long succession of acts. The million-plus fans at Woodstock, in 1967, represented the ultimate in the dream, the 'Sympathy For The Devil' stabbing at Altamont the worst nightmare.

Festivals are now part of the annual rock music round all over the world, Glastonbury and Reading having found a new (although, so far, weaker) rival in Phoenix, and the traditional package tour has been making a comeback. Not, of course, that the idea ever truly went away, for in the 70s the punk/new wave era gave us the Stiff Records tour with Elvis Costello, Ian Dury, Nick Lowe, Wreckless Eric and Lene Lovich, and even in the 80s, New Order and Echo and the Bunnymen used the pair-up-to-share-out formula to good effect.

"Natural successors to the variety shows of the music hall era, package tours really got off the ground in the 1950s."

"... a succession of rock bands, starved of places to play in the current recession, have recognised that shared billings are a way to improved work circumstances."

Soul music legend Willie Mitchell recently brought over his fellow Waylo Records' artists, including Ann Peebles and Otis Clay, for a couple of tours to earn rave reviews. Meanwhile, blues packages abound, giving us the chance to hear and see such legends as Buddy Guy and Otis Rush, and a succession of rock bands, starved of places to play in the current recession, have recognised that shared billings are a way to improved work circumstances.

In 1992 Metallica and Guns N' Roses teamed up for a major US tour, and from 1991 onwards the massive Lollapalooza events, the brainchild of Perry Farrell, then of Jane's Addiction and now of Porno For Pyros, had put such diverse noisemakers as Dinosaur Jr, Alice In Chains, Rage Against The Machine, Fishbone, Verve, Babes In Toyland, Primus and Arrested Development (93), and Red Hot Chili Peppers, Lush, Pearl Jam, Soundgarden, Ministry and Ice Cube (92), out on the American roads together.

Meanwhile, two years of its British equivalent Rollercoaster found The Jesus & Mary Chain persuading Blur, Dinosaur Jr and My Bloody Valentine to share the bill in rotating order at medium sized venues around Europe.

And nearly two decades after Stiff took their label mates out on tour together, the single label package is back too, with the Acid Jazz label having recently put its acts like Corduroy, the James Taylor Quartet, Galliano and Mother Earth in adjoining dressing rooms – proving that good things can still come in small packages ...

Rock

> *"The live album made a big comeback too, mostly thanks to MTV's Unplugged series, where artists are asked to perform live and acoustically for an invited audience."*

1993 will probably be remembered as the year that the British music industry took a pasting from Gerald Kaufman's Select Committee over its CD pricing policy.

However, ignoring the intriguing asides of the business, 1993 was actually quite a good year for rock music. Maybe not in Britain in terms of sales, but certainly in the breadth and scale of releases. Without doubt the two biggest name releases of the year came from U2 and REM.

In both cases the world was still reeling from the band's previous releases. REM hadn't toured to support sales of the previous year's *Out Of Time* album, but it sold in millions anyway. In September 92, they released *Automatic For The People*, and it seemed as if they had gone mad. Michael Stipe refused to talk about it. The album is laid-back, dark, acoustic and there's no Shiny, Happy People. It sold more than *Out Of Time*, gave the band three Top Ten hits and found its way into the Top Ten of Radio One listeners' all-time great album chart of June 1993.

U2 were touring the globe with their ZOO TV show as they announced a release in 1993. Originally it was to be a single. Then an EP. Finally, an album. *Zooropa* was recorded during a break in touring while in Dublin, mainly because, as Bono explained, "When we came off the ZOO TV tour we thought we could lead normal lives and then go back on the road in the summer. But it turns out that your whole way of thinking, your whole body has been geared toward the madness of ZOO TV. So we decided to put the madness on record." *Zooropa* is dense, varied and features Johnny Cash singing *The Wanderer*. *The Joshua Tree* it ain't.

The live album made a big comeback too, mostly thanks to MTV's *Unplugged* series, where artists are asked to perform live and acoustically for an invited audience. The show is broadcast on MTV, the lucky artist gets their own record company to release the end product and – in the case of Eric Clapton last year – get the biggest selling album of their career. 1993 saw Bruce Springsteen, Rod Stewart and Neil Young benefit most from *Unplugged* releases. For Springsteen it was a chance to prove to fans that, despite the relative failure of his simultaneously released studio albums of the previous year, he and his new band could kick ass. In truth Springsteen's *Plugged* is a neat live set and presents the best bits of both *Lucky Town* and *Human Touch*.

Rod Stewart released three albums in 1993, and not one of them contained a new Stewart composition. His *Unplugged – And Seated* had the ex-Mod on his stool throughout the set due to a footballing injury. He was ably assisted by Ron Wood and orchestra as he trawled through his back catalogue, drawing liberally from Faces days. The other two Stewart releases of the year were yet another *Best Of…*, and *Lead Vocalist* containing seven old Stewart numbers and five recently recorded versions of other people's songs. Apparently Stewart is thinking of re-recording *Sailing* as *Coasting*; "…we are coasting…".

Neil Young's *Unplugged* was possibly the best of the bunch in 1993. On it, Young runs through a set that takes in highlights of his 30-year career, from *Mr Soul* to *From Hank To Hendrix*, the latter taken from his *Harvest Moon* album released in November 1992.

Despite rumours that *Harvest Moon* was a 20-years late follow-up to *Harvest*, Young claimed, "This record has nothing to do with the past other than that you can always refer to it." A largely acoustic album with a mellow mood it is, Young says, "A more female record than any I've done."

Morrissey also put out a studio and live album in the space of 12 months. The studio set, *Your Arsenal*, was widely hailed – rightly- as the best solo effort he had released so far. Despite claims that songs such as *The National Front Disco* and *We'll Let You Know* are thinly veiled examples of Mozzer's inherent racism, his fans and Tony Parsons remained unconvinced. "Morrissey could invade Poland," wrote Parsons for Vox magazine in April 1993, "and I still wouldn't believe he is a Nazi." For his part, Morrissey exclaimed, "never explain, never complain." The live album was widely regarded – rightly – as a filler. *Beethoven Was Deaf* is a great title for a moderately successful attempt at capturing the high excitement of Morrissey in the flesh.

Your Arsenal was produced by Mick Ronson, once the driving force behind David Bowie's *Spiders From Mars*. During what proved to be the last year of his life, Ronson also contributed to David Bowie's long-awaited solo comeback album, *Black Tie, White Noise*. On *Black Tie*, Bowie recorded a version of Morrissey's *I Know It's Going To Happen Someday*. It was one of the few

▲ *Thirty years of Neil… forever Young*

◄ *Def or Deaf? Morrissey bowing to Bowie*

► *Lock up ya grandmothers – the Velvet Underground*

highpoints on a sorely disappointing album that had older critics cooing. Mainly because Bowie had ditched the dreadful sub-metal Tin Machine and made a record that sampled the best bits of Bowie from the 1970s.

The 1970s were very much in vogue for fashion designers during 1993. Many stars of that era made a return and spouted on about how awful it was. Aerosmith's Steven Tylar claimed that "surviving the 70s was a miracle." Listening to their smart-ass rawk and rawl *Get A Grip* you have to smile and be thankful that they did.

Leonard Cohen came back with the great, witty and droll *The Future*. Van Morrison released yet another fine if patchy collection of musical memories of his life, *Too Long In Exile*. Robert Plant, Billy Joel, Pete Townshend and even Mick Jagger released new albums and were declared the musical equivalent of protected buildings. Jagger's *Wandering Spirit* sounded a lot like the Rolling Stones circa 1973. A wise move but, "I didn't plan it to be like that," claimed Mick. Townshend's witty concept *Psychoderelict* album was funnier and more heartening than news that *Tommy – The Musical* was on its way to Britain after winning every Broadway award going. Billy Joel's *River Of Dreams* was a concept based on the singer working out his anger toward the manager and accountant who conspired to lose him a fortune —"I hate managers!" he screamed. "Screw 'em, screw 'em!"

Robert Plant wowed the crowds at Glastonbury and sounded a lot like, well, Robert Plant on his *Fate Of Nations*. In fact, 1993 was big on comebacks. After more than

25 years apart, The Velvet Underground toured. "Laughing" Lou Reed, John "Boyo" Cale, "Mad" Mo Tucker and Sterling "Who?" Morrison wowed Europe plenty in the summer of 93. Sade gave the world *Love Deluxe* and the world – except Britain – loved it. It sounded just like Sade. Terence Trent D'Arby dropped his trousers but not his arrogance and released *Symphony Or Damn*. Tom Waits put out the excellent, but far from easy-listening *Bone Machine*. Mike Scott, still trading as The Waterboys, released *Dream Harder* and it should have been titled *Try Harder*. The now solo Tears For Fears and OMD released new albums which sounded much like their old ones. The other half of Tears For Fears, Curt Smith produced a sprawling MOR album made in LA which sounded like it.

Prince put out another mixed album of mini-masterpieces and over-indulgent rubbish. Since it was titled the name of the symbol that appeared on the cover, and that is what the Purple One chooses to call himself now, it is his only eponymous release to date.

The Madchester scene might be dead and buried (where *are* the Stone Roses?) and Factory closed, but New Order continued on their less than merry way with *Republic* – although for how long is not too sure. New label bosses at London must be a little worried about tales of a split in the Order ranks, but at least they have the back catalogue to exploit.

Depeche Mode released *Songs Of Faith And Devotion* and proved that they are the best Brit synth-pop band who look like bikers around. Peter Gabriel released the shiny, unhappy *Us*

and provided the best live set seen (since Pink Floyd built their Wall) for his world tour. Donald Fagen released only his second solo album in 13 years, *Kamakiriad*. It sounded as if he went into the studio straight after the release of his last solo effort, *Night Fly*. "I did," he explained.

Sinead O'Connor released an album of show tunes, *Am I Not Your Girl*. Lush, beautifully arranged and touchingly sung, its impact was affected by her tearing up a picture of the Pope on live TV in America, claiming everyone was abused as children and paying an Irish paper to print her poem asking the world to leave her alone.

Two women who made their names and careers with bands, Maria McKee and Bjork, formerly of Lone Justice and The Sugarcubes respectively, produced odd, varied but highly entertaining solo albums. Maria's *You Gotta Sin To Be Saved* sounding a lot like Janis Joplin arguing with Van Morrison, Bjork's *Debut* sounding like Irving Berlin writing the history of Icelandic music.

Which only leaves Suede. The music press darlings of the year who could do no wrong and will save the business from itself. Armed with some coy sexual orientation — "I'm a bisexual who hasn't had a homosexual experience yet" (lead singer Brett Anderson) — and old David Bowie albums, Suede's debut album is well executed, stylized and familiar enough to sell well. Which it has. Whether Suede will have any lasting impact remains to be seen.

MAL PEACHEY

Heavy Rock

▲ It's been a good year for the Roses

> *"Despite the genre being constantly lambasted as rock'n'roll's half-witted, bastard son, it's the sheer excitement of its fans that has allowed it to endure."*

Ten years ago if you'd picked up a copy of metal mag Kerrang!, chances are you'd have known exactly what you were shelling out for. Iron Maiden, Judas Priest, Saxon, Motorhead, Motley Crue and more... a list that Rik Mayall could easily have got to grips with in the cult Comic Strip metal parody "Bad News". Pretty simple really. In the cold light of 1993, though, things have moved on a tad from your tried 'n' trusted crop of crotch-thrusting, leather-clad lotharios. Things have changed.

In fact, despite its reputation as an unashamedly conservative musical genre, heavy metal/hard rock/call-it-what-you-will has constantly evolved. Like dance music, it knows how to re-invent itself every couple of years. The last 12 months have probably provided the finest examples of this

chameleon-like quality, throwing up numerous subcultures. Now the whole caboodle has threatened to implode, weighed down by a horde of metal-styled train-spotters willing to argue the toss as to whether Florida nasties Deicide are still a pure death metal band, or whether they're Satanic enough to be a black metal outfit. To the outside world these rather chuckle-worthy categories are much of a muchness. It is, after all, all noise, but to devotees the world over they're a source of constant debate and passionate discussion.

Passion itself has been the key to the whole metal shebang since time immemorial, and little has changed on that score. Whether you happen to accost a 15-year-old Metallica fan, or a bearded thirtysomething Blue Oyster Cult apostle, the chances are you'll get the same level of rabid devotion from both parties. This is what's kept metal alive and screaming for something like 25 years. Despite the genre being constantly lambasted as rock'n'roll's half-witted, bastard son, it's the sheer excitement of its fans that has allowed it to endure.

Amazingly enough, though, looking back over 93 it's almost as if metal, in the broadest sense of the word, has become *hip*. Far from the tight-trousered tomfoolery of the 70s or the pretty boy pout of the 80s, the joy of loud, distorted guitars, pounding rhythms and wailing vocals has almost been embraced by what can only be tagged as the first wave of

right-on rivet-heads.

This is in no small way due to a number of wild cultural collisions. Not earth-shattering events, but the kind of head-on sound-crashes that have produced the plaid-wearing Seattle boom, and the re-emergence of the rap metal collaboration some seven years after Aerosmith walked this way and had their career resurrected by producer Rick Rubin and Run DMC. Consequently, Kerrang! '93 features the likes of grunge gurus Nirvana, Pearl Jam and Soundgarden rubbing be-cardiganed shoulders with socio-political rap ranters Rage Against The Machine or fierce funkateers Fishbone. Then, of course, there's the Holy Trinity of Guns N' Roses, Metallica and Bon Jovi among more the traditional hard rock heroes.

Essentially, with the all-pervading influence of hard rock, 93 has become something of an *Annus Metallus*, where the emphasis has shifted away from the cliched denim 'n' spandex factor. The clearest indication of this comes in the rather sprawling shape of the recently completed third Stateside Lollapalooza touring festival. Created three years ago by then-Jane's Addiction frontman Perry Farrell (now leading 93's Reading Festival headliners Porno For Pyros), Lollapalooza was designed as an umbrella for all kinds of aggressive music, blurring press-imposed boundaries and

◄ A shining example of 90s metal: Alice In Chains

also allowing forums for cultural debate on issues as diverse as abortion rights and the plight of the native American Indians.

This year's bill included Seattle's rising stars Alice In Chains, the aforementioned Rage Against The Machine, whacked out San Francisco funk punks Primus (kind of Tom Waits-mugs-Zappa in Bootsy Collins' backyard), Fishbone and the Metal thrash of Tool. Sidling up alongside this new breed of metal-conscious combos, mellow groovers Arrested Development, industrial dance kings Front 242, guitar hooligans Dinosaur Jr and all-girl wailers Babes In Toyland also helped blur the boundaries.

Alice In Chains, however, are a shining, twisted example of the current state of metal. Their influences draw unashamedly on old-style metal acts like Black Sabbath, Zeppelin and even Heart, but they've managed to assimilate the power of the 80s thrash metal explosion as pioneered by the likes of Slayer, Megadeth and Metallica, and the anti-star attitude of the US Hardcore scene. Tipped as the songwriters of the grunge generation alongside managerial stablemates Soundgarden, AIC are set to deal with the pressure drop of stadium excess.

The ascension of AIC to stadium-status has had a profound effect on some of metal's elder statesmen. Whereas some three years ago US hard rock harlequins Poison, Motley Crue and Kiss were able to rule the American arena roost, in 93 their power has waned. In a quest for added cred, Kiss's Gene Simmons has been seen hanging out at gigs by the likes of Babes In Toyland and Tool, and has been heard touting New York noise-sters Helmet as the future of rock 'n' roll. Very strange.

The malaise in old-styled mainstream metal has been compounded by a merry-go-round replacement of band members in some of the genre's biggest names. The tail end of 92 saw UK metal gods Judas Priest lose frontman Rob Halford in a bizarre exchange of faxes. Meanwhile, down LA way, Motley Crue lost frontman Vince Neil, Poison got earthy and replaced out-to-lunch guitarist CC DeVille, while hairspray and glam rags bit the dust. Back in Blighty, Iron Maiden announced that their most recent UK tour was to be their last with vocalist-cum-thespian Bruce Dickinson. In the turmoil, barely a week seemed to go by without a major act carelessly shedding a member or two.

On another footing, the last 12 months have seen the return of some serious hard rock legends. In a fit of affectation, Zep guitar dark lord Jimmy Page teamed up with ex-Deep Purple/Whitesnake/Robert Plant fancier David Coverdale to release the imaginatively titled *Coverdale/Page*. In reply, ex-Zep crooner

Plant resurfaced with his *Fate Of Nations* offering, which saw him steal the show effortlessly while managing to throw in a couple of rather nifty festival appearances alongside The Black Crowes, Lenny Kravitz and Def Leppard.

Elsewhere on the returning legend front, Ozzy Osbourne rounded off his farewell solo tour at the butt end of 92 with a series of expletives and the announcement that he would be reuniting the original 70s Black Sabbath line-up. Rather than chortle, the metal community looked on goggle-eyed as everyone from Irish proto-metallers Therapy? through to Soundgarden and Faith No More haggled for the support slot. At the eleventh hour, however, Ozzy shocked the metal world by cancelling his commitments due to 'personal reasons'.

While the nostalgia factor whirred into action, there was enough full-on metal action hitting the UK to infiltrate the mainstream and send the booking agents home happy. The Black Crowes loved-in at Glastonbury and headlined the Phoenix festival alongside Faith No More and Sonic Youth, while Def Leppard squashed in a 30,000 hometown Sheffield show at the Don Valley Stadium. Metallica, Bon Jovi and Guns N' Roses all lined up to play Milton Keynes Bowl in front of 60,000 people, with the latter doing a delirious two-night stint.

Meanwhile, Metallica wrapped up their two

year world tour and were estimated to have played to a mere 4.3 million people while selling a cool 12 million albums worldwide. The sheer size of these metal shows sounded the death knell for the yearly Castle Donington Monsters Of Rock festival and heralded new scenes of sheer power-soaked pandemonium.

The outdoor euphoria was matched by mainstream action from newfound traditionalists Ugly Kid Joe and UK hard rockers Little Angels, who took their fourth album *Jam* to the Number One slot followed by The Almighty, whose *Powertrippin* opus dented the Top Five. In earnest, it proved that even in an age when metal was seen to be fragmenting, the genre's ability to keep its commercial face remained intact.

And so to 94. A year which is bound to boast more crunching chaos and excess. Will the full-on 70s revival threatened by 92-93 emerge? Will 'Seattle' become a term of abuse? Will Axl lay claims to his sanity? Whatever the questions, the simple fact remains that while certain genres will scrabble to fill out their year with fake excitement, the metal contingent will be there in loud voice. Defiantly unfashionable.

PHIL ALEXANDER

▶ *Little Angels: delighting the record-buying public*

Black America's greatest gift to world culture, blues and jazz music, was spawned in the cottonfields and plantations of the Deep South – the cradle of the blues being a tiny triangle of Mississippi, known as the Delta, which contains no town of more than 10,000 people.

Yet in 1993 this still essentially ethnic music achieved mega-status here in Britain, thanks as much to its adoption by the TV advertising world as to wider recognition by rock critics and fans alike, with a whole new audience of switched-on groovers taking it to their hearts.

John Lee Hooker's hauntingly potent style is being used to promote blue jeans, the rich voice and strident guitar of Lonnie Brooks – once known as Guitar Junior – tries to convince us that there really is something special about Heineken and the voice of the late, great Muddy Waters lives again as the boomingly assertive tones of *I'm A Man* rattle TV speakers across the land.

The good news for the blues is that it has become a worldwide phenomenon – we even had a UK visit by Japan's top interpreter of the form, who revealed that clubs all over his country provide ready work for visiting American greats like Buddy Guy, Junior Wells and Otis Rush.

Across Europe, sales have held up strongly while other music forms have suffered a decline, and in its native America specialist blues labels like Alligator, Black Top and Delmark have been shipping out CDs, tapes and vinyl too in quantities they would not have dreamed of three or four years ago.

Blues clubs now abound Stateside and, rather than being hidden away in the inner city ghetto, are now midtown, middle-class and multi-racial, with a new generation of young blacks rediscovering the music which their grandparents cherished but which their parents turned their backs on during the assertive "I'm black and I'm proud" soul years of the 60s.

But it is the big open air festivals which have really been putting the message across and providing constant well-paid work for such

1993 the year in…

Blues & Jazz

Have I got blues for you: Buddy Guy's (left) gone big in Japan, John Lee Hooker's (above) the new jean genie and Gary Moore's (right) gone back to his roots

veterans as Albert Collins, Jimmy McCracklin, Koko Taylor and Little Milton, enthusiastically touted newer talents like Robert Cray, Sherman Robertson, Larry McCray and Jay Owens and such respected white exponents of the message as John Hammond, Walter Trout and Steve Roux.

Bobby "Blue" Bland and other soul crossover artists whose work has always displayed a touch of the blues have moved more assertively towards the style – notable among them being Johnny Taylor and his near namesake Little Johnnie Taylor, Latimore, Etta James and Otis Clay.

And, not before time, the mass blues audience of white art students and college graduates has largely turned its back on the once fashionable but sterile purism which in former times led them to boo many of the more inventive and progressive rhythm and blues artists. Now they're giving belated wide recognition to such highly creative veterans as Lowell Fulsom, Jimmy McCracklin and Little Milton, all of whom they previously dismissed offhand as being too commercial in orientation – thus missing out on some of the most exciting music to be heard.

Even in the blues' boom days of the 60s, when a listing in the New Orleans, Clarkesdale or Memphis phone book was all a blues singer needed to guarantee a UK album release, aficionados of the music never had it so good as they do today.

Specialist re-release labels like Ace, Charly and Demon assure a relentless flow of material from across the entire spectrum of the music, while Virgin's Pointblank label and the Indigo setup headed by the redoubtable Nike Vernon – who, in an earlier period, ran Blue Horizon and first put Fleetwood Mac and Chicken Shack onto record – ensure a reliable outlet for new recordings.

The market for home-grown blues is vibrant too. John Mayall, the granddaddy of 'em all, visited from his self-imposed Californian exile in the Spring, and British-based American exile Otis Grand has been pleasing his homeland audiences as well as those in his adopted country. Meanwhile, Gary Moore has become a guitar hero of Clapton proportions without turning his back on the blues music his appeal has always been rooted in.

Lower down the pecking order, there is a host of British blues bands following in the footsteps of the 60s acts like the Stones and the Animals, who used the blues as the stepping stone to bigger things and, these days, there is even the chance for some of them to make it really big in rock audience terms without in any way having to water down their music.

And, above all, BB King, as befits his name, remains the grand master of it all, striding like a colossus across the world music scene and commanding concert audiences of a size to make rock stars weep. The MCA Records veteran is just one of a number of people trying to ensure continued well-being of the blues by backing seminars, recording tutorials and generally preaching the creed.

Of course, there have been downers too. The loss last Christmas of the great Albert King and the more recent death of talented white American blues exponent John Campbell – ironically just as he was coming good after years of dues playing – have left a hole to be filled.

Jazz, too, has seen a steady toll of people who have been with us so long they almost seemed immortal. With the deaths in recent times of both Miles Davis and Dizzy Gillespie we have come to realise that so-called modern jazz is no longer so modern. It certainly isn't in its dotage, however, as formidable new talents like Britain's sax genius Courtney Pine have emerged to take the music on to new levels of creativity.

Moreover, the wholesale adoption of jazz funk and master cuts by discotheque audiences has assured the music of a whole new audience, many of whose members will surely be encouraged to explore further into the music, moving on from Roy Ayers and the jazz organist's more esoteric talents to ensure its continued commercial wellbeing at a time when its creative energies – encouraged in the UK by such live music outlets as Ronnie Scott's clubs in Birmingham and London and the Jazz Café, also in London – are at a new, exciting high.

ROGER ST PIERRE

Country

> *"The current Nashville theory is that rock music has lost its way and that Americans, battered by recession and crime, are turning to the mournful ballads of the music that Hank Williams once described as 'God's own lullabies'."*

In view of its current rude health it is hard to believe that, little more than a decade ago, country music was being written off by Uncle Tom Cobley and all as a lost cause. By the beginning of the 80s, the genre might not have been quite ready to hand in its dinner pail but, clearly, it had seen better days. After a decade of MOR-oriented Nash Trash, it was in dire need of renovation. Perhaps its credibility reached an all-time low with the release of *Urban Cowboy*, an atrocious bars'n'broncos movie starring the ever-hapless John Travolta.

Then, in the mid-80s, came the rise of New Country, a back-to-basics movement that included such promising talents as Dwight Yoakam, Steve Earle, Lyle Lovett, Randy Travis, Rosanne Cash and Nanci Griffith. Suddenly, it seemed that country music was about to break free of the preconceived mould of straw bales, blue jeans, chewing tobacco, Confederate flags and stout truck-drivers with CB radio.

In the last 12 months, the most ominous development in the country field has surely been the soaraway success of Billy Ray Cyrus's cornball *Achy Breaky Heart*. But there is little evidence to suggest that the insipid Cyrus Virus is about to precipitate a wholesale return to the gaudy excesses of the 70s. While the last 12 months have been a few furlongs short of a resoundingly classic year for country, there has been much to applaud for devotees and casual observers alike.

The current Nashville theory is that rock music has lost its way and that Americans, battered by recession and crime, are turning for emotional nutrition to the mournful ballads and plangent guitar sounds of the music that Hank Williams once described as "God's own lullabies". Certainly, in the States, country has never been hipper and its current resurgence is best symbolised by the phenomenal popularity of Garth Brooks, who has succeeded in doing for Nashville what Steven Spielberg consistently manages to do for Hollywood. Having launched himself into the superstar league with his 1992 album, *Ropin' The Wind*, this podgy, stetsoned thirty-something goes on outselling the likes of Guns N' Roses and Michael Jackson at home. While his radio-friendly mainstream style continues to be eyed suspiciously by the diehard purists, it has to be acknowledged that Brooks' commercial breakthrough has had a vital catalytic effect on country as a whole. Not least, the days are past when country music would be treated with a disdainful snort by the music press. These days, it is accorded the kind of respect reserved for jazz or blues.

Even so, Brooks' recent *The Chase* album failed to make the expected big killing in Britain, while his Christmas album, *Beyond The Season*, was given a resounding thumbs-down. Twenty years after Mike Harding sang, 'It's hard being a cowboy in Rochdale', country music remains something of a cult in this country, the convivial British world of country resembling some benign iceberg under the surface of transatlantic cultural currents.

Perhaps the most promising new name to emerge in the last 12 months has been Iris DeMent, a 32-year-old American whose 11-track debut album, *Infamous Angel*, has delighted critics and public alike on both sides of the Atlantic. Binding the melodic strains of country, folk and bluegrass to a twangy front-porch vibrato, DeMent has won herself comparisons with the likes of Loretta Lynn, Kitty Wells and the mighty June Carter Cash. Country music doesn't come much purer than this: raw and emotionally direct, steeped in a nostalgia for happier days and simpler times, it might have been made 40 or 50 years ago. Her down home, pretension-free style offers a timely antidote to the ostentatious posturing of Billy Ray Cyrus.

As DeMent recently remarked: "I would take it as a compliment if my music was regarded as old-fashioned. I guess I'm nostalgic by nature. I've always had a great curiosity about the 30s and 40s, when people would walk into houses and have conversations because there was nothing like television to distract them. That's what my music is trying to do: start a conversation. That might be an old-fashioned way of looking at things. But it tells me that my music crosses boundaries. It doesn't fit any particular time zone and that's fine by me."

DeMent is not the only newish country name

◀ *Joe Ely returned from the underground*

▶ *Iris Dement cemented her fan base*

o kick up a shindy in the last year. Among those poised for major breakthroughs are Travis Tritt, Alan Jackson and Clint Black. Arguably leading the pack is Reba McEntire, whose recent *It's Your Call* album chronicled the ups and downs of modern women through an appealing set of pop-flavoured country songs that included an indecently pretty duet with the equally promising Vince Gill. Likewise, Joy White's recent *Between Midnight And Hindsight* offered an impressive selection of pathos-soaked ballads and winsome honky-tonkery, topped off by a voice of eggshell fragility. Meanwhile, Jason dropped his last name along with his celebrated Scorchers and emerged with a knock-'em-dead ten-track solo album, *One Foot In The Honky Tonk*, that veered between the devilishly brash and the profoundly melancholic.

There were a whole host of not-so-new names who, in the last year, have made a sharp return to form. New Jersey's Mary Chapin Carpenter followed up her acclaimed debut, *Hometown Girl*, with the gorgeously introspective *Come On Come On*. The hugely influential Guy Clark re-emerged with the highly acclaimed *Boats To Build*, his most consistent collection of songs since the groundbreaking *Old No 1*. Dwight Yoakam had much to prove after a string of lacklustre releases and, while his recent *This Time* was too lushly sentimental to rank as a major comeback, it went some way to restoring him to his position among country's songwriting elite. After a lengthy hibernation, Joe Ely returned to the fold with *Love And Danger*, an album that provided a rough and ready blend of country, blues and rock. Lucinda Williams' *Sweet Old World* effortlessly fulfilled the promise of her acclaimed 1990 debut, while George Strait's excellent *Pure Country* finally delivered on the expectations of earlier albums like *Strait Country* and *Ocean Front Property*.

At the same time, there were a host of classic country names who were never far from the headlines. Most notably, the great Johnny Cash performed at Butlins on the same bill as the less than great Roy Hudd before hooking up with U2 for a track on their mega-selling *Zooropa* album. More recently, Cash has signed on the dotted line with Rick Rubin's Def American label and his forthcoming album, as yet untitled, is rumoured to be his most compelling for donkeys' years.

Following her triumphant chart-topping success with The KLF, Tammy Wynette delivered an exhaustive triple-pack CD set, *Tears Of Fire*, that offered ample reasons why she is still regarded as The First Lady Of Country. Willie Nelson emerged from his much-publicized tussles with the US tax authority to deliver *Across The Borderline*, a stunning return to form that included collaborations with Bob Dylan, Sinead

O'Connor and Paul Simon. Even the much-maligned Dolly Parton could be found on the brink of a miraculous recovery. Having penned the globally successful *I Will Always Love You* for Whitney Houston, she then weighed in with the star-studded album *Slow Dancing With The Moon* that included input from Chet Atkins and Emmylou Harris.

There was also plenty of activity on the country fringes too. While kd lang and Rosanne Cash have been veering further from their country roots with every release, most of the recent activity has been in the opposite direction with Robert Forster's *Calling From A Country Home*, Joan Baez's *Play Me Backwards* and Chuck Prophet's *Balinese Dancer* all absorbing the country flavour in their different ways. The last named, from the former Green On Red guitarist, offered a blistering set of country rock that established Prophet as one of the names to watch in the forthcoming year.

While all these convoluted plots were unfolding, one of New Country's original torchbearers, Lyle Lovett, was grabbing the tabloid headlines by making an honest woman out of Julia "Pretty Woman" Roberts. The announcement of this unlikely marriage might have left a million or so hopeful bachelors with their hearts in their boots, but at least there was the consolation of a plethora of good new country music to drown their sorrows to.

JON WILDE

Indie

> *At the end of the year, indiedom – for all its faults, all its failures – could flick through the singles pile and smile benignly.*

▲ *Pavement: they never walked alone*

July 1993 was a special month. Particularly for anyone with a receding hairline and a penchant for the more obscure things in life. It was then that Lady Fate, in her infinitely quirky wisdom, decided that two seminal independent labels of the late 70s should suddenly start breathing once again. Rough Trade records, after a series of financial catastrophes and alarming political decisions (cf massive staff lay-offs) was reactivated with Disco Inferno and Butterfly Child, two of the more esoteric bands doing the rounds. And the Postcard label – home of plaid long before Sub Pop – reappeared with Vic Godard and Orange Juice reissues. The Sound Of Young Scotland? Not really… .

Yet, seeing as how a substantial amount of record buyers from that post-punk period had eventually become cogs within the music industry machine, it was hard not to shed a nostalgic tear for an era when The Jam could get to Number One, flares hadn't yet been re-invented, people could wear long grey overcoats in the middle of summer without fear of a public beating and Sonic The Hedgehog was merely a greasy glimmer in the silicon chippy of life. Oh, and anything in a seven-inch sleeve could shift 10,000 units within milliseconds. Obviously.

Fundamentally, this was a return to old-fashioned values – however mythical – at a time when Manchester was stagnant, "Shoegazers" couldn't get arrested, not even for the most blatant of parking offences, and Techno (both musical and visual) was on the commercial rampage. Like, 15 years on the independent sector was struggling, and suddenly (KAPOW! WHAM! BLAM!) the superlabels were back! Saved at the bell! Possibly…

More intriguingly, the rebirth of cool types like Rough Trade and Postcard was a reminder of just how diluted the independent ethos had

become. A decade and a half on from the original scowling anti-establishment idealism, the 90s found label entrepreneurs, sly corporate tacticians and ambitious bands alike all gently massaging the rulebook for their own gains. What was once an 'Us And Them' situation was now 'Us And Them With A Few Thousand Floaters In The Middle Ground Grabbing The Best Of Both Worlds'.

Mandies – major-backed indie labels, literary fans – were on the agenda again after a faintly disastrous honeymoon period in the mid-80s when the likes of Blue Guitar and Elevation were set up to entice circa 86-era groups out of the ghetto. Now Hut (subsidized by Virgin), Dedicated (RCA/BMG), Parallel (London) and Free (Go! Discs) were attempting to correct previous mistakes, with varying degrees of success. The basic problem, however, is that indie bands are so defined because they rarely shift ocean tankers-full of units, and so rarely warrant enormous investment in the early stages of their careers. Bar the (very) occasional Suede-style success, money was thus being pumped into press-favoured groups and bank managers were going bonkers. Hey, can you name the 'alternative' band who'd spent so much money that by the time their debut LP was released it had to sell 240,000 copies simply to break even? No? Good.

Think small. Think smelly. Think Wiiija, Clawfist and Too Pure, a triumvirate of London-based labels with frayed shoestring budgets, an innate sense of what made music good and *exciting*, not to mention a unique feeling of backs-against-the-wall camaraderie. Clawfist had Gallon Drunk, Breed and Mambo Taxi. Too Pure discovered PJ Harvey and worked with Moonshake, Stereolab and

Th' Faith Healers. And Wiiija, having started somewhat grumpily with the likes of Bastard Kestrel and Thule, suddenly struck a golden pose with Jacob's Mouse and, more pertinently, Huggy Bear and Cornershop. Money was meticulously spent. The bands were carefully chosen. The original spirit (seven-inch singles! Wraparound sleeves!) fizzed. Wa-hay!

Huggy Bear and Cornershop were particularly significant arrivals, given that by the close of 1992 astute observers were keenly anticipating a timely resurgence in politically-fired music. Huggy Bear were influenced by American Riot Grrrls such as Bikini Kill, punk-splattered feminists who encouraged fellow (sic) women to clamber on stage and make a bloody racket. The Bears themselves managed this so successfully in the space of half a year they had amassed a bewildering array of achievements and controversies, including several Single Of The Week awards, abusing male photographers and – most notably – terrorizing tacky TV show "The Word". They also influenced legions of teenage girls and became embroiled in an insane struggle against any form of compromise. Women only gigs? This way please, Linus, Skin Teens, Bratmobile, Pussycat Trash, Sister George *et al.*

Cornershop were less militant, simply by virtue of being more media-friendly. Similarly ragged and raucous in the musical stakes, their grounding was an anti-Morrissey campaign inspired by the Singh "brothers' " first hand experience of racist abuse. By the time of their second single, the incendiary *Lock Stock And Double-Barrel* EP, they could almost play a thrilling live show.

It all fitted. Elsewhere, anger was an equally valid form of energy: the so-called crusty scene had been festering away from the media eye for a couple of years at free festivals and drop-out venues. So much so that by the time aggrieved ska popsters Back To The Planet signed to Parallel Records at the turn of the year they were pulling 1000 punters in London. BTTP blamed Teenage Mutant Ninja Turtles for the world's problems, which was rather disappointing, but behind them the likes of Senser (vicious rap/rockers), Blaggers ITA (even more vicious punk/ska activists) and Fun-da-Mental (slightly less vicious Asian hip-hoppers) were making right-on rackets and encouraging lesser sorts to go genre-mutating crazy. And when Credit To The Nation took the riff from *Smells Like Teen Spirit* and gave it a rap-stylee kicking in the form of *Call It What You Want*, it was an indictment of everything innovative and invigorating 1993 had thrown up.

All of which tended to conveniently disguise the fact that there wasn't much else going on, actually. And what was occurring elsewhere in the Indie Village was so absurdly disjointed as to make any logical analysis virtually impossible. Struggling against plummeting record sales (and therefore expectations), increasingly "generous" major labels, less tolerant retailers who favoured CD-only displays and Super Bloody Mario, it's hardly surprising that 92/93 will fail to go down in the annals of history as *anni miribiles*. Yeah, Teenage Fanclub finally broke into the Top 40, Belly's *Star* LP cracked the Top Five and Suede's stunning rise from toilet circuit losers to chart-topping pop poseurs *extraordinaire* was a delight to behold.

Yet for every Suede there were another hundred Revolvers, a thousand Fretblankets and a million Shrimptrators. New labels (Lemon? Nude? Parallel? Deceptive? Domino? Placebo? Guernica? Gift? Scared

Hitless???) seemingly appeared every week. Various big indie moneyspinners such as My Bloody Valentine, The Cocteau Twins, Therapy?, New Order and PJ Harvey were all enticed away into Majorland, while The Pixies split up. And – the rotten icing on the crumbling cake – Factory Records went bust. A bitter blow, as the label was actually negotiating a buy-out with London Records when it went under (Creation had already accepted a similar multi-zero offer from Sony), Factory's demise was exacerbated by posthumous bickering: the label blamed New Order for failing to finish their *Republic* album on schedule; New Order blamed Factory for sending the increasingly (and, as it transpired, terminally) unstable Happy Mondays to record in the Bahamas. Everyone else blamed The Adventure Babies, and Ian Curtis failed to return from the grave to save the day.

Fittingly, Manchester's once-vibrant guitar scene was quieter than a dead mouse, with only the awkwardly intense Molly Halfhead bothering to suggest there was anything indigenous left to challenge the Inspiral Carpets' abnormally consistent plundering of the garage scene. The Midlands was equally recalcitrant, with a scattering of longhaired guitar-grippers haplessly incapable of undermining the dominance of the Poppies/ Ned's/Stuffies axis. And so, in the absence of any post-modern punk revolutions in Norwich or Walthamstow, Americans once again had a clear path into the Pop Kids' wallets.

In the wake of Nirvana, the US corporate vehicle had decided that basic metal masquerading as grunge was the way ahead. Luckily, Smashing Pumpkins, Sebadoh and Pavement slipped through the major net in the UK, inspiring a laconic chase to discover the weirdest, wiggiest rockers in the Mid-West. Mercury Rev may have mastered the 'art' of fannying around, but they hadn't cornered the farty market if Archers Of Loaf, Radial Spangle, The Grifters, Trumans Water, Royal Trux and Thinking Fellers Union Local 282 were anything to go by on the wibble wibble front. On a more orthodox (ie take fewer drugs) level, Lotion, St Johnny, 81 Mulberry, Redhouse Painters and Further (armed with their excellent *Grip Tape* LP) were all

responsible for splendidly low-key releases (the pick of several thousand bands), proving that you don't *have* to be mad to work here but blahblahblah. And the acerbic, grinding Rocket From The Crypt still refused to tour Europe, in spite of some seriously delirious press interest. Buggers.

Madder Rose and Liz Phair revealed the softer underbelly of the US rock pig. And well-timed it was, too, as a new generation lurking in the American underground decided that the British "shambling" scene was the most influential musical statement of the past 30 years and Unrest, The Lotus Eaters and The Swirlies all did a fine job of pretending to have been born in Blighty.

Some things, natch, never changed: Depeche Mode stormed the world and made some magnificently expensive videos; The Shamen got to Number One and everyone who liked them in 89 decided they were rubbish; ice fairy pumpkin Bjork returned to charm the 501s off everyone who hated Einar Sugarcube; indie radio station XFM continued its fight for a permanent Londonwide licence with its Great Xpectations show at Finsbury Park (complete with The Cure, Sugar, Belly, Carter USM and 25,000 t-shirt wearers); The Stone Roses went on holiday; and Primal Scream took some drugs. Allegedly.

But at the end of the year, indiedom – for all its faults, all its failures – could flick through the singles pile and smile benignly. Compulsion's ribald *Casserole* EP, Animals That Swim's sneeringly seductive *Roy*, The Tindersticks' mesmerising *Marbles*, Huggy Bear's venomous *Her Jazz*, Gigolo Aunts' poptastic *Cope*, Collapsed Lung's rampantly rapped *Thundersley Invacar*, Wat Tyler's *Sexless*, a merciless parody of Madonna's *Sex* tome replete with wobbly arses hanging over garden walls… all of the above were reasons to be cheerful, and fine excuses to hang out down the Bull & Gate one more time. Just in case…

Yup, small-scale successes the lot of them, but hey, isn't that how Rough Trade and Postcard started all those years ago?

Don't bury it yet.

▼ *Huggy Bear: fighting sexism with sexism*

SIMON WILLIAMS

Dance

> *At one end, techno is the new indie music, bedroom music made by obsessives for other obsessives to pore over in their bedrooms. At the other, it's the new punk. Simple, hard driven beats getting thousands stomping like nutters at raves.*

Dance music has had a crazy year. Rave music has effectively disappeared, condemned to survive only as a pop aberration known as 2 Unlimited. House music has boomed as a distinctly British phenomenon, throwing up success stories like Sunscreem, M-People and The Shamen. And techno has miraculously re-invented itself as the bedroom music of the 90s, faceless machine music as a soundtrack for modern living. Ragga and swingbeat have crossed right over into pop culture, while dancing in a field has been effectively banished out of all legality. It's been an erratic year.

Not least for the Stereo MCs, who only 12 months ago, after two criminally-ignored albums, were seriously considering giving up. But somehow it has all come together, as the early punk-ish energy of tracks like *On 33* and the pop bliss of *Elevate My Mind* suddenly coalesced into their charged-up *Connected* album. With rapper Rob risking street cred to actually sing, the band's warmth became only too obvious as they gigged their way round Britain. Rob, looking like some maniac Van Gogh heroin addict, was soon whipping every crowd up into serious states of fevered dancing. The Stereos always were this good, but in some kind of strange universal telepathy, everyone suddenly just switched on and got it at the same time.

Sunscreem's breakthrough also came after plenty of trying. Always insisting on playing live, they had seen a year pass by as other artists simply mimed their way through three gigs a night, while they struggled to get their equipment right for just one night. Lucia, the dreadlocked, whirling dervish singer, and her five piece outfit kept at it though. *Love You More* broke them and then the hits flooded through as people remembered seeing this house band actually doing it for real. With a darker, fuller sound and lyrics that weren't afraid to discuss rape and ugliness, their music was house taken further yet. A far broodier beast than the disco-inspired original that DJ Frankie Knuckles first started spinning 15 years ago in Chicago's Warehouse club.

Mike Pickering made his name bringing house to the loved-up northern masses as resident DJ sensation in Manchester's Hacienda club. Master of smooth, flowing, hands-in-the-air excitement as a DJ, his M-People project has

▲ **The Prodigy: style and bounce**

been his vehicle for even wider success. Hooking up with belting Garage vocalist Heather Small, Pickering's M-People has hit with glorious, positive anthems that just stir it right up. At a time when the American Garage sound has lumbered into deeply repetitive, hi-hat dullness, M-People have switched the tables, belting out cracking songs with the chunkiest, glossiest house productions, beating the New York sound at its own game.

But this is all happening at the mass end of things. Dance music is still in a state of fevered evolution, throwing up brief, maniac trends. *Jungle* combined ridiculously fast breakbeats, ragga and rude boy jumping around and ended up sounding like The Specials fighting James Brown at 78 rpm. Rotterdam's *Gabber* briefly destroyed all-comers in northern techno quarters. Incredibly fast and dangerous, it burned bright enough to make your eyes hurt but it never sounded any better than machine gun fire on speed. And during spring, there was even a loopy fashion for helicopter noises.

'Progressive House', however, was the biggest disappointment of the year. Riding in on imaginative records like the chunky, hunky, hypnotic house of tracks like Gat Decor's *Passion* and DOP's *Groovy Beat*, it all ended with far too many producers rushing out formulaic house records with a heavy dub influence.

Likewise, the original energy of hardcore rave burned out as everyone struggled to do something new with breakbeats, banging piano

and screeching female vocals all at roughly 900 miles an hour. Only The Prodigy managed to keep it going with any style, ripping into it with a bounce and a musical sophistication that their rivals could only gawp at. But even Liam Howlett and his band of Essex ravers had bored of the genre's schoolkid following by the end of the year, switching to harder, less frantic, techno flavourings.

Despite the lingering death of rave's original bright-eyed blissed-out hopes, 1993 was nonetheless a breakthrough year. For this was the year of techno. Hard and determinedly electronic, techno began to prove itself as the music of the future. It was still too early for serious chart action, but for the first time techno started getting taken seriously by DJs, clubs and record buyers. The Aphex Twin, Future Sound Of London, Dance 2 Trance and Sven Vath started selling albums in reasonably significant numbers and the music couldn't stop going forward. That it actually sounded like the future, like some kind of Blade Runner version of music of the future, hasn't hurt it any either.

For a music as far from the black soul of house's disco roots as Slayer is from Whitney Houston, techno's struggle has always been in packing some emotion. Early innovators like Detroit's Derrick May and Juan Atkins might have been able to get away with elegant swirls of rhythm, but most bedroom chancers have got stuck in leaden, go-nowhere droning. It's the obsessives who've changed it, having worked out, largely through endlessly messing around with their machinery, how to wring out those special addictive noises that make any great record so fine. Future Sound Of London did it with *Papua New Guinea*, Jaydee did it with *Plastic Dreams*, Moby with *I Feel It* and CJ Bolland certainly did it with *Camargue*.

Not that these records were big sellers, but anyone hearing techno like this for the first time was immediately smitten. Warp found their series of 'Artificial Intelligence' albums from techno adventurers like Black Dog, B12 and Aphex Twin as Polygon Window steadily outselling each other. Less purist techno compilations have disappeared in increasingly large numbers as well. It's not a lot yet, but when you hear a track like Speedy J's *De-Orbit* or Hardfloor's driven *Hardtrance Acperience*, you can immediately hear that this is a completely new music; machine music so obviously devoid of the human warmth of, say, Stereo MCs, and yet beguiling nonetheless.

At one end, techno is the new indie music, bedroom music made by obsessives for other obsessives to pore over in their bedrooms. At the other, it's the new punk. Simple, hard driven beats getting thousands stomping like nutters at raves across northern Europe, dark clubs in London and one massive 2000 capacity club up north in Morley called The Orbit.

Techno certainly isn't, however, some neat new explosion. Already it's spinning off in new directions; feeding off world music in the Frankfurt trance music of Sven Vath and Dance 2 Trance; connecting across house's synapses in the work of instrumental sine surfers like Orbital and 808 State and packing rave's original charging energy with artists like Moby and The Prodigy at the controls.

Techno has also had a major influence on the crusty dance scene. In the small gap between anarcho disorganization and student parties, a club scene is growing up where the unwashed, pissed off and intellectually adventurous meet for wild nights of dub and techno-influenced sounds. London's MegaDog nights have led the way, and Britain's techno equivalent of

Lollopalooza, the Midi-Rain Tour, had Orbital, The Drum Club and Aphex Twin taking the vibe around the country to clubs nationwide swamped with people, ready to shake it all out.

Dance music is now old enough to be merely part of the fabric of life to anyone under 21, it's not as new as it once was. Its edges are consequently blurring all the time. One of the best dance albums this year came from former indie superstar and Sugarcubes singer, Bjork, as she hooked up with former Soul II Soul producer, Nellee Hooper for her *Debut* LP. Weird and oddball in a poppy kind of way, it wasn't pure dance, but it wasn't really anything else either.

And this is where it gets interesting. With rising bands like One Dove, Espiritu and Eskimos & Egypt mixing up rock, world music, rave and house for dancefloor action, Britain is keeping its head well up in the international dance music fraternity. And after the success of the Stereos, M-People and Sunscreem, all of these bands have the edge to breakthrough anytime soon. Perhaps.

DAVID DAVIES

▶ The Aphex Twin survived dance's identity crises

▼ Sunscreem say it in broken English

95

Soul

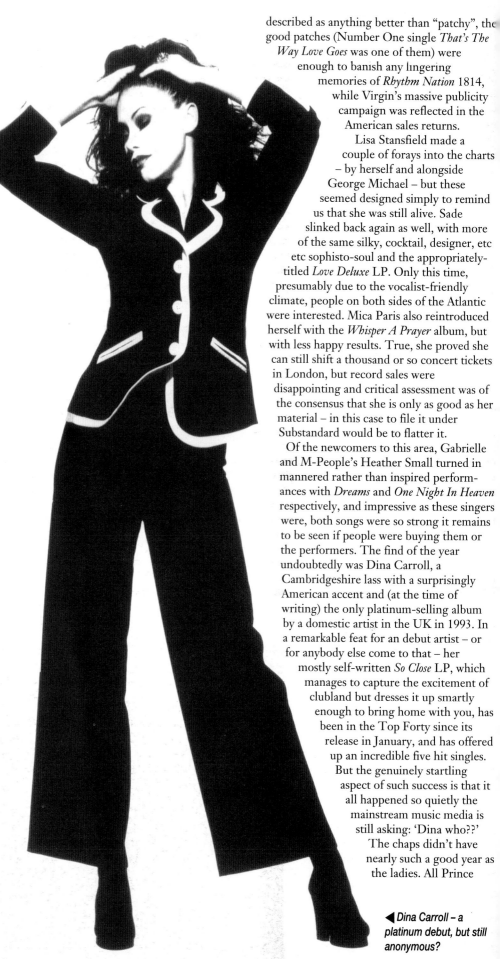

> *"Suddenly it wasn't about what you did with your samplers, computers or sequencers... what counted was how well whoever you had out front could sing."*

If the last 12 months are going to be remembered for anything, it'll be for the re-establishment of the human voice as a major force in popular music. So enormous was this revival of vocalism, it was almost as if the previous decade's advancements in studio technique hadn't happened. Across the stylistic board, artists, record companies and record buyers had rediscovered the irresistible appeal of the sound of singing. Suddenly it wasn't about what you did with your samplers, computers or sequencers, or the virtuoso level of your instrumentalists. What counted was how well whoever you had out front could sing. Understandably, nowhere was this more pronounced than in the voice-sensitive world of soul music.

Naturally, the established divas were prominent in this upsurge, and it was one of the best years ever for the crossover, glamorously upmarket pop singer. Whitney Houston's career curve suffered no ill effects whatsoever from marriage, motherhood and *The Bodyguard* (a blockbuster film that appeared to be testing co-star Kevin Costner's credibility and his audience's patience far more than La Houston's acting prowess) and she continued to prove that an absolute lack of communicated emotion was no barrier to success as long as your technique was flawless. As well as having a hit with Chaka Khan's stomping classic *I'm Every Woman* she had the Christmas Number One (and the year's only million-selling single) with *I Will Always Love You*, the film's interminable theme song .

Janet Jackson had a good year too, the fashionably lower-cased and bafflingly full stopped *janet.* being the first fruit borne of her multi-million dollar deal with Virgin Records. Once again she teamed up with Jam & Lewis. While the album cannot truthfully be

described as anything better than "patchy", the good patches (Number One single *That's The Way Love Goes* was one of them) were enough to banish any lingering memories of *Rhythm Nation* 1814, while Virgin's massive publicity campaign was reflected in the American sales returns.

Lisa Stansfield made a couple of forays into the charts – by herself and alongside George Michael – but these seemed designed simply to remind us that she was still alive. Sade slinked back again as well, with more of the same silky, cocktail, designer, etc etc sophisto-soul and the appropriately-titled *Love Deluxe* LP. Only this time, presumably due to the vocalist-friendly climate, people on both sides of the Atlantic were interested. Mica Paris also reintroduced herself with the *Whisper A Prayer* album, but with less happy results. True, she proved she can still shift a thousand or so concert tickets in London, but record sales were disappointing and critical assessment was of the consensus that she is only as good as her material – in this case to file it under Substandard would be to flatter it.

Of the newcomers to this area, Gabrielle and M-People's Heather Small turned in mannered rather than inspired perform-ances with *Dreams* and *One Night In Heaven* respectively, and impressive as these singers were, both songs were so strong it remains to be seen if people were buying them or the performers. The find of the year undoubtedly was Dina Carroll, a Cambridgeshire lass with a surprisingly American accent and (at the time of writing) the only platinum-selling album by a domestic artist in the UK in 1993. In a remarkable feat for an debut artist – or for anybody else come to that – her mostly self-written *So Close* LP, which manages to capture the excitement of clubland but dresses it up smartly enough to bring home with you, has been in the Top Forty since its release in January, and has offered up an incredible five hit singles. But the genuinely startling aspect of such success is that it all happened so quietly the mainstream music media is still asking: 'Dina who??' The chaps didn't have nearly such a good year as the ladies. All Prince

◀ Dina Carroll – a platinum debut, but still anonymous?

▲ janet.– lights camera – Jackson!

▼ Nu Colours: green shoots sighted in London

added to his repertoire was further proof that he's a bit bonkers. It was announced he'd changed his name to a, quite literally, unspeakable symbol – that of the combined male and female gender signs, as featured on his last album – and either he or his management figured it would be a good idea to price London concert tickets at £45 in the depths of a recession. Curiously, a couple of weeks before the event, there were still plenty of seats left.

Terence Trent D'Arby chose this year for his comeback, only to find it was far less eagerly anticipated than it might have been. Admittedly, *Symphony Or Damn* was enormously better than the unlistenable *Neither Fish Nor Big Selling Album*, but it would have had to go far to have been worse. It was entirely serviceable in itself, the real problem was that most people really didn't give a damn about Terence any more – in spite of his 'outrageously' stripping off in a best-selling music magazine. Sydney Youngblood came back to rather less than universal acclaim too – in fact it wouldn't be an exaggeration to say few people outside his immediate family noticed.

It was really left to those hardily perennial lurrve men Luther Vandross and Alexander O'Neal to, er, keep their end of things up. Their albums, *Never Let Me Go* and *Love Makes No Sense*, were respectable if hardly earth-shattering offerings. Interestingly , and still on the oldies 'trip', Al Green is about to release his first LP for yonks on which he sings about loving babes rather than Jesus. It's produced by Cox and Steele of The Fine Young

Cannibals and it'll be good to see what they can do with somebody who can really sing, as opposed to Roland Gift.

Maybe it was just the guys by themselves that weren't having too much luck: once they got plural it was a different matter. During the last 12 months, the US pop charts have been dominated by youthful singing groups, who are combining the post-adolescent excitement of hip-hop with the sweet harmonies of a bygone era. Boyz II Men, Portrait, Shai, Jodeci, Joe Public, Bell Biv Devoe, and girl groups En Vogue and Jade are the most recent success stories of a phenomena that's been building in urban America for the past five years.

Tagged "swingbeat" by its founding father Teddy Riley (production credits include Bobby Brown and Michael Jackson), it's post-hip hop musical expression that, according to its young protagonists, happened as an extension of rap as much as a reaction against it. About five years ago rap had taken itself so far up the blind alley of its obsessive macho posturing – musically, lyrically and attitood-wise – that it was beginning to alienate its target audience. Of black America's teenagers, the less extreme boys (who, in spite of media assumptions, were a majority) and virtually all girls were getting turned off by hip-hop's then practically intrinsic obnoxiousness. Having grown up with little other than rap, though, they had little choice outside adapting to it. They took hip-hop sounds and production techniques, blended in melodies (or at the very least melodic hooks) and sang over the top. Harmonising in groups, as so many already did in church, was a natural next step.

It was the combination of a spiky adolescent presentation – both the guy and the girl groups in expensive versions of street fashions and

obligatory shades and hats – and sweet, sexy singing that took in all the joys of teen life (love, hanging out, cars, the mall and so on) that made this style fly. Record companies found it far easier than rap to deal with – rap fell outside the average 40 year-old's past experiences, yet they could all remember The Temptations. Seven figure album sales were the order of the day for the above-mentioned acts, with the leaders in the field, Boyz II Men, En Vogue and Portrait, doing even better than that with, respectively, *Cooleyhighharmony*, *Funky Divas* and *Portrait*.

Such success has not gone unnoticed this side of the Atlantic either. The groups concerned have enjoyed singles hits, and there's a growing pool of homegrown talent. Again young, black, steeped in hip-hop and taught to sing in church, the market leaders are Kreuz (the first act signed by Motown UK, independently of the American parent company); Rhythm & Bass, who have been active for a while and are at last starting to get noticed; and the spectacular London five-piece Nu Colours, who have stirred a generous helping of rave music into their mix.

This less traditionally-corporate attitude, paying far more attention to what is happening on the streets, looks to be the direction Soul UK is moving in. A significant pointer occurred at a huge summer concert in London's Alexandra Park. Alexander O'Neal headlined but most people were there to see second-on-the-bill Dina Carroll, and Nu Colours took the stage with few in the audience knowing who they were but danced off with the biggest applause of the afternoon.

LLOYD BRADLEY

Reggae

> *"Both the reggae establishment and the younger, fresher end of the scale have pushed the music forward to the point where once again it's a pop chart contender to be taken seriously."*

The 12 months up until August was the best year for reggae music since 1977. Back then 'Rock Against Racism' meant huge shows headlined by the likes of Steel Pulse or Misty, with Elvis Costello or The Police propping up the bill and every university student owning a copy of Dillinger's *CB200* album. Or maybe this reggae resurgence harks back even further to the late 60s and the so-called Trojan Explosion, when "Top Of The Pops" was something of a second home for the likes of Desmond Dekker, Nicky Thomas and Bob & Marcia.

Since last summer, both the reggae establishment and the younger, fresher end of the scale have pushed the music forward to the point where once again it's a pop chart contender to be taken seriously. The Bob Marley box set, *Songs Of Freedom*, has won numerous 'Best Compilation Album' awards and gone on to become the second best-selling box set of all time (behind the remastered Led Zeppelin), with sales of just under a million. UB40 joined the big time, officially, when *Can't Help Falling In Love* took up virtual residency at Number One and the sales figures for *Labour Of Love II* passed the five million mark worldwide. Almost forgotten acts like Maxi Priest, Freddie McGregor, Burning Spear and Inner Circle resurfaced – and a posthumous Bob Marley got up in the Top 20 with *Iron Lion Zion*. But most remarkable amongst the old-timers was an unexpected endorsement of reggae by incoming US President Bill Clinton, when he personally invited Birmingham roots veterans Steel Pulse to the White House to play his inauguration ceremony.

As far as new acts (new to the mainstream, anyway) were concerned, the situation was even more spectacular. In March, for the first time ever, reggae singles occupied the top three positions in the singles charts: 1) Shaggy, *Oh Carolina*; 2) Snow, *Informer*; 3) Shabba Ranks, *Mr Loverman*. Whereas Shaggy was the tiny specialist label Greensleeves' first Number One in their 17-year history and sold 500,000-plus, Snow was perhaps the most surprising of this trio. His credentials were slightly left of centre compared to the average reggae star: the lad is a caucasian Canadian, but his follow-up album showed there's much more to him than a Vanilla Ice-type novelty value one hit wonder.

The music extended its territorial waters eastwards too, when Apache Indian blended reggae with bhangra (a speedy, bastardized Punjabi folk music) for the big-selling *Arranged Marriage*, and BMG licenced the Anglo-Asian Multitone label who were already established in such a market. Other majors dabbling in this area were Warners (they had signed Snow) and Sony Music, who already had Shabba Ranks on the Epic label and were proceeding further down that road when Columbia captured young roots stars Buju

▲ He's Snow Vanilla Ice

◄ Shaggy: Carolina on his mind?

anton, Super Cat and the worryingly-
monikered Mad Cobra. Newcomers Chaka
Demus & Pliers introduced themselves to the
pop charts and in the pure pop world, Ace Of
Base appropriated a straightforward reggae
rhythm to have a debut Number One.

Why reggae has reappeared with such a
vengeance is because people are getting to hear
it again, and it is making itself easy to listen to.
For a long time the dance music world has
flirted with reggae; as the house scene became
creatively bankrupt it began to dip into reggae
for its rhythm tracks on a greater and greater
scale. How this got over to the mainstream was
through the traditional singles buyers – teens
and early-20s – opting to tune in to
independent and pirate radio stations, where
dance music holds considerable sway. This far
less specialist audience do their record
shopping in chart return stores, thus reggae
was getting into the national charts and onto
the Radio One playlists.

Also, as far more reggae was being made
outside Jamaica and using American or British
samples, the whole feel of it had been altered.
It now sounded far more accessible to ears
brought up on rock or soul music and, on the
radio, sat far more comfortably alongside the
regular programming. It's no coincidence that
of the records that took the top three places,
two were made in New York and one in
Toronto.

Any way you add it up it's impressive, yet
given the creative and cultural void reggae had
buried itself under for the previous decade – since
the death of Bob Marley sank in completely –
this resurrection was little short of miraculous.
However, for a great many people the most
prominent memories of Last Year In Reggae
will be TV news footage of a cordon of heavily
armed police around the London dance hall Le
Palais. Or, equally unfortunately, of the music's
then biggest star on Channel 4's "The Word",
quoting the Bible as he argued that there was
nothing morally wrong with a record that
advocated shooting homosexuals.

The former occurred when the Champions
In Action Tour – a roadshow starring Tiger,
Sanchez, Daddy Screw and Terror Fabulous,
roots market stars who attract virtually no
mainstream interest – came to the venue on
Easter weekend. There were two incidents of
gunfire in the packed-to-over-capacity hall,
leaving two people injured and a couple of
holes in the ceiling. The latter involved
Shabba Ranks being questioned about Buju
Banton's reggae specialist chart topper *Boom
Bye Bye*, and his naively righteous, and
growlingly vociferous endorsement of its
violently homophobic lyric. Both were part of
reggae's most recent development, ragga, and
in neither case were industry insiders
particularly surprised that the style had
managed to score such damagingly high profile

own goals.

More or less ten years old, the
harsh, aggressively-paced style
evolved as technology increasingly
took over from musicians in the
studios. Originally known, for
obvious reasons, as 'digital reggae',
then 'dancehall' (it was then a club
rather than a stage orientated
music), as the rhythms became
faster and more intense and the
lyrics decreasingly politically
correct, it evolved into more a
soundtrack for an attitude than
merely a music. By the end of the
1980s it had taken its name from an
abbreviation of 'ragamuffin' – the
term Jamaica's dispossessed ghetto
youth apply to themselves – and
took on deliberately intimidating
qualities as the chest-beating
posturing seemed to be taken
seriously.

Although sex and violence have
always been part of Jamaican lyrics,
now the sex had no sense of humour
and what were called 'gun records'
appeared to be acted out on both
sides of the footlights: Buju Banton
was fined in the Cayman Islands for
firing a pistol outside a club; Super
Cat was acquitted in a murder trial
in New York; two Shabba Ranks
shows in the UK ended in
shootings; and a couple of days
before the Champions In Action
tour got to London, shots had been
fired into the ceiling of the Bristol nightclub it
was playing at.

When this culminated in the Le Palais
incident, headline writers, on both sides of
sociological divide, reached for the block
capitals. Away from the merely sensationalist,
the explanations on offer all seemed to link the
decampment, about five years ago, of reggae
from Jamaica to New York, Miami and
Washington. Once in the US, according to
popular theory, it rubbed shoulders with hip
hop, and while absorbing the state of the art
studio technique it also assimilated a new
attitude and new drugs. It was at this time that
rap was at crisis point as macho swaggering
had given way to armed violence, while crack
was approaching epidemic status in American
inner cities. And those same pundits were
equally unanimous on the notion that it was
going to take something of those dimensions
to turn things around.

In the aftermath of Champions In Action
and The Word, Ranks was dropped as support
on Bobby Brown's US tour; specialist record

shops and deejays, many of whom had openly
boycotted gun records for the last year or so,
became vocal in their condemnation of lyrical
irresponsibility; venues cancelled ragga dance
bookings (Part II of Champions In Action,
due a month after the first, was cancelled); and
large sections of its understandably appalled
fan base began to shy away. Naturally, given
these commercial pressures, a fair amount of
act cleaning up has gone on in the last four or
five months, curiously softening the music as
well as the attitude. Now it's fun rather than
an endurance test – Chaka Demus & Pliers
are shining examples of the new, lighter side
of ragga.

As far as the future goes, the reggae industry
is bullish. Perhaps understandably so. Given
the increased outlets, the enormous awareness
factor and the rediscovery of the idea that it's
about entertainment, this current momentum
shouldn't be a problem.

LLOYD BRADLEY

> *"Anyone prepared to pontificate a year ago would have labelled 'world' as peripheral, weird-beard, Guardian reader music. Things change."*

How to sum up 12 months that kicked off with the top young classical musicians from the east and the west (Nigel Kennedy and U Srinivas) jamming on some raggas, and culminated with a raggafied Baaba Maal as a fixture in national daytime radio play? Was 1993 the year international music finally broke through into the popular consciousness? Anyone prepared to pontificate a year ago would have labelled 'world' as peripheral, weird-beard, Guardian reader music. Things change. But what was unmistakable was that it became impossible to write about world without touching on every other genre. The cross-pollination that has been threatening for many years happened, and to a far greater extent than previously envisaged, leaving few people unaffected.

Any examination of world music in 93 has to take into account the success of ragga, with moral panics over sexism and violence seemingly enough to provide it with the popularity and credibility to become the most influential trend of the year. There was much to celebrate in the case of the eclectic Apache Indian, with his mix of ragga, rap and bangra, filtered through healthy dollops of city of Birmingham suss. How long will this phenomenon last? Months maybe, weeks probably, but at least we will be left with a legacy of some classic dancefloor material.

Perhaps then the time is right for a truly global, truly popular, pop music, in which case all praise the catalysts that are ragga, reggae, bangra, zouk… But anyone who remembers Mory Kante's brief flirtation with fame may adopt a more cynical line. Unless there is some convincing consolidation, who would bet against the successes of 92-93 being just another fad, albeit one that brings world ever closer to acceptability?

Baaba Maal's arrival was the achievement of the year. He'd been promising great things for years, but it took some Euro-centred magic dust from jazzman Simon Booth, in the producer's chair for *Lam Toro* (Mango), to make it happen. Roping in the Uilleann pipes of Davy Spillane, and adding a bit of rapping hardly affected the overall sound, but coupled with some major label marketing, they brought it to enough important ears to make it one of the albums of the year.

If there are competitors for that accolade, then the fresh, upfront funk of Egypt's Ali Hassan Kuban is certainly in with a shout –

▲ *Oumou Sangare, quite contrary*

Walk Like A Nubian (Piranha) was voted No 1 album on the pan-European World Music Chart. If you like sacrosanct, traditional African music, this is not the album for you. Try *En Mana Kuoyo* from Kenya's Ayub Ogada, a haunting, rhythmic introduction to the Luo people. Although dwarfed by the stadium spaces on tour with Peter Gabriel, it never hindered his ability to communicate with a new audience unused to this one-man band.

Western Africa enforced its position as second to Zaire in British popularity during the year. Malian music was still to the fore: Oumou Sangare proved with *Kosira* (World Circuit) and some stunning live performances that she has become a force to be reckoned with. Her calls for love and the empowerment of women may seem tame relative to western feminism, but they are little less than revolutionary in her own society. Ali Farka Tour had a memorable year too. Gigs were rare, but he produced his finest album to date with *The Source* (World Circuit), and can't have been hindered by a resurgence of interest in blues guitarist John Lee Hooker.

Elsewhere in Africa, some great names made stirring returns. Fela Kuti delivered *US (Underground System)* (Stern's) – a storming diatribe on economic imperialism that will appeal to anyone with a taste for thumping, committed music. His return to the British stage was an event worth celebrating, but whether his continuing legal problems will allow us another chance to see him has still to be decided. King Sunny Ade's long-awaited reappearance was no less brilliant, making it even more lamentable that Sunny usually languishes in the 'where are they now?' file, despite releasing an album every three months in Nigeria, each of which sells out in 12 hours. Flame Tree Records laudably promoted new Nigerian music, with fuji and juju albums from the young bucks snapping at the establishment's heels. Sir Shina Peters' debut, *Experience*, was the pinnacle of this burst, while Barrister's *New Fuji Garbage* (Globestyle) proved how vibrant the Lagos scene is at the moment.

Zaire remained the biggest draw for African music buyers, with two glorious soukous albums providing the lead. Papa Wemba's *Le Voyageur* (Real World) found him in innovative form, modernising his music to keep up with his threads. The Soukous Stars' *Mozanda* (Stern's) was a blistering showpiece for the Congolese rumba, some stunning guitars and voices. Madagascar had a great year, with the various artists compilation *A World Out Of Time* topping the best-seller lists in the States. Tarika Sammy toured extensively in the UK to great acclaim, appeared on Blue Peter, and released their finest recordings to date on *Fanafody* (Rogue). From India came the fast maturing U Srinivas and Company, taking the humble mandolin and producing divine, if unorthodox, Carnatic ragas. His dexterity on the fretboard would shame most guitarists, while his percussionists never shirked from demonstrating their explosive capabilities. At the other end of the age spectrum, Ravi Shankar's tribute to the recently deceased film-maker Satyajit Ray, *Farewell My Friend*, was an

▶ *Here comes the Sunny – King for Ade*

▼ *Ali Hassan Kuban – the new (Ban)man*

awe-inspiring and emotional album.

Events have kept Eastern Europe/Western Asia in the news throughout the year, and perhaps boosted interest in the indigenous cultures of these areas. A slow train coming which finally arrived was appreciation for Jewish Klezmer music, all but wiped out by 1945. The success of *Rhythm & Jews* (Piranha), the second album by the Klezmatics, was overwhelming. Find of the year were the shamans of Heart of Asia: visiting the UK for an eisteddfod performance, they decided to busk around Manchester rather than return immediately to Tuva, whereupon they were rediscovered and a return engagement is promised. Also debuting was Ashkhabad, a screaming, hard rock mix of Qawwali, rai, mbalax, and Islam from Turkmenistan. Their eponymous album on Real World was one of the year's spiritual highs, even if you missed their costumes.

From northern Europe came Finland's Varttina with the highly successful vocal textures of *Seleniko* (Sonet). From northern Africa and beyond came the Sephardic traditions of Middle Eastern and African Hebrews, strengthened and modernized by Zehava Ben, whose *Best of…* compilation (Hed Arzi) showcased influences as varied as India, Russia, Turkey, and European folk.

The Latin American scene continues to fill dancehalls around the country, although the news that the lambada is the craze in Southeast Asia should send a shiver up every spine. Brazil continues to dominate, although Colombia's ex-pat colony in Britain has at last been rewarded with some outstanding albums to back up the reputation of the live shows. Joe Arroyo's visits are always keenly anticipated, but close behind were storming appearances by Los Tupamares and Toto La Momposina. Toto has at last kicked out the ropy unpro-fessionalism that has dogged her and delivered a killer album for Real World, *La Candela Viva*. Sierra Maestra have been revitalizing the Cuban Son for a number of years, and an extensive UK tour brought them to wider attention.

Compared to France, where ragga DJs and zouk musicians have been

adopting styles to introduce exciting hybrids, British openness to experimentation has been hampered by the rewards on offer for homogeneity and the difficulty of finding new sounds to play with. Accommodation and integration are not words that sit well with our most profitable artists. Hats off then to a notable success during the year: the tenth anniversary of Stern's record shop in London. Ten years of providing music that no-one has heard of or is supposed to want. The shop, however, pales against the significance of Stern's distribution network. Wherever you buy world music in Britain, the chances are that someone from Stern's has laid their hands upon it.

From the successes to the collapse of WOMAD. A weekend in Brighton should have been a celebration of expansion through ten traumatic years. Instead the crowd stayed away, and when overseas festivals failed to materialise and rescue the cash flow, WOMAD called in the receivers. Bailed out by Peter Gabriel, they have turned around and had one of their busiest years yet, with five UK festivals. As long as there are some people willing to face the challenges of Nusrat Fateh Ali Khan or Guo Yue, there will be people reaping dividends from chartbound derivatives.

World music may be stronger and more influential than ever, or it may be so dissipated and integrated that the term now simply means 'those whose time is yet to come'. Whatever it is, when Gloria Estefan releases an album in Spanish, (*Mi Tierra*) what does that make her?

DAVID HUTCHEON

Pop

> **"** *The year ended with hope in its hip-flask and vomited all over 93's resolutions with another* display of cover fever. **"**

Twelve months ago the most successful new pop 'artiste' in Britain was a 30-year-old bloke that no-one had ever heard of, no-one had ever seen and who made a glib, monotone monstrosity out of a middle-aged pop tune of 15 years ago. It wasn't clever, it wasn't good-looking and it was very, very big indeed. Undercover he called himself, and every one of his blasted cover versions was enormous for the six months. When he eventually showed himself on "Top Of The Pops" he looked like a Deputy Assistant Ad Manager (Acting) for the Abbey National. This, of course, would never do. Pop, the

media pronounced, was dead.

Q magazine examined the evidence and blamed 'The Industry' (singles in decline, recessional caution, CD-domination - should have blamed themselves, eh, rock ironists?), Tony Parsons went on the telly and blamed the 70s revival, Sonic The Hedgehog and yoof-culture apathy, and Simon Bates held a debate on Radio One, where he mentioned that Tina Turner was really good while patronizing everyone. Pointless, really, the lot of it, but we all knew that something had gone horribly, horribly Pete Tong. Dance, after all, had invented the notion of the Faceless Pop Record and we'd seen the 'all-important' Top Ten clogged with the bleeps and blips of dance-pop anonymity for years, but the autumn of 92 was as woeful a time in pop as we'd *ever* seen.

As the twigs snapped under the flimsy beige loafers of crap pop covers (KWS' s *Rock You Baby*, Cover Girls' *Wishing On A Star*, Krush's *Walking On Sunshine*), the glittering tiara of pop rested solely on the head of our very 'own' Kylie with *What Kind Of Fool* as we tried to

ignore the resolutely less glittering sight of Billy Ray Cyrus and his bloody *Achy Breaky Heart*, swiftly followed by the lumbering perm of Jimmy Nail's *Ain't No Doubt*. We bemoaned the absence of the perverted trouserwear of Right Said Fred as *What A Day For A Day Dream* failed to ignite the chartways, Michael Jackson lost the plot completely and Take That were as fine a concept as ever, but their tunes were cobblers.

Inconceivably, it was the bleak hinterland of Walthamstow that produced our first proper pop sensation of the entire year. East 17 had a Staffordshire Bull Terrier, a gob-full of trash about smoking fags and losing their virginity to prostitutes and this was fairly a tonic to the idol-starved teensters who knew *House Of Love* was freshly-laundered dance-pop at its finest. Grown-up pop, on the other hand, was glum as ever. *Baby Don't Cry* went INXS as Annie Lennox went *Walking On Broken Glass* dressed up as an ostrich.

It was all taking on the unmistakable feel of the Brits' nominations, until the singular most glorious moment in 1992's patchy pop wilderness alighted. A chart-topping Legend had come among us and its name was *Ebeneezer Goode*. It was Mickey Mouse rave-up rubbish for the kiddies. It was also an insurrectionary pop grenade lodged in the intestinal bile of the pop establishment which had five-year-olds squealing from their playpens of the glories of top Grade A narcotics. "Ho ho ho!" went The Shamen and Mr C was a brand new wiggly-fingered superstar overnight. Now *that* was more like it.

Rave culture was standing proud once again, until... "No No! *No No* No No! - there's no lyrics!!" Such was the jest at 2 Unlimited's expense and the nation put its Vicks Vaporub to the back of the medicine cabinet. 2 Unlimited's Anita and Ray, however, also knew The Score; they and the Shamen have been the only recognizable, consistent pop heroes from the entire techno genre and for that we salute them.

None of this, however, sated our toughened urban pop kids. Dance was still, of course, The New Pop and a new US/Celtic flavour emerged with the House Of Pain's tremendous *Jump*. (Kriss Kross had limped out of sight, blubbing into their ill-arranged trousers earlier in the year with *I Missed The Bus*. Er, indeed.) The phase was quashed on its pogo-stick, however, by the on-coming assault of the pop traditionalists. Madonna returned, chests aloft to more global infamy with her busiest spell for years. The *Erotica* LP, the Sex extravaganza and the pervy film - none of them much cop at all. Erasure brought us *Abbaesque* nonsense, Prince proved as nuts as ever with his *My Name Is Prince* pop hoot, as did Shakespear's Sister with the goth-pop glimmering of *Hello (Turn Your Radio On)*.

All this, of course, was far too grown-up for pure pop and it was the tartan shorts of Boyz II Men that danced on the bus passes of the lot of them with its *Motownphilly* new-jack-swinger and the sensational lungs-akimbo pop belter *End Of The Road* (before Whitney Houston redefined the concept of power-ballad with the even more Bryan Adams-sized *I Will Always Love You*). Pop, thank goodness, was soon roundly fed up with incessant tonsil-quivering and turned, once again, to the knee for inspiration. Charles And Eddie's fragrant *Would I Lie To You* heralded the return of the decent dance experience before The Stereo MCs saved the world with *Connected*. The globe rejoiced on its axis as 'quality' dance-pop stormed the continents and brought us more political-knee-flailers from Arrested Development with *3 Years, 5 Months and 2 Days In The Life Of...*

The year ended with hope in its hip-flask and vomited all over 93's resolutions with *another* display of cover fever. The world did not need Faith No More's 'interpretation' of the Commodores' *Easy*, nor The Lemonheads' *Mrs Robinson*, but they were still better than Networks' *Run To You*. Sensitive-techno made a molecular comeback with The Beloved's *Sweet Harmony* and then fell into a coma again before blustering fem-stomp saviours En Vogue boggled our eyes with the glorious *Give It Up, Turn It Loose*, and their forbearers Sister Sledge caught on to the unabated disco revival with the re-released *We Are Family*.

From here, things took a traditional pre-Spring dip, saved only by Belly's *Feed The Tree* while we did our best to ignore Undercover's *I Wanna Stay With You*. The 1993 Brits Awards didn't ignore it, they gave it a shiny tribute for its mantelpiece. Watching at home, asleep, our tea-trays wobbled only momentarily as Bert from Suede did his finest impersonation of Julian Clary yet and stomped off in a petulant huff. The Future Of Every-

thing Ever? We shall see...

Normal transmission resumed with the rightful placing of the Stereo MCs as pop's new heroes of righteous-dance as *Ground Level* flew into the charts with much media merriment found in Rob's resemblance to Kirk Douglas in the Van Gogh bio-pic. (That and the rather less jovial 'he looks like he's dead!'). It was Rob Stereo who first mentioned the 'nice sounds' of something called Jamiroquai in print and within seconds, the be-hatted, Indian-loving, sparrow-chested, table-pounding rhetoric of Jay stormed the country as *Too Young To Die* doobied its way up the hit parade and the worthy dance-pop-jazz-fusion, er, 'Revolution' was with us.

Since then pop has embraced The Plot with a gusto not seen since the days of the indie-dance-pop crossover of 89/90, which was the last time pop was *truly* very incredible indeed. Black Box and The Happy Mondays - *them* were the days, Grandad. The drastic splintering of the entire pop genre - what the hell *is* pop these days, anyway? - the same generic breakdown which could so easily have obliterated it completely, might just prove to be its making. Pop, dance, rap, ragga, hip-hop, dancehall, soul, jazz, indie, grunge, crustie, rock... they're fast becoming a giant one-ness and there's pop heroes in there for us all.

We live in a time where the 'incendiary' Manic Street Preachers are teenage Pop Gods and a bloke who looks like Jesus with a sock on his head has one of the biggest pop hits of the year, ie the Spin Doctors with *Two Princes*. Which is all precisely as it should be. From the pure pop of Sybil's *When I'm Good And Ready* to the cultural first of - yes! - Bhangra-hip-hop in Apache Indian's *Arranged*

Marriage, the Nirvana-inspired rap creativity of Credit To The Nation's *Call It What You Want* and the spring/summer domination of ragga/dancehall, we're on the brink of Western pop throwing itself into the bubbliest cauldron of eclecticism since The Stone Roses pelted their paint pots off the head of a high court judge (or whatever it was).

Thus, for every UB40's *I Can't Help Falling In Love*, we've a JCOO1's *Cupid*. For every Gloria Estefan 'Megamix', a Utah Saints' *I Want You*, for every Lisa Stansfield's *I Swear*, a Gabrielle's *Dreams*. Much of the best pop is still of the Faceless Dance variety, of course, but, well, we should be used to that by now. If you want faces, even the old folks that went away and came back again haven't let us down: New Order, Pet Shop Boys, Terence 'Trout' D'Arby, Neneh Cherry, REM, Janet Jackson. Hell, even Take That's *Pray* is infinitely preferable to some George Michael-on-the-karaoke Queen cover. And Vanessa Paradis *is* the new Kylie.

Things, as the song said, can only get better, and they already have because pop is back from the alleged dead. What more do you want? A *real* revolution? As 'revolutionary' Jim from the Jesus and Mary Chain once said, "Music doesn't cause revolutions." And what does? "Machine guns."

Meantime, we have pop. Enjoy...

SYLVIA PATTERSON

E17 gave us the House of Love, Madonna the book of Sex, and Shakespear's Sister Bard out gracefully

Hearts on Sleeves

What will replace the one-time glories of the gatefold? **Kevin Greening** offers a personal view.

"My bedroom was a gallery for which the local high street record shop was the auction room – full of works by great masters whose brush strokes you could actually hear when you got them home."

When, at the age of eleven, I first glimpsed the hare-in-a-headlight expressions on their faces, the near-naked nubiles on the front cover of Roxy Music's *Country Life* had such an impact on me that I can only guess I had never until that moment seen a truly pornographic photo. This was in the days when a youngster could reasonably expect his developing taste in music to offend his parents' ears, and the sleeves of the records he was buying could be counted on to act as foot-high sentinels of depravity – the first thing Mum would see when she opened the bedroom door.

Twenty years ago, album covers were such bold statements. My point is this; it's probably fair to say until I was 20, the only *objets d'art* I owned were my records and the cardboard they came in. Album (and later 7-inch single) sleeve design was the closest I ever got to the right side of the turntable at an art exhibition. My bedroom was a gallery for which the local high street record shop was the auction room – full of works by great masters whose brush strokes you could actually *hear* when you got them home.

The purpose of sleeve art is changing. It has done since the pre-rock'n'roll days when you were lucky to get a graduation-style portrait of an artiste on an LP cover. Before TV and world tours, this photo might be the only image of the singer you were ever likely to see.

When the Beatles stared out from the front cover of *Rubber Soul* we began to feel that bands were using their album covers to communicate something of themselves to us. By the time Peter Blake's cut-out-and-keep paste-up appeared round the *Sgt Pepper* LP, the Beatles were in charge of their collective creative destiny; the sleeve design was like a bonus track to the record – as much a part of the concept as Lennon and McCartney's chord progressions. The seeds were sown for the increasingly pompous statements of the early 70s in which art houses like Hipgnosis and Roger Dean competed to produce ever more outlandish, other-wordly and abstract designs for the amusement of the bands and their fans.

For what it's worth, in a straw poll on my Virgin 1215 radio show, the album sleeves which scored best are almost all from this late-Beatles-to-late-Progressive era. However, these 'dinosaur designs' were to be wiped out by three cataclysmic climate changes: Fashion, Film and Format…

First with New Wave, the album sleeve was de-constructed along with the music – a good example was XTC's minimalist design for *Go 2*. This is a RECORD cover… Roger Dean and his squiggly typefaces and lunar landscapes were replaced overnight by safety-pin cynicism.

Soon afterwards came the video; the three-and-a-half minute commercial that TV stations actually pay record companies to play. It was a marketing breakthrough and before long fans were forming visual impressions of their heroes not from a few stills on a gatefold sleeve, nor even from in-the-flesh live appearances, but instead from plays on MTV and "Going Live!" More TV viewers saw Freddie Mercury vacuuming in drag or Annie Lennox dancing in a tuxedo than gig-goers ever witnessed either of them cross-dressing on stage. The sleeve designer had been superseded by the video director.

Thirdly and most recently came the format revolution. Already reduced in importance by the video, sleeve designs were reduced in *size* by the switch to CD. As a result, artwork had tended to become less intricate and less intriguing. The 5-inch square dimensions mean that necessarily passport-sized photos of band members are often ditched in favour of blurred colour washes with plenty of space left for the artiste's name and the obligatory 'includes previously unreleased bonus tracks' sticker.

It's ironic that, as product packaging in the supermarket has become more distinctive and eye-catching (Radion, Lynx, I Can't Believe It's Not Butter, $^*! Me If This Is Yogurt etc etc), the Perspex-Persil CD case had relegated the album cover to the second division of graphic design. Most compact disc inlays now contain less information about the product they advertise than the helpful leaflet which accompanied the fizzy drinks maker I bought recently. Even when the artwork does run to a few pages of lyrics, it's important to remember that the booklet can only be removed from the CD tray twice before it becomes irreparably frayed at the edges and cannot be re-inserted.

Of course there are exceptions. Pick up a Vaughan Oliver designed CD and you know you're buying a 4AD release; you feel from the artwork that musically the product is probably as good as (but sufficiently different from) everything else on 4AD. But, by and large, mediocrity rules.

Where are the post-vinyl counterparts of the Madonna album whose cover was infused with petchouli oil so pungent that it contaminated everything in my collection from McCartney to Marillion? Where are the post-analogue equivalents of sleeve design folklore classics like Thin Lizzy's *Black Rose* which went to the printers three times until the rose came back black enough – or Roxy Music's *For Your Pleasure* whose artwork featured Amanda Lear and a black panther pumped so full of valium for the photo shot that its eyes had to be painted open afterwards?

In short, without gatefold sleeves and 12-inch picture discs, who is making the exhibits for the teenagers' bedroom wall galleries of tomorrow?

**RESULT OF VIRGIN 1215
'BEST ALBUM SLEEVE POLL'**
· · · · · · · · · · · · · · · · · ·

① **Vaughan Oliver's collective
designs for 4AD**
② *Physical Graffiti* – **LED ZEP**
③ *Rubber Soul* – **BEATLES**
④ *White Album* – **BEATLES**
⑤ *Momentary Lapse of Reason* –
PINK FLOYD

"Most compact
disc inlays now
contain less
information about
the product they
advertise than the
helpful leaflet which
accompanied the
fizzy drinks maker
I bought recently."

a

BARRY ADAMSON
The Negro Inside Me (Mute)

"This isn't a film soundtrack but it walks that way. If *The Negro Inside Me* did have accompanying visuals it would involve a couple of car chases, a murder, a shag and a happy ending." **NME**

"...an attempt to blend the button-down elegance of the best movie with modern club beats. On paper, it's a disaster waiting to happen. On record, it feels strange at first; after a couple of plays, it's so seamless and effective that you have to wonder why it hasn't been attempted before." **Melody Maker**

"Once Barry Adamson made soundtracks for films that would never be made. Then he made soundtracks for films that would be made but you would never see. Now, he's back where he started." **Select**

ALICE IN CHAINS
Dirt (Columbia)

"Lyrically, as musically, this is a violent record, full of implicit and explicit threats. *Dirt* is a stunning album – beautiful, ugly, angry and ground-breaking. Alice In Chains have taken enormous risks. It's paid huge dividends."
Melody Maker

"It wouldn't be much of a surprise if this album was found to contain subliminal Satanic messages." **NME**

"...raises them to that level so far only achieved by the band they're most often accused of sounding like, Soundgarden. *Dirt* could well be the album that sees Alice in Chains clean up." **Metal CD**

AMERICAN MUSIC CLUB
Mercury (Virgin)

"Eitzel's still claiming to be, variously, a wino, a desperate man, a mess and a loser, but where *Mercury* cuts it over the virtually suicidal outlook of, say, Red House Painters, is in its sublime humour, which, whatever Eitzel might argue, is the humour of a great writer." **Select**

"A similar mixture of angst and whimsy has served Morrissey well over the years, but Eitzel is a much less flamboyant character. For all its intellectual clout, this album lacks charm." **The Times**

"Intensely brooding, strangely poetic and uniquely edgy, the latest album from this San Francisco five-piece should finally establish them as America's hippest rock band." **Esquire**

"Singer/songwriter Mark Eitzel could be a Poet Laureate for the grunge generation if only the Xers had the insight to realise. In the underrated stakes, this gem will, no doubt, sit alongside Talk Talk's last album."
The Face

TASMIN ARCHER
Great Expectations (EMI)
See The Year In Review

AUTEURS
New Wave (Hut)

"Luke Haines is a good lyricist, managing to play the roles of high-brow poet and seedy, streetwise urchin simultaneously. Musically, he's capable of churning out some damn fine guitar riffs which chime away in a wistful, melancholy fashion..."
Making Music

"The indie-glam saga continues with a touch of Bolan and early Bowie, roughly hewn guitars and more well-crafted 'tunes' than you could shake a platform-soled glitter stick at."
The Face

"There's enough here to suggest that The Auteurs are on the verge of something truly sublime. Indeed, compared to The Auteurs, most other rock 'n' roll contenders sound like they're farting through a keyhole." **Rock CD**

AZTEC CAMERA
Dreamland (WEA)

"*Dreamland* is a hard album to pull apart – lush, polished and smooth, it just kind of

swans around your head for a while. It would be great if halfway through, in the style of Sega's Pirate TV ads, some jarring noise-bleed march suddenly bootlegged in to wake you from this worthy slumber." **NME**

"Dreamland is not a disastrous album, but it is a disappointing one. Frame has the sleepwalking air of a man whose life – for the time being at least – is too strongly centred somewhere other than in his music." **Vox**

"Having spent more than a decade as the boy of great promise, one would have thought that Frame's ongoing apprenticeship might have provided some kind of sustained pay-off. As it is, he's once again left with everything to prove." **Rock CD**

b

THE B52'S
Good Stuff (WEA)

"...B52's fans won't be disappointed by *Good Stuff* – there's too much to like about it and it's still ahead of the pack – but as any dictionary will confirm, Good is not the same as Best." **Q**

"Somehow or other, they've been through a major career renaissance in the US, and have been elevated to 'rock institution' status. Sounds like cobwebby old twaddle... Isn't it about time The B52's got proper jobs?" **Sky**

"...one almost forgets the discipline it takes to carry off such whopping conceits of style and still make them accessible." **Vox**

JOAN BAEZ
Play Me Backwards (Virgin)

"Throughout the album she lowers her vocals, moving away from that shrill warbly sound that's made much of her output inaccessible. At times she comes across like Michelle Shocked's wiser aunt, at others she sounds as fresh-voiced as she ever did."
Rock CD

"...Joan Baez has succeeded against the odds with this album in adapting her straight-laced delivery to a body of songs styled in an elegantly fashionable new country vein. *Play Me Backwards* is an object lesson in what can be done with a seasoned talent given the right material..." **Q**

"...working hard to shrug off the po-faced, protest singer tag, her new album, recorded in Nashville, is stuffed with sharply-observed country-rock ballads." **The Daily Telegraph**

THE BEACH BOYS
Summer In Paradise (EMI)

"All the ingredients are there: snap-shots of past peaks ('vibration rhyming with 'excitation'), bap-bap-wa-oom bass notes, an imagined world inhabited by babes and surfers, every other title with the word 'summer' in it. Without Brian Wilson's touch the concoction seems merely comical. To think some of these people took part in *Pet Sounds*." **Q**

BELLY
Star (4AD)

"*Star* prefers insinuation to grabbing a fistful of heartstrings and giving them a hefty yank (geddit?) – which would seem to be the love technique of most other records right now."
Melody Maker

"You can put it on while you make breakfast, bounce around to it before you go out and still save it for soul-searching moments in the wee hours." **NME**

"...a debut LP that is a jingly jangly pop guitar education in itself. Sultry lead singer Tanya Donelly breathes sophistication over a background of real guitar energy... a dreamy and beautiful beginning for Belly."
Smash Hits

"Sensual, passionate, utterly compelling and although barely into '93, an album of the year. Here's hoping this release makes Ms Donnelly as big a star as the one she's created."
Rock CD

THE BELOVED
Conscience (East West)

"...still offering reassuring feel-good sentiments long after the second Summer Of Love receded into a drug-deranged trudge round England's brown and muddy fields."
The Independent

"...it seems ironic that music borne out of the frenetic activity of the dancefloor should end up sounding so listless." **The Times**

"This album is so chock-a-block with sentiment it will have you reaching for the Kleenex! If you're a fan of tinkly piano bits, tragic lyrics and true love you'll find it all pretty fabulous." **Smash Hits**

BJORK
Debut (One Little Indian)

"...the sound of 2003. If your ears are programmed to accept only words and sounds you expect to hear, then you'll hate *Debut*. But if you pin them right back and prepare yourself for something unique and radically different you might learn to love it." **Today**

"This is an album that believes music can be magical and special. It will either puzzle you or pull you into its spell. And if you fall into the latter category, *Debut* will make every other record you own seem flat, lifeless and dull by comparison." **NME**

"Coughing and spitting and hiccupping, Bjork is never the most understated of vocalists. She plays the wild-eyed urchin weirdo from Zog to the hilt here. Which is just as well..."
Melody Maker

"...what a relief it is to be able to hear her without that berk Einar prattling away over the top." **The Independent**

FRANK BLACK
Frank Black (4AD)

"Thankfully, *Frank Black* isn't merely the Pixies minus the civilising influence of Kim Deal. *Frank Black* isn't an attempt to take on grunge. And those who liked the petulant, random, abrasive, pyromaniac aspects of the Pixies might well be disappointed by this album. It's richer, smoother – you can see your face in its surfaces." **Melody Maker**

"All 15 tracks are shot through with Frank's shrewd goofy personality and queer, rare musical gift. The word 'genius' might not be too strong." **Select**

"Full of surprises and hidden goodies, this album grows on you with every play."
Making Music

"Like Byrne, Black exalts in the possibilities of American music: a lot of his songs rely on the big 'why not' factor and benign indulgence on the listener's part, which usually pays dividends." **The Independent**

BLUR
Modern Life Is Rubbish (Food/EMI)

"Blur never stop sounding exactly like Blur – waterfalls of guitars, whining Essex accents and hooklines as contagious as chickenpox. *Modern Life Is Rubbish* is as English as football pools, fish-fingers and Ford Escorts."
The Daily Telegraph

"*Modern Life Is Rubbish* has enough faults to give a surveyor nightmares...if they've made a mistake, then celebrate – at times it's a brilliant one." **NME**

"Blur are dead hard and they've got a big dog too. Yeah right! *Modern Life Is Rubbish* is about as tough as the annual I'm A Grandad Convention, but it is packed with fab groovy tunes." **Smash Hits**

"Blur storm off on an energised, infectious romp around contemporary little England, by way of an exuberant trawl through a highly-coloured patchwork of its pop past." **Q**

MICHAEL BOLTON
Michael Bolton: Timeless (The Classics) (Columbia)

"Thank you Michael. Run out of songs for the Christmas market, have we?" **NME**

"...the supersheen hi-gloss of the arrangements and production seem likely to guarantee pots of cash, multi-platinum sales and further Grammy glory in 1993." **Q**

BON JOVI
Bon Jovi: Keep The Faith (Jambco/Mercury)

"Slickly polished, *Keep The Faith* tootles around in a perfectly reasonable daytime radio manner, but with Nirvana to their right and Guns N' Roses to their left it can't stop that niche looking more and more precarious by the minute." **Select**

"As a man who initially formed his band to pick up 'chicks' rather than from a burning desire to say anything important or even vaguely personal, it's hardly surprising that passionate music fans shun Bon Jovi with a vengeance." **Making Music**

"Of course, one can never come right out and admit one likes Bon Jovi, unless it's to one's therapist, but they have a glaring gift for melodrama and cheap thrills." **The Guardian**

DAVID BOWIE
Black Tie White Noise (Arista)

"In an age so bereft of real heroes, one senses that punters and pundits alike are desperate to forgive him the sins of the 1980s and bring him back from the cold. As 1993 turns ever more inexorably into a re-run of 1973, it's time to greet again the man who fell on his feet." **The Times**

"...there will be no more disguises, no strange new characters to add to the rogue's gallery of his 1970s personae. Right from the start – a peal of church bells introducing a sax-based instrumental which Bowie composed to be played at his wedding ceremony – the album deals primarily with the moods and experiences of the 'real' David Bowie..." **Q**

"*Black Tie White Noise* is being touted as some sort of creative rebirth, but while it may be preferable to the worst moments of *Tin Machine* or *Never Let Me Down*, it's completely unconvincing." **Sky**

"Ultimately, what makes this the best album Bowie has made since the golden years of the 70s is that, finally, here is the voice of the man behind the masks." **The Daily Telegraph**

JAMES BROWN
Universal James (Scotti Brothers/Polydor)

"A pointless attempt to update James Brown for the 90s, *Universal James* is misconceived, mediocre and sad. And not very funky either." **Select**

"A judicious blend of tracks written and produced by either Brown himself, Soul II Soul's Jazzie B, or Clivilles & Cole, *Universal James* is certainly much better than Brown's first post-jail album, *Love Overdue*. Here, at least, the other guys are trying, even if James isn't sure." **The Independent**

"After his release two years ago, it took him only days to make a new album, *Love Overdue*. It was terrible and deservedly a failure. *Universal James* is a more considered attempt to re-establish his reputation." **The Daily Telegraph**

BUZZCOCKS
Trade Test Transmissions (Castle Communications)

"A surprisingly good return, and if Shelley's solitary pursuits don't drive him blind, these youngsters could go far." **Select**

"It's not great, but then none of the Buzzcocks' albums ever were. They were just these long 12-inch interludes between the singles." **NME**

"...there is little attempt to develop – they probably don't know, or want to know, how to do so – but, nevertheless, this is more than a collection of New Wave retreads." **Vox**

C

CHARLES & EDDIE
Duophonic (Stateside/Capitol)

"Relax and chill to the vibes on this railroad-track of sweet soul music. *Duophonic* envelops you like the softest silk sheet this side of Luther Vandross's laundry." **Smash Hits**

"Charles & Eddie don't demand to know what time it is, they have no detectable samples and they rarely touch bland. For a 1992 soul album, that's remarkable." **Q**

"The unnerving thing about the album is that although Charles and Eddie seem well-intentioned and do actually sound like Al and Marvin, there is a curious lack of vibe to it. *Duophonic* just seems too ingenious." **Vox**

NENEH CHERRY
Homebrew (Circa)

"It has been more than three years since Neneh Cherry's dynamic debut, *Raw Like Sushi*. Needless to say, sceptics were lining up to bang nails in her coffin and prance on her grave. Hats will have to be eaten, however, because *Homebrew* will do very nicely, thank you. The results sound loose and vaguely ramshackle, but direct and powerfully expressive." **The Guardian**

"Whether singing or rapping, she too often sounds like Cyndi Lauper in a sulk. Neneh Cherry, it seems, is an example of someone who can, with great panache, walk the walk, but fails dismally to talk the talk." **Select**

"Refreshingly, Neneh has avoided the temptation to tackle some grandiose concept, and instead has kept it simple and pretty rough, recording the tracks on a mobile studio and using rap and beatbox rhythms as building blocks for her songs." **Sky**

"...it's that kind of vivid, powerful experience that makes you wonder if everybody shouldn't take three years between albums." **Q**

THE CHRISTIANS
Happy In Hell (Island)

"*Happy In Hell* is the best Christians LP yet, their *Psychedelic Shack*. Still flabby in places and hardly innovative, but it's a start." **Select**

"The Christians have apparently forgotten that their real appeal, and what made them so refreshingly different, lay in their rough edges and all the Scally roots they left showing. By smoothing them all over, the band who should be kings could well find themselves lost in the crush. Which would be a tragic waste of talent." **Vox**

"...the songs rarely do more than mark time during the verses, but there's normally an awesome chorus pinned to the end of them, decked out with vocal harmonies on a choral scale." **Q**

ERIC CLAPTON
Unplugged (WEA)

"The album's accessibility and sense of fun will probably bring a sneer to the lips of the bluesier-than-thou brigade, but it's undoubtedly Clapton's most enjoyable album for years." **Q**

"Always unhappy in the limelight, you can see Clapton being a happy plucker about this anonymous little affair: being paid a packet for playing the blues, as he's always wanted to do." **Vox**

GARY CLARK
Ten Short Songs About Love (Circa)

"Clark maintains his uniqueness by stretching his melody lines and injecting his vocals with a lonesome poignancy that would be capable of turning *Itsy Bitsy Teeny Weeny Yellow Polka Dot Bikini* into something of an intense experience." **Q**

"Clark is far more than just another singer-songwriter – he is in the same league as Paddy McAloon... and they don't come any better than that. While his acoustic guitar gently sighs, Clark records the invisible wounds men and women inflict on each other." **The Daily Telegraph**

"Cocooned in his home studio, Gary Clark seems to have spent too long honing and refining his undeniable talents, dulling their previously-proven impact. Sadly, this soft soul soft soap just won't wash." **Vox**

LEONARD COHEN
The Future (Columbia)

"Never prolific, he has gone away and pondered for a few years before venturing into *The Future*, where he travels further into an existential wilderness which, somehow, contrives to be strangely comforting. Cohen's new music moves confidently between global chaos, apocalyptic dread and the compensating diversions of love and lust." **The Guardian**

"It's hard to explain Leonard's appeal to the uninitiated. Maybe it's because he's persevered with his craft in the face of adversity and ridicule, and risen to the status of cult hero despite them." **Making Music**

"The music's a faultless brew of folk, gospel and rock, too, the highlight being a Lanois-like gumbo mysticism to *Waiting For A Miracle*. And the killer couplet? 'There's a crack in everything/That's how the light gets in.' Absolutely." **Select**

MARC COHN
The Rainy Season (East West)

"When he's peppy he sounds like John Hiatt; when he's sensitive, he sounds like Jackson Browne. Skilful and sincere he may be, but Cohn still lacks the fire or the originality to be much more than a postscript to his 70s mentors." **Q**

"Ultimately, there's lots of craftsmanship, but nothing terribly interesting." **Vox**

CURVE
Radio Sessions (Anxious)

"Whether Curve's next proper release will reveal a giant leap away from their entrenched glitterdoom bridgehead remains to be seen. *Radio Sessions* merely suggests they may have worked this clinically beautiful seam to exhaustion." **NME**

"The trouble with a lot of these session albums is that they don't appear to offer you anything tastier than slightly less slick versions of songs which you already own. *Radio Sessions* gives you nothing that Curve's small-but-perfectly formed back catalogue hasn't already mesmerised you with." **Melody Maker**

"...only the vaguest glimmer of busked, recorded-in-a-day precariousness adds a further frisson to Curve's witchly glamour." **Vox**

JULIAN COPE
Jehovahkill (Island)

"*Jehovahkill* is Cope's best work since 1985's *Fried*, the fan-club totem. Julian Cope has beget a timeless work, for he is once again stoned, immaculate." **NME**

"Another double from Julian Cope, and this one's further out than even the shipping forecasts are prepared to go. You get grade-freakin'-A blowouts, a mad rush instrumental, some fine funk, some melodic pop heaven and more words than a South American football commentary..." **Select**

"His enormous new album takes his preoccupation with the fate of Planet Earth to new and fantastical extremes. The music is strange and often sombre in an early psychedelic fashion, though Cope's talent for

standing popular legends on their elbow is audible." **The Guardian**

"...while there are arguably no hits among these 16 tracks, this is an album that should most probably acquire a dedicated cult following." **Q**

JULIAN COPE
The Skellington Chronicles (Magog)

"'The Skellington Chronicles can't really be regarded as an official follow-up to *Jehovahkill* – that has yet to come – but as a cute and quirky sidestep it's a thoroughly entertaining rag-bag that proves Julian has lost none of his adventure or enthusiasm. Barmy but unbowed, the fully-fledged return of Julian Cope is imminent." **NME**

"...picks up where the original left off with a set of demoish, mostly acoustic strums, shot through with equal measures of self-deprecation, self-indulgence, wit and off-kilter songwriting genius." **Vox**

"Some records make you want to play air guitar. Others make you want to get out of your mind on dope and speed, take the rest of your life off, write a novel and fuck strangers naked in the stream. A clue: this record does not make you want to play air guitar." **Select**

ELVIS COSTELLO & THE BRODSKY QUARTET
The Juliet Letters (WEA)

"With each successive play, something new and unexpected is revealed. It's that rare thing, really: an album you know you're going to be

able to live with down the years." **Melody Maker**

"Like virtually all conjunctions of rock and classical elements, *The Juliet Letters* ends up as a battle, with neither side winning outright..." **The Independent**

"Costello's voice is familiar, of course, though devotees may find themselves nonplussed at hearing it in this setting. This is *The Letters'* weakest point – Elvis's voice cannot encompass the full range of imaginary lovers, losers, depressives, daydreamers and hucksters who've supposedly written these letters to Juliet Capulet. Better to have gone the whole hog and hired a classical singer, or possibly two." **The Guardian**

COVERDALE/PAGE
Coverdale/Page (EMI)

"A truly English sound, free of crass Americanisms and bloodrush modernism, this album screams classic from start to finish. It's every bit the opus to play the tennis racket to and grow your hair for. Page's production lets his fingers do the walking. Any lapsed and confused modern metal fan won't be disappointed." **Q**

"...an album that is far and away the most authoritative piece of work either musician has signed his name to in a decade at least." **The Times**

"*Coverdale/Page* is a bizarre, but not completely unwelcome throwback, a hulking great blues-rock album like they don't make 'em any more. David Coverdale and Jimmy Page, strange bedfellows indeed, proceed as if the last 20 years were merely a mirage..." **The Independent**

ICE CUBE
The Predator (Island)

"Terrifying but strangely compulsive too. Ice Cube probably won't be invited on Oprah Winfrey or put up for a Grammy, but that doesn't stop *The Predator* – despite its quota of dick-fixated misogyny – being a hell of a record." **Q**

"As a reaction to recent events, the only thing unexpected about *The Predator* is the extreme nature of its expression of hatred... the response from white America should register on the Richter scale." **NME**

"He has a point to make, and he makes it with conviction, style, and no little musicality. The

point is, the problem's not his, it's everybody's." **Making Music**

HOLGER CZUKAY
Moving Pictures (Mute)

"*Moving Pictures* isn't easy listening, whoopee fun, or even like any other ambient album. It beats with a mad heart in slow motion – and it's great." **NME**

"It's less specific and linear than his classic 1980 collage exercise *Movies*... it sounds like a Daniel Lanois atmosphere without the central focus of attention, a studio playing itself." **Q**

TERENCE TRENT D'ARBY
Symphony or Damn: The Tension Inside The Sweetness (Columbia)

"In the finest tradition of records made in home studios with only the occasional guest musician to interrupt the flow of genius, *Symphony Or Damn* sounds immediately different to the usual overbright contender. It's mixed weird. The voices are bigger than the drums. Guitars and keyboards jump out of speakers in real stereo. And the tunes don't sound plastic." **Q**

"Terence has gone all indie and bleak and serious in this, his third, and in terms of re-establishing himself as a major act, probably most crucial LP. And guess what? It works. It's pop, it's rock, it's soul. It's very good indeed." **Smash Hits**

DEACON BLUE
Whatever You Say, Say Nothing (Columbia)

"Ricky Ross can write strong songs... but collaborator-free, he seems to have run smack-bang into an artistic cul-de-sac. This album just isn't happening." **Q**

"...a belated jump onto the baggy bandwagon that lit out for the wasteland about the time of the last Happy Mondays album." **The Independent**

"There is some good stuff here and Deacon Blue might find success in the dance charts or recruiting U2 fans, but I don't think that this way they'll find themselves." **Making Music**

DENIM
Back In Denim (London)

"Beyond this LP, Denim are doomed. They have No Future. Lawrence has done what he set out to do. That's the beauty of Denim; they will never grow old or threadbare or fade." **NME**

"The music is pretty authentic, even beefier than the 70s sound, thanks to Leckie's production, but it's the lyrics which steal the show. And any song with the line 'there were lots of little Osmonds everywhere' has to be a winner." **Rock CD**

"'It' is 70s music, dredged up and remodelled in all its cheesy glory. 'It' is paid homage to on Denim's fun, fun, fun album *Back In Denim*." **Vox**

DEPECHE MODE
Songs Of Faith & Devotion (Mute)
See The Year in Review

DINOSAUR JR
Where You Been (Blanco Y Negro)

"On *Where You Been* the original slacker gets his shit together and reveals uncharacteristic signs of ambition (artistic and career-wise). J Mascis looks like he wants to go somewhere (artistically and commercially) with his music. He wants to put himself on the map, make his (land)mark, and *Where You Been* could do it for him." **Melody Maker**

"An album of great moments rather than a great album, *Where You Been* finds a band happy for others to squabble over their leftovers while determined to have a crack at 50 different new things. At the same time." **Select**

"At its best the formula is an irresistible combination of the powerful and the vulnerable. But Mascis is just as happy to deploy an acoustic guitar and a discreet string section to make his oddball points. *Where You Been* is a stirring and masterful achievement." **The Times**

DIRE STRAITS
On The Night (Vertigo)

"Throughout the album, charisma, pizzazz and rock 'n' roll abandon lie dormant, but Dire Straits have long since stopped worrying about such trifles. This live document adds nothing vital to their oeuvre. Then again, it takes nothing away. And that's the way they like it." **Rock CD**

"As 80s as Porsches, as unfashionable as Goth, Dire Straits rumble on, giving the punters what they want." **Vox**

"Knopfler does nothing with his songs other than deliver them – no new arrangements, no surprising diversions, no moments of musical transcendence. It's much like an overly expensive tour book... likely, before long, to be lost at the bottom of a box." **Q**

DURAN DURAN
Duran Duran (Parlophone)

"So they were better than the Spandaus after all..." **Select**

"...you're led to the unavoidable conclusion that this has distinguished itself as the worst album to be inflicted on the public since Kajagoogoo hung up their boots." **Rock CD**

IAN DURY
The Bus Driver's Prayer & Other Stories (Demon)

"Always more Vaudeville than rock 'n' roll, there is a quality to Ian Dury's writing which seems as timely now as it did during his *New Boots And Panties* heyday. The 'Ian Dury For Poet Laureate' campaign starts here." **Select**

"A dozen years on from his last good album, *Laughter*, this is true Dury, untrammelled and unmitigated. A quip, a laugh, a kick in the bollocks: this is exactly the kind of hard entertainment he's always striven for." **Q**

"If nothing else, *The Bus Driver* affirms that Dury is a national treasure and should have a preservation order slapped on him immediately!" **NME**

BOB DYLAN
Good As I Been To You (Columbia)

"There is a sense of a circle being drawn, the light beginning to fade on an illustrious career. But the force of some of these performances belie the suggestion that this is the work of a man for whom things are coming to an end. The very opposite in fact. *Good As I Been To You* is the sound of Dylan looking forward to another new morning." **Melody Maker**

"...when he's not singing in Dylan Caricature Voice, a hammered-flat nasal drone, you're reminded of the plaintive and captivating wail

of his first acoustic outings: a pleasant experience." **Select**

"This month, the cover of Q Magazine asks 'What's So Great About Bob Dylan?'. On the evidence of this all-acoustic set of elderly folk songs, the answer is 'nothing'." **The Guardian**

808 STATE
Gorgeous (ZTT)

"Proudly assembled using hardly any 'real' instruments whatsoever, as the endless list of gadgets in the back of the accompanying booklet shows, *Gorgeous* is a smoothly impressive demonstration that 808 State may be surreptitiously usurping the ground previously occupied by New Order and Depeche Mode." **The Guardian**

"...the weaknesses of over-familiarity are fully apparent. All the old ingredients are here – depth, melody, mood – but at times they are just that: old. *Gorgeous* too often leaves you wanting more." **Select**

"Why does so much of the highest-technology music sound so boring? Take 808 State's latest album. Bland and anonymous, there's considerably less here than meets the ear..." **The Independent**

EMF
Stigma (Parlophone)

"Buy it, crank it up and dance around until your ears bleed. Just unplug the expectation circuits first." **Select**

"Sensationally, the stroppy combo have managed to make discernible strides in songwriting and overall conception. James Atkins sings like... well, like a singer, which not even the most star-struck devotee could have suspected he was." **The Guardian**

"James Atkins' vocal still sounds weak, perched atop this thundering mix, but that's the point." **Making Music**

"...the Mef have chosen to go rockier on their next venture. Chuck away your Nirvana records, boys, because this is an unbelievably hardcore album." **Smash Hits**

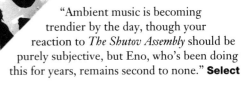

BRIAN ENO
Nerve Net (WEA)

"*Nerve Net* teases and twists through 12 distinctive tracks... the tunes explore a wide variety of musical landscapes." **Q**

"...fresh sonic ideas that are soothing, disturbing and, above all, accessible. A complete electric music for the mind and body for the 90s." **Select**

"The dalliances with World music and ambient noise of the intervening years coalesce into a dizzy and often dazzling mix of ethnic references, dub effects, eerie pulses and the sort of crazy funk you might expect a decade or so after *My Life In The Bush Of Ghosts*." **Vox**

BRIAN ENO
The Shutov Assembly (Opal)

"If further proof were needed that Eno is the undisputed master of his craft, then this gorgeous slab of unreal sublimity is it." **NME**

"The final product maps the other side of *Nerve Net*, slowing the pace and stripping back to a single idea – in contrast to its more commercial sibling's fidgeting and jerks with bizarre inspiration." **Vox**

"Ambient music is becoming trendier by the day, though your reaction to *The Shutov Assembly* should be purely subjective, but Eno, who's been doing this for years, remains second to none." **Select**

DONALD FAGEN
Kamakiriad (WEA)
See The Year in Review

THE FALL
The Infotainment Scam (Permanent)

"*The Infotainment Scam* is the most light-hearted Fall album ever, the concentrated vitriol of the past replaced by good-humoured piss-taking. The unique worldview and the pithy putdowns are still present and correct, but they're all the more effective for being delivered with a sly smile and a sprinkling of tangy, melodic sweetener." **Melody Maker**

"Off-kilter noises, feedback, backwards loops, synth flatulence, multi-tracked mumbling, out-of-control reverb, radio interference – your Fall album is infected with apparently random detail, while catchy, regal mainstream guitar and keyboard riffs sail through it like royalty on a press visit to bedlam." **Select**

"This is the closest that The Fall have yet come to carnival mood, and it is proof that terminal sourpuss Smith doesn't always need to take the piss. Fine music sometimes flows from hope and contentment." **Vox**

THE FARM
Love See No Colour (End Product/Columbia)

"It is, and no buts, a better record by far than *Spartacus* – which sounded fine under the Joe Bloggs reign of terror but has not aged gracefully. These songs are simply miles stronger..." **Select**

"Once upon a while ago The Farm used *Groovy Train* to hop aboard the gravy train. Now they're going nowhere." **Vox**

"The bustling, mechanical rhythm tracks have presumably been designed for all-night frugging, but the melodies are slight and repetitive, while the mix favours a blur of sound over clarity or crunch." **The Guardian**

BRYAN FERRY
Taxi (Virgin)

"Here, yet again, he irons the complexities and idiosyncrasies out of another selection of covers without breaking a sweat, for people who want to listen without breaking a sweat either." **The Independent**

"What *Taxi* consists of: Bryan staring dreamy-eyed into his record collection and then re-inventing it as the musical equivalent of a Vogue photo-shoot." **NME**

"There's no denying Ferry's knack for making the simplest songs sound vaguely sinister..." **Sky**

"Like all of Ferry's records, *Taxi* is exquisitely crafted and steeped in a kind of melancholy grandeur." **The Daily Telegraph**

TIM FINN
Before & After (Capitol)
"Now branching out again on his own, the former Split Enz main man has augmented the kind of tuneful, pert pop that Crowded House have patented with his own thirst for quirky story-telling and clever collaborations. The album gambols gently through a subtle range of styles and arrangements while retaining a strong sense of character..." **Q**

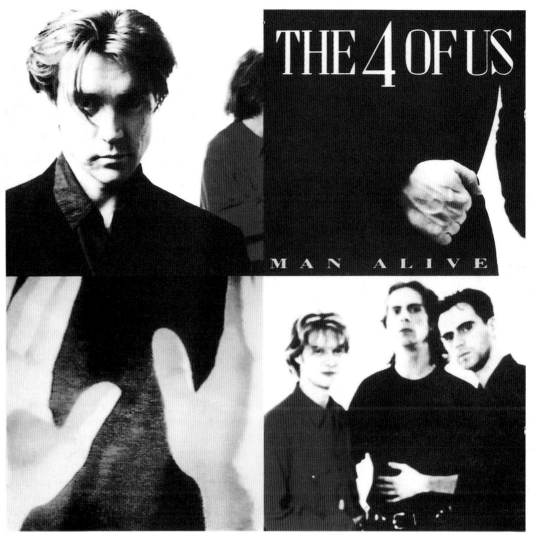

"The root problem this album will suffer is in grabbing the listener's attention...the album lacks a certain cohesion... It's worth the effort though. *Before And After* matures gracefully with every listen." **Vox**

FISHBONE
Give A Monkey A Brain And He'll Swear He's The Centre Of The Universe (Columbia)

"For all the lyrical fuss they kick up, they don't actually say much more than 'fuck this shit up'. And for all the musical styles they visit, they have no real identity. It's not even abstract, it's more like showing off." **NME**

"Fishbone skank on a dynamite fuse. They're exhilarating, dangerous and have no regard for their personal safety. The band to dance to when the ship's going down." **Melody Maker**

"Eventually Fishbone may well record a truly great record. But it won't sound anything like this." **Select**

THE 4 OF US
Man Alive (Columbia)

"*Man Alive* has spirit and vitality, unencumbered by bombastic Celtic rock ballast... a delicious, surprisingly diverting album." **Vox**

"A reckless abandon here is struggling to break free, but the corporate seatbelt is too tight." **Select**

"... confirmation that here is the best straight rock band to come out of Ireland in years." **Q**

THE FRANK & WALTERS
Trains, Boats & Planes (Go! Discs)

"For all of the lyrical disappointments, and the frustrating underachievement that is Edwyn Collins' production, *Trains, Boats And Planes* still haunts in the faintly scent of something different." **NME**

"The haircuts, the naivete, the gibberish and all that orange... if packets of Radion had guitars, wore Beatle wigs and were full of space-dust bon bons instead of washing powder, they'd be pretty much indistinguishable from The Frank And Walters." **Select**

"The Frank And Walters have tunes, they have words, they have chord sequences that make you go 'mmmmm'. And how can you resist a band with lines like 'What a hippy diddly crazy world'? Hummable humanity. Get it into your head." **Making Music**

ROBERT FRIPP/DAVID SYLVIAN
The First Day (Virgin)

"...the songs sound too contrived and riff-bound to allow either partner to shine. An experiment that probably shouldn't have been allowed out of the lab." **Q**

"...the best moments are the result of Fripp's transparent-sounding 'Frippertronic' style, glistening guitar loops sustained to infinity and layered like showers of diamonds. Sylvian meanwhile might have lost the visual fragility of his Japan years, but his voice is as emotionally amorphous as ever..."
The Independent

"...hovers dreamily into Eno-Fripp territory. What gives it Sylvian's signature, however, is the voice, and his willingness to follow a fascinating experiment through to its conclusion." **Vox**

g

PETER GABRIEL
Us (Virgin)
See: The Year in Review

GALLON DRUNK
From The Heart Of Town (Clawfist)

"*From The Heart Of Town* is a huge leap forwards. The rockabilly crooning, the Latin voodoo rhythms, the strategic blasts of feedback and silence now have a devastating power." **Select**

"At the height of the currently popular smiley-faced 70s revival, to sound like the Birthday Party is joltingly original. Gallon Drunk offer something feral, dark and potent." **Vox**

"Gallon Drunk's lasting achievement lies in how they've cast back to the pre-rock era, magnified those optimistic years into high melodrama and shot through a multitude of genres with their own punkish bravura and wicked humour." **NME**

BOB GELDOF
The Happy Club (Vertigo)

"Working with World Party's Karl Wallinger, Geldof has convinced himself that it's okay to dabble in diverse musical styles. Given that Bob actually seems to be revelling in the diversity, every attempt scores highly."
Rock CD

"Perhaps it's getting worn-out through use, but the Geldof voice is no longer what it was. It's a cruel irony, for in his efforts to slip the shackles of celebrity and re-establish himself as a working musician, the songs of Sir Bob have never been more interesting." **Q**

"Maybe it's time for Sir Bob to hang up his rock 'n' roll shoes and concentrate on a Breakfast TV career." **Vox**

h

HAPPY MONDAYS
...Yes Please! (Factory)

"...*Yes Please* is their morning-after album, with their Madchester glory days long gone. At least the band have recognised that there could be problems and have sought help in the shape of Tom Tom Clubbers Chris Frantz and Tina Weymouth, who have given the band a patina of crisp professionalism, which is probably the last thing they should have... too many tracks sound shapeless and hastily concocted. The only way is down, unfortunately."
The Guardian

"...*Yes Please* really is heartbreaking, because despite all the loathsome behaviour from the band's auto-destructive faction, a lot of people still want the Mondays to be as great as they should be. Maybe they will be again someday. Nevertheless, you have to suspect that at the moment this duff album is the least of Shaun Ryder's worries." **Select**

"Happy Mondays have always made music as lads not poets, but just as it seems they might finally have shambled and gambled an album too far, they come up with a clutch of cuts that restore your faith in all things grubby, grinning and gleeful...they've pulled it off again." **Q**

"...Shaun Ryder's lyrics are better than ever ('It took more than one man to change my name to Shanghai Lily' he croaks). Q. 'What is he on?' A. 'Everything' – allegedly."
Smash Hits

DEBORAH HARRY
Debravation (Chrysalis)

"A plethora of producers lends the album a disparate, crazy paving style which backfires badly; intended to show off her versatility, what it actually shows is in how many different ways she can be terrible." **The Independent**

"When it comes to female pop singers, it certainly beats most of the opposition. I don't know about you, but I've had it up to here with "tasteful", "cool" and "stylish" albums from your Micas, Dinas and Janets. *Debravation* is by turns cheap, trashy, tacky, funny, patchy and confused – and all the better for it." **Today**

"...the witching voice is intact, and *Debravation* shows it off better than any of her post-Blondie efforts, but the productions accorded Harry's latest collection of coitally inclined songs are still a decidedly mixed bunch." **The Observer**

hothouse flowers
songs from the rain

SOPHIE B. HAWKINS
Tongues & Tails (Columbia)

"What they call a 'priority act' in the record industry, semi-Bohemian New Yorker Sophie B Hawkins's debut nudges originality while remaining rooted in the traditional pop/rock concoctions of chart-toppers past and present... her selling point is a general air of sensual desire." **Q**

"It's to Sophie Hawkins' credit that she never loses sight of the power of a good melody, however sophisticated the song-structures – and her vocals throughout crackle with a passion..." **Vox**

HOTHOUSE FLOWERS
Songs From The Rain (London)

"The band nails down the song arrangements with a touch more firmness and overall precision than in the past, but generally they stick to what has become a clearly defined stylistic path. The only danger is that some people who think they have heard it all before may fail to give this beautiful album the close attention it so richly repays." **The Times**

"...it'll probably go down as their most consistent and satisfying effort to date. If somebody's got to do the cheerleading for us, these five Irishmen are still better equipped than most." **Q**

"Slickly produced by Stewart Levine (Simply Red), it has the right kind of sheen to attract some of Hucknall's fans, although to say it had enough sparkle for the Flowers to reach the *Stars* would be overstating the case." **Vox**

HOUSE OF LOVE
Audience With The Mind (Fontana)

"... an exercise in exorcism, a working out of neuroses, a case study in isolation. Raw and cynical in tone, with vocals sneering where they once cajoled... it's less Creation, more Armageddon. With guitars." **Melody Maker**

"*Audience With The Mind* finds Chadwick and band in calm repose. For the 1993 House Of Love there are no Joneses to keep up with." **Vox**

"Thoroughly back on the beam, The House Of Love have for the first time hitched good commerce to great music, and the marriage is built to last. Fans will love it, sceptics can only be impressed." **Select**

BILLY IDOL
Cyberpunk (Chrysalis)

"It'd be great to say that this was rock 'n' roll built by robots, a vision of how pop will be in the year 2077. But it's just not that interesting." **NME**

"...half of these tracks are turgid rockers of the highest order, and all the cyberpunk fantasies in the world won't make up for lyrics like '*It's the age of destruction in a world of corruption*'." **Vox**

"Cyberspace has been brilliantly defined as where you are when you're on the phone. *Cyberpunk* is the kind of album you could probably write during that phone call." **Select**

INSPIRAL CARPETS
Revenge Of The Goldfish (Mute)

"Post-baggy, post-shoegazing and post-grunge, *Revenge* puts The Inspirals in pole position among their various washed-out, self-imploding or missing-in-action Madchester peers." **Select**

"If there's a problem, it's with the lyrics, which sound like they were knocked out in the lavatory at the studio." **Rock CD**

"...too much goes in one ear and out the other. It also suffers from the dreaded 'lush production' and Boon's organ dominates, which is fine on the singles but wears thin over 40 minutes." **Making Music**

INXS
Welcome To Wherever You Are (Mercury)

"*Welcome To Wherever You Are* stands in relation to the rest of INXS's portfolio at much the same point as *Achtung Baby* does to the U2 canon, and indeed both albums mark a similar stage of development in their respective careers. INXS are hardly in the league of U2, but this album is a welcome and generous step in the right direction." **Q**

"Jolly horn-blowin' scarf-wavers with curious noises like vocals in a hose-pipe, posh blokes sampled off the radio and floaty keyboards in the ether. Gets a bit glum at times, of course, but mainly it's thinker's rock for gurls (much better than the usual buffoon's rock for the blokes)." **Smash Hits**

"INXS show little sign of progression, which is no big deal to them. They still do this stadium stuff better and more arrogantly than the rest. To plough on in this vein for another ten years won't upset the fans." **Select**

"As pop, *Welcome To Wherever You Are* isn't as perfect as Bolan or Abba, but Hutch would be the perfect pop star if only he'd get back together with Kylie." **Vox**

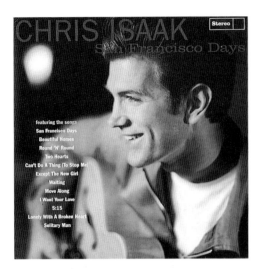

CHRIS ISAAK
San Francisco Days (WEA)

"Once again, Isaak's music is cool, hunky and tinted blue, though greatness has still not been thrust upon him. Quite nice if you want some unabashed retro in your life." **Sky**

"There are no impressive metaphors or clever tricks to hide behind, and so when he fails his songs can appear very mundane indeed. But when he succeeds – as he does on about half of this latest album – the result is majestic." **The Independent**

"...*San Francisco Days* is full of irresistible pop songs laced with a curious, almost ironic, melancholy." **Q**

JANET JACKSON
Janet. (Virgin)

"While her brother loops the loop on Planet Pepsi, it's hard to imagine the spotlight ever shifting to his sassy sis, but this modern hunk of an album should redress some of the balance." **NME**

"Despite the predictable production moves of Jam and Lewis on some songs, it was good for me. The earth moved; watch the units shift." **Vox**

"*Janet.* will please most people because it is crammed with the sort of tender joyous pop music that lingers long after smarter records have been forgotten." **The Daily Telegraph**

"Dammit, Janet! The last Jackson hero(ine) has carried peacock feathers to the dance. Holier than Mahalia." **Melody Maker**

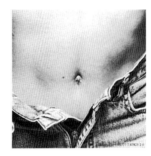

MICK JAGGER
Wandering Spirit (Atlantic)
See The Year in Review

WENDY JAMES
Now Ain't The Time For Your Tears (MCA)

"After the embarrassing fiasco of Transvision Vamp's unreleased third album, our Wendy romps back into view with a feisty collection of songs written specially for her by Elvis Costello." **Esquire**

"... Elvis' sneering bitterness isn't so unpalatable in someone else's mouth. And Wendy does bring to the songs a bruised diva's bar-room allure." **Select**

"... James herself is gloriously ill-equipped for the job, stumbling awkwardly round the phrases and experiencing great difficulty in hitting and holding the right notes." **The Independent**

THE JAYHAWKS
Hollywood Town Hall (Def American)

"They're from Minneapolis – it's worth mentioning because they sound like they're from way down South, where the rattlesnakes end up as neck-ties and where you get over losing your lover with a few tumblers of whisky and a good ol' country rock band, a band rather like the Jayhawks, if possible." **Select**

"The Jayhawks combine an appreciation of the best country rock tradition (Neil Young, Bob Dylan et al), with a blast of youthful passion.

Vocalist Mark Olson has a biting authentic rasp while guitarist Gary Louris plays with tremendous controlled aggression..." **The Times**

"There's a lot of jingly-jangly electric guitar, plenty of power, direct lyrics and excellent playing. Throw in at least six top-notch songs and you're talking about a band who could easily outsell REM given the right breaks." **Rock CD**

JELLYFISH
Spilt Milk (Virgin)

"Our heroes are entranced with childhood trivia – joining fan clubs, drinking Kool-Aid, worshipping girls from afar – but the fervour of their meditations makes something oddly profound out of hokey scenarios. Jellyfish might be funny but they're well beyond a joke." **Q**

"Now their pop comes bedecked with baubles and trinkets, garbed in mile-deep production and mile-wide orchestral and choral excess." **Vox**

"...this is a highly entertaining album which suggests that these Smurfs From Hell might just be the band to put the shang back in shang-a-lang-a-ding-dong." **Rock CD**

THE JESUS AND MARY CHAIN
Sound Of Speed (Blanco Y Negro)

"There is little doubt that The Jesus And Mary Chain are on something of a roll. If further proof were needed, *Sound Of Speed* provides it in spades, clubs and a selection of exotic trumps too diseased to even think about." **Select**

"... these two non-singers wanly aspire to the rich euphony of Brian Wilson. Though the Reed Brothers have extended their repertoire of racket to include unplugged guitar, their singing expresses only studied, sneering boredom..." **Q**

"The top ten hits might be few and far between, but the best, most twisted songs on display show that the aspirations here are to longevity and changing the shape of the musical map, rather than the cheap 'n' quick thrills and premature ejaculations of passing success. How many other current groups can make a compilation of A-sides, alternative takes, B-sides and cover versions actually worth enquiring about?" **NME**

JESUS JONES
Perverse (Food/EMI)

"By contemporary standards of mediocrity this is powerful stuff, but they aren't doing anything here that they didn't do at least as well on their first two albums. The Joneses make a big deal out of being 'different', but it sounds like they're playing safe."
The Guardian

"...despite the skip-load of technology which has been poured into *Perverse*, it doesn't sound dramatically different from the Jones' past efforts. Over the general sense of high-speed urgency, guitars crack and ricochet, sequencers blip, bass things go 'omp' and there are loads of nice vocal harmonies too." **Sky**

"...the true precursor of Jesus Jones is probably early Roxy Music, with its classicism bent into new, fantastic shapes by its futuristic zeal. If Edwards were a bit more louche and ironic, there'd be little to separate them."
The Independent

BILLY JOEL
River Of Dream (Columbia)

"Billy Joel is 42 years old, rich, happy and successful, and should have been grazing quietly in Barry Manilow country by now. Obviously no-one has told him." **Vox**

"From the evidence of *River of Dreams*, Billy's view of the world seems to be, in so many words, that its a terrible place really, but bearable if you manage to snare yourself a fantastic looking model to live with..."
The Independent

"Ex Bronx-boxer Billy Joel's raging bull tendencies feed this album. Perhaps with a former manager in his mind's eye, Joel throws words like punches. He gets through by sheer force of personality. He's a MOR ball of fire." **Q**

"...they make unfathomable 'noise' records with wonky vocals, buzzing noises and lyrics about how crap fame is. They also don't make particularly memorable LPs. Stick to the singles." **Smash Hits**

ELTON JOHN
The One (Rocket)

"...as usual in the Elton John canon of 30-odd albums, most of the tracks bespeak nothing brighter than the multi-millioned duo's unremitting toil – they are dust-caked miners for the heart of gold, not natural-born geniuses." **Q**

"With an average length of five minutes plus, all the songs would have benefited from savage trimming. As would the fringe." **Vox**

THE KINKS
Phobia (Columbia)

"Ray Davies' Kinks may be over 20 years past their peak but they still have their moments. Sadly, the band opt for an AOR production which, while it might shift units in the States, lessens the impact of some powerful songwriting." **Select**

"Though Davies sometimes sounds like a listed building – an archaism that we shouldn't knock down – he's still got the necessary guile. Ignore the chaff, parts of *Phobia*, at least, turn misery into an art form." **Vox**

"Ray Davies might think he's engaged on a spiritual quest, others will hear a losing battle with writer's block. Many fans would rather they didn't fight it out in public." **Q**

LENNY KRAVITZ
Are You Gonna Go My Way? (Virgin)
See The Year in Review

l

DANIEL LANOIS
For The Beauty Of Wynona (WEA)

"*Wynona* has the power of great fiction – uncertain but optimistic as it deals with nakedly personal stuff in often startling imagery – love in chains, abducted brides and dead trains – while offering sympathy to the downtrodden and glimpses into rural French Canada." **Q**

"On the whole, the album, which focuses on the small Canadian town of Wynona near where he grew up, is darker in tone than *Acadie*. Overall, there's much to enjoy... although Lanois' voice remains the weakest link in his design." **The Independent**

"He sounds like Paul Simon manque: small, sweet and desperately poetic. No wonder Canada is so famous for its waffle." **Vox**

LEMONHEADS
It's A Shame About Ray (Atlantic)

"You get a bit weary of albums that are obviously worked to death; you long for someone to go, 'OK, here's a bunch of songs I've just written, let's record them'. That's what it sounds like here..." **Making Music**

"The 12 tracks pass in a blistering, acoustic rush: throwaway and totally addictive. Get it before the summer's out." **Vox**

"With Lemonheads' former grunge excesses now streamlined, this album thrills at neighbourhood-waking volume." **Q**

THE LEMON TREES
Open Book (Oxygen)

"A worrying insight into what major record companies think makes an exciting new band. Sad, really." **Select**

"The songs on *Open Book* are all pop single length, have beginnings, middle-eights and catchy choruses – and all bear familiar-sounding hooklines." **Vox**

"*Open Book* is an exuberant collection of retro-pop gems, simply recorded with gameful gusto and full of natty ideas." **Q**

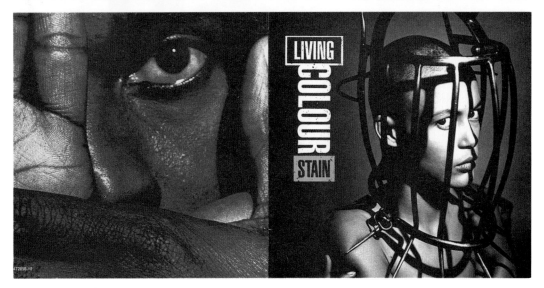

LITTLE ANGELS
Jam (Polydor)

"Certainly their best album to date, *Jam* is the perfect addition to any collection that's propped up with rock's pop purveyors, from Def Leppard to Bon Jovi. Whether it's enough of a quantum leap to completely cross them over remains debatable." **Q**

"Little Angels keep well away from Status Quo land and just play around in Extreme's sandpit when it comes to rockin'. An album packed to the rafters with noise, energy and hair."
Smash Hits

"...they follow in the footsteps of their fellow northerners, Def Leppard, peddling a carefully crafted amalgam of soft metal and pop. But occasionally, they strap on the acoustic guitars and drift into the tough-guys-can-be-sensitive-too mode that is the calling card of Extreme or Del Amitri." **The Times**

LIVING COLOUR
Stain (Epic)

"The cover of *Stain* is printed beneath red plastic, a neat metaphor for the bloody emotions in which it deals. The central image of slavery imposed on those too weak to defend themselves pervades every track. Living Colour feel the pain, really get it to work, then use that anger for everything it's worth."
Melody Maker

"While Hothouse Flowers and Lenny Kravitz have returned to the fray none the worse for having been away, Living Colour have not been so lucky. Their unyielding brand of political-thrash metal was par for the course at the time of their last album... it sounds, unintentionally, rather old-fashioned."
The Times

"...this album is for the benefit of fellow musos rather than fans, designed to showcase the band's versatility rather than make an ear-pleasing sound." **The Independent**

PAUL McCARTNEY
Off The Ground (Parlophone)

"Though most of *Off The Ground* is pleasantly innocuous, melodic pop tunes and trite lyrical diatribes against vivisection or in favour of everybody being friends, there is enough variegated inspiration and craft to tip the balance in its favour." **The Independent**

"Recorded live in the studio, McCartney and his band make a polite guitar and keyboard sound that lacks even a modicum of punch. Rock 'n' roll for the grandparental generation." **The Times**

"Nobody expects rigour from McCartney but once again slackness is endemic... expensively and carefully wrought fluff, flawed by its lack of what George Bush calls 'the vision thing'." **Q**

"The disc treats itself to a leisurely fadeout over which McCartney urges us all to become 'cosmically conscious'. If I had as much money as him, I'd buy the cosmos and have done with it. However honourable, Planet McCartney bears no relation to life as most know it."
The Guardian

MARIA McKEE
You Gotta Sin To Get Saved (Geffen)

"The LP's forte is shoulder-heaving, wrenched ballads (ouch!), sepia laments, though McKee never sounds truly wracked. It's not enough. We're looking for the world here."
Melody Maker

"Nothing on McKee's second solo album

equals the sobbing bathos of *Show Me Heaven*, the power ballad that topped the singles chart for four weeks in 1990. Most of the ten country-rock tunes lack a certain je ne sais quoi in the personality department."
The Guardian

"Grungesters will probably hate this, but for those of us who are not hell-bent on morbid introspection, *You Gotta Sin To Get Saved* is a breath of fresh air." **Making Music**

IAN McNABB
Truth & Beauty (This Way Up)

He's a dreamer, an unashamed one, and when you've got dreams as kaleidoscopic as these... This is a lovely record, a true one-off. REM maniacs, please take a chance." **Select**

Truth And Beauty isn't Ian McNabb's great masterpiece by any means. That is still to come. But for those of us who believe in this guy's songwriting flair and warm-hearted opinions, it's a much welcome return."
Melody Maker

"...McNabb has completely regained his knack for constructing literate songs that poke the listener in the gut and linger persistently in the memory." **Rock CD**

MADNESS
Madstock (Go! Discs)

"It sounds just like a jukebox playing Madness records, with a bit of crowd noise overdubbed on top, prompting the suspicion that perhaps not every note the faithful heard that weekend was made by live musicians. It's high time the Madness back catalogue was retired to the great loony bin in the sky." **Sky**

"The wonder of Madstock was that instead of trading on affectionate memories, Madness honoured them, and this LP does too." **Select**

"...there are those fun-filled festive shows to look forward to. Hey, doesn't Gary Glitter do fun-filled festive shows too? The past is catching up with us." **Vox**

MADONNA
Erotica (Maverick/Sire)

"When *Erotica* the album is good – ie when it's funny, original, lively and, yes, sexy – it's about as good as the modern media event gets. Because this is a media event in a way that pop records never were once upon a time. You've seen the pictures, you've wondered whether you can afford the £25 for the book (for your own personal use, of course). Now hear the accompanying soundtrack." **NME**

"*Erotica* has been expertly designed to hit a dance/rave audience while achieving mainstream pop crossover. But efficiency has been at the expense of joie de vivre. Perhaps Madonna doesn't even like sex very much. It's a job, though." **The Guardian**

"You didn't get inside her pants, though it felt like you had her from every angle, but when the teasing subsided you got a glimpse of the real Madonna." **Vox**

"Madonna mixed up? The signs are that, once she's popped her kit back on and realised we like her for herself, it'll all turn out nicely." **Q**

MANIC STREET PREACHERS
Gold Against The Soul (Columbia)

"The Manics are in this far without a map – now that all their bedroom manifestos have been realised, they don't know what's required of them." **NME**

"*Gold Against The Soul* crystallises all that adolescent turmoil. In sound and sentiment, it's no less than the spiritual heir to *Appetite For Destruction*." **Melody Maker**

"The heroic vocal and fuzzed-up guitar emulate your Bon Jovis so perfectly that you suspect parody, except that the singer's newly-grown beard says otherwise." **The Guardian**

JOHN MARTYN
Couldn't Love You More (Permanent)

"There are moments when this could be a Chris Rea record. There are moments when he outdoes Van Morrison with jazzy Celtic soul. This is the aural equivalent of one of those days when it's about to rain but never quite gets around to it." **Rock CD**

"Cushioned on smoothly upholstered rhythms and haloed by the smokiest winebar saxophone, Martyn sounds like he's doing his damnedest to plug into the Simply Red fan-base. And he's doing it in the most eco-friendly way: by recycling highlights of his own back catalogue in new, luxury versions." **Q**

BRIAN MAY
Back To The Light (Parlophone)

"Maybe in his will Freddie Mercury left Brian May his vocal chords, because here on May's debut solo LP he sounds unnervingly like King Fred." **Select**

EROTICA
This version contains language that some people might find offensive

Erotica Madonna

"...he is too frequently eclipsed by the awe-inspiring arrangements, where Freddie would have flown high above them." **Vox**

"...May was always an important behind-the-scenes figure, his input on the Queen sound and recording sessions more than vital. Anyone who thought Queen was a one-man band is way off the mark." **Rock CD**

MEGADETH
Countdown To Extinction (Capitol)

"The trouble is it's not quite... y'know... out there. Mustaine's voice has always been a problem and the laughable 'Rockschool' predictability of some of the riffs spoils things. After five albums you have to wonder if they'll ever get there." **Select**

"...if Metallica whetted your appetite for power, aggression and volume with attitude, Megadeth will take you one louder." **Q**

"These days he is off drugs, and Megadeth's music, like Metallica's, is slower and more melodic. Mustaine can still play a mean riff, but *Countdown To Extinction* rarely rises above average." **Vox**

MIDNIGHT OIL
Earth & Sun & Moon (Columbia)

"Recorded 'virtually live', the album has a beguiling neo-60s feel, bolstered by a frisson of swirly psychedelia... Ultimately, it's the Oils' winning way with a chorus which prevails..." **Q**

"Peter Garrett's eco-rock

posse sound tired and somewhat directionless on this, their ninth album." **Vox**

"Never one to mince his words, Peter Garrett has always worn his heart on his sleeve. However, this time, Australia's leading agit rockers have made an album where all the tunes are as strong and impassioned as the sentiment expressed within." **Rock CD**

STEVE MILLER
Wide River (Polydor)

"Unfortunately for his real fans, Miller has been discovered by the AOR-meets-MTV generation and turned into a nostalgia peddler. *Wide River* should be given a wide berth; Miller lite is dishwater weak." **Vox**

"Miller's first album since 1988, a silence only broken by the little matter of an international Number One three years ago with a re-released *The Joker*. Nothing here is fated to be that successful, but from time to time *Wide River* does show Miller's knack for skilful arrangements and simple hooks." **Q**

MORRISSEY
Your Arsenal (HMV)

"The Smiths split up five years ago. The signs are that, at long last, Morrissey is getting over it." **Select**

"Whether *Your Arsenal* is Morrissey's final flourish, or the first sign of a powerful new direction, remains to be seen, but it is

undoubtedly a pleasing work from a writer who, these days, irritates and inspires in equal measure." **Vox**

"He experiments further with the outmoded rockabilly he and his band seem so keen on, adding glam rock punches alongside the obligatory gloom and despondency. Intriguing but patchy." **Smash Hits**

"*Your Arsenal* is his best solo work yet and easily stands comparison with the best of The Smiths." **Q**

MORRISSEY
Beethoven Was Deaf (HMV)

"'Thank you, I love you, goodbye,' he tells the French at the end. He sounds delighted, you should be too. This album captures Morrissey at his most audacious, ingenious and abandoned." **Rock CD**

"All that's missing is a touch of danger, of devil, of the unexpected. The crowd sound like they're having the original bon temps. Robbed of the sight of the most engaging torso in rock, the delights for the listener are proportionally less." **Q**

"Perhaps a declaration of rights would be expecting too much, but if not Morrissey, who else is there to believe in?" **Vox**

"Beethoven was indeed deaf, and, halfway through this record, how I envied him." **Melody Maker**

VAN MORRISON
Too Long In Exile (Polydor)

"*Too Long In Exile* represents a resounding return to form and it settles for the blues. Never has one man's regression therapy

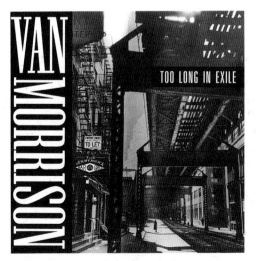

sounded this exhilarating. And if it ain't curing his blues, it's sure making the rest of the world feel a whole lot better." **Melody Maker**

"God help anyone who suggests that the album might benefit from some levity (a bit of rapping, perhaps, or a tuba solo). Needless to say this new album doesn't exactly torment the humour bugs. Nice album cover, but it's difficult to shake the feeling that you're meant to listen in reverential silence." **The Guardian**

"If his last few albums have suggested a performer settling into a contemplative and mellow mid-life, *Too Long In Exile* works as a vivid reappraisal of earlier influences, a celebration of his blues and jazz roots."
The Daily Telegraph

MUDHONEY
Piece Of Cake (Reprise)

"The Muds don't have the nervy poppiness of Pearl Jam, but instead they like to create a feedback-crazed heads-down charge. Noisy but nice..." **Sky**

"*Piece Of Cake* has a plaything quality running through it: a record to be cranked up loud, hit with a hammer – but never really forgotten."
NME

"Mudhoney drag the joke out over 17 tracks, of which four are just a few seconds of noise... While it's tempting to give Mudhoney the benefit of the doubt, *Piece Of Cake* should be treated with extreme caution." **Metal CD**

n

NED'S ATOMIC DUSTBIN
Are You Normal? (Sony)

"That *Are You Normal?* sounds more like a band's greatest hits collection than just their second album has everything to do with fine songwriting and virtually nothing to do with a propensity for playing seven gigs before teatime." **Select**

"...denuded of the energy crackle of their gigs, *Are You Normal?* is a limply-unaffecting listen." **Vox**

"This is fresh, frenzied and the perfect soundtrack for music festival regulars to practise stage-diving techniques." **Rock CD**

AARON NEVILLE
The Grand Tour (A&M)

"The trademark shivering warble is much in evidence, but the greatest Neville Brother sounds uninspired by the material... Neville needs a quirky producer like Don Was or Daniel Lanois to drag him from the middle of the road, find some real songs and bring out his soul." **Q**

"*The Grand Tour* is less beguiling than his last solo album, *Warm Your Heart,* and less varied than the cosmopolitan mixture of styles he records with the Nevilles." **Vox**

NEW ORDER
Republic (London)

"This record is within shouting distance of greatness. It is dance music that doesn't have its head in the clouds, pop music with a brain. On *Republic,* New Order sound miserable as sin. It suits them." **The Daily Telegraph**

"...you'd have thought it impossible for New Order to return without making sorry spectacles of themselves, but they can keep you both weightless in space and fully-anchored to

the ground on this showing... Rediscover them." **NME**

"New Order albums tend to creep up on a listener slowly, gradually seducing and exciting. *Republic* has been spinning away for three days now and, already, it suggests that New Order have moved to an even higher plateau. Marvellous in the extreme." **Rock CD**

"...the album does miss the dance tracks they've come up with in the past, leaving them sounding like easy-listening for the right-on." **Smash Hits**

NINE INCH NAILS
Broken (Island)

"*Broken* shows all the signs that Trent Reznor has shaken off the shackles of influence and found his own suitably idiosyncratic niche." **NME**

"You can't fake something like this – like a harrowing rape account, it's an intensely vicious and shocking 30 minutes. *Broken* is unremitting and superlatively brilliant." **Making Music**

"*Broken* may border on the unlistenable, but there's something here worth investigating." **Metal CD**

NIRVANA
Incesticide (Geffen)
See The Year in Review

SINEAD O'CONNOR
Am I Not Your Girl? (Chrysalis)

"The arrangements work well enough, featuring a brash and blowsy horn section and a rhythm section which has big-band bop deftly nailed down. Miserably, however, Sinead consistently fails to take the measure of the material." **The Guardian**

"A brave attempt that doesn't quite cut it. But overall the orchestral arrangements nicely embellish her still folksy-sounding vocals, all adding up to an album that almost succeeds." **Rock CD**

"...the real disappointment is that too often she mistakes restraint for subtlety. On virtually every track she is produced down to a barely audible whisper." **Q**

MIKE OLDFIELD
Tubular Bells II (WEA)

"...whatever goes into producer Trevor Horn's studio fairy-dust, it makes your record-player at home sound like a million dollars. This time, audiophiles will not be able to beef about a 100 hertz mains hum spoiling this pristine recording. That's progress – just about the only 'progress' you will find two decades on from that original zenith of progressive rock." **Q**

"Hi-fi buffs could no doubt indulge in hours of textual analysis of versions one or two. Others should be warned that beyond the arguable appeal of the original, this is music for train spotters." **Vox**

OMD
Liberator (Virgin)

"A month or two back, the quality press was full of journalistic fogies wringing their word processors in despair at the death of 'real' pop music. *Liberator* rams the doom merchants' words straight back down their throats." **Vox**

"If nothing else, *Liberator* shows that OMD songwriter/curator Andy McCluskey can still

turn out a catchy tune without so much as rumpling his cardigan. If the tunes here sound familiar, maybe it's because much of today's dance-pop is descended from OMD's early sound. It's really not bad." **The Guardian**

"OMD are back, and they're pretty much as they left us in 1990. These sleek, shiny songs hark back to their 80s heyday. Pleasant, disposable stuff." **Select**

THE ORB
UfOrb (Big Life)

"It sounds like a homemade soundtrack from a DIY sci-fi movie... can't see how this would be of any earthly use to man or beast. Apart from the fact that it is quite handy for testing the stereo picture in your headphones." **Sky**

"...explorations of sounds and feelings take up the rest of the LP in The Orb's attractive style – sometimes floating, sometimes powering on, mixing beats and rhythms with soundscapes and sound effects..." **Q**

OZRIC TENTACLES
Jurassic Shift (Dovetail)

"In 1976, this type of thing was top of the corporate rock agenda, seemingly force-fed to a nation by sandal-wearing men with pony-tails. It was used to shut out the alternative. Now, in 1993, this soaring, rambling, grandiloquent noise is about as alternative as you can get." **Melody Maker**

"*Jurassic Shift* would fall by the travelling wayside were it not for the variety of the ingredients and the way they're mixed. Bubble and squeak new age synths, crunchy guitars and funky bass lines – something for everyone." **Vox**

ON
O

"...Ozric Tentacles would have to be more resolved than their carefully hippified presentation suggests, or they'd never have survived a decade and five albums." **Q**

p

ROBERT PALMER
Ridin' High (EMI)

"*Ridin' High* finds Batley's most distinguished crooner singing a bunch of 'standards'. In this post-modern wilderness, it's impossible to sing them in the way Bing or Frank did, but Palmer knows his way around the material, and performs it sympathetically enough to make this more than an in-joke." **The Guardian**

"Hernia-inducingly painful though it is to admit, this set of big band torch songs from the eternal smoothie is not that bad." **Select**

"...Bob pinching Sinatra classics and singing them pretty well. Pleasantly tongue-in-cheek, if not exactly cutting-edge stuff..." **Sky**

PERE UBU
The Story Of My Life (Fontana)

"...pioneers of industrial shuffle-funk and fragmented, factory-floor lyricism. But Thomas and his grey-templed team are beginning to sound quaintly nostalgic and somewhat lost." **NME**

"...their tenth LP proper is typical of their work: amazing, galumphing, creepy, sad, occasionally very poppy. Ubu never make unjust demands on one's emotions, leavening pain with humour." **The Independent**

PJ HARVEY
Rid Of Me (Island)

"Polly Harvey is, without doubt, a compelling, powerful songwriter and performer. *Rid Of Me* will not be her best album, but it feeds the myth, builds her fledgling power and satisfies for now." **NME**

"...someone seems to have forgotten to tell them that a good album requires good songs. *Rid Of Me* consists of 14 tracks, most of which are constructed to the same formula: chugging guitar and small voice exploding into an ear-splitting cacophony." **Making Music**

"With *Rid Of Me*, Harvey seems to have shifted emphasis and gone on the offensive. The rawness of the music, which previously smacked of inexperience rather than intent, is now both brutal and vindictive." **Vox**

"This is an album which will be showered with knee-jerk praise and bought, initially, in substantial quantities. But don't be surprised if in six months time you find it sitting at the bottom of a pile that's hardly been played at all." **Q**

ROBERT PLANT
Fate Of Nations (Fontana)

"Robert Plant hasn't changed his style much. *Fate Of Nations* sounds smooth but signifies little. They'll love it at Kensington Market." **Vox**

"...the venerable vocalist's most ambitiously constructed album to date: loud, proud and positive proof that he's one of the few 70s survivors with his marbles intact. Long may his trousers tremble." **Q**

PM DAWN
The Bliss Album..? (Gee Street)

"Like all great vocal groups, from The Beach Boys to the Temptations, PM Dawn have their own distinctive harmonic formula. But after two long LPs... the formula is starting to get a little too familiar." **The Independent**

"...right now, after Rodney King, the LA riots,

Ice T's battle with Warners and Malcolm X, this just seems like a whiff of air-freshener in a pervading atmosphere of bullshit." **Select**

"Pop rap passes that 'difficult' second album test. Just." **The Face**

"They have been called hippies, loonies and many other names. But right now nobody is making better records than PM Dawn." **The Daily Telegraph**

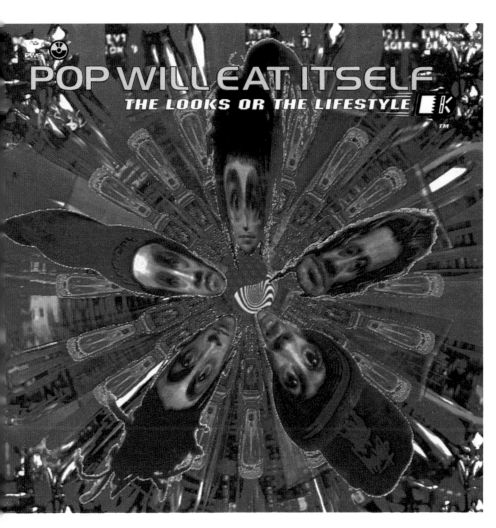

POP WILL EAT ITSELF
The Looks Or The Lifestyle (RCA)

"The lifeless, technological comedy of the last two LPs is replaced by the head-on collision of man and machine, creativity and Atari, which first caught our attention with *Box Frenzy*. Poppies say Grrr again." **Select**

"The Poppies' fourth LP finds them in familiar territory, mixing bad-assed dancefloor attitude with a self-deprecating bar-room wit that instantly betrays their Stourbridge roots." **Vox**

"Their time may never really have come, but Pop Will Eat Itself still sound like no other group." **Q**

PORNO FOR PYROS
Porno For Pyros (WEA)

"Much is constructed within the dub and slappy rhythms Farrell's always been so fond of, at the risk of alienating his more blinkered metal followers (hurrah!)... Like some wide-eyed, global village idiot, Perry Farrell is on the edge, whether he knows it or not."
Melody Maker

"No doubt things'll come together on future albums, but after a lot of effort and positive bias, this one's merely get-into-able and fairly sexy. Judging by the high criteria Farrell has set for himself, you have to admit, it's a let-down." **Select**

"...fans pining for Jane's Addiction will be pleased to hear that the solo Farrell is proceeding along much the same lines. In other words, he still sings like an ostrich caught on a barbed-wire fence, and his music is still based on a kind of hypertense scuzz-funk..." **Sky**

"Porno For Pyros take off exactly where Jane's Addiction left off and while their progressive garage rock is occasionally a little too predictable, Farrell's performance reinstates him not as Lollapalooza's wise elder statesman but as its wild and irresponsible spirit. May he never mature." **Q**

PRINCE & THE NEW POWER GENERATION
Symbol (Paisley Park/Warner Bros)

"All that's missing is a sense that Prince has anything much to sing about, beyond the threadbare fare of sex and partying. Allegedly, the album is a 'rock soap opera' recounting 'the relationship between a pop superstar and the princess of a fictional Middle Eastern kingdom', but there's scant evidence of this in the lyrics." **The Guardian**

"This album might have been applauded if it came from a more anonymous group, but for Prince that's not an adequate excuse... this particular genius must try harder." **Rock CD**

"If impersonation and parody is what the concept is all about, fine. But Prince should be more aware of how self-mimicry shows up the failing of the real thing." **Select**

"It's overlong and drags a bit in the middle, but represents a massive workload and a fearsome talent. The need to stress his own abilities (musical and otherwise) seems unnecessary, but I guess even Renaissance sex gods have their failings." **Making Music**

PUBLIC ENEMY
Greatest Misses (Columbia)

"*Greatest Misses* is a fine compilation album, so don't come to it expecting another *Black Planet*. At this time, it's probably the only record Public Enemy could, or should, have made." **NME**

"As tough as ever, they punch to the gut of everything they hate – namely, racism and abuse of power. Public Enemy take no prisoners. Whatever you think of them, you can't shut 'em down." **Smash Hits**

"More tuff stuff from rap's mission control. Fierce, funky, prescient and political." **I-D**

RADIOHEAD
Pablo Honey (Parlophone)

"They roam through shoegazing and punk and end up in bed with... none of them. Told you they weren't fashionable." **Select**

"Ultimately, *Pablo Honey* flounders on a misconceived desire to be something rather more than the sum of its parts." **Vox**

"The vigour of Radiohead live loses a great deal of fun in translation to plastic, but the best bits rival Nirvana, Dinosaur Jr and even the mighty Sugar." **Q**

GERRY RAFFERTY
On A Wing & A Prayer (A&M)

"Rafferty's lugubrious delivery, overlong arrangements and swathes of unnecessary strings combine to make everything sound much of a muchness. Fine for fans but no hits and little he hasn't done better before." **Q**

"A welcome return for a class act... a textbook example of the songwriting art which should provide Undercover with more material worth butchering in the years ahead." **Vox**

RAMONES
Mondo Bizarro (Chrysalis)

"They sing of which they know, and if it's something you don't want to hear, they play it fast enough to get it over with. Funny. Fast. Fabulous." **Select**

"For three-chord wonders who became famous over 15 years ago, the 'brothers' Ramone have aged remarkably well." **Q**

"Funny, but *Mondo Bizarro* sounds and feels just right. Strange, because like an old pair of DMs, you don't normally think of the Ramones as refreshing." **Vox**

CHRIS REA
God's Great Banana Skin (East West)

"Rea's songs convey a sense of unhurried distance, but while some might consider the material here to be ideal auto-route music, the pieces are little more than variations on a theme of cruel melancholy. Very nice, if you like your wallpaper tasteful." **The Guardian**

"His 12th collection may not be designed to set the pulse racing but in edging between the often mawkish sentiment of *Auberge* and the thematic despair of *The Road To Hell*, he's unearthed a comforting middle ground and

realised what is probably his most satisfying album to date." **Q**

REM
Automatic For The People (WEA)

"After a lot of listens, I still don't know where to put it in the REM canon. Sometimes it recalls the quieter parts of *Out Of Time* (some of the tracks date back to those sessions). But I'm still pining for some of the growling, two-fisted attack of *Document* or *Green*."
The Guardian

"*Automatic For The People* is melancholia-a-go-go, but it's not depressed. If your life is horrible, if your scene is at an all-time low, if you're recently bereaved, its emotional power may prove a touch overwhelming. But if you're happy it will enrich your life like discovering a new colour." **Select**

"... it is the way in which they trawl so many sources for inspiration – from Southern country twang to the Celtic folk of Northern Europe – and yet still sound like an authentic part of the rock 'n' roll tradition that is their particular claim to greatness." **The Times**

"There are touches of class here, but if we worked in A&R at Warner Bros, we'd be urging Michael to take Axl Rose classes." **Sky**

KEITH RICHARDS
Main Offender (Virgin)

"The music here is a rare example of music growing old gracefully and with dignity. It's all classic stuff. You thought rock 'n' roll was dead. You were looking in the wrong direction." **NME**

"The Indestructible One is in such good voice throughout that you can overlook the fact that most of these pieces are a single idea stretched

to inordinate lengths rather than songs as we know them." **The Guardian**

"Sure, Richards is a dreadful singer, but not even Jagger would sing an entire song with a cod West Indian accent. Now, that's entertainment!" **Select**

JONATHAN RICHMAN
I, Jonathan (Rounder)

"See him gazing out of the sleeve, all wide-eyed innocence in a hooped tee-shirt, and you realise straight away that little has changed in Jonathan Richman's world. He still appears to regard naivety as one of the highest human virtues. The music's still minimalist, the lyrics full of wonder at the small joys of life."
Melody Maker

"Rock 'n' roll basics are where Jonathan's still at: hollow handclaps, beach bongos, Link Wray at low volume and an endearing garage naivety that's been honed over the years into his own private world of wonderment." **Select**

SADE
Love Deluxe (Epic)

"The first lady of wallpaper soul proves that she has lost none of her featherlite touch when it comes to creating music so smooth and discreet that it makes dead silence sound crude and raucous... listeners should set their alarm clocks before slipping *Love Deluxe* onto the mini-stack." **Sky**

"It's often a toss-up whether these songs are subtly evocative or plain dull, possibly depending on how much lager you've drunk or whether or not it's the middle of the night."
The Guardian

"... it was always the voice that made Sade special. And here it is stronger, and at the same time, more haunting than ever." **Soul CD**

ST ETIENNE
So Tough (Heavenly)

"Sarah Cracknell's airy, sweet voice surfs on just the right side of cloying, while uncanny tunes are pieced together by Pete Wiggs and Bob Stanley. *So Tough* is thus an inspired, evocative and quite beautiful London album."
Q

"*So Tough* is a marked improvement on their *Foxbase Alpha* debut, with far fewer of the tracks sounding like half-finished backing tracks, though there are still a few tracks that

ade love deluxe

SENSELESS THINGS
Empire Of The Senseless (Epic)

"With a more sympathetic, hammerhead production, the Things are bolshier and genuinely noisier than ever before. Trouble is, having sorted out the left to the jaw they've apparently lost the right hook. This is not what you might call a chorus-heavy album." **Select**

"...the Senseless Things have struggled to sustain their workmanlike effervescence over an album's duration. That said, *Empire Of The Senseless* is undoubtedly their best shot yet." **Vox**

"These punky scuzzballs have come a long way since their frenetic, three-chord singles of the late 80s. This is heavy-duty rawwk and raawl, surprisingly well-crafted and confident, and laden with killer singles." **The Face**

THE SHAMEN
Boss Drum (One Little Indian)

"Forget dodgy hippy notions for a moment, just wallow in this Virtual Reality festival mudbath of high-velocity optimism and chemically-enhanced idealism." **NME**

"*Boss Drum* sounds like the commercial masterplan, but they've spectacularly lost the plot." **Q**

"Bit of a non-stop jamboree this album, with all bases in Dancefloooronia well and truly covered. I haven't got a clue what they're going on about and to be honest I couldn't give a fig. This is weird but quite, quite wonderful." **Smash Hits**

SONIC YOUTH
Dirty (DGC)

"Yet again they make you vaguely hanker after some American urban dream; yet again they make the guitar sound like the funkiest camera in the war zone. So rock has got to learn to take on techno? Get out of here." **Select**

"...a measure of clarity in their record production might encourage to the surface qualities which Sonic Youth perhaps only dimly suspect they possess. Until then, it seems likely that the band are destined to remain godparents or midwives to the new scene, but never the main event." **Q**

"Almost ten years ago Sonic Youth opined that 'confusion is sex', and *Dirty* demonstrates

---

suffer from the group's pick 'n' mix approach to sampling." **The Independent**

"Trapped in a world of kinky boots, loon pants and bowl haircuts, St Etienne slap together a saucy 60s feel with a groovy 90s beat. An album stuffed with the fun and frolics of summer... shame it's February, eh?" **Smash Hits**

SAW DOCTORS
All The Way From Tuam (Solid)

"It makes The Pogues sound like The Prodigy. Moreover, it sounds like it was made by a bunch of blarneying bogtrotters with peat for brains. It is complete and utter shite." **Melody Maker**

"Proceedings are well-moulded by Levellers' producer Phil Tennant who gives things an unpronounced rock edge, although even he can do little to rescue Dave Carton's leaden voice. This long record gets a little longer with each listen." **Select**

"An apparently unquenchable stream of melody and a lyrical honesty that eats your heart from the inside." **Rock CD**

STEREO MC'S *CONNECTED*

brilliantly that for a mind-boggling sensory turn-on there's still no-one to touch them."
Vox

SPIN DOCTORS
Pocket Full Of Kryptonite (Epic)

"... an unholy melding of The Grateful Dead, the Steve Miller Band, and any other Yankee rock bores who reached their nadir of tedium in the early 70s. This is a record that could bore a stiff stiff. Avoid it like you would a roving gang of Jehovah's Witnesses."
Melody Maker

"...don't believe the hype about the Spin Doctors. *Pocket Full Of Kryptonite* sounds like a compilation of out-of-date rockers Lynyrd Skynyrd and Steve Miller." **Sky**

"*Pocket Full Of Kryptonite* lacks a feeling of genuine currency. That it's difficult to tie down to any particular point in the last decade is likely to prove detrimental to its success this side of the pond." **Vox**

"With such an imaginative succession of fresh takes on the gritty, guitar group format, Spin Doctors prove to be neither an out-and-out retro band like The Black Crowes, nor in the post-grunge Pearl Jam mould. No matter what time their watches are reading, or the contents

of their pockets, this album is full of dynamite." **Q**

STEREO MCs
Connected (4th & Broadway)

"*Connected* cements the Stereos' position as purveyors of a unique sound, which owes as much to live funk and soul as to rap. A killer LP." **Select**

"Lyrically, they indulge themselves in the rather tired rapping obsessions with urban decay and 'one love'. Nevertheless, a valiant, if underachieving effort."
Q

"The group specialise in loose, long-running grooves with surprisingly few synthetic additives. We think you'll like them..." **Sky**

"The Stereos continue to mine an earthly funk vein – rap with choruses you can sing along to." **I-D**

STING
Ten Summoner's Tales (A&M)

"Thankfully, *Ten Summoner's Tales* claws back some of the pop territory that had been largely abandoned on his previous solo outings, resulting in the most approachable of his post-Police works." **The Independent**

"... it's not a sin to be literate, even in rock 'n' roll. And let it be said that it's not stopped him making a truly cracking album. *Ten Summoner's Tales* assails you with sheer enthusiasm at every turn. Nothing but fine." **Q**

"*Ten Summoner's Tales* is Sting stripped down, in the company of a tight, disciplined group of musicians, an album that is direct and affecting, starker than previous heavyweight efforts. This is: Sting Something Simple." **Vox**

"All his ludicrous pretensions and arty conceits might remain intact, but Sting's latest album offers a not entirely unappealing mix of downbeat pop and jazz-inflected R&B."
Esquire

IZZY STRADLIN
Ju Ju Hounds (Geffen)

"The pure enjoyment of playing music for music's sake infuses every song and *Ju Ju Hounds* consequently sounds relaxed, honest, and completely human. Its vibe is elusive, and needs to be tracked down, but it's well worth the effort." **Making Music**

"...Stradlin brings verve and love to his work and the drooling beast is once more revived. Indoor fun at its best." **NME**

SUEDE
Suede (Nude)

"The overwhelming feeling towards the debut album by Suede is one of relief that it finally made it here. In the wake of the media froth, anticlimax hangs heavy in the air, very much the same as when, getting on for ten years ago, the first Smiths album appeared." **NME**

"There's a feeling in the air that they haven't fully let themselves go yet; that they'll be more shocking or blunt next time out. As debuts go this isn't exactly Suede in flames; but what a smouldering attempt." **Select**

"This is music for the boys who don't dance, who prefer an evening's self-pitying wallow in their bedroom; delirious ballads hold gentle sway here – some betraying their obvious Smiths influence." **The Independent**

"This is not a second coming for Ziggy Stardust – or The Smiths, for that matter. Suede are ultimately a self-styled and self-obsessed package. Their own brand of rock 'n' roll, sex-on-a-stick appeal and funny shirts have been distilled into a crafty and provocative debut album." **Vox**

"What does it take to turn you on???"
Melody Maker

SUGAR
Copper Blue (Creation)

"For a man who sounds like he's been to hell and back and been burned along the way, Mould has returned to heal old wounds. With Sugar and *Copper Blue* he's made a great start." **NME**

"Sugar couldn't have timed their debut LP better. With a new member of the Husker Du generation currently breaking out of every other town in the country, Bob Mould should be able to cash in on his rich legacy at last." **Vox**

"The only substantial criticism concerns Mould's voice, about which he seems to remain unnecessarily unconfident. It's a frail but raging human plaint immersed in the surf of guitar noise, swept along with meanings obscured, but with its harmonies heading for the sun." **Q**

SUGAR
Beaster (Creation)

'Rarely has a band rocked out with such bleak intensity and utter conviction. A vast cathedral of noise and despair, erected and demolished in half an hour flat, this is an album which has to be heard to be believed." **The Times**

'Sugar are about the turmoil of the interior life, which is maybe why an album like *Beaster* is best listened to loud, on the headphones at home rather than live, where Sugar are too awkward somehow to conform to the traditional requirements of upbeat solidarity and fist-pumping communion." **Melody Maker**

'*Beaster* is like *Copper Blue* with the smooth corners removed. It's totally wonderful. It could have you in tears at the end. You'll get no new Sugar LP until 1994, but that's OK. It'll take you years to tire of this." **Select**

"...the dark but insidiously catchy companion to *Copper Blue* confirms what those in the know had predicted; Sugar are definitely The Next Big Thing." **The Daily Telegraph**

THE SUNDAYS
Blind (Parlophone)

"Harriet sings her guts out, hitting that flesh-crawling note at just the right moment before letting the crashing chorus carry along. Melancholia has seldom sounded so attractive." **Select**

"The Sundays are too fastidious for the flat-out gimmickry of pop, yet lack the dark obsessiveness that their brand of soul-mining requires. For now, they're in Palookaville." **The Guardian**

"*Blind* is dreamy, Wheeler's vocals stretching her high range around the melody and back again before matching up with the insistent but pleasant guitar fills." **Rock CD**

---

t

ICE T
Home Invasion (Virgin)

"Of the split with Warners, little is said, save for the dramatic vignette which prefaces *It's On*, sardonically equating record distribution with drug-dealing. But even this is a re-hash of

Ice's old shtick about 'dope rhythms and dope beats', just a different angle on the metaphor." **The Independent**

"...a hell of a lot more convincing than the trashy *Body Count* album, T reaffirms his commitment to his ghetto roots, slams rappers who make 'weak-ass dance music 'cos they couldn't stay down with the hardcore', and parades his lurid sexual fantasies..." **Sky**

"Ice T rides the fast-bucking rhythm with acrobatic balance, drawing up battle plans and targeting the Republican backyard for the hip-hop invasion. Rap never sounded so mean, so sane, so villainous." **Vox**

TELEVISION
Television (Capitol)

"It's cool listening, it would make a pretty good Tom Verlaine solo LP... But it's not the Television we know and worship." **Select**

"Anyone not up on Verlaine's post-Television work will be surprised at how understated this is. It's still a very, very fine album." **Q**

"A nice idea, but given Television's pre-eminence as a guitar band, they could have been so much flasher, so much less well-mannered. In the circumstances I'll happily wait until 2006 for the fourth record." **Vox**

THE THE
Dusk (Epic)
See The Year in Review

THERAPY?
Nurse (A&M)

"Therapy? kick off sounding like Nirvana and end with a final guitar stroke that imitates The Beatles. In between, *Nurse* is solid Therapy? Pure and simply staggering." **NME**

"You realise that Therapy?, damn silly question mark and all, will soon be a household name." **Select**

"...not to say that Therapy? are starved of originality. But ultimately this, their third elpee, does echo other bands including the frenetic vocals of That Petrol Emotion..." **Rock CD**

THUNDER
Laughing On Judgement Day (EMI)

"For what it's worth, W Axl Rose reckons Thunder to be the best rock band to come out of Britain since Led Zeppelin. A potent mix of guitar-heavy hard rock diluted by an occasional exquisite ballad, *Laughing On Judgement Day* is strong evidence to support Rose's opinion." **Q**

"Everything is brilliantly sung by Bowes. How can Thunder fail? Even miserable old Axl Rose likes 'em." **Vox**

TIN MACHINE
Live – Oy Vey Baby (Victory/London)

"This rib-crackingly titled live album offers ample evidence that, despite their elegantly tailored suits, haircuts and equipment, Tin Machine are rooted in nostalgia for the late 60s. They have a long way to go before sniffing the vapour trails of Hendrix, Cream and The Who..." **Q**

"...put the still-born mutant that is Tin Machine out of its – and our – misery..." **NME**

PETE TOWNSHEND
PsychoDerelict (East West)

"The music dating back from the 70s is really good, and even some of the new stuff isn't terrible, but *Psychoderelict* is let down by awful dialogue." **Q**

"If only the songs here were as strong as The Who's best work I would say buy this record. As it is, I say borrow it, enjoy the story and cherish Pete Townshend as one of the few rock stars of integrity and passion." **Today**

THE TRAGICALLY HIP
Fully Completely (MCA)

"...an effortlessly powerful but beautifully streamlined rock record that bristles with capacious melodies, dark intent and a big, driving guitar sound. Comparisons with mid-term REM might prove helpful..." **Q**

"... the marvel of this album is its gorgeous guitar textures, so clean and warm yet hard enough to give a tense, edgy quality to most of the songs. It is quite the most sensual sound I have heard this year." **The Times**

"...it's an also-ran album from an outfit who might have been contenders had they chosen rather more mainstream and melodic material." **Vox**

U2
Zooropa (Island)
See The Year in Review

UB40

UB40
Promises & Lies (Virgin)

"It's a modern reflection of the way in which, under Bob Marley's leadership, reggae music came to represent a symphony for the downtrodden." **The Independent**

"Their 857th LP and they're still making reggae for people who don't like reggae. Makes Shaggy seem like the revolution itself!" **Smash Hits**

"Their work is evenly divided between bittersweet love songs and gritty social protest.

They effortlessly combine the romantic conceits of lovers' rock and the legacy of Bob Marley." **The Daily Telegraph**

"Aficionados might scowl a little... it'll sell by the bucketload." **Vox**

VAN HALEN
Live: Right Here Right Now (WEA)

"They've traded their Baywatch bubblegum sorcery of yore for a lead-plated rock dullness. Poodle parlour bimbo rock has never sounded so uninteresting." **NME**

"Sammy Hagar was the inaugural member of the spandex bollocks through the mangle school of rock, and his howling at the moon sits surprisingly neatly with frequently melodic riff action cooked up by the Van Halen brothers and friends..." **Q**

"This is an exhaustive, not to say exhausting, account of HM personified. Ear insurance is recommended." **Vox**

SUZANNE VEGA
99.9F (A&M)

"She is still a more self-contained and contemplative soul than the Toris and Sophies who have emerged during her absence, but the charms of Vega's album are no less insistent for that." **Q**

"...this fourth studio album is such a decisive step forward that she can no longer be sidelined as an artist of minority appeal. *99.9F* comes complete with a library of production sounds: industrial clattering and banging, Attractions-type rock romps, robust pop and the purest of acoustic guitar settings." **Vox**

VEGAS
Vegas (RCA)

"They only sound like Eurythmics meeting the Colourfield, like Hall and Stewart. With the depth of experience these two have they could and should have stuck their necks out. Instead, what they intended to be 'a studio experiment' is a tame and

---

depressingly safe affair." **Select**

"Stewart dominates much of the material and it's only later that Hall makes his musical presence felt... Vegas is an exercise in perfect pop and this unlikely partnership could well yield a few hit singles." **Rock CD**

"If this conjures up visions of the desert rather than the glitzy metropolis dumped in the middle of it, then you're on the right track... *Vegas* started off as an experiment, and really should have stayed that way." **Vox**

VERVE
A Storm In Heaven (Hut)

"It's a collection of some of the prettiest noise ever to escape from amplifiers. At best you'll believe a man can fly." **NME**

"Music to make your head melt. Verve have already achieved transcendence – their music sounds like it's been around for centuries waiting to be brought into being and will linger for centuries to come, somehow, somewhere." **Melody Maker**

"The first album from the Wigan band seduces you into a shadow world somewhere between ambient, chill-out and straightforward indie rock. This hypnotic collection feels like an album of the year." **The Guardian**

THE WATERBOYS
Dream Harder (Geffen)
See The Year in Review

VEGAS

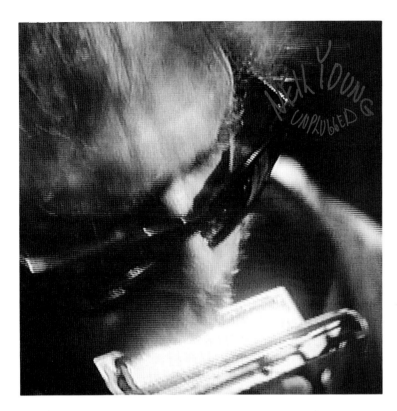

ROGER WATERS
Amused To Death (Columbia)

"Lyrically, the album is a catalogue of sixth-form cliches – the futility of war, the mindlessness of television, the ubiquity of American fast food. Stanley Kubrick's *2001* makes a guest appearance ('The monkey sat on a pile of stones/And stared at the broken bones in his hand'); you thought that movie was fantastic when you were 17, and Waters apparently still does." **Q**

"He should stop trying to be Pink Floyd, he should drop the dodgy concepts and get back to writing songs; songs that needn't be thematically linked, songs that rhyme, songs that don't need QMSound (TM) to make their impact." **Vox**

PAUL WELLER
Paul Weller (Go! Discs)

"Highly influenced by 60s soul and soft psychedelia, Paul Weller's first solo LP is a corker, combining lots of sexy guitar work, clever lyrics and some smooth soulful vocals. A top notch debut." **Smash Hits**

"...the real disaster here is a musical one: most of the vocal melodies are amateurish and lazy, laid across a platform of cod 70s soul and 60s cool jazz that's so shambolic it sounds as if the musicians learned the songs as they went along." **Vox**

"...a decent record for a bastard hot sticky day. Bring on the Pimms and let's have a sing-song round the old Hammond because Paul Weller is back. Nearly anyway." **NME**

WORLD PARTY
Bang! (Ensign)

"*Bang!* feels so all-embracing and just plain big, it's practically an environment in itself. If they built cities out of Karl Wallinger's music, we'd all live happily ever after." **Q**

"Imagine *Sign O' The Times* or *U Got The Look* with the really ace bits taken out and the crappy mid-80s samples kept in. All those people in possession of the good groove take one step forward. Not so fast Karl..." **Select**

"*Bang!* fails to excite like its predecessors. As parties go, this one needs a new manifesto." **Vox**

ROBERT WYATT
A Short Break (Voiceprint)

"...this mini-album hints that Wyatt may finally be hitting a new creative groove. *A Short Break* is a gem despite, or maybe because of, its rough, homemade feel." **Select**

"This mini-CD ('20 minutes at home' as he calls it) comprises five songs recorded on a four-track this summer, and if it hardly qualifies as a major statement, it's appealingly intimate, the equivalent of a fireside chat with one of Britain's most enduring oddballs." **Q**

"...a sort of musical clearing-of-the-throat before he begins his next magnum opus." **Vox**

NEIL YOUNG
Harvest Moon (Reprise)
See The Year in Review

NEIL YOUNG
Unplugged (Reprise)

"The astonishing thing about this recording isn't the songs or its placing, so much as the way Neil makes everything sound so effortless. *Unplugged* is a rare, rare moment, one to be cherished." **Melody Maker**

"Young has taken 'unplugged' literally – what you get is 65 minutes of the lank-haired one, his guitar and unobtrusive backing band. This has its pitfalls, chief among them that with Young acoustic often equals dreary." **The Guardian**

"In a stroke, Neil has summoned up ghosts, captured the flavour of an age and marked his own cheery-sad passage through life – no small achievement." **Vox**

"All that remains is to shoot the member of the audience who thought it appropriate to whoop his approval during *The Needle And The Damage Done*. Such is the strength of this set that his shame is likely to pursue him down the years." **Q**

WARREN ZEVON
Learning To Flinch (Giant)

"On this record, the piano tracks surpass the guitar ones mostly because he plays the piano like it's his friend, and treats his guitar like shit; again, it would work visually, but irritates secondhand." **Vox**

"Zevon unadorned, slashing at an acoustic guitar or banging the piano to deliver his vivid songs of boxing and booze, mad superstars and headless Thomson gunners directly into the DAT machine. Acolytes will automatically invest in *Learning To Flinch*. Those who remain curious about him could do worse." **Q**

Thunder from down under

Jonathan Coleman leans over the edge of the Pacific basin and reflects on how Australia and New Zealand managed to produce Rolf, the boys from INXS **and** the Rolling Clones.

"... At first it was so difficult to get hold of any new music that radio stations used to pay Qantas air crews to act as scouts ..."

One of the most rewarding things about doing radio shows in the UK has been the reaction to the music I've been playing from Oz and NZ. People will ring up and say "Thanks for playing that old Sherbet track" and it seems like they know more about the band than I do. That's probably a sign that there's more and more crossover: so many Ozzies have transplanted themselves into the UK along with all the TV shows, and a lot of Brits have had a stint working or travelling down under.

It wasn't always like that. In the 50s and 60s, Australia and New Zealand were still pretty isolated – not just geographically – and the only exposure to good music came from the UK or the US (that's not to downgrade the local talent). They represented a kind of Shangri-La to anyone into music around that time: the feeling we had was that if you made it in Australia, that was all well and good, but any local acclaim just didn't count unless you could be successful overseas.

Part of the reason for this was that all the music we heard seemed to come from Britain or the States. At first it was so difficult to get hold of any new music that radio stations used to pay Qantas air crews to act as scouts, pick up the latest releases on their stopovers and bring them back so they could be played on the Top 40 shows. The local musicians would then record cover versions of the singles, and we all grew up listening to those imports and those covers – I've often thought that that's probably why Australian bands like INXS and Midnight Oil instinctively developed such an internationally acceptable sound.

Apart from the Seekers, and showbiz acts like the enduring Rolf Harris, the first band I really remember breaking out of Australia were the Easybeats. Harry Vanda and George Young would later be instrumental in getting AC/DC off the ground with George's two younger brothers. The Easybeats' *Friday on My Mind* was really the first international rock Number One from an Australian band – David Bowie did a cover version of the song on *Pin Ups* – and their influence was later felt by INXS who were seen as having the same kind of edge to their music.

The traditional route was for bands to start getting something going in Australia and then head off to London – if you look back there was a continual stream of bands seeking fame and fortune, from the Easybeats and The Master's Apprentices to John Farnham, and the Bee Gees of course. Many of these guys had been born in the UK and moved out to Australia at an early age, just like me, so it was a natural thing (thank God for the assisted passage scheme to Australia in the 50s and 60s).

When I started playing keyboards in bands I remember the Bee Gees rehearsing in a garage down the road at Bronte Beach, Sydney. When they first made a ripple they were TV personalities, on black and white teen shows – "Let's welcome the Gibb Brothers". Another guy from my early days was Dave Evans, who was the original singer in the first manifestation of AC/DC. Dave was auditioned by Harry Vanda and George Young and lasted for about 8 months before they fell out "for artistic differences". Harry and George were effectively acting as producers for AC/DC and decided to take the band down the hard rock route; at the time they'd been much more like the Faces.

I was playing in a blues band at the time, the Rugcutters (don't tell me you don't remember the Rugcutters), on electric piano and synth, and working in advertising, writing copy and jingles. It came to the point where I had to decide whether to keep struggling on as a muso or do a proper job. I did neither and became a TV presenter and part-time DJ instead, and left the music up to the rest of them (sort of).

Through the 70s we still felt a long way from the action, but bands like Zoot, Axiom and Flying Circus were keeping the flag aloft in Europe and we used to get all the US and UK TV shows ("Top of the Pops", for example, was shown once in a while on Australian TV). Then gradually we started to become part of the circuit for world tours. One of the first concerts I went to was Led Zep at the Sydney Showground somewhere around 1972, and Joe Cocker had come down on the Mad Dogs and Englishmen tour a couple of years earlier. One of the best things I saw at the time was a bill featuring Deep Purple, Free and Manfred Mann at the Randwick Racecourse for $4 – I wish tickets were still that cheap.

The Aussie musos would go along and try to emulate the sounds they heard, so if Led Zep had Orange amps, an original Les Paul and a violin bow, suddenly everyone would go out and try and get hold of the same equipment. We got to be very good at imitation – and maybe that's part of the reason the whole clone band thing would become so big (but so embarrassing!).

Live music has always been huge in Australia, but the demand was always for songs that everybody knew. Over in Western Australia the pubs (and what we call pubs can have audiences of up to 3000) first got into the cover bands with the Beatniks doing Beatles numbers and the Rolling Clones paying homage to Mick and co. The whole performance was almost like cabaret, with endless costume changes from bands like Bjorn Again. At first it was distinctly uncool to like them, but suddenly the whole thing picked up and created its own credibility. It's significant that some of the glam rock dinosaurs can still get regular club tours in Australia, and over

here you'd only catch them playing cross-Channel ferries, if you're lucky.

Despite all this imitation, there have always been bands sticking to their original material – in recent years just look at bands like INXS, Midnight Oil, Devinyls and Split Enz. The punk movement had a major impact as well – and the Stiff bands all toured, encouraging local bands to be that much more outrageous and develop their own identities. Then in the early 80s Boy George and Marilyn came over, although Marilyn got involved in some trouble in a Sydney bar (nudge, nudge). I actually did a piece on TV about the incident and put a chalk mark on the floor marking the spot where Marilyn got punched out! Sorry, Marilyn. Squeeze came across too and appeared on my TV show "Wonder World"; it was Jools Holland's 21st birthday and he didn't know anyone so we spent the evening together, drinking and solving the problems of the world.

As well as this move towards individuality a critical turning point was the ruling which obliged Australian radio to play a hefty percentage of Australian music; all of a sudden they had to programme in a lot more of the local bands and that helped them get much wider recognition not only in Oz but overseas. The ones who made it internationally we all know, but there were some great bands that never crossed over internationally and are well worth checking out on re-release.

Cold Chisel – Jimmy Barnes' original band – were huge but never got exposure outside Australia, along with the Sonny Boys, the Rock Melons, the Angels (with Doc Neeson) and Rose Tattoo, fronted by Angry Anderson, who only broke through as a solo artist when his song *Suddenly* was used for Charlene and Scott's wedding in "Neighbours".

On Virgin 1215 I've been putting in 2 or 3 songs from homegrown bands every morning. This is my Thunder from Down Under spot and it gives me a chance to keep in touch with what's going on and coming through from Oz. Some of my faves from 1993: The Cruel Sea with their movie music cum indie sound with lots of Ry Cooder-ish slide guitar; Baby Animals (who toured with Bryan Adams) and their hard-edged, raunchy, rocky approach; Black Sorrows who are a kind of mix between Van Morrison and zydeco music; and Paul Kelly, who's quite simply one of the best songwriters around ... and many more.

So if you're the least bit interested in Oz or NZ music, hassle your local record shop, or me at 1215.

"I remember the Bee Gees rehearsing in a garage down the road at Bronte Beach, Sydney. When they first made a ripple they were TV personalities, on black and white teen shows – 'Let's welcome the Gibb Brothers'".

books

◆ SIMPLY MICK: MICK HUCKNALL OF SIMPLY RED THE INSIDE STORY
Robin McGibbon and Rob McGibbon
(Weidenfeld and Nicolson, £15.99)
Simply Mick brims over with gushing sentiment and flowery prose, but still makes for an entertaining read. Bequeathed by the mother who abandoned him as a baby with "the drive and determination to go after what one wanted, and the ruthless singlemindedness to make sure one got it", Mick needed all this instinct for self-preservation to get him through his tortuous school life. "His hair was a red rag to the bullies," and old acquaintances testify how "he really was an odd looking character, particularly in sports gear". But Mick's childhood talent as an impresario went from strength to strength, and his formative years as band leader show how seriously he took himself, sometimes to an obnoxious degree.

◆ INCREDIBLY STRANGE MUSIC: VOLUME ONE
V Vale and Andrea Juno (editors)
(RE/Search Publications/Airlift Book Company, £15.99)

This book is a wonderfully absurd tribute to the dying days of independent record labels and quirky recordings. In interviews with collectors we are enlightened as to such classics as *Muhammad Ali Fights Tooth Decay* and Barbara Cartland's *Album Of Love Songs Especially For You*. Eccentrics and purveyors of kitsch are given their due in this celebration of recorded eccentricity.

Best moments include *The Addicts Sing*, by Nine Former Addicts, and interviews with drag queen Lypsinka and The Cramps' resident pussycat, Lux Interior. *Incredibly Strange Music* is funny and camp – roll on Volume Two!

◆ ELVIS
Dave Marsh
(Omnibus £12.95)
Dave Marsh's biography, first published in 1981, returns with a new introduction. It contains a comprehensive analysis on The King's position in the rock'n'roll scheme of things, and a superb photographic documentation of his life and times. With its reliance on factual evidence, as opposed to gossip and hearsay, and its in-depth assessment of the actual records and films, this work restores Elvis's dignity and is a deliberate antidote to Albert Goldman's sensationalist biography. The only drawback is the painstaking critique of the ghastly films, most of which could have been justifiably ignored.

However, the insight gained into the Colonel's limiting publishing deal, and Elvis's ultimate transcendence of those limitations, renders the project totally worthwhile. Marsh paints a touching portrait of Elvis's conventional aspirations even while he was initially seen by conservative America as the devil incarnate.

◆ THE GUINNESS ENCYCLOPEDIA OF POPULAR MUSIC
Colin Larkin (editor)
(Guiness £225)
This work comprises four volumes, each one a tome, and a 100-page bibliography and 400-page index. This door-stopper of an encyclopedia of popular music is a truly awe-inspiring work covering artists, bands and genres from 1900 to the present day. The style of the book is bright and breezy, while still managing to incorporate some telling anecdotes; stories of how songs came to be written and recorded and 'Where are they now'-type items abound. This is a landmark in the charting of popular culture, a Who's Who of rock which encompasses everything and everyone. As an archivist's reference book or a record-buyer's bedtime read, it's a must.

◆ FEEL LIKE GOING HOME
Peter Guralnick
(Penguin £9.99)
This is a classic of blues and rock'n'roll portraiture, first published in 1971. For those who missed it the first time round it is a timeless account of the blues greats like Muddy Waters, Howlin' Wolf and Skip James. Guralnick has the edge with his writing on these original talents, mainly because he was on the scene before they became wary of media exposure. Also he doesn't neglect the lesser known, like Johnny Shines and Robert Pete Williams, whose influence is too often overlooked.

His accounts are both eloquent and informative, giving insight into the nuances of his subject's personalities while still doing critical justice to their music.

◆ ACROSS THE GREAT DIVIDE: THE BAND & AMERICA
Barney Hoskyns
(Viking £16.99)
The Band were self-effacing as individuals, but together they influenced the course of American music in a major way. Their cultural influences, spanning R&B, gospel and folk-lore, and Robbie Robertson's picturesque songwriting combined to create an inimitable style.

After paying their dues in the early 60s with Ronnie Hawkins, they eventually teamed up with Bob Dylan for his 1966 UK tour. And it was this fortuitous liaison that finally brought the big time to their door.

Since there was little in the group members' private lives apart from the music, Hoskyns concentrates on the albums, analyzing each one with meticulous attention, and bringing much critical insight to their powerful legacy. The Band's downfall is mapped, from the head-turning success of their self-titled second album to the sad low-key suicide of the alcoholic Richard Manuel.

◆ NICO: THE LIFE AND LIES OF AN ICON
Richard Witts
(Virgin £16.99)
At the age of 21, Nico (formerly Christa Paffgen) fled Berlin to bask in the artistic hothouse of 1960s Paris. Quickly immersing herself in the more artistic side of 60s rebellion, she landed a role in Fellini's *La Dolce Vita*, went on to flirt with the swinging London scene, before finally ending up as part

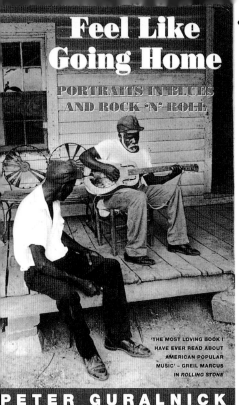

Feel Like Going Home

PORTRAITS IN BLUES AND ROCK 'N' ROLL

'THE MOST LOVING BOOK I HAVE EVER READ ABOUT AMERICAN POPULAR MUSIC' - GREIL MARCUS IN *ROLLING STONE*

PETER GURALNICK

of Warhol's entourage at The Factory. Subsequently her deathly voice and detached beauty brought her to the attention of The Velvet Underground and a string of lovers including Jim Morrison, Brian Jones and Jackson Browne. The rest, as they are inclined to say, is history.

In this revealing biography, the author colourfully evokes the decade and Nico's life in it, and writes in a compassionate style as he documents the eventual heroin-tainted decline of an ultimately tragic figure who could never understand why she failed to scale the heights of mass popularity enjoyed by so many of her her contemporaries.

◆ DOWN THUNDER ROAD – THE MAKING OF BRUCE SPRINGSTEEN
Marc Elliot, with the participation of Mike Appel
(Plexus £9.99)
When Bruce Springsteen finally made it big with the 1975 album *Born To Run*, Mike Appel, the man who had managed his affairs since the nowhere days of 1972, must have been rubbing his hands with glee. So when he was un-ceremoniously dropped in favour of former Rolling Stone scribe Jon Landau, it was hardly surprising that he immediately instigated legal proceedings that prevented 'The Boss' from recording a follow-up until the dispute was settled.

Since then, Appel has become Springsteen's personal *bête noire*, and now for the first time he tells his side of the story. Beginning with a riveting description of the power struggle that developed between himself and Landau, the book goes on to reveal that no-one fought harder to champion his *protégé's* talent than Appel, who went on to suffer considerable

personal hardship as a result.

Needless to say, Springsteen does not come across well, and instead of the slick wordsmith we might be entitled to expect we are presented with a picture of an inarticulate and ignorant individual whose ultimate response to tough questioning about his business affairs is to throw a foul-mouthed tantrum.

◆ U2: WIDE AWAKE IN AMERICA
Carter Alan
(Boxtree £7.99)
American broadcaster and journalist Carter takes us right through the phenomenal rise of U2 in America to the *Achtung Baby* LP and the Zoo TV tour. For someone who's had the ear of the band more or less from the start of their career, this could have been done with more anecdotal aplomb. Nevertheless, Carter's comprehensive interviewing technique does shed some light on their personal foibles, and his documentation of their live work is exhaustive. He also takes an impartial look at the music, including the backlash which followed *Rattle and Hum*. His insider's perspective affords a solid overview of the U2 phenomenon in America.

◆ NEIL YOUNG: DON'T BE DENIED
John Einarson
(Omnibus £9.99)
Essentially a fan's supplement, this account of Neil Young's formative years in Canada is not supposed to be a definitive biography. Einarson deals affectionately with Neil's one-parent childhood and his days in 'The Squires', predecessors to Buffalo Springfield and Crazy Horse. The song lyrics are given an autobiographical context, among them *Long May You Run* – a tribute to the hideous 1948 Buick Roadmaster hearse that carried The Squires from gig to gig. Although *Don't Be Denied* goes on to describe Young's Californian experiences, it's mainly an acknowledgment of his Canadian roots, with which Neil has always stayed in touch. Maybe this is part of the man's unpretentious appeal and the lasting respect he has earned from the fickle music press.

◆ MORRISSEY AND MARR: THE SEVERED ALLIANCE
Johnny Rogan
(Omnibus, £9.99)
Johnny Rogan's weighty exposé of one of the seminal bands of the 80s is quite an achieve-ment, and he leaves few stones unturned in his analysis of the Morrissey/Marr alliance. We trace Morrissey's rather morbid pre-occupations back to mothers gossiping about the Moors Murders at the school gates before moving on to identify some of the magic engendered by his relationship with Marr. Morrissey has not authorized the book;

indeed, he has publicly wished Johnny Rogan a slow and painful death in an M3 pile-up. Nevertheless, this is a story that had to be told and is done so here with an aficionado's eye for detail.

STRANGE DAYS

My Life With And Without
JIM MORRISON
·
PATRICIA KENNEALY

'The first good book on Jim Morrison.'
New York Daily News

◆ STRANGE DAYS: MY LIFE WITH AND WITHOUT JIM MORRISON.
Patricia Kennealy
(HarperCollins £16.99)
Strange Days is a detailed and lively narrative, lent authenticity by its author's status as the other woman in Morrison's life. Patricia Kennealy succeeds in fleshing out the accepted myth, revealing Morrison to be a charismatic and psychologically complex character. She does not, however, gloss over the more irritating and pretentious aspects of his personality, though is keen to refute rumours of Morrison's sexual inadequacy and place herself back in her rightful position as number one in the legend's life. Not without a certain dramatic tension, *Strange Days* is a welcome and sincere appreciation of the doomed would-be poet.

◆ ABBA GOLD: THE COMPLETE STORY
John Tobler
(Century 22 Ltd £12.95)

This blow-by-blow account of the Supergroup's career is laid out in a yearly format, putting the albums and songs in the context of events within the group. This makes for fairly soapy reading, Tobler's style managing to be both obsequious and perfunctory. One searches the pages for any whiff of a human failing which would make them seem more real. When Bjorn and Agnetha have a baby they time it carefully, as "careers would be adversely affected if a new baby were to arrive at an inopportune time". When they separate it takes "little time to work out that there was no need for their private tragedy to affect their best friends".

For those nostalgia buffs, however, the photographs take some beating. Jumpsuits tucked into boots, glitter encrusted flamenco flares and matching 'theme' outfits for the girls… good grief, it could be 1993! This is ABBA, whose greatest achievement, apparently, was "loosening the grip of the English-speaking nations on the world charts, even if it was only for a decade."

◆ SHE'S A REBEL – THE HISTORY OF WOMEN IN ROCK AND ROLL
Gillian S Gaar
(Seal Press $16.95 plus p&p from 3131 Western Avenue, Suite 410, Seattle, Washington 98121-1028, USA)

With a title like this you have to hope for an essential read, and Gaar doesn't disappoint. Her analysis of the status and significance of women in popular music over the last 40 years is an ambitious subject, to which she does justice. They're all here, the Blues mamas, the Motown posse, folksy songwriters and queens of punk. This is somewhat limited in biographic detail due to the sheer volume of artistes covered, and as a radical feminist Gaar's appraisal of women's impact on rock is ultimately pessimistic. Sexism is, of course, still rife in this industry, permeated with macho values, but long may the rebels rock the boat.

videos

■ THE LEMONHEADS
2 Weeks In Australia (East West £10.99)
In which Evan Dando and fellow 'heads' David Ryan and Nic Dalton strum and hum their way across the Land Of Oz. Mixed in with pano-ramic views of the outback and the videos for

Mrs Robinson, It's A Shame About Ray, My Drug Buddy, Half The Time and *Confetti*, we find previously unseen performances of six other viewer-friendly Lemon songs, including Alison's *Starting To Happen* and *Rockin' Stroll*. In addition, we get Evan looking tanned and hunky by the lake, Evan looking tanned and hunky at the in-store promo and Evan looking tanned and hunky as he talks us through the intricate Aboriginal-styled carvings on Nic's guitar, which tell the story of The Lemonheads so far. Combined with a nice line in gentle self-deprecating humour, this makes for an entertaining 45 minutes.

■ NEIL YOUNG
MTV Unplugged (Warner Music Video £10.99)
Swapping amps for acoustics and that inimitable shambling stoop for a stool, the grizzled granddaddy of grunge sits down to regale an irritatingly sycophantic audience with a 14-strong selection of songs. Old favourites such as *Mr Soul, Helpless, Pocahontas* and *Like A Hurricane* are tackled solo before a group of homely-looking friends, including Nils Lofgren on accordion, join in on newer material – *From Hank To Hendrix, Look Out For My Love* and *Unknown Legend* – taken from *Harvest Moon*. Positive proof that there is life after 40.

■ PUBLIC ENEMY
The Enemy Strikes Live (Sony Music Video £11.99)
"To those who don't know what a rap concert is like, here's a peek at rap at its best," says the sleeve, and for once the action lives up to the

hype as Chuck E, Flavor Flav, Terminator X and the precision-drilled Security Of The First World power their way through a typically uncompromising 60-minute set, recorded live at The Apollo Theatre in New York. A further ten minutes of footage is added through the inclusion of controversial promos for *By The Time I Get To Arizona, Shut 'Em Down, Night Train* and *Hazy Shade Of Criminal*, the latter juxtaposing images of Mike Tyson and Judge Clarence Thomas and making telling points about racism, injustice and the shortcomings of the American dream.

■ MADNESS
Madstock The Movie (GO Discs £13.99)
Although it paled by comparison to Divine Madness (the longform video compilation released the previous February), Madstock gave still-thirsty Madness fans something extra to suck on in 1992. Concentrating exclusively on the live performance of the Camden Crombie-ites, back to full strength with the return of Mike Barson, the movie captured the spirit, if not quite the enthusiasm (Suggs looks decidedly jaded at times), of the band's early jape-filled days and provides many an opportunity – with *Bed And Breakfast Man, The Prince, One Step Beyond, Embarrassment, House Of Fun* and, of course, *Baggy Trousers* to name but a few – for the adoring fez-topped audience to have a good old Norf London knees up.

■ CROWDED HOUSE
I Like To Watch (PMI £10.99)
Despite the sleazy connotations of the title, this was all good clean fun as the jovial antipodeans took us on a tour of the promo

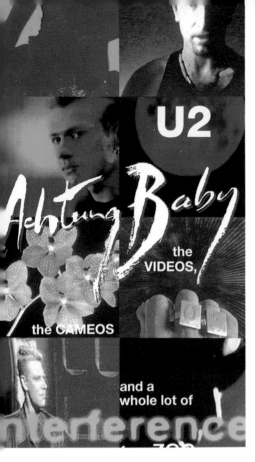

videos for 13 songs taken from their three albums to date. The gaps between the musical bits are filled with the slightly bizarre sight of drummer Paul Hester practising yoga in his polka dot jammies, Neil Finn playing with his collection of clockwork toys and Nick Seymour showing off his car, plus amusing backstage Crowded House-type snippets. Although at times the busyness of the videos detracts from the quality of the songs, there's still plenty to enjoy.

■ JIMI HENDRIX
At Woodstock (BMG £11.99)
If you were to ask a random group of thirtysomethings to recall the most memorable moment of the legendary Woodstock festival, it's as likely as Thora Hird being cast as the shrewish old granny in a Yorkshire-based comedy that they'd say the bit where Hendrix plays *Star Spangled Banner*. This golden moment, plus everything that went before (*Voodoo Chile, Fire, Red House*, etc) and after it (*Purple Haze, Hear My Train A' Comin'*, etc) during Hendrix's debut set with his new Band Of Gypsies was captured and condensed onto video by the legendary DA Pennebaker. Slip it on and wait for the nostalgia hit.

■ THE ROLLING STONES
The Stones In The Park (BMG £11.99)
Staged in London's Hyde Park, this was the event that brought half a million people together with the Stones for what became a tribute to the recently departed Brian Jones. It was the day that Mick Jagger, looking like mutton dressed up as, er, mutton, read awkwardly from the works of Shelley, released

several million Cabbage Whites into the air and introduced Jones' replacement, Mick Taylor, to the band's small but loyal fan base. Despite a decidedly wobbly *Sympathy For The Devil*, the whole event was underpinned by a solid r 'n' b groove, and at the end of the day everybody – the freaky dancers, the spaced-out chicks and the Angels – had a great time.

■ OTIS REDDING
Remembering Otis (VVL £10.99)
In 1967 Otis Redding, Booker T And The MGs and Sam And Dave toured Europe as the Stax-Volt soul revue. Later in the same year, Otis and Booker T appeared at the Monterey pop festival. Ace documentary maker DA Pennebaker was present on both occasions, capturing the former event in grainy monochrome and the latter in glorious technicolour. In the British segment Otis rips through soul greats like *My Girl, Satisfaction, Try A Little Tenderness* and *Shake* (showing that while he could sing like an angel he couldn't dance for toffee), while Sam And Dave contribute crowd-pleasing versions of *Hold On* and *When Something Is Wrong With My Baby* and Booker T slides in a cool 'n' groovy *Green Onions*.

In sunny California Otis adds *I've Been Loving You Too Long* and *Respect* to the set and proves, if further proof were needed, that when it came to showmanship and delivery he was, indeed, 'the tops'.

■ U2
Achtung Baby The Videos (Polygram £12.99)
Zoo TV plus… frantic cut-up-and-keep video

scrapbook of the band's past triumphs… impressionistic views of Berlin… great quotes ("I don't think the lyrics are worth a shite. I think it's all about drums")… four jerks with a police escort… wibbly wobbly videos shot in Arabian towns… dayglo groovers… Trabants all over the shop… three very different versions of *Even Better Than The Real Thing* and *One* plus *The Fly* and *Mysterious Ways*… slow motion buffalos… belly dancers dancing by the light of the silvery moon… action from Zoo TV tour… electric blue… Wim Wenders… until the end of the world… transmission ends. Click! Get the message?

■ THE SHAMEN
Boss Video (VVL £10.99)
Clockwork toys freaking out in a sepia-tinted scrapyard, a comedian-cum-magician roaming about the streets of London in silly hat and cloak, a spooky shot of Colin Angus and the late Will Sin walking out of the ocean and the sight of the three current members of the trippy chart-toppers strolling through the trees in full Camelot get-up are just some of the 'treats' to be found in this companion piece to the *Boss Drum* album. Tracks include *Ebeneezer Goode, LSI, Make It Mine* and *Progen/Move Any Mountain*. Drop it in the water supply and hold your neighbourhood to ransom.

■ BLONDIE
The Best Of… (Video Collection £6.99)
Ignore the so-called storyline about the cigar-chewing taxi driver taking you on a tour of dodgy New York locations and let the 16 hit singles – representing the most perfect of all marriages between New Wave energy and perfect pouting punk pop – draw you in. Thrill to the sight of Debbie in swimsuit and box jacket on *Denis*; marvel at the power of Clem Burke's punchy percussion and the sound of Chris Stein and Frank Infante's twitchy twanging on *Detroit 442*; swoon to the swaying reggae tones of *Tide Is High*. In short, singalong to the whole kit and caboodle because nothing like this will happen again. Ever.

■ BETTY WRIGHT
All The Way Live (PMI £12.99)
Recorded at the Hammersmith Odeon (now Labatt's Apollo), this video captures Betty Wright at her very best. She puts together a fine show in which the band's funky licks and punchy horns underpin perfectly her in-your-face raps and songs about the trials and tribulations suffered by the modernday woman. Once she has the audience eating out of her hand she takes the opportunity to indulge her prodigious talent for mimicry. During the medley that comprises *Clean Up Woman*, Al Green, The O'Jays and Tina Turner all come in for some good natu…

stick. As subsequent shots of the crowd show, her efforts are wholly appreciated, especially by the women whose gleeful smiles contrast tellingly with the sheepish hope-she-doesn't-pick-on-me grins of the men. Result: Women 1, Men nil.

■ THE ORB
The Video (Big Life £13.99)
When cerebral New Age pranksters The Orb crafted the visual accompaniment to their UFOrb album, they resisted the temptation for nervy subliminal-style image-flashes. Instead they created something that, in keeping with the cosily blissed out soundtrack, you could relax to. Needless to say, the overall effect is psychedelic in the extreme, as little fluffy clouds move snail-like across a backdrop further illuminated with images of dolphins, UFOs (natch) multi-coloured sunsets and happy campers trancing it up at their 1992 Brixton bash.

■ LOU REED
Magic And Loss – Live In Concert (Warner Music Video £10.99)
Looking like a college professor who's mistakenly got himself a footballer's haircut, Reed turns in a thoughtful, dignified and thoroughly unsentimental performance as he salutes the memory of his long-time colleague and tunesmith Doc Pomus, and an unknown woman called Rita. The atmosphere is cool, calm and considered, and even the rockier numbers are pastel coloured. But what prompted Reed to follow the Magic And Loss songs with an encore of Velvets standards when there was no audience to demand it is anyone's guess.

■ THE FATIMA MANSIONS
Y'Knaa (Radioactive £n/a)
Since withdrawn from sale, but available in the bargain bins, Cathal Coughlan and Co. perform five of their thought-provoking videos. *Blues For Ceausescu*, which juxtaposes shots of crucifixes with a 'great dictators of our time'-type collage and the sight of Cathal being womanhandled by a dominatrix; Only *Losers Take The Bus*, in which yer man takes the opportunity to menace innocent passers-by with a wild eyed rant; *Shiny Happy People*, which adds a new pornographic dimension to the REM classic; *1000%*, a comparatively restrained performance piece; and *Go Home Bible*, which features stomach-churning scenes of a man eating a bible. Don't try this one at home.

▲ *A hair-raising performance from Matt Dillon in Singles*

● SINGLES (15)
Set against the backdrop of a singles rooming house (hence the title) in Grungeville USA, ie Seattle, this finely-observed and wittily written story follows the adventures of six confused teenagers struggling to find their identities. Matt Dillon, as Cliff the singer in a bargain basement rock band, and Bridget Fonda as Janet his waitress girlfriend, play the main protagonists. But there are also sharply drawn performances from Campbell Scott, Kyra Sedgewick, Sheila Kelley and Jim True, and these add extra depth to the drama. With a good script and a soundtrack provided by Seattle's finest – Pearl Jam (who also appear as members of Cliff's band), Soundgarden, Alice In Chains *et al* – there's enough here to please both the diehard grunge fan and her starry eyed boyfriend.

● THE CURE
Show (PG)
Given the potential dream combination of Robert Smith and director Tim Pope, The Cure's last foray into full length film territory, The Cure In Orange, left a lot of people disappointed. This latest effort – helmed by Aubrey Powell and Leroy Brown – more than makes up for it. Filmed at Detroit's Aubern Palace arena during the American stint of last year's Wish tour, Show benefits massively

from a 16-strong camera crew whose mission is to dash in and out of the performers, recording every facial twitch and sweat droplet. Inevitably, Smith gets the lion's share of attention, although bassist Simon Gallup and the since-departed guitarist and brother-in-law of Bob, Porl Thompson, do their best to upstage him with a double-headed master-class in the art of rock 'n' roll posing. Music-wise we're talking the bulk of the *Wish* set plus old favourites such as *Love Cats* and *Boys Don't Cry* thrown in to show that there was always more to this band than gloomy rumblings and tortured barnets.

● WILD WEST (15)
This quirky Southall-bound tale follows the fortunes of the most unlikely musical amalgamation – a Pakistani Country And Western band. While the plot is standard fare for this sort of story – ie one minute the band are up and on a roll, the next they're down in the dumps – there's enough in the way of off-the-wall comic action and characters to capture and keep the interest. Most of all it's fun, and you don't get much of that to the British movie pound.

● PETER'S FRIENDS (15)
In which Renaissance man Kenneth Branagh yet (Dead) again bows to Hollywood (why can't British films nod towards European film-making?) in a shameless, archly Anglisized version of The Big Chill – with an updated 80s soundtrack. The music isn't as classic as the Chill's (can you name a Peter's tune?) but as a marketing tool aimed at those who want to re-hear snatches of semi-memorable 80's tracks this does the trick, presumably.

As a film it's a cringe-worthy story in which Stephen Fry acts the amiable toff with a heart of gold and a crumbling ancestral pile, who organizes a New Year's reunion for his old college pals, (self-indulgently played by Branagh, Emma Thomson, Rita Rudner, Imelda Staunton, Tony Slattery and Alphonsia Emmanuel). Only Hugh Laurie extricates himself with any dignity. Who cares? The film (and video) was a hit.

● TINA: WHAT'S LOVE GOT TO DO WITH IT (15)
This uplifting bio-pic takes us from Tina's (or Anna Mae Bullock, as she was then known) earliest days as a naughty schoolgirl being expelled from the gospel choir for improv-izing, right up to her present-day status as ageing rock 'n' roll goddess. In between we get the full story of her tempestuous marriage to Ike, who, considering his reputation, gets a fairly sympathetic treatment, and a bundle of hits including *River Deep Mountain High*, *Nutbush City Limits*, *Shake A Tail Feather* and *Proud Mary*. Starring Angela Basset and Larry Fishburne in the central roles, the film focuses mainly on the Ike and Tina partnership, although there is a rather hasty glossary of the latter's solo career tacked on at the end for good measure.

● BOB ROBERTS (15)
Tim Robbins followed up his highly-regarded performance in The Player with his own directorial debut Bob Roberts, the story of a hokey folk singer who runs for President on a manifesto somewhere to the right of extreme. What makes it interesting is not so much the revelation that American politics is rotten to the core – we all knew that anyway – but the unexpectedly sinister twist to a satirical tale and the use of Robbins' self-penned songs and clever adaptation of old Bob Dylan record sleeves and videos to illustrate his point.

● THE BODYGUARD (15)
Kevin Costner stars as an ex-Secret Service agent turned bodyguard who is hired to protect a pop mega-star, Whitney Houston, who has been receiving far from friendly letters and packages from one of her 'fans'. Although at first they regard each other with mutual hostility, the pair eventually become lovers. No surprises there, or anywhere else for that matter.

The script is one dimensional, the *denouement* predictable and, although Houston is unsurprisingly convincing as the pop star, Costner is too clean-cut to sustain the image of a gun-toting hard man. Nevertheless, a very popular film on both sides of the Atlantic. And for those who love Whitters, there's the added bonus of the hit-strewn soundtrack.

● THE FIVE HEARTBEATS (15)
Although it only graced the cinema screens for a short time, this fictitious story of an ambitious soul band, directed by Robert 'Hollywood Shuffle' Townsend, is well worth catching on video.

Starring in the lead role of singer/songwriter Donald "Duck" Matthews, Townsend spins a

▲ *Bernhard reflects on 30 years of US tack*

convincing tale of the trials and tribulations that afflict a band – not only when they're struggling but also when they make it. Drug problems, personality clashes and the less salubrious aspects of the music biz are dealt with with the minimum of sensationalism. The soundtrack, which sports a satisfyingly original set of 60s/70s-style songs, is guaranteed to leave you wanting more.

● SANDRA BERNHARD: WITHOUT YOU I'M NOTHING (18)
A big screen version of Bernhard's hit off-Broadway show, wherein the current co-star of C4's "Roseanne" takes us by the hand and leads us through 30 years of tacky American culture.The story goes like this: Bernhard returns to her LA club roots where despite, or more truthfully because of, her ego expanding success in New York, she is quickly consigned to the obscurity of the so-called Parisian Rooms. Once installed, Bernhard embraces a series of sharply-observed stage personas which she peppers with startlingly original interpretations of classic pop songs like *Little Red Corvette*, only to be confronted with a mainly black audience who show as much interest as an empty bank account. Until, that is, the arrival of a no-hope stripper – a not-so-thinly disguised dig at her former pal Madonna. As always, Bernhard is witty and abrasive in equal amounts. This video proves once and for all that she is one of the most vital comedienne's around.

▼ *Hands up who's voting? The persuasive Bob Roberts*

▲ Take That Take That award

THE BEAT (Carlton)
Giving a lesson to all would-be presenters about how to impose your personality without being irritatingly obtrusive, Gary Crowley almost single-handedly hauled the music programme genre back from the brink of absurdity.

Crowley's mixture of matey populism, relaxed interview technique and enthusiasm for the subject helped "The Beat" succeed where others failed. Combining tour dates, film reviews and an eclectic selection of bands – everyone from Bang Bang Machine, Eskimo's In Egypt and Pulp, through Stereo MCs and Suede to Deacon Blue and Del Amitri – "The Beat" was essential late-night viewing for anyone interested in sucking on the multi-flavoured lollipop that constitutes contemporary culture.

BPM (Carlton)
Presented by Crowley's ex-school chum, co-collaborator on the punk fanzine The Modern World and MARRS DJ Dave Dorrell, BPM took over from Pete Waterman's late-night plebutantes ball, "The Hitman And Her".

Essentially hipper and trendier, "BPM" ventured into the clubs, like Ministry Of Sound, where "The Hitman" would have been refused entry for flouting the establishment's door policy. Result: a raver's, rather than a voyeur's, eye view of what was down and happening across the nation's dance floors.

NAKED CITY (C4)
Fronted by the ebullient Johnny Vaughan and teenage wunderkind Caitlin Moran, "Naked City" introduced us to the delights of Busk Or Bust and Cred Or Dead. In the former, tip-top celebs (Jason Donovan, Shaggy, The Bee Gees, etc) would don the dark glasses and open the guitar case for a spot in which they

▼ City folk Johnny and Caitlin

▲ Mark, Dani, Katie and Terry spread "The Word"

would compete with less well-known street-artistes (Shaky Jake and Jolly Wolly) to see who could take the most cash: in the latter a star would talk about their unusual habits or pastimes just to see how embarrassingly hopeless they were.

In between, we got the likes of Bjork, heavy metal gay band RPLA, Courtney Love, up and coming grungers Smashing Pumpkins and doyens of dance One Dove entertaining us with their own particular brand of music.

THE WORD (C4)
With stand-up comic Mark Lamaar added to strengthen the line up and Dani Behr introduced as the pneumatic replacement for the game but gormless Amanda De Cadenet, "The Word" and Terry Christian stumbled lamely on. Wallowing in the kind of shambolic amateurism which, in time (remember how crap – great bands aside – "Ready Steady Go" really was), will see it accorded 'classic youth programme' status.

High spots included Kurt Cobain's on-air announcement – "Courtney Love is the best fuck in the world" – L7's public, pants-down, protest and Mark Lamaar giving nit-wit, bible-quoting, homophobe Shabba Ranks a right royal roasting. Low points the mercifully short-lived broadcasting career of Amanda's brother Bruiser and the twerp who ate maggots.

HYPNOSIS (C4)
The fusion of video snapshots and a relentlessly dance-driven soundtrack made Hypnosis the ideal programme for dance enthusiasts who couldn't wait up for "BPM".

Comprising club calls and scene breakdowns from around the country, plus video interrogations of the top DJs whose tunes are setting the nation's dance floors alight, "Hypnosis" threatens to 'revolutionize the way

SMASH HITS POLL WINNERS
Best British group: Take That
Best British single: *A Million Love Songs*, Take That
Best LP: *Take That And Party*, Take That
Best video: *I Found Heaven*, Take That
Best dance act: Marky Mark
Best male solo artist: Michael Jackson
Best indie act: The Farm
Best rock outfit: Extreme
Best DJ: Bruno Brooks
Smash hits/Radio 1 Best New Act: The Shamen
Worst video: *Ebeneezer Goode*, The Shamen
Worst group: New Kids On The Block
Worst male singer: Jason Donovan
Worst female singer: Dannii Minogue

BRITS
Best British male: Mick Hucknall
Best British female artist: Annie Lennox
Best British album: *Diva*, Annie Lennox
Best producer: Peter Gabriel
Best British newcomer: Tasmin Archer
Best international solo artist: Prince
Best international group: REM
Best international newcomer: Nirvana
Best live act: U2
Best soundtrack: Wayne's World
Best video: *Stay*, Shakespeares Sister
Best single: *Could It Be Magic*, Take That
Best classical recording: Nigel Kennedy
Outstanding contribution: Rod Stewart

The mantle – y appealing Brit

GRAMMY AWARDS

Album of the year: *Unplugged*, Eric Clapton
Record/Song of the year: *Tears In Heaven*, Eric Clapton
Best short video: *Digging In The Dirt*, Peter Gabriel
Best long video: *Why*, Annie Lennox
Best new age artist: Enya, *Shepherd Moons*
Best rock performance by a group: U2, *Achtung Baby*
Best producer: Brian Eno and Daniel Lanois, LA Reid and Babyface.
Best new artist: Arrested Development
Best female pop song: *Ingénue*, kd lang
Best r 'n' b song: *End Of The Road*, Boyz II Men,
Best hard rock performance: Red Hot Chilli Peppers, *Blood Sugar Sex Magic*
Best metal performance: *Wish*, Nine Inch Nails
Best alternative album: *Bone Machine*, Tom Waits
Best reggae album: *Xtra Naked*, Shabba Ranks

IVOR NOVELLO AWARDS

Best contemporary song/Best selling song/International hit of the year: Peter Dale and Mick Leeson for *Would I Lie To You*, Charles And Eddie.
Songwriters of the year: The Shamen
Best song musically and lyrically: *Why*, Annie Lennox
PRS most performed work: *Deeply Dippy*, Right Said Fred.
Best song from a film: *Tears In Heaven*, Eric Clapton.

MTV AWARDS (Sept 92)

Best video/direction/editing: *Right Now*, Van Halen
Best breakthrough video/art direction: *Give It Away*, Red Hot Chilli Peppers
Viewers choice award: Under the Bridge, Red Hot Chilli Peppers
Best video from a film: *Bohemian Rhapsody*, Wayne's World
Best choreography: *My Lovin'*, En Vogue
Best rap video: *Tennessee*, Arrested Development
Best metal/hard rock video: *Enter Sandman*, Metallica

IRISH RECORDED MUSIC AWARDS

Best international act/best album: REM
International newcomer: Curtis Stigers
International country album: *Ropin' The Wind*, Garth Brooks
Irish album: *Man Alive*, 4 Of Us
Irish female artist: Enya
Irish male artist: Paul Brady
Best Irish artist: The Stunning
Best new act: Elanor McEvoy
Hall of Fame award: Van Morrison

▲ *'Revolutionize… sight and sound' – Hypnosis*

we perceive the sight and sound' experience. And it just might too…

▶ RAW POWER (ITV)
Designed to cover anything that could remotely come under the heading 'hard rock', ie everything from Napalm Death to Dan Reed Network, "Raw Power" covered its ground – promo videos, live acts, gig guides, celeb interviews and club round-ups plus all the gossip (from the irrepressible Krusher) – with admirable efficiency and the minimum of intervention from VJ Ann Park. Apart from a more user-friendly slot and a surprise home visit from Slash, what more could any heavy metal fan want? No frills, no fuss and loads of riffs.

▶ RAW SOUP (Carlton)
A mixture of "Reportage", "The Word" and "The Tube", "Raw Soup" started off shaky and ended up strong. The improvement was due less to a strong and adventurous musical policy – Senser rubbing shoulders with Jamiroquai, The Frank And Walters with plucky little Euro-songbird Sonia – than to the increasingly confident way in which co-hosts Paul Tonkinson and Miranda Sawyer handled presentational chores and spiky studio-floor discussions.

▶ NO STILETTOS (BBC Scotland)
Introduced by charismatic beanpole Eddi Reader, who also performed three numbers per programme with her band The Patron Saints Of Imperfection, "No Stilettos" boasted not only the most telegenic of TV music venues so far – The Cottier, a de-consecrated church starting a second career as a theatre come restaurant – but a host of left-of-centre favourites. These included The Lemonheads, Pulp, Cranberries, American Music Club, Edwyn Collins and Ian McNabb.

▶ LATER (BBC2)
Hosted by the genial Jools Holland, "Later" benefitted from a change to a more viewer-friendly Friday night slot and the introduction

of a more eclectic musical menu.

The latter enabled the likes of Leonard Cohen – who raised his grizzled mug on The Beeb for the first time since he appeared with Julie Felix 20-odd years hence – to provide a rare main course to Jellyfish's frothy starter. At a later date, the acidic tartness of PJ Harvey's striking prose was soothed by the uplifting spiritual Sounds Of Blackness. As the man said, there's something for everyone and you can take the kids.

▶ DANCE ENERGY HOUSE PARTY (Channel 4)
Despite its slightly contrived format, "House Party", fronted by the endearingly daft

Miranda and Paul: vital ingredients for a good "Raw Soup"

Normski, was never less than entertaining. Within the happening portals of chez 'Ski, The Shamen could be found cheek-by-jowl with Neneh Cherry, and The Charlatans with Lisa Stansfield. As if to justify her much reported quote that "comedy is the rock 'n' roll of the 90s", Janet Street-Porter added Vas Blackwood (aka Winston in "The Lenny Henry Show") as comic support, and a good time was had by all. Yo!, and, indeed, ho, ho.

▶ **TOP OF THE POPS** (BBC 1)
For 1992/93 the burning question for television's longest running pop show was 'will it still be here in 12 months time?' After an alarming slump in viewing figures, from an all-time high of 15 million down to a low point of six million, much to-ing but mainly fro-ing of new presenters (Tony Dortie and Mark Franklin were the sole survivors of the five new presenters who replaced DJ celebs) and lashings of 'it's gonna get the chop tomorrow'-type speculation, another Great British institution was saved. But for how long?

▶ **139** (Cable only)
If you could ignore the irritatingly repetitive news bulletins and the prattle of some of the less competent VJs, MTV offered something for everyone 24 hours of every day.

Ray Cokes finished miles ahead of the pack as the man most likely to go far-ther. His "Big Picture Show", featuring interviews with film stars, directors and producers, could always be relied on to come up with something amusing and off the wall. As, too, could MTV's "Most Wanted" featuring the most in-demand artists, the most unusual performances and more viewer inter-action than you could shake a stick at.

Otherwise Paul King with his Indie-oriented "120 Minutes", the informative top 40 show "Hit List UK" and Dennis Leary "Station-Ident" rants all hit the spot.

fanzines & auctions

fanzines...a selection

● **BRAIN DAMAGE**
The International Pink Floyd Magazine.
Pink Floyd have no official fanzines, but Brain Damage is a comprehensive contribution to the unofficial ones that exist. First issued in 1986 and now published in the USA (since Jan 1993), Brain Damage enjoys a readership of around 5,000 worldwide. Quite glossy, well presented, more of a magazine than a fanzine, it includes information on other contacts/fanzines, re-releases, book reviews, and many other items of interest to the Pink Floyd devotee.

The editor, Glen Povey, recently visited Eugene den Ouden in Holland, who has spent years installing a fully automated miniature construction of *The Wall* show, and there's a review of a recently unearthed rarity ; a video of Syd Barrett pre-Floyd and out of his box.

There's plenty of info re Floyd's current activities; David Gilmour's involvement in Paul Rodgers' tribute to blues great Muddy Waters, for example. Plus this year marks the 20th anniversary of the release of *Dark Side Of The Moon*, so there's plenty of news re promotional items from EMI and the Pink Floyd Fan Convention.

Brain Damage is available from Glenn Povey, PO Box 385, Uxbridge, Middlesex, UB9 5DZ (£2.50 plus p&p)

● **STRANGETHINGS**
The Emotional Fish Fanzine.
Strangethings is only in its second incarnation and young and fresh in tone. Written by Andrew Unsworth, a devotee of the outfit, and dedicated to keeping fans in touch with An Emotional Fish's progress, reminding them of their roots and history, and maybe making a few conversions along the way! This is presented in an A5 format, with a rather off-putting capital typeface, interspersed with blurred and grainy black and white photographs.

However, you can't help but be infected by Andy's love of his subject, and this has the ring of unspoilt fandom about it.

Available for £1.20 from Andrew Unsworth,

4 Windmill Lane, Dublin 2, Ireland (Please enclose SAE).

● **BE GLAD...FOR THE SONG HAS NO ENDING**
All things Incredible (String Band)
Published twice a year, Be Glad… is, as stated on the cover, an appreciation of The Incredible String Band past and present. Lovingly crafted, this publication bears testament to editor Andy Roberts' obsession with all things Incredible over the last 20 odd years. For £3, not only do you get loads of info, reviews, and articles of interest, but also a free facsimile concert handbill – a very nice touch.

Themes remain true to IBS's rustic concerns; one article investigates the megaliths and myths of the Penwern area, "where much of the script for the film *Be Glad For The Song Has No Ending* was dreamed, written and acted out". This fanzine is a solid attempt to record IBS history previously unavailable to the public, and certainly keeps the faith for the dream-believers.

Available from Andy Roberts, 84 Elland Road, Brighouse, West Yorkshire, HD6 2QR (£3 inc p&p)

● **FACELIFT**
The Canterbury Scene and Beyond.
This fanzine, as its title depicts, covers what's broadly known as the Canterbury Scene – bands such as Soft Machine, Caravan, Hatfield and the North, Egg, National Health, and In Cahoots, and solo player such as Robert Wyatt, Kevin Ayres, Steve Hillage, etc. This comprehensive title also covers anything it considers worthwhile in the psychedelic, experimental, progressive and jazz fields.

While Facelift is a little dry, it will certainly appeal to those who take this type of music seriously. Issue ten includes a 26 page interview with Richard Sinclair, spanning his time with The Wilde Flowers, Caravan, Hatfield and the North, Camel, In Cahoots, and others. Other items of interest in the previous issue include interviews with Dagmar Kruse, Jakko (Level 42), and an ecstatic review of Kevin Ayres' live show at the Shaw Theatre in April 92.

Available from Phil Howitt, 39 Nicholas Road, Manchester M21 1LG (£1.20 inc p&p)

● **HIGHWAY TWELVE**
A kd langzine.
Highway Twelve is a typical in-joke fanzine. All gushing and girlie, this gets plenty of schoolgirl mileage out of lang's on-stage innuendos and rumoured song-sources; "the songs on *Ingénue* were written about her experience of falling in love for the first time", it

Christie's South Kensington

gushes. However, there's a decent biography in issue one, a thorough coverage of the kd lang convention and a definitive discography. This follows the traditional fanzine remit of mythologizing its subject in a refreshingly irreverent manner.

Available from Lin Murdoch and Jan Cormack, 19 Wood Street, Torry, Aberdeen AB1 3QD (£1.50 inc p&p)

● DARK STAR
Mike Oldfield Magazine.

Dark Star could just as easily be called *Tubular Bells*, as the main content of the fanzine is a celebration of this (not surprisingly as Mike Oldfield's reputation rests upon the success of *Tubular Bells* 20 years ago). So if *Tubular Bells* was a life-changing experience for you, this could be your kind of fanzine. Other items include a lengthy review of Mike Oldfield live at the Royal Albert Hall, complete with fascinating reprints of the six different access passes one may have spotted backstage. Available from Chris Dewey, 7 Stockley Road, Wareham, Dorset BH20 4EZ (£4 for two issues)

● WHERE'S ERIC!
All things Clapton

Where's Eric is a well-presented update on Eric Clapton's activities, covering events he has appeared at and events he was rumoured to appear at, but didn't. There is a review of Eric's secret gig in support of Alcoholics Anonymous in Issue 5, and his appearance in the not-so-worthy Japanese TV commercial for cigarettes. Truly for aficionados, there is also the set list for the Albert Hall gig and a re-run of the 1980 Friday Rock Show Interview with Clapton by Tommy Vance. Available From A E Edser, 74 Lowbrooks Drive, Woodlands Park, Maidenhead, Berkshire SL6 3XR (£1.75 per issue)

auctions...majorpopsales

If you're wondering what makes an item particularly valuable or sought after, apparently it's the items that have an immediate association with the artist. For example, song lyrics penned by the artist, and showing some of the mechanics of writing the song, are always in demand. Clothes which are habitually worn and authenticated by photographs are worth more than stage costumes donned only once, borne out by the highest ever price being fetched in auction last year for Lennon's old leather jacket (the one he wore before he changed his whole style) – £23,000.

The same logic applies to guitars: one that was actually used for recordings and gigs and is authethenticated by photographs, would be worth more than just another guitar from a star's collection.

★ CHRISTIE'S

Christie's Auction of Pop took place on Friday 14th May, and Beatles memorabilia took up a large portion of the lots. A scribbled playlist by Lennon went for £1,980 (reserve price £1,500-2000) and a pair of his old Chelsea Boots (RP £3,000-5,000) went for £3,080.

Stage outfits can be worth a hefty sum too, depending on their pedigree; Marc Bolan's one piece flared jumpsuit of burgundy satin, embroidered with silver and blue sequins (RP £150-250) spelling "Marc", fetched £330, and a more rare stage outfit of James Brown, comprising a typically understated, ornate scarlet four-arch crown and a full length cape of ermine and velvet (RP £8,000-12,000) fetched a mere £6,600. More contemporary items were there too; a signed cover of *One Step Beyond* by Madness (RP £200-400) went for £286. Prize for Kitsch instrument of the year went to Gene Simmons' Kramer Axe Solidbody Guitar (RP £1,500-2,500), shaped like, yes, a huge axe. One of the financial coups of the event was a black boned satin bustier of Madonna's, signed "Madonna" in gold felt-pen, and well authenticated by publicity photographs. Reserved at £4,500-6,500, this fetched a modest £8,580.

★ BONHAMS

Earlier on in the year, Bonhams' Entertainment Sale offered up some interesting Beatles paraphernalia. A metallic saucepan lid and a pie tin (both reserved at £200-300) signed by well-known culinary couple John Lennon and Yoko Ono fetched £260 and £160 respectively.

Silver, Gold and Platinum discs were well represented by the likes of Duran Duran (*Notorious*) Foreigner (*Agent Provocateur*), The Dave Clark Five (*Twenty Five Thumping Great Hits*), Eurythmics (*Sweet Dreams*), Black Sabbath (*Technical Ecstasy*), John Lennon (*Imagine*), Diana Ross And The Supremes (*Twenty Golden Greats*) and Roxy Music (*Flesh And Blood*). Of these, only *Imagine* (£320) and The Supremes (£260)

'Donna's old undies... a snip at £8,500

fetched more than their reserve price. The others went for less or remained unsold.

★ SOTHEBY'S

Sotheby's had its 1993 pop sale on 29 July, and plenty of signed photographs and records featured on the list of lots, the most notable signature being Jim Morrison's autographed piece of paper (reserved at £500-600) dedicated 'to the LA Woman'.

Other sought-after items included posters, especially psychedelic ones. A Jimi Hendrix concert poster from the Milwaukee Auditorium gig of May 1, 1970 was reserved at £1,500-1,800, despite its slightly shabby state. Slightly more poignant was a letter (written in 1965 and reserved at £250-300) from Brian Jones to a fan in which the original Stone pleaded "which are your favourite tracks? I'd love to know, honestly.")

Elsewhere a Who set-list taped to the underside of Keith Moon's Timpani drumskin was available for between £1,500-1,800. Song lyrics penned by the artist were also available in spades. A sheet of typed lyrics complete with ballpoint corrections, for Dylan's *Most Likely You Go Your Way And I'll Go Mine*, was available for between £2,500-3,500, while the words to Blondie's *Dreaming*, scribbled by Debbie Harry in blue felt pen on yellow lined paper (ouch!) and including a lip print in red, was put on offer for the relatively paltry sum of £200-300.

At the top of the list for lyrics, however, was John Lennon's original manuscript for *I Am The Walrus*, which was reserved at a massive £40,000-50,000.

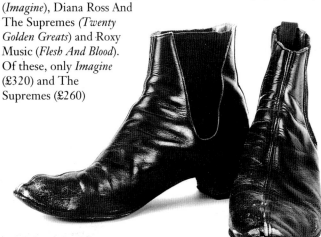

Lennon's boots were made for walking at £3,000

Christie's South Kensington

the year in charts...

...a whole undiluted 52 weeks' worth of hard chart information, guaranteed to satisfy the most ferocious appetite for stats, and to resolve the latest of late-night arguments.

On the following pages we give you the Top 20 UK albums, Top 10 UK singles, plus the Top 5 UK indie albums and Top 5 UK dance singles for every week from September 1992 to August 1993, courtesy of CIN.

Plus the Top 20 US albums and Top 10 US singles for the same period, brought to you by kind permission of Billboard Publications Inc.

AND right here, the Top 10 albums from each of the Virgin Labatt's Album Charts broadcast from the launch of the station to the end of August 1993.

We'll be asking questions later.

The Virgin Labatt's Album Chart

Labatt's *Canadian Lager* ™

With albums now outselling singles three to one, particularly among serious rock fans, the three-hour Virgin Labatt's Album Chart has become the most significant chart on music radio.

Album sales recorded at 1,550 record shop tills across the country are electronically monitored right up to midnight on each Saturday, allowing Chart Show host Russ Williams to present the best tracks from the best-selling albums every Sunday afternoon at 4 pm. Compiled by Gallup, the chart – like Virgin 1215 and Labatt's – is totally dedicated to people of discerning taste, and reflects Labatt's commitment to music.

The first ever Virgin Labatt's Album Chart was broadcast on Sunday 2nd May...

Week Ending 1st May

1	**Automatic For The People** R.E.M.	Warner Bros.
2	**Bang** World Party	Ensign
3	**Ten Summoner's Tales** Sting	A&M
4	**Duran Duran** Duran Duran	Parlophone
5	**Get A Grip** Aerosmith	Geffen
6	**The Infotainment Scan** Fall	Permanent
7	**Unplugged** Eric Clapton	Reprise/Duck
8	**3 Years, 5 Months & 2 Days In The Life** Arrested Development	Cooltempo
9	**In Concert – MTV Plugged** Bruce Springsteen	Columbia
10	**Black Tie White Noise** David Bowie	Arista/BMG

Week Ending 8th May

1	**Republic** New Order	London
2	**Automatic For The People** R.E.M.	Warner Bros.
3	**Ten Summoner's Tales** Sting	A&M
4	**Symphony Or Damn** Terence Trent D'Arby	Columbia
5	**Banba** Clannad	RCA
6	**Bang** World Party	Ensign
7	**Duran Duran** Duran Duran	Parlophone
8	**Rid Of Me** PJ Harvey	Island
9	**Unplugged** Eric Clapton	Reprise/Duck
10	**Get A Grip** Aerosmith	Geffen

Week Ending 15th May

1	**Automatic For The People** R.E.M.	Warner Bros.
2	**Republic** New Order	London
3	**On The Night** Dire Straits	Vertigo
4	**Home Movies – The Best** Everything But The Girl	Blanco Y Negro
5	**Ten Summoner's Tales** Sting	A&M
6	**Banba** Clannad	RCA
7	**Blues Alive** Gary Moore	Virgin
8	**Duran Duran** Duran Duran	Parlophone
9	**Symphony Or Damn** Terence Trent D'Arby	Columbia
10	**Beethoven Was Deaf** Morrissey	HMV

Week Ending 22nd May

1	**Automatic For The People** R.E.M.	Warner Bros.
2	**Republic** New Order	London
3	**On The Night** Dire Straits	Vertigo
4	**Home Movies – The Best** Everything But The Girl	Blanco Y Negro
5	**Keep The Faith** Bon Jovi	Jambco/Mercury
6	**Live At The Royal Albert Hall** Wet Wet Wet/Wren Orchestra	Precious Organisation
7	**Blues Alive** Gary Moore	Virgin
8	**Banba** Clannad	RCA
9	**Ten Summoner's Tales** Sting	A&M
10	**Sleepwalking** Kingmaker	Scorch/Chrysalis

Week Ending 29th May

1	**Automatic For The People** R.E.M.	Warner Bros.
2	**Kamakiriad** Donald Fagen	Reprise
3	**Dream Harder** Waterboys	Geffen
4	**Fate Of Nations** Robert Plant	ES Paranza/Fontana
5	**Unplugged ... And Seated** Rod Stewart	Warner Bros.
6	**Pocket Full Of Kryptonite** Spin Doctors	Epic
7	**Keep The Faith** Bon Jovi	Jambco/Mercury
8	**Republic** New Order	London
9	**Home Movies – The Best** Everything But The Girl	Blanco Y Negro
10	**Ten Summoner's Tales** Sting	A&M

Week Ending 5th June

1	**Automatic For The People** R.E.M.	Warner Bros.
2	**Too Long In Exile** Van Morrison	Exile/Polydor
3	**Unplugged ... And Seated** Rod Stewart	Warner Bros.
4	**Pocket Full Of Kryptonite** Spin Doctors	Epic
5	**Kamakiriad** Donald Fagen	Reprise
6	**Dream Harder** Waterboys	Geffen
7	**Connected** Stereo MC's	4th + B'way
8	**Keep The Faith** Bon Jovi	Jambco/Mercury
9	**Fate Of Nations** Robert Plant	ES Paranza/Fontana
10	**Ten Summoner's Tales** Sting	A&M

Week Ending 12th June

1	**What's Love Got To Do With It** Tina Turner	Parlophone
2	**Automatic For The People** R.E.M.	Warner Bros.
3	**Pocket Full Of Kryptonite** Spin Doctors	Epic
4	**Elemental** Tears For Fears	Mercury
5	**Unplugged ... And Seated** Rod Stewart	Warner Bros.
6	**Connected** Stereo MC's	4th + B'way
7	**Too Long In Exile** Van Morrison	Exile/Polydor
8	**Kamakiriad** Donald Fagen	Reprise
9	**Ten Summoner's Tales** Sting	A&M
10	**Keep The Faith** Bon Jovi	Jambco/Mercury

Week Ending 18th June

1	**What's Love Got To Do With It** Tina Turner	Parlophone
2	**Unplugged ... And Seated** Rod Stewart	Warner Bros.
3	**Unplugged** Neil Young	Reprise
4	**Automatic For The People** R.E.M.	Warner Bros.
5	**Pocket Full Of Kryptonite** Spin Doctors	Epic
6	**Ten Summoner's Tales** Sting	A&M
7	**Connected** Stereo MC's	4th + B'way
8	**Too Long In Exile** Van Morrison	Exile/Polydor
9	**Elemental** Tears For Fears	Mercury
10	**Liberator** OMD	Virgin

Week Ending 26th June

1	**Unplugged ... And Seated** Rod Stewart	Warner Bros.
2	**Pocket Full Of Kryptonite** Spin Doctors	Epic
3	**Automatic For The People** R.E.M.	Warner Bros.
4	**What's Love Got To Do With It** Tina Turner	Parlophone
5	**Unplugged** Neil Young	Reprise
6	**Ten Summoner's Tales** Sting	A&M
7	**Gold Against The Soul** Manic Street Preachers	Columbia
8	**Muddy Water Blues** Paul Rodgers	London
9	**Connected** Stereo MC's	4th + B'way
10	**Keep The Faith** Bon Jovi	Jambco/Mercury

Week Ending 3rd July

1	**Unplugged ... And Seated** Rod Stewart	Warner Bros.
2	**Pocket Full Of Kryptonite** Spin Doctors	Epic
3	**Ten Summoner's Tales** Sting	A&M
4	**Automatic For The People** R.E.M.	Warner Bros.
5	**What's Love Got To Do With It** Tina Turner	Parlophone
6	**Unplugged** Neil Young	Reprise
7	**Connected** Stereo MC's	4th + B'way
8	**Muddy Water Blues** Paul Rodgers	London
9	**Gold Against The Soul** Manic Street Preachers	Columbia
10	**Keep The Faith** Bon Jovi	Jambco/Mercury

Week Ending 10th July

1	**Zooropa** U2	Island
2	**Debut** Bjork	One Little Indian
3	**Unplugged ... And Seated** Rod Stewart	Warner Bros.
4	**Pocket Full Of Kryptonite** Spin Doctors	Epic
5	**Automatic For The People** R.E.M.	Warner Bros.
6	**Ten Summoner's Tales** Sting	A&M
7	**Bigger, Better, Faster, More!** 4 Non Blondes	Interscope/East West
8	**What's Love Got To Do With It** Tina Turner	Parlophone
9	**Unplugged** Neil Young	Reprise
10	**Keep The Faith** Bon Jovi	Jambco/Mercury

Week Ending 17th July

1	**Promises And Lies** UB40	Virgin
2	**Zooropa** U2	Island
3	**Unplugged ... And Seated** Rod Stewart	Warner Bros.
4	**Pocket Full Of Kryptonite** Spin Doctors	Epic
5	**Bigger, Better, Faster, More!** 4 Non Blondes	Interscope/East West
6	**Automatic For The People** R.E.M.	Warner Bros.
7	**Ten Summoner's Tales** Sting	A&M
8	**Debut** Bjork	One Little Indian
9	**Unplugged** Neil Young	Reprise
10	**What's Love Got To Do With It** Tina Turner	Parlophone

Week Ending 24th July

1	**Promises And Lies** UB40	Virgin
2	**Zooropa** U2	Island
3	**Siamese Dream** Smashing Pumpkins	Hut
4	**Pocket Full Of Kryptonite** Spin Doctors	Epic
5	**Bigger, Better, Faster, More!** 4 Non Blondes	Interscope/East West
6	**Automatic For The People** R.E.M.	Warner Bros.
7	**Unplugged ... And Seated** Rod Stewart	Warner Bros.
8	**Ten Summoner's Tales** Sting	A&M
9	**Debut** Bjork	One Little Indian
10	**Keep The Faith** Bon Jovi	Jambco/Mercury

Week Ending 31st July

1	**Promises And Lies** UB40	Virgin
2	**Zooropa** U2	Island
3	**Automatic For The People** R.E.M.	Warner Bros.
4	**Bigger, Better, Faster, More!** 4 Non Blondes	Interscope/East West
5	**Pocket Full Of Kryptonite** Spin Doctors	Epic
6	**Unplugged ... And Seated** Rod Stewart	Warner Bros.
7	**Siamese Dream** Smashing Pumpkins	Hut
8	**Ten Summoner's Tales** Sting	A&M
9	**Debut** Bjork	One Little Indian
10	**Sex And Religion** Vai	Relativity

Week Ending 7th August

1	**Promises And Lies** UB40	Virgin
2	**Zooropa** U2	Island
3	**Automatic For The People** R.E.M.	Warner Bros.
4	**River Of Dreams** Billy Joel	Columbia
5	**Pocket Full Of Kryptonite** Spin Doctors	Epic
6	**Bigger, Better, Faster, More!** 4 Non Blondes	Interscope/East West
7	**Unplugged ... And Seated** Rod Stewart	Warner Bros.
8	**Ten Summoner's Tales** Sting	A&M
9	**Keep The Faith** Bon Jovi	Jambco/Mercury
10	**Siamese Dream** Smashing Pumpkins	Hut

Week Ending 14th August

1	**Promises And Lies** UB40	Virgin
2	**Zooropa** U2	Island
3	**River Of Dreams** Billy Joel	Columbia
4	**Pocket Full Of Kryptonite** Spin Doctors	Epic
5	**Automatic For The People** R.E.M.	Warner Bros.
6	**Bigger, Better, Faster, More!** 4 Non Blondes	Interscope/East West
7	**Unplugged ... And Seated** Rod Stewart	Warner Bros.
8	**What's Love Got To Do With It** Tina Turner	Parlophone
9	**Ten Summoner's Tales** Sting	A&M
10	**Debut** Bjork	One Little Indian

Week Ending 21st August

1	**Promises And Lies** UB40	Virgin
2	**Pocket Full Of Kryptonite** Spin Doctors	Epic
3	**Zooropa** U2	Island
4	**River Of Dreams** Billy Joel	Columbia
5	**Keep The Faith** Bon Jovi	Jambco/Mercury
6	**Automatic For The People** R.E.M.	Warner Bros.
7	**Antmusic - The Very Best Of Adam Ant** Adam Ant	Arcade
8	**Bigger, Better, Faster, More!** 4 Non Blondes	Interscope/East West
9	**Unplugged ... And Seated** Rod Stewart	Warner Bros.
10	**What's Love Got To Do With It** Tina Turner	Parlophone

Week Ending 28th August

1	**Promises And Lies** UB40	Virgin
2	**Levellers** Levellers	China
3	**Pocket Full Of Kryptonite** Spin Doctors	Epic
4	**River Of Dreams** Billy Joel	Columbia
5	**Zooropa** U2	Island
6	**Antmusic - The Very Best Of Adam Ant** Adam Ant	Arcade
7	**Keep The Faith** Bon Jovi	Jambco/Mercury
8	**Automatic For The People** R.E.M.	Warner Bros.
9	**Bigger, Better, Faster, More!** 4 Non Blondes	Interscope/East West
10	**What's Love Got To Do With It** Tina Turner	Parlophone

uk albums

1	**Kylie Greatest Hits** Kylie Minogue	Pwl International
2	**Laughing On Judgement Day** Thunder	EMI
3	**Best...I** The Smiths	WEA
4	**Dangerous** Michael Jackson	Epic
5	**Take That & Party** Take That	RCA
6	**Diva** Annie Lennox	RCA
7	**The Greatest Hits 1966-1992** Neil Diamond	Columbia
8	**Back To Front** Lionel Richie	Motown
9	**Some Gave All** Billy Ray Cyrus	Mercury
10	**We Can't Dance** Genesis	Virgin
11	**Bobby** Bobby Brown	MCA
12	**Stars** Simply Red	East West
13	**Welcome To Wherever You Are** Inxs	Mercury
14	**The Definitive Patsy Cline** Patsy Cline	Arcade
15	**Shepherd Moons** Enya	Warner Brothers
16	**Nevermind** Nirvana	DGC
17	**Growing Up In Public** Jimmy Nail	East West
18	**Divine Madness** Madness	Virgin Television
19	**Up** Right Said Fred	Tug
20	**Jon Secada** Jon Secada	SBK

us albums

1	**Some Gave All** Billy Ray Cyrus	Mercury
2	**Ten** Pearl Jam	Epic Associated
3	**Totally Krossed Out** Kris Kross	Ruffhouse
4	**Boomerang** Soundtrack	Laface
5	**Temple Of The Dog** Temple Of The Dog	A&M
6	**Countdown To Extinction** Megadeth	Capitol
7	**MTV Unplugged EP** Mariah Carey	Columbia
8	**The One** Elton John	MCA
9	**Blood Sugar Sex Magik** Red Hot Chili Peppers	Warner Bros
10	**Ropin' The Wind** Garth Brooks	Liberty
11	**Funky Divas** En Vogue	Atco Eastwest
12	**Mo' Money** Soundtrack	Perspective
13	**Use Your Illusion!** Guns N' Roses	Geffen
14	**OOOOOOOHHH...On The TLC Top** TLC	Laface
15	**Brand New Man** Brooks & Dunn	Arista
16	**Metallica** Metallica	Elektra
17	**House Of Pain** House Of Pain	Tommy Boy
18	**Adrenalize** Def Leppard	Mercury
19	**3 Years 5 Months & 2 Days In The Life** Arrested Development	Chrysalis
20	**No Fences** Garth Brooks	Liberty

uk singles

1	**Rhythm Is A Dancer** Snap	Logic Uk
2	**The Best Things In Life Are Free** Luther Vandross & Janet Jackson	Perspective
3	**Baker Street** Undercover	Pwl International
4	**Achy Breaky Heart** Billy Ray Cyrus	Mercury
5	**Just Another Day** Jon Secada	SBK
6	**Ebeneezer Goode** The Shamen	One Little Indian
7	**Don't You Want Me** Felix	Deconstruction
8	**Walking On Broken Glass** Annie Lennox	RCA
9	**Too Much Love Will Kill You** Brian May	Parlophone
10	**Rock Your Baby** Kws	Network

us singles

1	**End Of The Road (From Boomerang)** Boyz II Men	BIV
2	**Baby Baby Baby** TLC	Laface
3	**November Rain** Guns N' Roses	Geffen
4	**Humpin' Around** Bobby Brown	MCA
5	**This Used To Be My Playground** Madonna	Sire
6	**Move This** Technotronic Featuring Ya Kid K	SBK
7	**Stay** Shakespear's Sister	London
8	**Baby Got Back** Sir Mix-A-Lot	DEF American
9	**Giving Him Something He Can Feel** En Vogue	Atco Eastwest
10	**Just Another Day** Jon Secada	SBK

indy albums

1	**Red Heaven** Throwing Muses	4Al
2	**Levelling The land** The Levellers	Chin
3	**Turns Into Stone** The Stone Roses	Silverton
4	**Full On.. Mask Hysteria** Altern 8	Networ
5	**Screamadelica** Primal Scream	Creatio

dance singles

1	**Ebeneezer Goode** The Shamen	One Little India
2	**The Future Music** Liquid	XLXL
3	**Young Disciples (EP)** Young Disciples	Talkin Lou
4	**Cry Freedom** Mombassa	Union Cit
5	**High** Hyper Go Go	Deconstructio

After 47 consecutive weeks in the Top Ten, Simply Red's Stars bows out. The only album to better this? It's Dire... Meanwhile, as Billy Ray Cyrus drops off the Number One spot, the Shamen's Ebeneezer Goode enters at Number Six – the group's highest debut entry following two previous Top Ten singles. Newcomer Dr Alban made Number 18 with It's My Life. The former Nigerian dentist from Stockholm was Number One in Austria, the Netherlands and Germany at this time. He gave up drilling to run a club and clothes shop... oh, and record too.

uk albums

1	**Tubular Bells II** Mike Oldfield	WEA
2	**Tourism** Roxette	EMI
3	**Kylie Greatest Hits** Kylie Minogue	Pwl International
4	**Back To Front** Lionel Richie	Motown
5	**Diva** Annie Lennox	RCA
6	**Unplugged** Eric Clapton	Duck
7	**Best...I** The Smiths	WEA
8	**Paul Weller** Paul Weller	Go! Discs
9	**The Greatest Hits 1966-1992** Neil Diamond	Columbia
10	**Dangerous** Michael Jackson	Epic
11	**America's Least Wanted** Ugly Kid Joe	Mercury
12	**Some Gave All** Billy Ray Cyrus	Mercury
13	**Laughing On Judgement Day** Thunder	EMI
14	**The Definitive Patsy Cline** Patsy Cline	Arcade
15	**Stars** Simply Red	East West
16	**We Can't Dance** Genesis	Virgin
17	**Nevermind** Nirvana	DGC
18	**Welcome To Wherever You Are** Inxs	Mercury
19	**Take That & Party** Take That	RCA
20	**Shepherd Moons** Enya	Warner Brothers

us albums

1	**Some Gave All** Billy Ray Cyrus	Mercury
2	**Bobby** Bobby Brown	MCA
3	**Ten** Pearl Jam	Epic Associated
4	**Unplugged** Eric Clapton	Duck
5	**Beyond The Season** Garth Brooks	Liberty
6	**Totally Krossed Out** Kris Kross	Ruffhouse
7	**Boomerang** Soundtrack	Laface
8	**Temple Of The Dog** Temple Of The Dog	A&M
9	**The One** Elton John	MCA
10	**Countdown To Extinction** Megadeth	Capitol
11	**Funky Divas** En Vogue	Atco Eastwest
12	**MTV Unplugged EP** Mariah Carey	Columbia
13	**Adrenalize** Def Leppard	Mercury
14	**Blood Sugar Sex Magik** Red Hot Chili Peppers	Warner Bros
15	**Ropin' The Wind** Garth Brooks	Liberty
16	**House Of Pain** House Of Pain	Tommy Boy
17	**Use Your Illusion!** Guns N' Roses	Geffen
18	**OOOOOOOHHH...On The TLC Top** TLC	Laface
19	**3 Years 5 Months & 2 Days In The Life** Arrested Development	Chrysalis
20	**What's The 411?** Mary J. Blige	Uptown

uk singles

1	**Rhythm Is A Dancer** Snap	Logic Uk
2	**Ebeneezer Goode** The Shamen	One Little Indian
3	**Baker Street** Undercover	Pwl International
4	**The Best Things In Life Are Free** Luther Vandross & Janet Jackson	Perspective
5	**Achy Breaky Heart** Billy Ray Cyrus	Mercury
6	**Too Much Love Will Kill You** Brian May	Parlophone
7	**Just Another Day** Jon Secada	SBK
8	**It's My Life** Dr Alban	Logic
9	**Walking On Broken Glass** Annie Lennox	RCA
10	**Don't You Want Me** Felix	Deconstruction

us singles

1	**End Of The Road (From Boomerang)** Boyz II Men	BIV
2	**Baby Baby Baby** TLC	Laface
3	**Humpin' Around** Bobby Brown	MCA
4	**November Rain** Guns N' Roses	Geffen
5	**Stay** Shakespear's Sister	London
6	**Giving Him Something He Can Feel** En Vogue	Atco Eastwest
7	**Sometimes Love Just Ain't Enough** Patty Smith	MCA
8	**Just Another Day** Jon Secada	SBK
9	**Jump Around** House Of Pain	Tommy Boy
10	**Move This** Technotronic Featuring Ya Kid K	SBK

indy albums

1	**Fontanelle** Babes in Toyland	Southern
2	**Red Heaven** Throwing Muses	4AD
3	**Levelling the Land** The Levellers	China
4	**Screamadelica** Primal Scream	Creation
5	**Turns into Stone** The Stone Roses	Silvertone

dance singles

1	**The Mighty Ming!** Brothers Love Dubs	Stress
2	**Hypnosis** Psychotropic	O2 O2
3	**Praise** Inner City	Ten
4	**Ebeneezer Goode** The Shamen	One Little Indian
5	**Bass Shake** Urban Shakedown/Micky Finn	Urban

indy albums

1	**Fontanelle** Babes in Toyland	Southern
2	**Levelling the Land** The Levellers	China
3	**Red Heaven** Throwing Muses	4AD
4	**Oomalama** Eugenius	Paperhouse
5	**Bleach** Nirvana	Tupelo

dance singles

1	**Give You** Djaimin	Cooltempo
2	**On A Mission** Aloof	Cowboy
3	**Walkin' On** Sheer Bronze	Black Pearl
4	**Praise** Inner City	Ten
5	**Push Push** Orinigal Rockers	Cake

uk singles

1	**Ebeneezer Goode** The Shamen	One Little Indian
2	**Baker Street** Undercover	Pwl International
3	**Rhythm Is A Dancer** Snap	Logic Uk
4	**It's My Life** Dr Alban	Logic
5	**Too Much Love Will Kill You** Brian May	Parlophone
6	**The Best Things In Life Are Free** Luther Vandross & Janet Jackson	Perspective
7	**Just Another Day** Jon Secada	Sbk
8	**My Destiny** Lionel Richie	Motown
9	**Theme From M.A.S.H.** Manic Street Preachers	Columbia
10	**House Of Love** East 17	London

us singles

1	**End Of The Road (From Boomerang)** Boyz II Men	BIV
2	**Baby Baby Baby** TLC	Laface
3	**Humpin' Around** Bobby Brown	MCA
4	**Stay** Shakespear's Sister	London
5	**November Rain** Guns N' Roses	Geffen
6	**Sometimes Love Just Ain't Enough** Patty Smith	MCA
7	**Jump Around** House Of Pain	Tommy Boy
8	**Just Another Day** Jon Secada	SBK
9	**The One** Elton John	MCA
10	**She's Playing Hard To Get** Hi-Five	Jive

us albums

1	**Some Gave All** Billy Ray Cyrus	Mercury
2	**Beyond The Season** Garth Brooks	Liberty
3	**Unplugged** Eric Clapton	Duck
4	**Ten** Pearl Jam	Epic Associated
5	**Bobby** Bobby Brown	MCA
6	**Boomerang** Soundtrack	Laface
7	**Totally Krossed Out** Kris Kross	Ruffhouse
8	**Temple Of The Dog** Temple Of The Dog	A&M
9	**What's The 411?** Mary J. Blige	Uptown
10	**Funky Divas** En Vogue	Atco Eastwest
11	**Adrenalize** Def Leppard	Mercury
12	**The One** Elton John	MCA
13	**3 Years 5 Months & 2 Days In The Life** Arrested Development	Chrysalis
14	**House Of Pain** House Of Pain	Tommy Boy
15	**Countdown To Extinction** Megadeth	Capitol
16	**Blood Sugar Sex Magik** Red Hot Chili Peppers	Warner Bros
17	**MTV Unplugged EP** Mariah Carey	Columbia
18	**Singles** Soundtrack	Epic Soundtrax
19	**Ropin' The Wind** Garth Brooks	Liberty
20	**No Fences** Garth Brooks	Liberty

uk albums

1	**Tubular Bells II** Mike Oldfield	WEA
2	**The Best Of Belinda Vol 1** Belinda Carlisle	Virgin
3	**Tourism** Roxette	EMI
4	**Back To Front** Lionel Richie	Motown
5	**Kylie Greatest Hits** Kylie Minogue	Pwl International
6	**Diva** Annie Lennox	RCA
7	**Unplugged** Eric Clapton	Duck
8	**Amused To Death** Roger Waters	Columbia
9	**Best...I** The Smiths	WEA
10	**Copper Blue** Sugar	Creation
11	**The Definitive Patsy Cline** Patsy Cline	Arcade
12	**The Greatest Hits 1966-1992** Neil Diamond	Columbia
13	**Stars** Simply Red	East West
14	**Nevermind** Nirvana	DGC
15	**The Looks Or The Lifestyle** Pop Will Eat Itself	RCA
16	**Dangerous** Michael Jackson	Epic
17	**Welcome To Wherever You Are** Inxs	Mercury
18	**We Can't Dance** Genesis	Virgin
19	**Some Gave All** Billy Ray Cyrus	Mercury
20	**99.9 Degrees F** Suzanne Vega	A&M

indy albums

1	**Copper Blue** Sugar	Creation
2	**Stranglers in the Night** Stranglers	Psycho
3	**Fontanelle** Babes in Toyland	Southern
4	**Screamadelica** Primal Scream	Creation
5	**Levelling the Land** The Levellers	China

dance singles

1	**Fire/Jericho** The Prodigy	XL
2	**I Feel Love** Messiah/Preciou Wilson	Kickin
3	**Radiccio (EP)** Orbital	Internal
4	**Give You** Djaimin	Cooltempo
5	**Saved My Life** Lil'Louis & The World	ffrr

uk singles

1	**Ebeneezer Goode** The Shamen	One Little Indian
2	**It's My Life** Dr Alban	Logic
3	**Baker Street** Undercover	Pwl International
4	**Rhythm Is A Dancer** Snap	Logic Uk
5	**Too Much Love Will Kill You** Brian May	Parlophone
6	**Iron Lion Zion** Bob Marley & The Wailers	Tuff Gong
7	**Theme From M.A.S.H.** Manic Street Preachers	Columbia
8	**My Destiny** Lionel Richie	Motown
9	**The Best Things In Life Are Free** Luther Vandross & Janet Jackson	Perspective
10	**Just Another Day** Jon Secada	SBK

us singles

1	**End Of The Road (From Boomerang)** Boyz II Men	BIV
2	**Sometimes Love Just Ain't Enough** Patty Smith	MCA
3	**Baby Baby Baby** TLC	Laface
4	**Humpin' Around** Bobby Brown	MCA
5	**November Rain** Guns N' Roses	Geffen
6	**Stay** Shakespear's Sister	London
7	**Jump Around** House Of Pain	Tommy Boy
8	**Just Another Day** Jon Secada	SBK
9	**She's Playing Hard To Get** Hi-Five	Jive
10	**Please Don't Go** K.W.S.	Next Plateau

us albums

1	**Some Gave All** Billy Ray Cyrus	Mercury
2	**Unplugged** Eric Clapton	Duck
3	**Ten** Pearl Jam	Epic Associated
4	**Beyond The Season** Garth Brooks	Liberty
5	**Bobby** Bobby Brown	MCA
6	**What's The 411?** Mary J. Blige	Uptown
7	**Boomerang** Soundtrack	Laface
8	**Totally Krossed Out** Kris Kross	Ruffhouse
9	**Funky Divas** En Vogue	Atco Eastwest
10	**I Still Believe In You** Vince Gill	MCA
11	**Blood Sugar Sex Magik** Red Hot Chili Peppers	Warner Bros
12	**Temple Of The Dog** Temple Of The Dog	A&M
13	**The One** Elton John	MCA
14	**3 Years 5 Months & 2 Days In The Life** Arrested Development	Chrysalis
15	**Adrenalize** Def Leppard	Mercury
16	**Singles** Soundtrack	Epic Soundtrax
17	**Metallica** Metallica	Elektra
18	**Honeymoon In Vegas** Soundtrack	Epic Soundtrax
19	**House Of Pain** House Of Pain	Tommy Boy
20	**Ropin' The Wind** Garth Brooks	Liberty

uk albums

1	**The Best Of Belinda Vol 1** Belinda Carlisle	Virgin
2	**III Sides To Every Story** Extreme	A&M
3	**Boss Drum** The Shamen	One Little Indian
4	**Tubular Bells II** Mike Oldfield	WEA
5	**Back To Front** Lionel Richie	Motown
6	**Diva** Annie Lennox	RCA
7	**Am I Not Your Girl?** Sinead O'Connor	Ensign
8	**Unplugged** Eric Clapton	Duck
9	**Tourism** Roxette	EMI
10	**Kylie Greatest Hits** Kylie Minogue	Pwl International
11	**The Singles Collection** The Four Tops	Polygram TV
12	**Nevermind** Nirvana	DGC
13	**Stars** Simply Red	East West
14	**Best...I** The Smiths	WEA
15	**Welcome To Wherever You Are** Inxs	Mercury
16	**The Definitive Patsy Cline** Patsy Cline	Arcade
17	**Dangerous** Michael Jackson	Epic
18	**The Greatest Hits 1966-1992** Neil Diamond	Columbia
19	**Amused To Death** Roger Waters	Columbia
20	**Rush Street** Richard Marx	Capitol

indy albums

1	**Boss Drum** The Shamen	One Little Indian
2	**Copper Blue** Sugar	Creation
3	**Number 10** JJ Cale	Silvertone
4	**...XYZ** Moose	Hut
5	**Screamadelica** Primal Scream	Creation

dance singles

1	**I'm Gonna Get You** Bizarre Inc/Angie Brown	Vinyl Solution
2	**Fire/Jericho** The Prodigy	XL
3	**Don't Go** Awesome 3	Citybeat
4	**Dub War** Dance Conspiracy	XL
5	**Xpand Ya Mind (Expansions)** Wag Ya Tail	PWL Sanctuary

uk singles

1	**Ebeneezer Goode** The Shamen	One Little Indian
2	**It's My Life** Dr Alban	Logic
3	**Baker Street** Undercover	Pwl International
4	**Sleeping Satellite** Tasmin Archer	EMI
5	**Iron Lion Zion** Bob Marley & The Wailers	Tuff Gong
6	**End Of The Road** Boyz II Men	Motown
7	**My Destiny** Lionel Richie	Motown
8	**Too Much Love Will Kill You** Brian May	Parlophone
9	**Theme From M.A.S.H.** Manic Street Preachers	Columbia
10	**Rhythm Is A Dancer** Snap	Logic Uk

us singles

1	**End Of The Road (From Boomerang)** Boyz II Men	BIV
2	**Sometimes Love Just Ain't Enough** Patty Smith	MCA
3	**Humpin' Around** Bobby Brown	MCA
4	**Baby Baby Baby** TLC	Laface
5	**Jump Around** House Of Pain	Tommy Boy
6	**She Playing Hard To Get** Hi-Five	Jive
7	**November Rain** Guns N' Roses	Geffen
8	**Please Don't Go** K.W.S.	Next Plateau
9	**Just Another Day** Jon Secada	SBK
10	**Stay** Shakespear's Sister	London

us albums

1	**Some Gave All** Billy Ray Cyrus	Mercury
2	**Ten** Pearl Jam	Epic Associated
3	**Unplugged** Eric Clapton	Duck
4	**Beyond The Season** Garth Brooks	Liberty
5	**Bobby** Bobby Brown	MCA
6	**What's The 411?** Mary J. Blige	Uptown
7	**Singles** Soundtrack	Epic Soundtrax
8	**Totally Krossed Out** Kris Kross	Ruffhouse
9	**Funky Divas** En Vogue	Atco Eastwest
10	**Boomerang** Soundtrack	Laface
11	**The One** Elton John	MCA
12	**Blood Sugar Sex Magik** Red Hot Chili Peppers	Warner Bros
13	**Greatest Misses** Public Enemy	DEF Jam
14	**3 Years 5 Months & 2 Days In The Life** Arrested Development	Chrysalis
15	**Temple Of The Dog** Temple Of The Dog	A&M
16	**I Still Believe In You** Vince Gill	MCA
17	**Adrenalize** Def Leppard	Mercury
18	**No Fences** Garth Brooks	Liberty
19	**Ropin' The Wind** Garth Brooks	Liberty
20	**Wynonna** Wynonna	Curb

uk albums

1	**Gold – Greatest Hits** Abba	Polydo
2	**Tubular Bells II** Mike Oldfield	WEA
3	**The Best Of Belinda Vol 1** Belinda Carlisle	Virgir
4	**Back To Front** Lionel Richie	Motowr
5	**Boss Drum** The Shamen	One Little Indian
6	**Am I Not Your Girl?** Sinead O'Connor	Ensign
7	**III Sides To Every Story** Extreme	A&M
8	**Unplugged** Eric Clapton	Duck
9	**Diva** Annie Lennox	RCA
10	**Songs Of Freedom** Bob Marley	Tuff Gong
11	**Tourism** Roxette	EMI
12	**Kylie Greatest Hits** Kylie Minogue	Pwl International
13	**Stars** Simply Red	East West
14	**Greatest Misses** Public Enemy	Def Jam
15	**Welcome To Wherever You Are** Inxs	Mercury
16	**Dangerous** Michael Jackson	Epic
17	**Nevermind** Nirvana	DGC
18	**We Can't Dance** Genesis	Virgin
19	**The Singles Collection** The Four Tops	Polygram TV
20	**The Greatest Hits 1966-1992** Neil Diamond	Columbia

Woolies start their first in-store chart with Tasmin Archer's Sleeping Satellite at Number One. The northern lass debuts at Number One in the CIN charts too following other memorable Bradford hitmakers Smokie and Kiki Dee. In the USA, Boyz II Men's End Of The Road stays at Number One for the tenth week in a row – the longest-running US Number One in the past decade.

indy albums

1	**Boss Drum** The Shamen	One Little Indian
2	**Abba-esque (The remixes)** Erasure	Mute
3	**Copper Blue** Sugar	Creation
4	**Number 10** JJ Cale	Silvertone
5	**Screamadelica** Primal Scream	Creation

dance singles

1	**Trip II The Moon (Kaleido...)** Acen	Production House
2	**I'm Gonna Get You** Bizarre Inc/Angie Brown	Vinyl Solution
3	**Jump Around** House of Pain	Ruffness
4	**Excited** M-People	Deconstruction
5	**Nush** Nush	X:treme

uk singles

1	**Ebeneezer Goode** The Shamen	One Little Indian
2	**It's My Life** Dr Alban	Logic
3	**Sleeping Satellite** Tasmin Archer	EMI
4	**End Of The Road** Boyz II Men	Motown
5	**Baker Street** Undercover	Pwl International
6	**I'm Gonna Get You** Bizarre Inc	Vinyl Solution
7	**Iron Lion Zion** Bob Marley & The Wailers	Tuff Gong
8	**My Destiny** Lionel Richie	Motown
9	**My Name Is Prince** Prince And The N.P.G.	Paisley Park
10	**Sentinel** Mike Oldfield	WEA

us singles

1	**End Of The Road (From Boomerang)** Boyz II Men	BIV
2	**Sometimes Love Just Ain't Enough** Patty Smith	MCA
3	**Jump Around** House Of Pain	Tommy Boy
4	**Humpin' Around** Bobby Brown	MCA
5	**Baby Baby Baby** TLC	Laface
6	**She Playing Hard To Get** Hi-Five	Jive
7	**Please Don't Go** K.W.S.	Next Plateau
8	**People Everyday** Arrested Development	Chrysalis
9	**When I Look Into Your Eyes** Firehouse	Epic
10	**I'd Die Without You (From Boomerang)** P.M. Dawn	Gee Street

us albums

1	**The Chase** Garth Brooks	Liberty
2	**Unplugged** Eric Clapton	Duck
3	**Some Gave All** Billy Ray Cyrus	Mercury
4	**Ten** Pearl Jam	Epic Associated
5	**Beyond The Season** Garth Brooks	Liberty
6	**Singles** Soundtrack	Epic Soundtrax
7	**Broken** Nine Inch Nails	Nothing
8	**Bobby** Bobby Brown	MCA
9	**What's The 411?** Mary J. Blige	Uptown
10	**III Sides To Every Stoy** Extreme	A&M
11	**Greatest Hits** Queen	Hollywood
12	**Funky Divas** En Vogue	Atco Eastwest
13	**Totally Krossed Out** Kris Kross	Ruffhouse
14	**Boomerang** Soundtrack	Laface
15	**No Fences** Garth Brooks	Liberty
16	**Greatest Misses** Public Enemy	DEF Jam
17	**Blood Sugar Sex Magik** Red Hot Chili Peppers	Warner Bros
18	**Ropin' The Wind** Garth Brooks	Liberty
19	**Temple Of The Dog** Temple Of The Dog	A&M
20	**Brand New Man** Brooks & Dunn	Arista

uk albums

1	**Automatic For The People** R.E.M.	Warner Bros
2	**Us** Peter Gabriel	Real World
3	**Gold – Greatest Hits** Abba	Polydor
4	**Tubular Bells II** Mike Oldfield	WEA
5	**Timeless (the Classics)** Michael Bolton	Columbia
6	**Back To The Light** Brian May	Parlophone
7	**The Best Of Belinda Vol 1** Belinda Carlisle	Virgin
8	**Back To Front** Lionel Richie	Motown
9	**Boss Drum** The Shamen	One Little Indian
10	**Greatest Hits** The Police	A&M
11	**Diva** Annie Lennox	RCA
12	**Experience** The Prodigy	Xl Recordings
13	**Unplugged** Eric Clapton	Duck
14	**Yes Please** Happy Mondays	Factory
15	**III Sides To Every Story** Extreme	A&M
16	**Am I Not Your Girl?** Sinead O'Connor	Ensign
17	**Dangerous** Michael Jackson	Epic
18	**Happy In Hell** The Christians	Island
19	**Stigma** EMF	EMI
20	**Tourism** Roxette	EMI

us albums

1. **The Chase** — Garth Brooks — Liberty
2. **Us** — Peter Gabriel — Geffen
3. **Some Gave All** — Billy Ray Cyrus — Mercury
4. **Unplugged** — Eric Clapton — Duck
5. **Timeless (The Classics)** — Michael Bolton — Columbia
6. **Dirt** — Alice In Chains — Columbia
7. **Ten** — Pearl Jam — Epic Associated
8. **Beyond The Season** — Garth Brooks — Liberty
9. **What's The 411?** — Mary J. Blige — Uptown
10. **Singles** — Soundtrack — Epic Soundtrax
11. **Bobby** — Bobby Brown — MCA
12. **Brand New Man** — Brooks & Dunn — Arista
13. **I Still Believe In You** — Vince Gill — MCA
14. **Broken** — Nine Inch Nails — Nothing
15. **Ropin' The Wind** — Garth Brooks — Liberty
16. **No Fences** — Garth Brooks — Liberty
17. **Totally Krossed Out** — Kris Kross — Ruffhouse
18. **Greatest Hits** — Queen — Hollywood
19. **Funky Divas** — En Vogue — Atco Eastwest
20. **Boomerang** — Soundtrack — Laface

uk singles

1. **Sleeping Satellite** — Tasmin Archer — EMI
2. **End Of The Road** — Boyz II Men — Motown
3. **Ebeneezer Goode** — The Shamen — One Little Indian
4. **I'm Gonna Get You** — Bizarre Inc — Vinyl Solution
5. **It's My Life** — Dr Alban — Logic
6. **Love Song** — Simple Minds — Virgin
7. **My Name Is Prince** — Prince And The N.P.G. — Paisley Park
8. **Tetris** — Dr Spin — Carpet
9. **A Million Love Songs** — Take That — RCA
10. **Baker Street** — Undercover — Pwl International

us singles

1. **End Of The Road (From Boomerang)** — Boyz II Men — BIV
2. **Sometimes Love Just Ain't Enough** — Patty Smith — MCA
3. **Jump Around** — House Of Pain — Tommy Boy
4. **Humpin' Around** — Bobby Brown — MCA
5. **She Playing Hard To Get** — Hi-Five — Jive
6. **Please Don't Go** — K.W.S. — Next Plateau
7. **I'd Die Without You (From Boomerang)** — P.M. Dawn — Gee Street
8. **When I Look Into Your Eyes** — Firehouse — Epic
9. **Baby Baby Baby** — TLC — Laface
10. **People Everyday** — Arrested Development — Chrysalis

indy albums

1. **Boss Drum** — The Shamen — One Little Indian
2. **Yes Please** — Happy Mondays — Factory
3. **Abba-esque (The Remixes)** — Erasure — Mute
4. **Copper Blue** — Sugar — Creation
5. **Eleventeen** — Daisy Chainsaw — Deva

dance singles

1. **Hurt You So** — Jonny L — Yoyo
2. **Perfect Motion** — Sunscreem — Sony
3. **Peace + Loveism** — Sonz Of A Loop Da Loop Era — SuburbanBase
4. **Jump Around** — House of Pain — Ruffness
5. **I'm Gonna Get You** — Bizarre Inc/Angie Brown — Vinyl Solution

uk albums

1. **Symbol** — Prince And The New Power Generation — Paisley Park
2. **Automatic For The People** — R.E.M. — Warner Bros
3. **Gold – Greatest Hits** — Abba — Polydor
4. **Tubular Bells II** — Mike Oldfield — WEA
5. **Timeless (the Classics)** — Michael Bolton — Columbia
6. **Us** — Peter Gabriel — Real World
7. **Back To Front** — Lionel Richie — Motown
8. **The Best Of Belinda Vol 1** — Belinda Carlisle — Virgin
9. **Back To The Light** — Brian May — Parlophone
10. **Kiss This** — The Sex Pistols — Virgin
11. **Greatest Hits** — The Police — A&M
12. **Diva** — Annie Lennox — RCA
13. **Unplugged** — Eric Clapton — Duck
14. **Boss Drum** — The Shamen — One Little Indian
15. **Dangerous** — Michael Jackson — Epic
16. **Woodface** — Crowded House — Capitol
17. **Revenge Of The Goldfish** — Inspiral Carpets — Cow
18. **Broken** — Nine Inch Nails — Island
19. **Experience** — The Prodigy — XI Recordings
20. **III Sides To Every Story** — Extreme — A&M

us albums

1. **The Chase** — Garth Brooks — Liberty
2. **Automatic For The People** — R.E.M. — Warner Bros
3. **Some Gave All** — Billy Ray Cyrus — Mercury
4. **Unplugged** — Eric Clapton — Duck
5. **Timeless (The Classics)** — Michael Bolton — Columbia
6. **Us** — Peter Gabriel — Geffen
7. **Ten** — Pearl Jam — Epic Associated
8. **Dirt** — Alice In Chains — Columbia
9. **Beyond The Season** — Garth Brooks — Liberty
10. **What's The 411?** — Mary J. Blige — Uptown
11. **Brand New Man** — Brooks & Dunn — Arista
12. **I Still Believe In You** — Vince Gill — MCA
13. **Ropin' The Wind** — Garth Brooks — Liberty
14. **Wynona** — Wynona — Curb
15. **Bobby** — Bobby Brown — MCA
16. **Totally Krossed Out** — Kris Kross — Ruffhouse
17. **Singles** — Soundtrack — Epic Soundtrax
18. **Boomerang** — Soundtrack — Laface
19. **No Fences** — Garth Brooks — Liberty
20. **3 Years 5 Months & 2 Days In The Life** — Arrested Development — Chrysalis

uk singles

1. **Sleeping Satellite** — Tasmin Archer — EMI
2. **End Of The Road** — Boyz II Men — Motown
3. **I'm Gonna Get You** — Bizarre Inc — Vinyl Solution
4. **Erotica** — Madonna — Maverick/Sire
5. **Keep The Faith** — Bon Jovi — Jambco
6. **Tetris** — Dr Spin — Carpet
7. **It's My Life** — Dr Alban — Logic
8. **Ebeneezer Goode** — The Shamen — One Little Indian
9. **A Million Love Songs** — Take That — RCA
10. **People Everyday** — Arrested Development — Cooltempo

us singles

1. **End Of The Road** — Boyz II Men — BIV
2. **Sometimes Love Just Ain't Enough** — Patty Smith — MCA
3. **Erotica** — Madonna — Maverick/Sire
4. **I'd Die Without You** — P.M.Dawn — Gee Street
5. **Jump Around** — House Of Pain — Tommy Boy
6. **How Do You Talk To An Angel** — The Heights — Capitol
7. **She's Playing Hard To Get** — Hi-Five — Jive
8. **When I Look Into Your Eyes** — Firehouse — Epic
9. **People Everyday** — Arrested Development — Chrysalis
10. **Please Don't Go** — K.W.S. — Next Plateau

indy albums

1. **Revenge Of The Goldfish** — Inspiral Carpets — Mute
2. **Boss Drum** — The Shamen — One Little Indian
3. **Yes Please** — Happy Mondays — Factory
4. **It's It** — The Sugarcubes — One Little Indian
5. **Copper Blue** — Sugar — Creation

dance singles

1. **Liberation** — Liberation — ZYX
2. **People Everyday** — Arrested Development — Cooltempo
3. **It Will Make Me Crazy** — Felix — Deconstruction
4. **I Trance You** — Gypsy — Limbo
5. **Hurt You So** — Jonny L — Yoyo/Tuchwood

uk albums

1. **Glittering Prize – Simple Minds 81/92** — Simple Minds — Virgin
2. **Erotica** — Madonna — Maverick/Sire
3. **Symbol** — Prince And The New Power Generation — Paisley Park
4. **Automatic For The People** — R.E.M. — Warner Bros
5. **Gold – Greatest Hits** — Abba — Polydor
6. **Timeless (The Classics)** — Michael Bolton — Columbia
7. **Once In A Lifetime** — Talking Heads — EMI
8. **Tubular Bells II** — Mike Oldfield — WEA
9. **Back To Front** — Lionel Richie — Motown
10. **The Best Of Belinda Vol 1** — Belinda Carlisle — Virgin
11. **Us** — Peter Gabriel — Real World
12. **Greatest Hits** — The Police — A&M
13. **Diva** — Annie Lennox — RCA
14. **Woodface** — Crowded House — Capitol
15. **Back To The Light** — Brian May — Parlophone
16. **Unplugged** — Eric Clapton — Duck
17. **Kiss This** — The Sex Pistols — Virgin
18. **Boss Drum** — The Shamen — One Little Indian
19. **Dangerous** — Michael Jackson — Epic
20. **Curtis Stigers** — Curtis Stigers — Arista

uk albums

1	**Glittering Prize – Simple Minds 81/92** Simple Minds	Virgin
2	**Erotica** Madonna	Maverick/Sire
3	**Timeless (The Classics)** Michael Bolton	Columbia
4	**Gold – Greatest Hits** Abba	Polydor
5	**Automatic For The People** R.E.M.	Warner Bros
6	**Symbol** Prince And The New Power Generation	Paisley Park
7	**Once In A Lifetime** Talking Heads	EMI
8	**Great Expectations** Tasmin Archer	EMI
9	**Tubular Bells II** Mike Oldfield	WEA
10	**The Best Of Belinda Vol 1** Belinda Carlisle	Virgin
11	**Back To Front** Lionel Richie	Motown
12	**Cooleyhighharmony** Boyz II Men	Motown
13	**Are You Normal?** Ned's Atomic Dustbin	Furtive
14	**Diva** Annie Lennox	RCA
15	**Blind** The Sundays	Parlophone
16	**Boss Drum** The Shamen	One Little Indian
17	**Curtis Stigers** Curtis Stigers	Arista
18	**Into The Light** Hank Marvin	Polydor
19	**Greatest Hits** The Police	A&M
20	**Jehovakill** Julian Cope	Island

us albums

1	**The Chase** Garth Brooks	Liberty
2	**Automatic For The People** R.E.M.	Warner Bros
3	**Unplugged** Eric Clapton	Duck
4	**Some Gave All** Billy Ray Cyrus	Mercury
5	**Symbol** Prince And The N.P.G.	Paisley Park
6	**Timeless (The Classics)** Michael Bolton	Columbia
7	**Ten** Pearl Jam	Epic Associated
8	**Us** Peter Gabriel	Geffen
9	**What's The 411?** Mary J. Blige	Uptown
10	**Dirt** Alice In Chains	Columbia
11	**Beyond The Season** Garth Brooks	Liberty
12	**Brand New Man** Brooks & Dunn	Arista
13	**Wynona** Wynona	Curb
14	**Boomerang** Soundtrack	Laface
15	**Bobby** Bobby Brown	MCA
16	**I Still Believe In You** Vince Gill	MCA
17	**Ropin' The Wind** Garth Brooks	Liberty
18	**Totally Krossed Out** Kris Kross	Ruffhouse
19	**3 Years 5 Months & 2 Days In The Life** Arrested Development	Chrysalis
20	**Funky Divas** En Vogue	ATCO

uk singles

1	**End Of The Road** Boyz II Men	Motown
2	**Sleeping Satellite** Tasmin Archer	EMI
3	**Erotica** Madonna	Maverick/Sire
4	**I'm Gonna Get You** Bizarre Inc	Vinyl Solution
5	**Keep The Faith** Bon Jovi	Jambco
6	**People Everyday** Arrested Development	Cooltempo
7	**A Million Love Songs** Take That	RCA
8	**Tetris** Dr Spin	Carpet
9	**(Take A Little) Piece Of My Heart** Erma Franklin	Epic
10	**Run To You** Rage	Pulse 8

us singles

1	**End Of The Road** Boyz II Men	BIV
2	**Sometimes Love Just Ain't Enough** Patty Smith	MCA
3	**I'd Die Without You** P.M.Dawn	Gee Street
4	**How Do You Talk To An Angel** The Heights	Capitol
5	**Erotica** Madonna	Maverick/Sire
6	**Jump Around** House Of Pain	Tommy Boy
7	**She's Playing Hard To Get** Hi-Five	Jive
8	**Free Your Mind** En Vogue	ATCO
9	**Rhythm Is A Dancer** Snap	Arista
10	**People Everyday** Arrested Development	Chrysalis

indy albums

1	**Boss Drum** The Shamen	One Little Indi
2	**Sleepwalking** Magnum	Music For Natio
3	**Revenge Of The Goldfish** Inspiral Carpets	Mu
4	**Body Exit Mind** New Fast Automatic Daffs	Play It Again Sa
5	**Yes Please** Happy Mondays	Facto

dance singles

1	**When You Gonna Learn?** Jamiroquai	Acid Ja
2	**People Everyday** Arrested Development	Cooltem
3	**Liberation** Liberation	Z
4	**L.S.D. (EP)** Kaotic Chemistry	Moving Shado
5	**Run To You** Rage	Pulse

uk albums

1	**Glittering Prize – Simple Minds 81/92** Simple Minds	Virgin
2	**Erotica** Madonna	Maverick/Sire
3	**Timeless (The Classics)** Michael Bolton	Columbia
4	**Gold – Greatest Hits** Abba	Polydor
5	**Live** AC/DC	Atco
6	**Automatic For The People** R.E.M.	Warner Bros
7	**Cooleyhighharmony** Boyz II Men	Motown
8	**Back To Front** Lionel Richie	Motown
9	**The Best Of Belinda Vol 1** Belinda Carlisle	Virgin
10	**Love Deluxe** Sade	Epic
11	**Tubular Bells II** Mike Oldfield	WEA
12	**Great Expectations** Tasmin Archer	EMI
13	**Symbol** Prince And The New Power Generation	Paisley Park
14	**Once In A Lifetime** Talking Heads	EMI
15	**Boom Boom** John Lee Hooker	Point Blank
16	**Diva** Annie Lennox	RCA
17	**Boss Drum** The Shamen	One Little Indian
18	**Curtis Stigers** Curtis Stigers	Arista
19	**Greatest Hits** The Police	A&M
20	**Take That & Party** Take That	RCA

us albums

1	**The Chase** Garth Brooks	Liberty
2	**Erotica** Madonna	Maverick/Sire
3	**Unplugged** Eric Clapton	Duck
4	**Some Gave All** Billy Ray Cyrus	Mercury
5	**Automatic For The People** R.E.M.	Warner Bros
6	**Timeless (The Classics)** Michael Bolton	Columbia
7	**Ten** Pearl Jam	Epic Associated
8	**Symbol** Prince And The N.P.G.	Paisley Park
9	**Pure Country** George Strati	MCA
10	**What's The 411?** Mary J. Blige	Uptown
11	**Us** Peter Gabriel	Geffen
12	**Dirt** Alice In Chains	Columbia
13	**Beyond The Season** Garth Brooks	Liberty
14	**Boomerang** Soundtrack	Laface
15	**Brand New Man** Brooks & Dunn	Arista
16	**Wynona** Wynona	Curb
17	**Bobby** Bobby Brown	MCA
18	**No Fences** Garth Brooks	Liberty
19	**I Still Believe In You** Vince Gill	MCA
20	**Funky Divas** En Vogue	ATCO

uk singles

1	**End Of The Road** Boyz II Men	Motown
2	**People Everyday** Arrested Development	Cooltempo
3	**Run To You** Rage	Pulse 8
4	**Sleeping Satellite** Tasmin Archer	EMI
5	**I'm Gonna Get You** Bizarre Inc	Vinyl Solution
6	**Boss Drum** The Shamen	One Little Indian
7	**Erotica** Madonna	Maverick/Sire
8	**A Million Love Songs** Take That	RCA
9	**Supermarioland** Ambassadors Of Funk	Living Beat
10	**Who Needs Love (Like That)** Erasure	Mute

us singles

1	**End Of The Road** Boyz II Men	BIV
2	**How Do You Talk To An Angel** The Heights	Capitol
3	**I'd Die Without You** P.M.Dawn	Gee Street
4	**Sometimes Love Just Ain't Enough** Patty Smith	MCA
5	**Erotica** Madonna	Maverick/Sire
6	**Jump Around** House Of Pain	Tommy Boy
7	**Rhythm Is A Dancer** Snap	Arista
8	**Rump Shaker** Wreckx-N-Effect	MCA
9	**Real Love** Mary J Blige	Uptown
10	**What About Your Friends** TLC	Laface

indy albums

1	**Boss Drum** The Shamen	One Little India
2	**Revenge Of The Goldfish** Inspiral Carpets	Mut
3	**Sleepwalking** Magnum	Music For Nation
4	**Copper Blue** Sugar	Creatio
5	**Body Exit Mind** New Fast Automatic Daffs	Play It Again San

dance singles

1	**Let Me Be Your Fantasy** Baby D	Production House
2	**Soul Freedom – Free Your Soul** Degrees Of Motion	Esquire
3	**People Everyday** Arrested Development	Cooltempo
4	**That Piano Track** Outrage	Junior Boys Own
5	**Understand This Groove** Franke	China

indy albums

	Boss Drum	
	The Shamen	One Little Indian
	Energique	
	Bizzare Inc	Vinyl Solution
	Revenge Of The Goldfish	
	Inspiral Carpets	Mute
	Copper Blue	
	Sugar	Creation
	Transition	
	Walter Trout Band	Provogue

dance singles

	Let Me Be Your Fantasy	
	Baby D	Production House
	Who Pays The Piper	
	Gary Clail/On-U Sound	Perfecto
	People Everyday	
	Arrested Development	Cooltempo
	Never Let Her Slip Away	
	Undercover	PWL
	It's Just A Feeling	
	Terrorize	Hamster

It was 40 years ago today: the first NME UK charts began with Al Martino at Number One with Here In My Heart on the Capitol label. Now it's Charles & Eddie's turn on the same label with Would I Lie To You?.

uk singles

#		
1	**End Of The Road**	
	Boyz II Men	Motown
2	**Would I Lie To You?**	
	Charles And Eddie	Capitol
3	**People Everyday**	
	Arrested Development	Cooltempo
4	**Boss Drum**	
	The Shamen	One Little Indian
5	**Run To You**	
	Rage	Pulse 8
6	**Be My Baby**	
	Vanessa Paradis	Remark
7	**Never Let Her Slip Away**	
	Undercover	Pwl International
8	**Supermarioland**	
	Ambassadors Of Funk	Living Beat
9	**I'm Gonna Get You**	
	Bizarre Inc	Vinyl Solution
10	**Who Needs Love (Like That)**	
	Erasure	Mute

us singles

#		
1	**How Do You Talk To An Angel**	
	The Heights	Capitol
2	**End Of The Road**	
	Boyz II Men	BIV
3	**I'd Die Without You**	
	P.M.Dawn	Gee Street
4	**If I Ever Fall In Love**	
	Shai	Gasoline Alley
5	**Sometimes Love Just Ain't Enough**	
	Patty Smith	MCA
6	**Rump Shaker**	
	Wreckx-N-Effect	MCA
7	**Rhythm Is A Dancer**	
	Snap	Arista
8	**What About Your Friends**	
	TLC	Laface
9	**Erotica**	
	Madonna	Maverick/Sire
10	**Jump Around**	
	House Of Pain	Tommy Boy

us albums

#		
1	**The Chase**	
	Garth Brooks	Liberty
2	**Timeless (The Classics)**	
	Michael Bolton	Columbia
3	**Unplugged**	
	Eric Clapton	Duck
4	**Erotica**	
	Madonna	Maverick/Sire
5	**Some Gave All**	
	Billy Ray Cyrus	Mercury
6	**Automatic For The People**	
	R.E.M.	Warner Bros
7	**Pure Country**	
	George Strati	MCA
8	**Ten**	
	Pearl Jam	Epic Associated
9	**What's The 411?**	
	Mary J. Blige	Uptown
10	**Symbol**	
	Prince And The N.P.G.	Paisley Park
11	**Boomerang**	
	Soundtrack	Laface
12	**Beyond The Season**	
	Garth Brooks	Liberty
13	**Us**	
	Peter Gabriel	Geffen
14	**Brand New Man**	
	Brooks & Dunn	Arista
15	**Dirt**	
	Alice In Chains	Columbia
16	**Harvest Moon**	
	Neil Young	Warner Bros
17	**Bobby**	
	Bobby Brown	MCA
18	**Wynona**	
	Wynona	Curb
19	**I Still Believe In You**	
	Vince Gill	MCA
20	**3 Years 5 Months & 2 Days In The Life**	
	Arrested Development	Chrysalis

uk albums

#		
1	**Keep The Faith**	
	Bon Jovi	Mercury
2	**Glittering Prize – Simple Minds 81/92**	
	Simple Minds	Virgin
3	**Timeless (The Classics)**	
	Michael Bolton	Columbia
4	**God's Great Banana Skin**	
	Chris Rea	East West
5	**Gold – Greatest Hits**	
	Abba	Polydor
6	**Greatest Hits**	
	Gloria Estefan	Epic
7	**Erotica**	
	Madonna	Maverick/Sire
8	**Automatic For The People**	
	R.E.M.	Warner Bros
9	**Harvest Moon**	
	Neil Young	Reprise
10	**Back To Front**	
	Lionel Richie	Motown
11	**Cooleyhighharmony**	
	Boyz II Men	Motown
12	**Boss Drum**	
	The Shamen	One Little Indian
13	**Tubular Bells II**	
	Mike Oldfield	WEA
14	**The Best Of Belinda Vol 1**	
	Belinda Carlisle	Virgin
15	**Diva**	
	Annie Lennox	RCA
16	**Curtis Stigers**	
	Curtis Stigers	Arista
17	**Indian Summer**	
	Go West	Chrysalis
18	**Good As I Been To You**	
	Bob Dylan	Columbia
19	**3 Years, 5 Months & 2 Days In The Life**	
	Arrested Development	Cooltempo
20	**Take That & Party**	
	Take That	RCA

uk singles

#		
1	**Would I Lie To You**	
	Charles And Eddie	Capitol
2	**End Of The Road**	
	Boyz II Men	Motown
3	**People Everyday**	
	Arrested Development	Cooltempo
4	**I Will Always Love You**	
	Whitney Houston	Arista
5	**Never Let Her Slip Away**	
	Undercover	Pwl International
6	**Boss Drum**	
	The Shamen	One Little Indian
7	**Invisible Touch (live)**	
	Genesis	Virgin
8	**Be My Baby**	
	Vanessa Paradis	Remark
9	**Temptation (Brothers In Rhythm Remix)**	
	Heaven 17	Virgin
10	**Run To You**	
	Rage	Pulse 8

us singles

#		
1	**How Do You Talk To An Angel**	
	The Heights	Capitol
2	**If I Ever Fall In Love**	
	Shai	Gasoline Alley
3	**I'd Die Without You**	
	P.M.Dawn	Gee Street
4	**End Of The Road**	
	Boyz II Men	BIV
5	**Rump Shaker**	
	Wreckx-N-Effect	MCA
6	**Rhythm Is A Dancer**	
	Snap	Arista
7	**What About Your Friends**	
	TLC	Laface
8	**Sometimes Love Just Ain't Enough**	
	Patty Smith	MCA
9	**Real Love**	
	Mary J. Blige	Uptown
10	**Jump Around**	
	House Of Pain	Tommy Boy

us albums

#		
1	**Timeless (The Classics)**	
	Michael Bolton	Columbia
2	**The Chase**	
	Garth Brooks	Liberty
3	**Love Deluxe**	
	Sade	Epic
4	**Unplugged**	
	Eric Clapton	Duck
5	**Keep The Faith**	
	Bon Jovi	Mercury
6	**Some Gave All**	
	Billy Ray Cyrus	Mercury
7	**Pure Country**	
	George Strati	MCA
8	**Automatic For The People**	
	R.E.M.	Warner Bros
9	**Erotica**	
	Madonna	Maverick/Sire
10	**Ten**	
	Pearl Jam	Epic Associated
11	**What's The 411?**	
	Mary J. Blige	Uptown
12	**Beyond The Season**	
	Garth Brooks	Liberty
13	**Boomerang**	
	Soundtrack	Laface
14	**Brand New Man**	
	Brooks & Dunn	Arista
15	**Live**	
	AC/DC	ATCO
16	**Dirt**	
	Alice In Chains	Columbia
17	**I Still Believe In You**	
	Vince Gill	MCA
18	**Symbol**	
	Prince And The N.P.G.	Paisley Park
19	**Bobby**	
	Bobby Brown	MCA
20	**Wynona**	
	Wynona	Curb

uk albums

#		
1	**Cher's Greatest Hits: 1965-1992**	
	Cher	Geffen
2	**Glittering Prize – Simple Minds 81/92**	
	Simple Minds	Virgin
3	**Timeless (The Classics)**	
	Michael Bolton	Columbia
4	**Greatest Hits**	
	Gloria Estefan	Epic
5	**Keep The Faith**	
	Bon Jovi	Mercury
6	**Automatic For The People**	
	R.E.M.	Warner Bros
7	**Gold – Greatest Hits**	
	Abba	Polydor
8	**Erotica**	
	Madonna	Maverick/Sire
9	**God's Great Banana Skin**	
	Chris Rea	East West
10	**Boss Drum**	
	The Shamen	One Little Indian
11	**Back To Front**	
	Lionel Richie	Motown
12	**The Best Of Belinda Vol 1**	
	Belinda Carlisle	Virgin
13	**Take That & Party**	
	Take That	RCA
14	**Cooleyhighharmony**	
	Boyz II Men	Motown
15	**Tubular Bells II**	
	Mike Oldfield	WEA
16	**Hormonally Yours**	
	Shakespears Sister	London
17	**Follow Your Dream**	
	Daniel O'Donnell	Ritz
18	**Diva**	
	Annie Lennox	RCA
19	**Curtis Stigers**	
	Curtis Stigers	Arista
20	**Harvest Moon**	
	Neil Young	Reprise

indy albums

#		
1	**Boss Drum**	
	The Shamen	One Little Indian
2	**Energique**	
	Bizzare Inc	Vinyl Solution
3	**Inspiringly Titled...**	
	Mega City Four	Big Life
4	**Revenge Of The Goldfish**	
	Inspiral Carpets	Mute
5	**Copper Blue**	
	Sugar	Creation

dance singles

#		
1	**Temptation (Remix)**	
	Heaven 17	Virgin
2	**Funky Guitar**	
	TC 1992	Union City
3	**Out Of Space**	
	The Prodigy	XL Recordings
4	**Follow Me**	
	Aly-Us	Cooltempo
5	**Let Me Be Your Fantasy**	
	Baby D	Production House

149

indy albums

1	**Boss Drum** The Shamen	One Little Indian
2	**Back In Denim** Denim	Boy's Own
3	**Revenge Of The Goldfish** Inspiral Carpets	Mute
4	**Yerself Is Steam/Lego My Ego** Mercury Rev	Beggars Banquet
5	**Copper Blue** Sugar	Creation

dance singles

1	**Funky Guitar** TC 1992	Union City
2	**Out Of Space** The Prodigy	XL Recordings
3	**Temptation (Remix)** Heaven 17	Virgin
4	**Who Can Make Me Feel Good?** Bassheads	Deconstruction
5	**Follow Me** Aly-Us	Cooltempo

uk singles

1	**Would I Lie To You?** Charles And Eddie	Capitol
2	**I Will Always Love You** Whitney Houston	Arista
3	**End Of The Road** Boyz II Men	Motown
4	**Temptation (Brothers In Rhythm Remix)** Heaven 17	Virgin
5	**Never Let Her Slip Away** Undercover	Pwl International
6	**Out Of Space (remix)** The Prodigy	Xl Recordings
7	**People Everyday** Arrested Development	Cooltempo
8	**Yesterdays/November Rain** Guns N' Roses	Geffen
9	**Boss Drum** The Shamen	One Little Indian
10	**Invisible Touch (live)** Genesis	Virgin

us singles

1	**I Will Always Love You** Whitney Houston	Arista
2	**How Do You Talk To An Angel** The Heights	Capitol
3	**If I Ever Fall In Love** Shai	Gasoline Alley
4	**Rump Shaker** Wreckx-N-Effect	MCA
5	**I'd Die Without You** P.M.Dawn	Gee Street
6	**End Of The Road** Boyz II Men	BIV
7	**Rhythm Is A Dancer** Snap	Arista
8	**Real Love** Mary J. Blige	Uptown
9	**What About Your Friends** TLC	Laface
10	**Good Enough** Bobby Brown	MCA

us albums

1	**The Chase** Garth Brooks	Liberty
2	**Timeless (The Classics)** Michael Bolton	Columbia
3	**Unplugged** Eric Clapton	Duck
4	**Some Gave All** Billy Ray Cyrus	Mercury
5	**Love Deluxe** Sade	Epic
6	**Pure Country** George Strati	MCA
7	**Keep The Faith** Bon Jovi	Mercury
8	**Automatic For The People** R.E.M.	Warner Bros
9	**Ten** Pearl Jam	Epic Associated
10	**Erotica** Madonna	Maverick/Sire
11	**Beyond The Season** Garth Brooks	Liberty
12	**What's The 411?** Mary J. Blige	Uptown
13	**Boomerang** Soundtrack	Laface
14	**Bobby** Bobby Brown	MCA
15	**Brand New Man** Brooks & Dunn	Arista
16	**Dirt** Alice In Chains	Columbia
17	**Greatest Hits** Gloria Estefan	Epic
18	**Live** AC/DC	ATCO
19	**I Still Believe In You** Vince Gill	MCA
20	**Totally Krossed Out** Kris Kross	Ruffhouse

uk albums

1	**Pop! – The First 20 Hits** Erasure	Mute
2	**Cher's Greatest Hits: 1965-1992** Cher	Geffen
3	**Live – The Way We Walk Vol 1 The Shorts** Genesis	Virgin
4	**The Freddie Mercury Album** Freddie Mercury	Parlophone
5	**Glittering Prize – Simple Minds 81/92** Simple Minds	Virgin
6	**Timeless (the Classics)** Michael Bolton	Columbia
7	**Greatest Hits** Gloria Estefan	Epic
8	**Gold – Greatest Hits** Abba	Polydor
9	**Automatic For The People** R.E.M.	Warner Bros
10	**The Celts** Enya	WEA
11	**Erotica** Madonna	Maverick/Sire
12	**Keep The Faith** Bon Jovi	Mercury
13	**God's Great Banana Skin** Chris Rea	East West
14	**The Best Of Belinda Vol 1** Belinda Carlisle	Virgin
15	**Take That & Party** Take That	RCA
16	**Back To Front** Lionel Richie	Motown
17	**Boss Drum** The Shamen	One Little Indian
18	**Tubular Bells II** Mike Oldfield	WEA
19	**Hormonally Yours** Shakespears Sister	London
20	**Diva** Annie Lennox	RCA

indy albums

1	**Pop! – The First 20 Hits** Erasure	Mute
2	**Boss Drum** The Shamen	One Little Indian
3	**The Curse** Throwing Muses	4AD
4	**Let's Knife** Shonen Knife	August
5	**Copper Blue** Sugar	Creation

dance singles

1	**Let Me Be Your Underwear** Club 69	ffrr
2	**Rump Shaker** Wreckx-N-Effect	MCA
3	**Show Some Love** Jaco	Warp
4	**Lion Rock** Lion Rock	Deconstruction
5	**So Close** Dina Carroll	A&M

uk singles

1	**I Will Always Love You** Whitney Houston	Arista
2	**Would I Lie To You?** Charles And Eddie	Capitol
3	**Heal The World** Michael Jackson	Epic
4	**Temptation (Brothers In Rhythm Remix)** Heaven 17	Virgin
5	**Out Of Space (remix)** The Prodigy	Xl Recordings
6	**End Of The Road** Boyz II Men	Motown
7	**Never Let Her Slip Away** Undercover	Pwl International
8	**Tom Traubert's Blues** (Waltzing Matilda) Rod Stewart	Warner Bros
9	**I Still Believe In You** Cliff Richard	EMI
10	**People Everyday** Arrested Development	Cooltempo

us singles

1	**I Will Always Love You** Whitney Houston	Arista
2	**If I Ever Fall In Love** Shai	Gasoline Alley
3	**Rump Shaker** Wreckx-N-Effect	MCA
4	**How Do You Talk To An Angel** The Heights	Capitol
5	**I'd Die Without You** P.M.Dawn	Gee Street
6	**Rhythm Is A Dancer** Snap	Arista
7	**Real Love** Mary J. Blige	Uptown
8	**Good Enough** Bobby Brown	MCA
9	**What About Your Friends** TLC	Laface
10	**End Of The Road** Boyz II Men	BIV

us albums

1	**The Predator** Ice Cube	Priority
2	**The Bodyguard** Soundtrack	Arista
3	**The Chase** Garth Brooks	Liberty
4	**Timeless (The Classics)** Michael Bolton	Columbia
5	**Unplugged** Eric Clapton	Duck
6	**Some Gave All** Billy Ray Cyrus	Mercury
7	**Pure Country** George Strati	MCA
8	**Love Deluxe** Sade	Epic
9	**Breathless** Kenny G	Arista
10	**Automatic For The People** R.E.M.	Warner Bros
11	**Beyond The Season** Garth Brooks	Liberty
12	**Ten** Pearl Jam	Epic Associated
13	**Keep The Faith** Bon Jovi	Mercury
14	**Home For Christmas** Amy Grant	A & M
15	**What's The 411?** Mary J. Blige	Uptown
16	**Erotica** Madonna	Maverick/Sire
17	**Bobby** Bobby Brown	MCA
18	**A Very Special Christmas 2** Various Artists	A & M
19	**Brand New Man** Brooks & Dunn	Arista
20	**Totally Krossed Out** Kris Kross	Ruffhouse

uk albums

1	**Pop! – The First 20 Hits** Erasure	Mute
2	**Cher's Greatest Hits: 1965-1992** Cher	Geffen
3	**Live – The Way We Walk Vol 1 The Shorts** Genesis	Virgin
4	**Timeless (The Classics)** Michael Bolton	Columbia
5	**Greatest Hits** Gloria Estefan	Epic
6	**The Freddie Mercury Album** Freddie Mercury	Parlophone
7	**Glittering Prize – Simple Minds 81/92** Simple Minds	Virgin
8	**Gold – Greatest Hits** Abba	Polydor
9	**Automatic For The People** R.E.M.	Warner Bros
10	**The Celts** Enya	WEA
11	**Take That & Party** Take That	RCA
12	**The Best Of Belinda Vol 1** Belinda Carlisle	Virgin
13	**Erotica** Madonna	Maverick/Sire
14	**Boss Drum** The Shamen	One Little Indian
15	**Keep The Faith** Bon Jovi	Mercury
16	**God's Great Banana Skin** Chris Rea	East West
17	**Diva** Annie Lennox	RCA
18	**Back To Front** Lionel Richie	Motown
19	**Follow Your Dream** Daniel O'Donnell	Ritz
20	**Stars** Simply Red	East West

us albums

	The Bodyguard Soundtrack	Arista
	Unplugged Eric Clapton	Duck
	The Predator Ice Cube	Priority
	Timeless (The Classics) Michael Bolton	Columbia
	The Chase Garth Brooks	Liberty
	Home For Christmas Amy Grant	A & M
	Some Gave All Billy Ray Cyrus	Mercury
	Breathless Kenny G	Arista
	A Very Special Christmas 2 Various Artists	A & M
0	**Beyond The Season** Garth Brooks	Liberty
1	**Love Deluxe** Sade	Epic
2	**Pure Country** George Strati	MCA
3	**Automatic For The People** R.E.M.	Warner Bros
4	**Christmas Album** Neil Diamond	Columbia
5	**Ten** Pearl Jam	Epic Associated
6	**What's The 411?** Mary J. Blige	Uptown
7	**Erotica** Madonna	Maverick/Sire
8	**Bobby** Bobby Brown	MCA
9	**Totally Krossed Out** Kris Kross	Ruffhouse
20	**Keep The Faith** Bon Jovi	Mercury

uk singles

1	**I Will Always Love You** Whitney Houston	Arista
2	**Heal The World** Michael Jackson	Epic
3	**Would I Lie To You** Charles And Eddie	Capitol
4	**Slam Jam** The WWF Superstars	Arista
5	**Temptation (Brothers In Rhythm Remix)** Heaven 17	Virgin
6	**Tom Traubert's Blues** (Waltzing Matilda) Rod Stewart	Warner Bros
7	**I Still Believe In You** Cliff Richard	EMI
8	**Out Of Space (Remix)** The Prodigy	XI Recordings
9	**Could It Be Magic** Take That	RCA
10	**Deeper And Deeper** Madonna	Maverick/Sire

us singles

1	**I Will Always Love You** Whitney Houston	Arista
2	**If I Ever Fall In Love** Shai	Gasoline Alley
3	**Rump Shaker** Wreckx-N-Effect	MCA
4	**In The Still Of The Night** Boyz II Men	Motown
5	**How Do You Talk To An Angel** The Heights	Capitol
6	**I'd Die Without You** P.M.Dawn	Gee Street
7	**Rhythm Is A Dancer** Snap	Arista
8	**Good Enough** Bobby Brown	MCA
9	**Real Love** Mary J. Blige	Uptown
10	**What About Your Friends** TLC	Laface

indy albums

1	**Pop! – The First 20 Hits** Erasure	Mute
2	**Boss Drum** The Shamen	One Little Indian
3	**Copper Blue** Sugar	Creation
4	**The Curse** Throwing Muses	4AD
5	**Hi-Tech/No Get Me** Yellow Magic Orchestra	Internal

dance singles

1	**Song of Life** Leftfield	Hard Hands
2	**As Always** Secret Life	Cowboy
3	**Terminator (EP)** Metalheads	Synthetic Hardcore
4	**One In Ten** 808 State/UB40	ZTT
5	**Metropolis** Metropolis	Union City

By December over 1,000 different records had charted in one year – hundreds of them cover versions. You also have to search through nine places in the UK album charts before you alight on a collection of new songs, and even Automatic For The People is two months old chart-wise. Covers madness reaches fever pitch when Bad Seed Nick Cave and Pogue Shane MacGowan try a little Christmas crooning with What A Wonderful World . It debuts at... er, Number 72. It's only the 15th cover version of a UK Number One to hit the charts in 1992.

uk albums

1	**Cher's Greatest Hits: 1965-1992** Cher	Geffen
2	**Pop! – The First 20 Hits** Erasure	Mute
3	**Live – The Way We Walk Vol 1 The Shorts** Genesis	Virgin
4	**Timeless (The Classics)** Michael Bolton	Columbia
5	**Greatest Hits** Gloria Estefan	Epic
6	**Glittering Prize – Simple Minds 81/92** Simple Minds	Virgin
7	**Gold – Greatest Hits** Abba	Polydor
8	**The Freddie Mercury Album** Freddie Mercury	Parlophone
9	**Automatic For The People** R.E.M.	Warner Bros
10	**Stars** Simply Red	East West
11	**Back To Front** Lionel Richie	Motown
12	**Erotica** Madonna	Maverick/Sire
13	**Dangerous** Michael Jackson	Epic
14	**God's Great Banana Skin** Chris Rea	East West
15	**Take That & Party** Take That	RCA
16	**The Celts** Enya	WEA
17	**Boss Drum** The Shamen	One Little Indian
18	**Diva** Annie Lennox	RCA
19	**The Best Of Belinda Vol 1** Belinda Carlisle	Virgin
20	**Duophonic** Charles And Eddie	Capitol

---

us albums

1	**The Bodyguard** Soundtrack	Arista
2	**Timeless (The Classics)** Michael Bolton	Columbia
3	**The Chase** Garth Brooks	Liberty
4	**Some Gave All** Billy Ray Cyrus	Mercury
5	**Home For Christmas** Amy Grant	A & M
6	**Unplugged** Eric Clapton	Duck
7	**A Very Special Christmas 2** Various Artists	A & M
8	**Christmas Album** Neil Diamond	Columbia
9	**Breathless** Kenny G	Arista
10	**Beyond The Season** Garth Brooks	Liberty
11	**Pure Country** George Strati	MCA
12	**The Predator** Ice Cube	Priority
13	**Love Deluxe** Sade	Epic
14	**Automatic For The People** R.E.M.	Warner Bros
15	**Ten** Pearl Jam	Epic Associated
16	**Greatest Hits** Gloria Estefan	Epic
17	**What's The 411?** Mary J. Blige	Uptown
18	**Totally Krossed Out** Kris Kross	Ruffhouse
19	**Bobby** Bobby Brown	MCA
20	**Brand New Man** Brooks & Dunn	Arista

uk singles

1	**I Will Always Love You** Whitney Houston	Arista
2	**Heal The World** Michael Jackson	Epic
3	**Would I Lie To You?** Charles And Eddie	Capitol
4	**Slam Jam** The WWF Superstars	Arista
5	**Could It Be Magic** Take That	RCA
6	**Deeper And Deeper** Madonna	Maverick/Sire
7	**Phorever People** The Shamen	One Little Indian
8	**In My Defence** Freddie Mercury	Parlophone
9	**Tom Traubert's Blues** (Waltzing Matilda) Rod Stewart	Warner Bros
10	**Boney M Megamix** Boney M	Arista

us singles

1	**I Will Always Love You** Whitney Houston	Arista
2	**If I Ever Fall In Love** Shai	Gasoline Alley
3	**Rump Shaker** Wreckx-N-Effect	MCA
4	**In The Still Of The Night** Boyz II Men	Motown
5	**I'd Die Without You** P.M.Dawn	Gee Street
6	**How Do You Talk To An Angel** The Heights	Capitol
7	**Rhythm Is A Dancer** Snap	Arista
8	**Good Enough** Bobby Brown	MCA
9	**Real Love** Mary J. Blige	Uptown
10	**What About Your Friends** TLC	Laface

indy albums

1	**Pop! – The First 20 Hits** Erasure	Mute
2	**Boss Drum** The Shamen	One Little Indian
3	**Levelling The Land** The Levellers	China
4	**Copper Blue** Sugar	Creation
5	**Revenge Of The Goldfish** Inspiral Carpets	Mute

dance singles

1	**SL2** SL2	XL Recordings
2	**Deeper and Deeper** Madonna	Maverick/Sire
3	**I Got My Education** Uncanny Alliance	A&M
4	**One In Ten** 808 State/UB40	ZTT
5	**Alive and Kicking** East Side Beat	ffrr

uk albums

1	**Cher's Greatest Hits: 1965-1992** Cher	Geffen
2	**Pop! – The First 20 Hits** Erasure	Mute
3	**Timeless (The Classics)** Michael Bolton	Columbia
4	**Greatest Hits** Gloria Estefan	Epic
5	**Live – The Way We Walk Vol 1 The Shorts** Genesis	Virgin
6	**Glittering Prize – Simple Minds 81/92** Simple Minds	Virgin
7	**The Freddie Mercury Album** Freddie Mercury	Parlophone
8	**Gold – Greatest Hits** Abba	Polydor
9	**Back To Front** Lionel Richie	Motown
10	**Stars** Simply Red	East West
11	**Take That & Party** Take That	RCA
12	**Dangerous** Michael Jackson	Epic
13	**Automatic For The People** R.E.M.	Warner Bros
14	**Boss Drum** The Shamen	One Little Indian
15	**Erotica** Madonna	Maverick/Sire
16	**God's Great Banana Skin** Chris Rea	East West
17	**Diva** Annie Lennox	RCA
18	**The Best Of Belinda Vol 1** Belinda Carlisle	Virgin
19	**Follow Your Dream** Daniel O'Donnell	Ritz
20	**The Celts** Enya	WEA

Dec'92:13th-19th

Dec'92: 20th-26th

uk albums

1	**Cher's Greatest Hits: 1965-1992** Cher	Geffen
2	**Greatest Hits** Gloria Estefan	Epic
3	**Pop! – The First 20 Hits** Erasure	Mute
4	**Live – The Way We Walk Vol 1 The Shorts** Genesis	Virgin
5	**Timeless (The Classics)** Michael Bolton	Columbia
6	**The Freddie Mercury Album** Freddie Mercury	Parlophone
7	**Glittering Prize – Simple Minds 81/92** Simple Minds	Virgin
8	**Stars** Simply Red	East West
9	**Take That & Party** Take That	RCA
10	**Gold – Greatest Hits** Abba	Polydor
11	**Back To Front** Lionel Richie	Motown
12	**Dangerous** Michael Jackson	Epic
13	**Boss Drum** The Shamen	One Little Indian
14	**Automatic For The People** R.E.M.	Warner Bros
15	**Erotica** Madonna	Maverick/Sire
16	**The Greatest Hits 1966-1992** Neil Diamond	Columbia
17	**Incesticide** Nirvana	DGC
18	**The Force Behind The Power** Diana Ross	EMI
19	**Diva** Annie Lennox	RCA
20	**The Best Of Belinda Vol 1** Belinda Carlisle	Virgin

us albums

1	**The Bodyguard** Soundtrack	Arista
2	**Home For Christmas** Amy Grant	A & M
3	**Timeless (The Classics)** Michael Bolton	Columbia
4	**The Chase** Garth Brooks	Liberty
5	**Some Gave All** Billy Ray Cyrus	Mercury
6	**Unplugged** Eric Clapton	Duck
7	**A Very Special Christmas 2** Various Artists	A & M
8	**Christmas Album** Neil Diamond	Columbia
9	**Breathless** Kenny G	Arista
10	**Beyond The Season** Garth Brooks	Liberty
11	**Pure Country** George Strait	MCA
12	**Automatic For The People** R.E.M.	Warner Bros
13	**Ten** Pearl Jam	Epic Associated
14	**Love Deluxe** Sade	Epic
15	**Greatest Hits** Gloria Estefan	Epic
16	**Aladdin** Soundtrack	Walt Disney
17	**Totally Krossed Out** Kris Kross	Ruffhouse
18	**The Predator** Ice Cube	Priority
19	**Brand New Man** Brooks & Dunn	Arista
20	**What's The 411?** Mary J. Blige	Uptown

uk singles

1	**I Will Always Love You** Whitney Houston	Arista
2	**Heal The World** Michael Jackson	Epic
3	**Would I Lie To You?** Charles And Eddie	Capitol
4	**Could It Be Magic** Take That	RCA
5	**Phorever People** The Shamen	One Little Indian
6	**Slam Jam** The WWF Superstars	Arista
7	**Boney M Megamix** Boney M	Arista
8	**Miami Hit Mix/Xmas Thru' Your Eyes** Gloria Estefan	Epic
9	**Tom Traubert's Blues (Waltzing Matilda)** Rod Stewart	Warner Bros
10	**Deeper And Deeper** Madonna	Maverick/Sire

us singles

1	**I Will Always Love You** Whitney Houston	Arista
2	**Rump Shaker** Wreckx-N-Effect	MCA
3	**If I Ever Fall In Love** Shai	Gasoline Alley
4	**In The Still Of The Night** Boyz II Men	Motown
5	**I'd Die Without You** P.M.Dawn	Gee Street
6	**Rhythm Is A Dancer** Snap	Arista
7	**Good Enough** Bobby Brown	MCA
8	**Saving Forever For You** Shanice	Giant
9	**How Do You Talk To An Angel** The Heights	Capitol
10	**Real Love** Mary J. Blige	Uptown

indy albums

1	**Pop! - The First 20 Hits** Erasure	Mute
2	**Boss Drum** The Shamen	One Little Indian
3	**Levelling The Land** The Levellers	China
4	**Copper Blue** Sugar	Creation
5	**Screamadelica** Primal Scream	Creation

dance singles

1	**Song Of Life** Leftfield	Hard Hands
2	**Hardtrance Acperience EP** Hardfloor	Harthouse UK
3	**Rock The House** Source Feat Nicole	React
4	**Way In My Brain/Drumbeats** SL2	XL Recordings
4	**One In Ten** 808 State/UB40	ZTT

Jan'93: 27th Dec-2nd Jan

uk albums

1	**Cher's Greatest Hits: 1965-1992** Cher	Geffen
2	**Greatest Hits** Gloria Estefan	Epic
3	**Timeless (The Classics)** Michael Bolton	Columbia
4	**Pop! – The First 20 Hits** Erasure	Mute
5	**Live – The Way We Walk Vol 1 The Shorts** Genesis	Virgin
6	**Glittering Prize – Simple Minds 81/92** Simple Minds	Virgin
7	**The Freddie Mercury Album** Freddie Mercury	Parlophone
8	**Stars** Simply Red	East West
9	**Take That & Party** Take That	RCA
10	**Gold – Greatest Hits** Abba	Polydor
11	**Boss Drum** The Shamen	One Little Indian
12	**Back To Front** Lionel Richie	Motown
13	**Dangerous** Michael Jackson	Epic
14	**Automatic For The People** R.E.M.	Warner Bros
15	**Erotica** Madonna	Maverick/Sire
16	**The Greatest Hits 1966-1992** Neil Diamond	Columbia
17	**Diva** Annie Lennox	RCA
18	**The Force Behind The Power** Diana Ross	EMI
19	**The Best Of Belinda Vol 1** Belinda Carlisle	Virgin
20	**God's Great Banana Skin** Chris Rea	East West

us albums

1	**The Bodyguard** Soundtrack	Arista
2	**Home For Christmas** Amy Grant	A & M
3	**Timeless (The Classics)** Michael Bolton	Columbia
4	**The Chase** Garth Brooks	Liberty
5	**Some Gave All** Billy Ray Cyrus	Mercury
6	**Unplugged** Eric Clapton	Duck
7	**A Very Special Christmas 2** Various Artists	A & M
8	**Christmas Album** Neil Diamond	Columbia
9	**Breathless** Kenny G	Arista
10	**Beyond The Season** Garth Brooks	Liberty
11	**Pure Country** George Strait	MCA
12	**Automatic For The People** R.E.M.	Warner Bros
13	**Ten** Pearl Jam	Epic Associated
14	**Love Deluxe** Sade	Epic
15	**Greatest Hits** Gloria Estefan	Epic
16	**Aladdin** Soundtrack	Walt Disney
17	**Totally Krossed Out** Kris Kross	Ruffhouse
18	**The Predator** Ice Cube	Priority
19	**Brand New Man** Brooks & Dunn	Arista
20	**What's The 411?** Mary J. Blige	Uptown

uk singles

1	**I Will Always Love You** Whitney Houston	Arista
2	**Heal The World** Michael Jackson	Epic
3	**Would I Lie To You?** Charles And Eddie	Capitol
4	**Could It Be Magic** Take That	RCA
5	**Slam Jam** The WWF Superstars	Arista
6	**Phorever People** The Shamen	One Little Indian
7	**Boney M Megamix** Boney M	Arista
8	**Tom Traubert's Blues (waltzing Matilda)** Rod Stewart	Warner Bros
9	**Miami Hit Mix/Xmas Thru' Your Eyes** Gloria Estefan	Epic
10	**Someday (I'm Coming Back)** Lisa Stansfield	Arista

us singles

1	**I Will Always Love You** Whitney Houston	Arista
2	**Rump Shaker** Wreckx-N-Effect	MCA
3	**If I Ever Fall In Love** Shai	Gasoline Alley
4	**In The Still Of The Night** Boyz II Men	Motown
5	**I'd Die Without You** P.M.Dawn	Gee Street
6	**Rhythm Is A Dancer** Snap	Arista
7	**Good Enough** Bobby Brown	MCA
8	**Saving Forever For You** Shanice	Giant
9	**How Do You Talk To An Angel** The Heights	Capitol
10	**Real Love** Mary J. Blige	Uptown

indy albums

1	**Pop! - The First 20 Hits** Erasure	Mute
2	**Boss Drum** The Shamen	One Little Indian
3	**Levelling The Land** The Levellers	China
4	**Copper Blue** Sugar	Creation
5	**Screamadelica** Primal Scream	Creation

dance singles

1	**Song Of Life** Leftfield	Hard Hands
2	**Hardtrance Acperience EP** Hardfloor	Harthouse UK
3	**Rock The House** Source Feat Nicole	React
4	**Way In My Brain/Drumbeats** SL2	XL Recording
5	**One In Ten** 808 State/UB40	ZTT

indy albums

1. **Pop! – The First 20 Hits** — Erasure — Mute
2. **Boss Drum** — The Shamen — One Little Indian
3. **Levelling The Land** — The Levellers — China
4. **Copper Blue** — Sugar — Creation
5. **Screamadelica** — Primal Scream — Creation

dance singles

1. **Exterminate!** — Snap — Arista
2. **Mr. Wendale/Revolution** — Arrested Development — Cooltempo
3. **Broken English** — Sunscreem — Sony
4. **New Emotion EP** — Time Frequency — Internal Affairs
5. **Song Of Life** — Leftfield — Hard Hands

Whitney Houston runs into 1993 still at Number One after six weeks. By March it had sold 1 1/2 million copies. Dutch duo 2 Unlimited's No Limit was the highest new year entry at Number Four. Suddenly Whitney is looking threatened. Can 2 Unlimited finally put an end to her spectacular reign at the top of the charts...?

indy albums

1. **Boss Drum** — The Shamen — One Little Indian
2. **Pop! – The First 20 Hits** — Erasure — Mute
3. **Copper Blue** — Sugar — Creation
4. **Levelling The Land** — The Levellers — China
5. **Screamadelica** — Primal Scream — Creation

dance singles

1. **The Love I Lost** — West End featuring Sybil — PWL Sanctuary
2. **It's Gonna Be A Lovely Day** — Soul System/Michelle Visage — Arista
3. **Exterminate!** — Snap — Arista
4. **Show Me Love** — Robin S — Champion
5. **Mr. Wendale/Revolution** — Arrested Development — Cooltempo

uk singles

1. **I Will Always Love You** — Whitney Houston — Arista
2. **Heal The World** — Michael Jackson — Epic
3. **Could It Be Magic** — Take That — RCA
4. **Would I Lie To You** — Charles And Eddie — Capitol
5. **Phorever People** — The Shamen — One Little Indian
6. **Slam Jam** — The WWF Superstars — Arista
7. **Exterminate** — Snap Feat Niki Haris — Arista
8. **Mr Wendal/revolution** — Arrested Development — Cooltempo
9. **Out Of Space (remix)** — The Prodigy — XI Recordings
10. **Miami Hit Mix/Xmas Thru' Your Eyes** — Gloria Estefan — Epic

us singles

1. **I Will Always Love You** — Whitney Houston — Arista
2. **Rump Shaker** — Wreckx-N-Effect — MCA
3. **If Ever I Fall In Love** — Shai — Gasoline Alley
4. **In The Still Of The Night** — Boyz II Men — Motown
5. **I'd Die Without You** — P.M. Dawn — Gee Street
6. **Rhythm Is A Dancer** — Snap — Arista
7. **Saving Forever For You** — Shanice — Giant
8. **Good Enough** — Bobby Brown — MCA
9. **What About Your Friends** — TLC — Laface
10. **Real Love** — Mary J. Blige — Uptown

uk singles

1. **I Will Always Love You** — Whitney Houston — Arista
2. **Exterminate** — Snap Feat Niki Haris — Arista
3. **Could It Be Magic** — Take That — RCA
4. **Mr Wendal/revolution** — Arrested Development — Cooltempo
5. **Heal The World** — Michael Jackson — Epic
6. **I'm Easy** — Faith No More — Slash
7. **Phorever People** — The Shamen — One Little Indian
8. **Would I Lie To You** — Charles And Eddie — Capitol
9. **Get The Girl! Kill The Baddies!** — Pop Will Eat Itself — RCA
10. **The Devil You Know** — Jesus Jones — Food

us singles

1. **I Will Always Love You** — Whitney Houston — Arista
2. **If Ever I Fall In Love** — Shai — Gasoline Alley
3. **In The Still Of The Night** — Boyz II Men — Motown
4. **Rump Shaker** — Wreckx-N-Effect — MCA
5. **Saving Forever For You** — Shanice — Giant
6. **Rhythm Is A Dancer** — Snap — Arista
7. **I'd Die Without You** — P.M. Dawn — Gee Street
8. **Good Enough** — Bobby Brown — MCA
9. **What About Your Friends** — TLC — Laface
10. **Deeper And Deeper** — Madonna — Maverick/Sire

us albums

1. **The Bodyguard** — Soundtrack — Arista
2. **Unplugged** — Eric Clapton — Duck/Reprise
3. **Breathless** — Kenny G — Arista
4. **Timeless (The Classics)** — Michael Bolton — Columbia
5. **The Chase** — Garth Brooks — Liberty
6. **Ten** — Pearl Jam — Epic Associated
7. **Some Gave All** — Billy Ray Cyrus — Mercury
8. **Automatic For The People** — R.E.M. — Warner Bros.
9. **Home For Christmas** — Amy Grant — A&M
10. **Hard Or Smooth** — Wreckx-N-Effect — MCA
11. **A Very Special Christmas 2** — Various Artists — A&M
12. **It's Your Call** — Reba McEntire — MCA
13. **Pure Country (Soundtrack)** — George Strait — MCA
14. **What's The 411?** — Mary J. Blige — Uptown
15. **Love Deluxe** — Sade — Epic
16. **OOOOOOOHHH... On The TLC Tip** — TLC — Laface
17. **If I Ever Fall In Love** — Shai — Gasoline Alley
18. **3 Years 5 Months & 2 Days In The Life** — Arrested Development — Chrysalis
19. **Totally Krossed Out** — Kris Kross — Ruffhouse
20. **The Predator** — Ice Cube — Priority

us albums

1. **The Bodyguard** — Soundtrack — Arista
2. **The Chase** — Garth Brooks — Liberty
3. **Timeless (The Classics)** — Michael Bolton — Columbia
4. **Unplugged** — Eric Clapton — Duck/Reprise
5. **Some Gave All** — Billy Ray Cyrus — Mercury
6. **Breathless** — Kenny G — Arista
7. **Ten** — Pearl Jam — Epic Associated
8. **If I Ever Fall In Love** — Shai — Gasilone Alley
9. **It's Your Call** — Reba McEntire — MCA
10. **Hard Or Smooth** — Wreckx-N-Effect — MCA
11. **What's The 411?** — Mary J. Blige — Uptown
12. **Pure Country (Soundtrack)** — George Strait — MCA
13. **Automatic For The People** — R.E.M. — Warner Bros.
14. **3 Years 5 Months & 2 Days In The Life** — Arrested Development — Chrysalis
15. **Love Deluxe** — Sade — Epic
16. **The Chronic** — Dr. Dre — Death Row
17. **Bobby** — Bobby Brown — MCA
18. **Metallica** — Metallica — Elektra
19. **OOOOOOOHHH... On The TLC Tip** — TLC — Laface
20. **Brand New Man** — Brooks & Dunn — Arista

uk albums

1. **Cher's Greatest Hits: 1965-1992** — Cher — Geffen
2. **Pop! – The First 20 Hits** — Erasure — Mute
3. **Take That & Party** — Take That — RCA
4. **Greatest Hits** — Gloria Estefan — Epic
5. **Live – The Way We Walk Vol 1 The Shorts** — Genesis — Virgin
6. **Glittering Prize – Simple Minds 81/92** — Simple Minds — Virgin
7. **Boss Drum** — The Shamen — One Little Indian
8. **Automatic For The People** — R.E.M. — Warner Bros
9. **Dangerous** — Michael Jackson — Epic
10. **Gold – Greatest Hits** — Abba — Polydor
11. **Stars** — Simply Red — East West
12. **Timeless (The Classics)** — Michael Bolton — Columbia
13. **Back To Front** — Lionel Richie — Motown
14. **Erotica** — Madonna — Maverick/Sire
15. **The Freddie Mercury Album** — Freddie Mercury — Parlophone
16. **3 Years, 5 Months & 2 Days In The Life** — Arrested Development — Cooltempo
17. **The Best Of Belinda Vol 1** — Belinda Carlisle — Virgin
18. **Nevermind** — Nirvana — DGC
19. **Duophonic** — Charles And Eddie — Capitol
20. **Incesticide** — Nirvana — DGC

uk albums

1. **Cher's Greatest Hits: 1965-1992** — Cher — Geffen
2. **Take That & Party** — Take That — RCA
3. **Boss Drum** — The Shamen — One Little Indian
4. **Automatic For The People** — R.E.M. — Warner Bros
5. **Pop! – The First 20 Hits** — Erasure — Mute
6. **Greatest Hits** — Gloria Estefan — Epic
7. **Live – The Way We Walk Vol 1 The Shorts** — Genesis — Virgin
8. **Glittering Prize – Simple Minds 81/92** — Simple Minds — Virgin
9. **Gold – Greatest Hits** — Abba — Polydor
10. **3 Years, 5 Months & 2 Days In The Life** — Arrested Development — Cooltempo
11. **Back To Front** — Lionel Richie — Motown
12. **Timeless (The Classics)** — Michael Bolton — Columbia
13. **Stars** — Simply Red — East West
14. **Incesticide** — Nirvana — DGC
15. **Only Yesterday** — The Carpenters — A&M
16. **The Freddie Mercury Album** — Freddie Mercury — Parlophone
17. **Erotica** — Madonna — Maverick/Sire
18. **Dangerous** — Michael Jackson — Epic
19. **Hit Parade 2** — The Wedding Present — RCA
20. **Unplugged** — Eric Clapton — Duck

indy albums

1	**Boss Drum**	
	The Shamen	One Little Indian
2	**Pop! – The First 20 Hits**	
	Erasure	Mute
3	**Copper Blue**	
	Sugar	Creation
4	**Levelling The Land**	
	The Levellers	China
5	**Screamadelica**	
	Primal Scream	Creation

dance singles

1	**We Are Family ('93 Mixes)**	
	Sister Sledge	Atlantic
2	**Open Your Mind**	
	Usura	Deconstruction
3	**The Love I Lost**	
	West End featuring Sybil	PWL Sanctuary
4	**Show Me Love**	
	Robin S	Champion
5	**It's Gonna Be A Lovely Day**	
	Soul System/Michelle Visage	Arista

uk singles

1	**I Will Always Love You**	
	Whitney Houston	Arista
2	**Exterminate**	
	Snap Feat Niki Haris	Arista
3	**I'm Easy**	
	Faith No More	Slash
4	**Could It Be Magic**	
	Take That	RCA
5	**The Love I Lost**	
	West End Featuring Sybil	PWL Sanctuary
6	**Mr Wendal/revolution**	
	Arrested Development	Cooltempo
7	**We Are Family ('93 Mixes)**	
	Sister Sledge	Atlantic
8	**Open Your Mind**	
	Usura	Deconstruction
9	**Sweet Harmony**	
	The Beloved	East West
10	**Steam**	
	Peter Gabriel	Real World

us singles

1	**I Will Always Love You**	
	Whitney Houston	Arista
2	**If Ever I Fall In Love**	
	Shai	Gasoline Alley
3	**In The Still Of The Night**	
	Boyz II Men	Motown
4	**Rump Shaker**	
	Wreckx-N-Effect	MCA
5	**Saving Forever For You**	
	Shanice	Giant
6	**Rhythm Is A Dancer**	
	Snap	Arista
7	**Good Enough**	
	Bobby Brown	MCA
8	**Deeper And Deeper**	
	Madonna	Maverick/Sire
9	**A Whole New World (Aladdin's Theme)**	
	Peabo Bryson and Regina Belle	Columbia
10	**I'd Die Without You**	
	P.M. Dawn	Gee Street

us albums

1	**The Bodyguard**	
	Soundtrack	Arista
2	**The Chase**	
	Garth Brooks	Liberty
3	**Some Gave All**	
	Billy Ray Cyrus	Mercury
4	**Unplugged**	
	Eric Clapton	Duck/Reprise
5	**Timeless (The Classics)**	
	Michael Bolton	Columbia
6	**Breathless**	
	Kenny G	Arista
7	**Ten**	
	Pearl Jam	Epic Associated
8	**It's Your Call**	
	Reba McEntire	MCA
9	**Pure Country (Soundtrack)**	
	George Strait	MCA
10	**Brand New Man**	
	Brooks & Dunn	Arista
11	**If I Ever Fall In Love**	
	Shai	Gasoline Alley
12	**The Chronic**	
	Dr. Dre	Death Row
13	**Love Deluxe**	
	Sade	Epic
14	**Hard Or Smooth**	
	Wreckx-N-Effect	MCA
15	**Bobby**	
	Bobby Brown	MCA
16	**3 Years 5 Months & 2 Days In The Life**	
	Arrested Development	Chrysalis
17	**What's The 411?**	
	Mary J. Blige	Uptown
18	**Totally Krossed Out**	
	Kris Kross	Ruffhouse
19	**Automatic For The People**	
	R.E.M.	Warner Bros.
20	**A Lot About Livin'**	
	Alan Jackson	Arista

uk albums

1	**Live – The Way We Walk Vol 2: The Longs**	
	Genesis	Virgin
2	**Connected**	
	Stereo Mc's	4th+b'Way
3	**Automatic For The People**	
	R.E.M.	Warner Bros
4	**3 Years, 5 Months & 2 Days In The Life**	
	Arrested Development	Cooltempo
5	**Take That & Party**	
	Take That	RCA
6	**Boss Drum**	
	The Shamen	One Little Indian
7	**Cher's Greatest Hits: 1965-1992**	
	Cher	Geffen
8	**Into The Skyline**	
	Cathy Dennis	Polydor
9	**Live – The Way We Walk Vol 1 The Shorts**	
	Genesis	Virgin
10	**Greatest Hits**	
	Gloria Estefan	Epic
11	**Pop! – The First 20 Hits**	
	Erasure	Mute
12	**Glittering Prize – Simple Minds 81/92**	
	Simple Minds	Virgin
13	**Gold – Greatest Hits**	
	Abba	Polydor
14	**Incesticide**	
	Nirvana	DGC
15	**Back To Front**	
	Lionel Richie	Motown
16	**Stars**	
	Simply Red	East West
17	**Only Yesterday**	
	The Carpenters	A&M
18	**Timeless (The Classics)**	
	Michael Bolton	Columbia
19	**Keep The Faith**	
	Bon Jovi	Mercury
20	**Unplugged**	
	Eric Clapton	Duck

uk singles

1	**I Will Always Love You**	
	Whitney Houston	Arista
2	**Exterminate**	
	Snap Feat Niki Haris	Arista
3	**The Love I Lost**	
	West End Featuring Sybil	PWL Sanctuary
4	**No Limit**	
	2 Unlimited	PWL Continental
5	**We Are Family ('93 Mixes)**	
	Sister Sledge	Atlantic
6	**I'm Easy**	
	Faith No More	Slash
7	**Open Your Mind**	
	Usura	Deconstruction
8	**Sweet Harmony**	
	The Beloved	East West
9	**Mr Wendal/revolution**	
	Arrested Development	Cooltempo
10	**Could It Be Magic**	
	Take That	RCA

us singles

1	**I Will Always Love You**	
	Whitney Houston	Arista
2	**If Ever I Fall In Love**	
	Shai	Gasoline Alley
3	**In The Still Of The Night**	
	Boyz II Men	Motown
4	**Saving Forever For You**	
	Shanice	Giant
5	**Rump Shaker**	
	Wreckx-N-Effect	MCA
6	**A Whole New World (Aladdin's Theme)**	
	Peabo Bryson and Regina Belle	Columbia
7	**Deeper And Deeper**	
	Madonna	Maverick/Sire
8	**Good Enough**	
	Bobby Brown	MCA
9	**Rhythm Is A Dancer**	
	Snap	Arista
10	**7**	
	Prince And The N P G	Paisley Park

indy albums

1	**Boss Drum**	
	The Shamen	One Little Indian
2	**Pop! – The First 20 Hits**	
	Erasure	Mute
3	**Copper Blue**	
	Sugar	Creation
4	**Surfing On Sine Waves**	
	Polygon Window	Warp
5	**Levelling The Land**	
	The Levellers	China

dance singles

1	**Things Can Only Get Better**	
	Dream	Magnet
2	**Open Your Mind**	
	Usura	Deconstruction
3	**We Are Family ('93 Mixes)**	
	Sister Sledge	Atlantic
4	**Dreams Of Heaven**	
	Ground Level	Faze
5	**Show Me Love**	
	Robin S	Champion

us albums

1	**The Bodyguard**	
	Soundtrack	Arista
2	**Breathless**	
	Kenny G	Arista
3	**Unplugged**	
	Eric Clapton	Duck/Reprise
4	**Some Gave All**	
	Billy Ray Cyrus	Mercury
5	**The Chase**	
	Garth Brooks	Liberty
6	**Timeless (The Classics)**	
	Michael Bolton	Columbia
7	**The Chronic**	
	Dr. Dre	Death Row
8	**If I Ever Fall In Love**	
	Shai	Gasoline Alley
9	**Ten**	
	Pearl Jam	Epic Associated
10	**Hard Or Smooth**	
	Wreckx-N-Effect	MCA
11	**Aladdin**	
	Soundtrack	Walt Disney
12	**Love Deluxe**	
	Sade	Epic
13	**It's Your Call**	
	Reba McEntire	MCA
14	**Pure Country (Soundtrack)**	
	George Strait	MCA
15	**Brand New Man**	
	Brooks & Dunn	Arista
16	**What's The 411?**	
	Mary J. Blige	Uptown
17	**Bobby**	
	Bobby Brown	MCA
18	**3 Years 5 Months & 2 Days In The Life**	
	Arrested Development	Chrysalis
19	**Jon Secada**	
	Jon Secada	SBK
20	**Pocket Full Of Kryptonite**	
	Spin Doctors	Epic Associated

uk albums

1	**Live – The Way We Walk Vol 2: The Longs**	
	Genesis	Virgin
2	**So Close**	
	Dina Carroll	A&M
3	**Automatic For The People**	
	R.E.M.	Warner Bros
4	**3 Years, 5 Months & 2 Days In The Life**	
	Arrested Development	Cooltempo
5	**Connected**	
	Stereo Mc's	4th+b'Way
6	**Take That & Party**	
	Take That	RCA
7	**Boss Drum**	
	The Shamen	One Little Indian
8	**Cher's Greatest Hits: 1965-1992**	
	Cher	Geffen
9	**Live – The Way We Walk Vol 1 The Shorts**	
	Genesis	Virgin
10	**Us**	
	Peter Gabriel	Real World
11	**Pop! – The First 20 Hits**	
	Erasure	Mute
12	**Keep The Faith**	
	Bon Jovi	Mercury
13	**Gold – Greatest Hits**	
	Abba	Polydor
14	**Greatest Hits**	
	Gloria Estefan	Epic
15	**Glittering Prize – Simple Minds 81/92**	
	Simple Minds	Virgin
16	**Into The Skyline**	
	Cathy Dennis	Polydor
17	**Appolonia**	
	Bm Ex	Union City
18	**The Juliet Letters**	
	Elvis Costello & The Brodsky Quartet	Warner Bros
19	**Stars**	
	Simply Red	East West
20	**Inspector Morse Vol 3**	
	Barrington Pheloung	Virgin

us albums

1	**The Bodyguard** Soundtrack	Arista
2	**Breathless** Kenny G	Arista
3	**Unplugged** Eric Clapton	Duck/Reprise
4	**The Chronic** Dr. Dre	Death Row
5	**Some Gave All** Billy Ray Cyrus	Mercury
6	**If I Ever Fall In Love** Shai	Gasoline Alley
7	**Timeless (The Classics)** Michael Bolton	Columbia
8	**Aladdin** Soundtrack	Walt Disney
9	**Hard Or Smooth** Wreckx-N-Effect	MCA
10	**Ten** Pearl Jam	Epic Associated
11	**The Chase** Garth Brooks	Liberty
12	**Love Deluxe** Sade	Epic
13	**Pocket Full Of Kryptonite** Spin Doctors	Epic Associated
14	**3 Years 5 Months & 2 Days In The Life** Arrested Development	Chrysalis
15	**What's The 411?** Mary J. Blige	Uptown
16	**It's Your Call** Reba McEntire	MCA
17	**Jon Secada** Jon Secada	SBK
18	**Bobby** Bobby Brown	MCA
19	**Automatic For The People** R.E.M.	Warner Bros.
20	**Pure Country (Soundtrack)** George Strait	MCA

uk singles

1	**I Will Always Love You** Whitney Houston	Arista
2	**No Limit** 2 Unlimited	PWL Continental
3	**The Love I Lost** West End Featuring Sybil	PWL Sanctuary
4	**Exterminate** Snap Feat Niki Haris	Arista
5	**Deep** East 17	London
6	**Ordinary World** Duran Duran	EMI
7	**Open Your Mind** Usura	Deconstruction
8	**Sweet Harmony** The Beloved	East West
9	**How Can I Love You More(Remixes)** M – People	Decon
10	**We Are Family ('93 Mixes)** Sister Sledge	Atlantic

us singles

1	**I Will Always Love You** Whitney Houston	Arista
2	**If Ever I Fall In Love** Shai	Gasoline Alley
3	**A Whole New World (Aladdin's Theme)** Peabo Bryson and Regina Belle	Columbia
4	**In The Still Of The Night** Boyz II Men	Motown
5	**Saving Forever For You** Shanice	Giant
6	**Rump Shaker** Wreckx-N-Effect	MCA
7	**Ordinary World** Duran Duran	Capitol
8	**7** Prince And The N P G	Paisley Park
9	**Deeper And Deeper** Madonna	Maverick/Sire
10	**Mr Wendal** Arrested Development	Chrysalis

indy albums

1	**Boss Drum** The Shamen	One Little Indian
2	**Appolonia** B M EX	Union City
3	**Pop! - The First 20 Hits** Erasure	Mute
4	**Copper Blue** Sugar	Creation
5	**Surfing On Sine Waves** Polygon Window	Warp

dance singles

1	**I Lift My Cup** Gloworm	Pulse
2	**How Can I Love You More (Remixes)** M.People	RCA
3	**Things Can Only Get Better** Dream	Magnet
4	**Dreams Of Heaven** Ground Level	Faze
5	**Breakbeat Pressure Part 1 & 2** DJSS	Formation

Whitney finally loses her grip on the top of the charts, knocked off by Dutch dance duo 2 Unlimited. In its time at Number One, *I Will Always Love You* sold an incredible 1.2 million copies in the U.K., making it the first double platinum seller since 1991, when Bryan Adams irritated a nation for endless weeks with *Everything I Do*. Bryan, however, was following in the footsteps of the master: in 1986 Paul McCartney went double platinum with *Mull Of Kintyre*.

uk albums

1	**Jam** Little Angels	Polydor
2	**Dusk** The The	Epic
3	**So Close** Dina Carroll	A&M
4	**Live – The Way We Walk Vol 2: The Longs** Genesis	Virgin
5	**3 Years, 5 Months & 2 Days In The Life** Arrested Development	Cooltempo
6	**Perverse** Jesus Jones	Food
7	**Automatic For The People** R.E.M.	Warner Bros
8	**Gorecki Symphony 3** Zinman/Upshaw/London Sinfonietta	Elektra Nonesuch
9	**Connected** Stereo Mc's	4th+b'Way
10	**Boss Drum** The Shamen	One Little Indian
11	**Take That & Party** Take That	RCA
12	**Cher's Greatest Hits: 1965-1992** Cher	Geffen
13	**Indian Summer** Go West	Chrysalis
14	**Live – The Way We Walk Vol 1 The Shorts** Genesis	Virgin
15	**Keep The Faith** Bon Jovi	Mercury
16	**Us** Peter Gabriel	Real World
17	**Funky Divas** En Vogue	East West America
18	**Gold – Greatest Hits** Abba	Polydor
19	**Pop! – The First 20 Hits** Erasure	Mute
20	**Glittering Prize – Simple Minds 81/92** Simple Minds	Virgin

---

us albums

1	**The Bodyguard** Soundtrack	Arista
2	**Breathless** Kenny G	Arista
3	**The Chronic** Dr. Dre	Death Row
4	**Unplugged** Eric Clapton	Duck/Reprise
5	**Some Gave All** Billy Ray Cyrus	Mercury
6	**Timeless (The Classics)** Michael Bolton	Columbia
7	**Ten** Pearl Jam	Epic Associated
8	**If I Ever Fall In Love** Shai	Gasoline Alley
9	**Aladdin** Soundtrack	Walt Disney
10	**Pocket Full Of Kryptonite** Spin Doctors	Epic Associated
11	**Hard Or Smooth** Wreckx-N-Effect	MCA
12	**3 Years 5 Months & 2 Days In The Life** Arrested Development	
13	**It's Your Call** Reba McEntire	MCA
14	**The Chase** Garth Brooks	Liberty
15	**Love Deluxe** Sade	Epic
16	**Bobby** Bobby Brown	MCA
17	**What's The 411?** Mary J. Blige	Uptown
18	**Jon Secada** Jon Secada	SBK
19	**Brand New Man** Brooks & Dunn	Arista
20	**Automatic For The People** R.E.M.	Warner Bros.

uk singles

1	**No Limit** 2 Unlimited	PWL Continental
2	**I Will Always Love You** Whitney Houston	Arista
3	**Little Bird** Annie Lennox	RCA
4	**The Love I Lost** West End Featuring Sybil	PWL Sanctuary
5	**Deep** East 17	London
6	**Ordinary World** Duran Duran	EMI
7	**Exterminate** Snap Feat Niki Haris	Arista
8	**Stairway To Heaven** Rolf Harris	Vertigo
9	**Sweet Harmony** The Beloved	East West

us singles

1	**I Will Always Love You** Whitney Houston	Arista
2	**A Whole New World (Aladdin's Theme)** Peabo Bryson and Regina Belle	Columbia
3	**If Ever I Fall In Love** Shai	Gasoline Alley
4	**Saving Forever For You** Shanice	Giant
5	**Ordinary World** Duran Duran	Capitol
6	**In The Still Of The Night** Boyz II Men	Motown
7	**Mr Wendal** Arrested Development	Chrysalis
8	**7** Prince And The N P G	Paisley Park
9	**Rump Shaker** Wreckx-N-Effect	MCA
10	**I'm Every Woman** Whitney Houston	Arista

indy albums

1	**Boss Drum** The Shamen	One Little Indian
2	**Pop! - The First 20 Hits** Erasure	Mute
3	**Appolonia** B M EX	Union City
4	**Copper Blue** Sugar	Creation
5	**Levelling The Land** The Levellers	China

dance singles

1	**All This Love I'm Giving** Music & Mystery/Gwen McCrae	KTDA
2	**Little Bird/Love Song For A...** Annie Lennox	RCA
3	**I Lift My Cup** Gloworm	Pulse
4	**Take Off Some Time** New Atlantic	3 Beat
5	**How Can I Love You More (RMX)** M.People	RCA

uk albums

1	**Pure Cult** The Cult	Beggars Banquet
2	**Star** Belly	4ad
3	**3 Years, 5 Months & 2 Days In The Life** Arrested Development	Cooltempo
4	**Funky Divas** En Vogue	East West America
5	**Off The Ground** Paul McCartney	Parlophone
6	**Gorecki Symphony 3** Zinman/Upshaw/London Sinfonietta	Elektra Nonesuch
7	**Automatic For The People** R.E.M.	Warner Bros
8	**The Madman's Return** Snap	Arista
9	**So Close** Dina Carroll	A&M
10	**Connected** Stereo Mc's	4th+b'Way
11	**Live – The Way We Walk Vol 2: The Longs** Genesis	Virgin
12	**Jam** Little Angels	Polydor
13	**Boss Drum** The Shamen	One Little Indian
14	**Take That & Party** Take That	RCA
15	**Indian Summer** Go West	Chrysalis
16	**Dusk** The The	Epic
17	**Gorgeous** 808 State	Ztt
18	**Keep The Faith** Bon Jovi	Mercury
19	**Cher's Greatest Hits: 1965-1992** Cher	Geffen
20	**Diva** Annie Lennox	RCA

uk albums

1	**Words Of Love** Buddy Holly & The Crickets	Polygram TV
2	**Conscience** The Beloved	East West
3	**Automatic For The People** R.E.M.	Warner Bros
4	**Pure Cult** The Cult	Beggars Banquet
5	**Funky Divas** En Vogue	East West America
6	**Gorecki Symphony 3** Zinman/Upshaw/London Sinfonietta	Elektra Nonesuch
7	**3 Years, 5 Months & 2 Days In The Life** Arrested Development	Cooltempo
8	**So Close** Dina Carroll	A&M
9	**Take That & Party** Take That	RCA
10	**Where You Been** Dinosaur Jr	Blanco Y Negro
11	**Diva** Annie Lennox	RCA
12	**Wandering Spirit** Mick Jagger	Atlantic
13	**Connected** Stereo Mc's	4th+b'Way
14	**Love Makes No Sense** Alexander O'Neal	Tabu/a&m
15	**Live – The Way We Walk Vol 2: The Longs** Genesis	Virgin
16	**The Madman's Return** Snap	Arista
17	**Star** Belly	4ad
18	**Indian Summer** Go West	Chrysalis
19	**Off The Ground** Paul McCartney	Parlophone
20	**Boss Drum** The Shamen	One Little Indian

us albums

1	**The Bodyguard** Soundtrack	Arista
2	**Breathless** Kenny G	Arista
3	**The Chronic** Dr. Dre	Death Row
4	**Some Gave All** Billy Ray Cyrus	Mercury
5	**Unplugged** Eric Clapton	Duck/Reprise
6	**If I Ever Fall In Love** Shai	Gasoline Alley
7	**Pocket Full Of Kryptonite** Spin Doctors	Epic Associated
8	**Ten** Pearl Jam	Epic Associated
9	**Aladdin** Soundtrack	Walt Disney
10	**Timeless (The Classics)** Michael Bolton	Columbia
11	**Hard Or Smooth** Wreckx-N-Effect	MCA
12	**In God We Trust** Brand Nubian	Elektra
13	**3 Years 5 Months & 2 Days In The Life** Arrested Development	Chrysalis
14	**Lose Control** Silk	Keia
15	**It's Your Call** Reba McEntire	MCA
16	**The Chase** Garth Brooks	Liberty
17	**Love Deluxe** Sade	Epic
18	**What's The 411?** Mary J. Blige	Uptown
19	**Bobby** Bobby Brown	MCA
20	**Automatic For The People** R.E.M.	Warner Bros.

uk singles

1	**No Limit** 2 Unlimited	PWL Continental
2	**Why Can't I Wake Up With You?** Take That	RCA
3	**Little Bird** Annie Lennox	RCA
4	**I Will Always Love You** Whitney Houston	Arista
5	**I'm Every Woman** Whitney Houston	Arista
6	**Deep** East 17	London
7	**Stairway To Heaven** Rolf Harris	Vertigo
8	**The Love I Lost** West End Featuring Sybil	PWL Sanctuary
9	**Ordinary World** Duran Duran	EMI
10	**How Can I Love You More (remixes)** M-people	Deconstruction/RCA

us singles

1	**I Will Always Love You** Whitney Houston	Arista
2	**A Whole New World (Aladdin's Theme)** Peabo Bryson and Regina Belle	Columbia
3	**Ordinary World** Duran Duran	Capitol
4	**I'm Every Woman** Whitney Houston	Arista
5	**Saving Forever For You** Shanice	Giant
6	**Mr Wendal** Arrested Development	Chrysalis
7	**If Ever I Fall In Love** Shai	Gasoline Alley
8	**7** Prince And The N P G	Paisley Park
9	**In The Still Of The Night** Boyz II Men	Motown
10	**Hip Hop Hooray** Naughty By Nature	Tommy Boy

indy albums

1	**Star** Belly	4AD
2	**Boss Drum** The Shamen	One Little Indian
3	**Pop! – The First 20 Hits** Erasure	Mute
4	**Copper Blue** Sugar	Creation
5	**Appolonia** B M EX	Union City

dance singles

1	**I'm Every Woman** Whitney Houston	Arista
2	**Feel** Sandy B	Mercury
3	**Little Bird/Love Song For A...** Annie Lennox	RCA
4	**Ground Level** Stereo MCs	Gee Street
5	**The Theme/Euphoria** House Crew	Production House

A bit of Brit does you good: kd lang re-entered the album charts at Number 15 with Ingenue, almost a full year after its original entry at Number 28. The reason? Probably her very romping duet with Erasure's Andy Bell at the Brits Awards.

---

uk albums

1	**Walthamstow** East 17	London
2	**Automatic For The People** R.E.M.	Warner Bros
3	**Diva** Annie Lennox	RCA
4	**Duran Duran (the Wedding Album)** Duran Duran	Parlophone
5	**Take That & Party** Take That	RCA
6	**Words Of Love** Buddy Holly & The Crickets	Polygram TV
7	**Funky Divas** En Vogue	East West America
8	**3 Years, 5 Months & 2 Days In The Life** Arrested Development	Cooltempo
9	**Dangerous** Michael Jackson	Epic
10	**Pure Cult** The Cult	Beggars Banquet
11	**Stars** Simply Red	East West
12	**Gorecki Symphony 3** Zinman/Upshaw/London Sinfonietta	Elektra Nonesuch
13	**Connected** Stereo Mc's	4th+b'Way
14	**So Close** Dina Carroll	A&M
15	**Ingenue** kd lang	Sire
16	**Conscience** The Beloved	East West
17	**Us** Peter Gabriel	Real World
18	**Great Expectations** Tasmin Archer	EMI
19	**The Very Best Of Sister Sledge 1973-93** Sister Sledge	East West
20	**Boss Drum** The Shamen	One Little Indian

us albums

1	**The Bodyguard** Soundtrack	Arista
2	**Breathless** Kenny G	Arista
3	**The Chronic** Dr. Dre	Death Row
4	**Unplugged** Eric Clapton	Duck/Reprise
5	**Some Gave All** Billy Ray Cyrus	Mercury
6	**Aladdin** Soundtrack	Walt Disney
7	**Pocket Full Of Kryptonite** Spin Doctors	Epic Associated
8	**Timeless (The Classics)** Michael Bolton	Columbia
9	**If I Ever Fall In Love** Shai	Gasoline Alley
10	**It's Your Call** Reba McEntire	MCA
11	**Wandering Spirit** Mick Jagger	Atlantic
12	**Dangerous** Michael Jackson	Epic
13	**Ten** Pearl Jam	Epic Associated
14	**Lose Control** Silk	Keia
15	**Reachin'** Digable Planets	Pendulum
16	**Love Deluxe** Sade	Epic
17	**Off The Ground** Paul McCartney	Capitol
18	**3 Years 5 Months & 2 Days In The Life** Arrested Development	Chrysalis
19	**Hard Or Smooth** Wreckx-N-Effect	MCA
20	**Live: The Way We Walk Vol 2:** The Longs Genesis	Atlantic

uk singles

1	**No Limit** 2 Unlimited	PWL Continental
2	**Why Can't I Wake Up With You?** Take That	RCA
3	**Little Bird** Annie Lennox	RCA
4	**I'm Every Woman** Whitney Houston	Arista
5	**Are You Gonna Go My Way?** Lenny Kravitz	Virgin America
6	**Give In To Me** Michael Jackson	Epic
7	**Deep** East 17	London
8	**I Feel You** Depeche Mode	Mute
9	**I Will Always Love You** Whitney Houston	Arista
10	**The Love I Lost** West End Featuring Sybil	PWL Sanctuary

us singles

1	**I Will Always Love You** Whitney Houston	Arista
2	**A Whole New World (Aladdin's Theme)** Peabo Bryson and Regina Belle	Columbia
3	**Ordinary World** Duran Duran	Capitol
4	**I'm Every Woman** Whitney Houston	Arista
5	**Nuthin' But A "G" Thang** Dr. Dre	Death Row
6	**Mr Wendal** Arrested Development	Chrysalis
7	**7** Prince And The N P G	Paisley Park
8	**Saving Forever For You** Shanice	Giant
9	**Hip Hop Hooray** Naughty By Nature	Tommy Boy
10	**Informer** Snow	Eastwest

indy albums

1	**Star** Belly	4AD
2	**Boss Drum** The Shamen	One Little Indian
3	**Pop! – The First 20 Hits** Erasure	Mute
4	**Copper Blue** Sugar	Creation
5	**See Nothing, Hear Nothing...** The Levellers	China

dance singles

1	**Buruchacca** Mukkaa	Limbo
2	**Took My Love** Bizarre Inc/Angie Brown	Vinyl Solution
3	**Reminisce** Mary J Blige	MCA
4	**I'm Every Woman** Whitney Houston	Arista
5	**Till We Meet Again** Inner City	Ten

indy albums

1	**Star** Belly	4AD
2	**Boss Drum** The Shamen	One Little Indian
3	**Pop! – The First 20 Hits** Erasure	Mute
4	**Copper Blue** Sugar	Creation
5	**See Nothing, Hear Nothing...** The Levellers	China

dance singles

1	**Ethnic Prayer** Havana	Limbo
2	**Give It To You** Martha Wash	RCA
3	**Do You Have The Power?** Boomshanka	Cowboy
4	**Took My Love** Bizarre Inc/Angie Brown	Vinyl Solution
5	**Journey From The Light** 4 Hero	Reinforced

uk singles

1	**No Limit** 2 Unlimited	PWL Continental
2	**Give In To Me** Michael Jackson	Epic
3	**Little Bird** Annie Lennox	RCA
4	**Are You Gonna Go My Way?** Lenny Kravitz	Virgin America
5	**Oh Carolina** Shaggy	Greensleeves
6	**I'm Every Woman** Whitney Houston	Arista
7	**Animal Nitrate** Suede	Nude
8	**Why Can't I Wake Up With You?** Take That	RCA
9	**I Feel You** Depeche Mode	Mute
10	**Deep** East 17	London

us singles

1	**A Whole New World (Aladdin's Theme)** Peabo Bryson and Regina Belle	Columbia
2	**I Will Always Love You** Whitney Houston	Arista
3	**Ordinary World** Duran Duran	Capitol
4	**Informer** Snow	Eastwest
5	**Nuthin' But A "G" Thang** Dr. Dre	Death Row
6	**I'm Every Woman** Whitney Houston	Arista
7	**Mr Wendal** Arrested Development	Chrysalis
8	**Hip Hop Hooray** Naughty By Nature	Tommy Boy
9	**Don't Walk Away** Jade	Giant
10	**Bed Of Roses** Bon Jovi	Jambco

us albums

1	**The Bodyguard** Soundtrack	Arista
2	**Breathless** Kenny G	Arista
3	**The Chronic** Dr. Dre	Death Row
4	**Some Gave All** Billy Ray Cyrus	Mercury
5	**Unplugged** Eric Clapton	Duck/Reprise
6	**Pocket Full Of Kryptonite** Spin Doctors	Epic Associated
7	**Aladdin** Soundtrack	Walt Disney
8	**It's Your Call** Reba McEntire	MCA
9	**Ten** Pearl Jam	Epic Associated
10	**Dangerous** Michael Jackson	Epic
11	**3 Years 5 Months & 2 Days In The Life** Arrested Development	Chrysalis
12	**Lose Control** Silk	Keia
13	**If I Ever Fall In Love** Shai	Gasoline Alley
14	**Timeless (The Classics)** Michael Bolton	Columbia
15	**Reachin'** Digable Planets	Pendulum
16	**Native Tongue** Poison	Capitol
17	**Love Deluxe** Sade	Epic
18	**Jon Secada** Jon Secada	SBK
19	**Hard Or Smooth** Wreckx-N-Effect	MCA
20	**Wandering Spirit** Mick Jagger	Atlantic

uk albums

1	**Diva** Annie Lennox	RCA
2	**Automatic For The People** R.E.M.	Warner Bros
3	**Rod Stewart Lead Vocalist** Rod Stewart	Warner Bros
4	**Unplugged** Eric Clapton	Duck
5	**Words Of Love** Buddy Holly & The Crickets	Polygram TV
6	**Dangerous** Michael Jackson	Epic
7	**So Tough** Saint Etienne	Heavenly
8	**Take That & Party** Take That	RCA
9	**Walthamstow** East 17	London
10	**If I Was: The Best Of** Midge Ure & Ultravox	Chrysalis
11	**Connected** Stereo Mc's	4th+b'Way
12	**So Close** Dina Carroll	A&M
13	**Duran Duran (The Wedding Album)** Duran Duran	Parlophone
14	**Ingenue** kd lang	Sire
15	**Stars** Simply Red	East West
16	**Funky Divas** En Vogue	East West America
17	**3 Years, 5 Months & 2 Days In The Life** Arrested Development	Cooltempo
18	**Great Expectations** Tasmin Archer	EMI
19	**Stain** Living Colour	Epic
20	**Native Tongue** Poison	Capitol

uk singles

1	**No Limit** 2 Unlimited	PWL Continental
2	**Oh Carolina** Shaggy	Greensleeves
3	**Give In To Me** Michael Jackson	Epic
4	**Are You Gonna Go My Way?** Lenny Kravitz	Virgin America
5	**Little Bird** Annie Lennox	RCA
6	**I'm Every Woman** Whitney Houston	Arista
7	**Animal Nitrate** Suede	Nude
8	**Fear Of The Dark (Live)** Iron Maiden	EMI
9	**Stick It Out** Right Said Fred And Friends	Tug
10	**Bad Girl** Madonna	Maverick/Sire

us singles

1	**Informer** Snow	Eastwest
2	**A Whole New World (Aladdin's Theme)** Peabo Bryson and Regina Belle	Columbia
3	**Nuthin' But A "G" Thang** Dr. Dre	Death Row
4	**Ordinary World** Duran Duran	Capitol
5	**I'm Every Woman** Whitney Houston	Arista
6	**Freak Me** Silk	Keia
7	**I Will Always Love You** Whitney Houston	Arista
8	**Mr Wendal** Arrested Development	Chrysalis
9	**Don't Walk Away** Jade	Giant
10	**Bed Of Roses** Bon Jovi	Jambco

indy albums

1	**So Tough** Saint Etienne	Heavenly
2	**New Wave** The Auteurs	Hut
3	**Star** Belly	4AD
4	**Pop! – The First 20 Hits** Erasure	Mute
5	**Boss Drum** The Shamen	One Little Indian

dance singles

1	**Too Young To Die** Jamiroquai	Sony
2	**Lost In Music (Remix)** Sister Sledge	Atlantic
3	**Show Me Love** Robin S	Champion
4	**Crystal Clear** The Grid	Virgin
5	**So Deep** The Reese Project	Network

us albums

1	**Unplugged** Eric Clapton	Duck/Reprise
2	**The Bodyguard** Soundtrack	Arista
3	**19 Naughty III** Naughty By Nature	Tommy Boy
4	**Breathless** Kenny G	Arista
5	**Live: Right Here, Right Now** Van Halen	Warner Bros.
6	**Some Gave All** Billy Ray Cyrus	Mercury
7	**Duran Duran** Duran Duran	Capitol
8	**The Chronic** Dr. Dre	Death Row
9	**3 Years 5 Months & 2 Days In The Life** Arrested Development	Chrysalis
10	**Pocket Full Of Kryptonite** Spin Doctors	Epic Associated
11	**Ten** Pearl Jam	Epic Associated
12	**Dangerous** Michael Jackson	Epic
13	**Lose Control** Silk	Keia
14	**It's Your Call** Reba McEntire	MCA
15	**Aladdin** Soundtrack	Walt Disney
16	**Jon Secada** Jon Secada	SBK
17	**If I Ever Fall In Love** Shai	Gasoline Alley
18	**Ingenue** kd lang	Sire
19	**Hard Workin' Man** Brooks & Dunn	Arista
20	**12 Inches Of Snow** Snow	Eastwest

uk albums

1	**Are You Gonna Go My Way?** Lenny Kravitz	Virgin America
2	**Ten Summoner's Tales** Sting	A&M
3	**Unplugged** Eric Clapton	Duck
4	**Whatever You Say, Say Nothing** Deacon Blue	Columbia
5	**Automatic For The People** R.E.M.	Warner Bros
6	**Diva** Annie Lennox	RCA
7	**Dangerous** Michael Jackson	Epic
8	**Rod Stewart, Lead Vocalist** Rod Stewart	Warner Bros
9	**Ingenue** kd lang	Sire
10	**Take That & Party** Take That	RCA
11	**So Close** Dina Carroll	A&M
12	**If I Was: The Best Of** Midge Ure & Ultravox	Chrysalis
13	**Great Expectations** Tasmin Archer	EMI
14	**Words Of Love** Buddy Holly & The Crickets	Polygram TV
15	**Funky Divas** En Vogue	East West America
16	**Walthamstow** East 17	London
17	**Stars** Simply Red	East West
18	**Connected** Stereo Mc's	4th+b'Way
19	**3 Years, 5 Months & 2 Days In The Life** Arrested Development	Cooltempo
20	**Rage Against The Machine** Rage Against The Machine	Epic

indy albums

1	**So Tough** Saint Etienne	Heavenly
2	**Feels Like Rain** Buddy Guy	Silvertone
3	**Star** Belly	4AD
4	**Boss Drum** The Shamen	One Little Indian
5	**New Wave** The Auteurs	Hut

dance singles

1	**Show Me Love** Robin S	Champion
2	**Too Young To Die** Jamiroquai	Sony
3	**Crystal Clear** The Grid	Virgin
4	**Don't Walk Away** Jade	Giant
5	**Time To Get Up** Liquid	XL Recordings

uk singles

1	**Oh Carolina** Shaggy	Greensleeves
2	**No Limit** 2 Unlimited	PWL Continental
3	**Mr Loverman** Shabba Ranks	Epic
4	**Stick It Out** Right Said Fred And Friends	Tug
5	**Give In To Me** Michael Jackson	Epic
6	**Are You Gonna Go My Way?** Lenny Kravitz	Virgin America
7	**Little Bird** Annie Lennox	RCA
8	**Informer** Snow	Atlantic
9	**Shortsharpshock EP** Therapy?	A&M
10	**Too Young To Die** Jamiroquai	Sony S2

us singles

1	**Informer** Snow	Eastwest
2	**Nuthin' But A "G" Thang** Dr. Dre	Death Row
3	**Freak Me** Silk	Keia
4	**A Whole New World (Aladdin's Theme)** Peabo Bryson and Regina Belle	Columbia
5	**I'm Every Woman** Whitney Houston	Arista
6	**Ordinary World** Duran Duran	Capitol
7	**Don't Walk Away** Jade	Giant
8	**Mr Wendal** Arrested Development	Chrysalis
9	**I Have Nothing** Whitney Houston	Arista
10	**Bed Of Roses** Bon Jovi	Jambco

us albums

1	**Unplugged** Eric Clapton	Duck/Reprise
2	**The Bodyguard** Soundtrack	Arista
3	**Breathless** Kenny G	Arista
4	**19 Naughty III** Naughty By Nature	Tommy Boy
5	**The Chronic** Dr. Dre	Death Row
6	**Some Gave All** Billy Ray Cyrus	Mercury
7	**3 Years 5 Months & 2 Days In The Life** Arrested Development	Chrysalis
8	**Pocket Full Of Kryptonite** Spin Doctors	Epic Associated
9	**Hard Workin' Man** Brooks & Dunn	Arista
10	**Lose Control** Silk	Keia
11	**Duran Duran** Duran Duran	Capitol
12	**Ten** Pearl Jam	Epic Associated
13	**Dangerous** Michael Jackson	Epic
14	**Aladdin** Soundtrack	Walt Disney
15	**Jon Secada** Jon Secada	SBK
16	**It's Your Call** Reba McEntire	MCA
17	**If I Ever Fall In Love** Shai	Gasoline Alley
18	**Live: Right Here, Right Now** Van Halen	Warner Bros.
19	**Slow Dancing With The Moon** Dolly Parton	Columbia
20	**12 Inches Of Snow** Snow	Eastwest

uk albums

1	**Are You Gonna Go My Way?** Lenny Kravitz	Virgin America
2	**Unplugged** Eric Clapton	Duck
3	**Ingenue** kd lang	Sire
4	**The Dark Side Of The Moon** Pink Floyd	Harvest
5	**Ten Summoner's Tales** Sting	A&M
6	**Diva** Annie Lennox	RCA
7	**Songs From The Rain** Hothouse Flowers	London
8	**Automatic For The People** R.E.M.	Warner Bros
9	**Frank Black** Frank Black	4ad
10	**Dangerous** Michael Jackson	Epic
11	**Rod Stewart, Lead Vocalist** Rod Stewart	Warner Bros
12	**Whatever You Say, Say Nothing** Deacon Blue	Columbia
13	**So Close** Dina Carroll	A&M
14	**Stars** Simply Red	East West
15	**Funky Divas** En Vogue	East West America
16	**Take That & Party** Take That	RCA
17	**Rage Against The Machine** Rage Against The Machine	Epic
18	**Other Voices/Other Rooms** Nanci Griffith	MCA
19	**Connected** Stereo Mc's	4th+b'Way
20	**Their Greatest Hits** Hot Chocolate	EMI

Oh Carolina by Shaggy was written 35 years ago and took eight weeks to shoot up from Number 62 to Number One. With Shabba Ranks and Snow also muscling into the Top Ten, this month marked the official reggae revival. You'd have to go back over 20 years to find anything close to such an impact from the reggae collective.

indy albums

1	**Frank Black** Frank Black	4AD
2	**Yeah Yeah/Our Troubled...** Bikini Kill/Huggy Bear	Catcall/Wiija
3	**So Tough** Saint Etienne	Heavenly
4	**Feels Like Rain** Buddy Guy	Silvertone
4	**Boss Drum** The Shamen	One Little Indian

dance singles

1	**I Believe In You** Our Tribe	ffrreedom
2	**Show Me Love** Robin S	Champion
3	**Pressure Us** Sunscreem	Sony
4	**Jump They Say** David Bowie	Arista
5	**Mr. Loverman** Shabba Ranks	Epic

uk singles

1	**Oh Carolina** Shaggy	Greensleeves
2	**Informer** Snow	Atlantic
3	**Mr Loverman** Shabba Ranks	Epic
4	**No Limit** 2 Unlimited	PWL Continental
5	**Young At Heart** The Bluebells	London
6	**Are You Gonna Go My Way?** Lenny Kravitz	Virgin America
7	**Cats In The Cradle** Ugly Kid Joe	Vertigo
8	**Peace In Our Time** Cliff Richard	EMI
9	**Give In To Me** Michael Jackson	Epic
10	**Jump They Say** David Bowie	Arista

us singles

1	**Informer** Snow	Eastwest
2	**Freak Me** Silk	Keia
3	**Nuthin' But A "G" Thang** Dr. Dre	Death Row
4	**Don't Walk Away** Jade	Giant
5	**Ordinary World** Duran Duran	Capitol
6	**I Have Nothing** Whitney Houston	Arista
7	**I'm Every Woman** Whitney Houston	Arista
8	**A Whole New World (Aladdin's Theme)** Peabo Bryson and Regina Belle	Columbia
9	**Mr Wendal** Arrested Development	Chrysalis
10	**Bed Of Roses** Bon Jovi	Jambco

us albums

1	**Unplugged** Eric Clapton	Duck/Reprise
2	**Ten Summoner's Tales** Sting	A&M
3	**The Bodyguard** Soundtrack	Arista
4	**Breathless** Kenny G	Arista
5	**Pocket Full Of Kryptonite** Spin Doctors	Epic Associated
6	**The Chronic** Dr. Dre	Death Row
7	**19 Naughty III** Naughty By Nature	Tommy Boy
8	**Some Gave All** Billy Ray Cyrus	Mercury
9	**3 Years 5 Months & 2 Days In The Life** Arrested Development	Chrysalis
10	**Lose Control** Silk	Keia
11	**Till Death Do Us Part** Geto Boys	Rap-A-Lot
12	**Hard Workin' Man** Brooks & Dunn	Arista
13	**Dangerous** Michael Jackson	Epic
14	**12 Inches Of Snow** Snow	Eastwest
15	**It's Your Call** Reba McEntire	MCA
16	**Slow Dancing With The Moon** Dolly Parton	Columbia
17	**Ten** Pearl Jam	Epic Associated
18	**Are You Gonna Go My Way** Lenny Kravitz	Virgin
19	**If I Ever Fall In Love** Shai	Gasoline Alley
20	**Jon Secada** Jon Secada	SBK

uk albums

1	**Their Greatest Hits** Hot Chocolate	EMI
2	**Amazing Things** Runrig	Chrysalis
3	**Are You Gonna Go My Way?** Lenny Kravitz	Virgin America
4	**Coverdale Page** Coverdale Page	EMI
5	**Unplugged** Eric Clapton	Duck
6	**Ingenue** kd lang	Sire
7	**Ten Summoner's Tales** Sting	A&M
8	**Diva** Annie Lennox	RCA
9	**Automatic For The People** R.E.M.	Warner Bros
10	**The Very Best Of Randy Crawford** Randy Crawford	Dino
11	**The Ultimate Glenn Miller** Glenn Miller	Bluebird
12	**The Dark Side Of The Moon** Pink Floyd	Harvest
13	**So Close** Dina Carroll	A&M
14	**Rod Stewart, Lead Vocalist** Rod Stewart	Warner Bros
15	**Dangerous** Michael Jackson	Epic
16	**Stars** Simply Red	East West
17	**Whatever You Say, Say Nothing** Deacon Blue	Columbia
18	**Take That & Party** Take That	RCA
19	**Songs From The Rain** Hothouse Flowers	London
20	**Great Expectations** Tasmin Archer	EMI

us albums

1. **The Bodyguard** — Soundtrack — Arista
2. **Breathless** — Kenny G — Arista
3. **Unplugged** — Eric Clapton — Duck/Reprise
4. **Ten Summoner's Tales** — Sting — A&M
5. **Coverdale/Page** — Coverdale/Page — Geffen
6. **Pocket Full Of Kryptonite** — Spin Doctors — Epic Associated
7. **The Chronic** — Dr. Dre — Death Row
8. **Lose Control** — Silk — Keia
9. **19 Naughty III** — Naughty By Nature — Tommy Boy
10. **12 Inches Of Snow** — Snow — Eastwest
11. **3 Years 5 Months & 2 Days In The Life** — Arrested Development — Chrysalis
12. **Some Gave All** — Billy Ray Cyrus — Mercury
13. **Till Death Do Us Part** — Geto Boys — Rap-A-Lot
14. **Dangerous** — Michael Jackson — Epic
15. **Ten** — Pearl Jam — Epic Associated
16. **Hard Workin' Man** — Brooks & Dunn — Arista
17. **It's Your Call** — Reba McEntire — MCA
18. **If I Ever Fall In Love** — Shai — Gasoline Alley
19. **Are You Gonna Go My Way?** — Lenny Kravitz — Virgin
20. **Slow Dancing With The Moon** — Dolly Parton — Columbia

uk singles

1. **Young Heart Run Free** — 20/20 Vision — Wis
2. **Oh Carolina** — Shaggy — Greensleeves
3. **Informer** — Snow — Atlantic
4. **Mr Loverman** — Shabba Ranks — Epic
5. **No Limit** — 2 Unlimited — PWL Continental
6. **Fever** — Madonna — Maverick/Sire
7. **Cats In The Cradle** — Ugly Kid Joe — Vertigo
8. **When I'm Good And Ready** — Sybil — PWL International
9. **Jump They Say** — David Bowie — Arista
10. **Show Me Love** — Robin S — Champion

us singles

1. **Informer** — Snow — Eastwest
2. **Freak Me** — Silk — Keia
3. **Nuthin' But A "G" Thang** — Dr. Dre — Death Row
4. **I Have Nothing** — Whitney Houston — Arista
5. **Don't Walk Away** — Jade — Giant
6. **I'm Every Woman** — Whitney Houston — Arista
7. **Ordinary World** — Duran Duran — Capitol
8. **Mr Wendal** — Arrested Development — Chrysalis
9. **Cat's In The Cradle** — Ugly Kid Joe — Stardog
10. **Bed Of Roses** — Bon Jovi — Jambco

indy albums

1. **Frank Black** — Frank Black — 4AD
2. **Feels Like Rain** — Buddy Guy — Silvertone
3. **Boss Drum** — The Shamen — One Little Indian
4. **So Tough** — Saint Etienne — Heavenly
5. **Star** — Belly — 4AD

dance singles

1. **U Got 2 Know** — Cappella — Internal
2. **Show Me Love** — Robin S — Champion
3. **Quoth** — Polygon Window — Warp
4. **Love The Life** — JTQ With Noel McKoy — Big Life
5. **Don't Walk Away** — Jade — Giant

In 1980 Chrissie Hynde and co became the first band to debut with a first album at Number One. But none have done it with such subsequent elan till Suede in April. True, they were nowhere close to beating Frankie Goes To Hollywood's debut Pleasuredome , with its first-week sales of 1/4 million, but they outsold Depeche Mode by four to one.

uk albums

1. **Songs Of Faith And Devotion** — Depeche Mode — Mute
2. **Taxi** — Bryan Ferry — Virgin
3. **A Real Live One** — Iron Maiden — EMI
4. **Their Greatest Hits** — Hot Chocolate — EMI
5. **Are You Gonna Go My Way?** — Lenny Kravitz — Virgin America
6. **Unplugged** — Eric Clapton — Duck
7. **Diva** — Annie Lennox — RCA
8. **The Very Best Of Randy Crawford** — Randy Crawford — Dino
9. **The Bliss Album?...(Vibrations Of Love...)** — PM Dawn — Gee Street
10. **Ingenue** — kd lang — Sire
11. **Automatic For The People** — R.E.M. — Warner Bros
12. **So Close** — Dina Carroll — A&M
13. **Ten Summoner's Tales** — Sting — A&M
14. **Coverdale Page** — Coverdale Page — EMI
15. **Home Invasion** — Ice-T — Rhyme Syndicate
16. **The Dark Side Of The Moon** — Pink Floyd — Harvest
17. **3 Years, 5 Months & 2 Days In The Life** — Arrested Development — Cooltempo
18. **Amazing Things** — Runrig — Chrysalis
19. **Dangerous** — Michael Jackson — Epic
20. **The Greatest Hits** — Boney M — Telstar

---

us albums

1. **Songs Of Faith And Devotion** — Depeche Mode — Sire/Reprise
2. **The Bodyguard** — Soundtrack — Arista
3. **Breathless** — Kenny G — Arista
4. **Unplugged** — Eric Clapton — Duck/Reprise
5. **Ten Summoner's Tales** — Sting — A&M
6. **Pocket Full Of Kryptonite** — Spin Doctors — Epic Associated
7. **12 Inches Of Snow** — Snow — Eastwest
8. **The Chronic** — Dr. Dre — Death Row
9. **Lose Control** — Silk — Keia
10. **Coverdale/Page** — Coverdale/Page — Geffen
11. **19 Naughty III** — Naughty By Nature — Tommy Boy
12. **Some Gave All** — Billy Ray Cyrus — Mercury
13. **3 Years 5 Months & 2 Days In The Life** — Arrested Development — Chrysalis
14. **Home Invasion** — Ice-T — Rhyme Syndicate
15. **Dangerous** — Michael Jackson — Epic
16. **Ten** — Pearl Jam — Epic Associated
17. **It's Your Call** — Reba McEntire — MCA
18. **Hard Workin' Man** — Brooks & Dunn — Arista
19. **Are You Gonna Go My Way?** — Lenny Kravitz — Virgin
20. **If I Ever Fall In Love** — Shai — Gasoline Alley

uk singles

1. **Young At Heart** — The Bluebells — London
2. **Oh Carolina** — Shaggy — Greensleeves
3. **Informer** — Snow — Atlantic
4. **Mr Loverman** — Shabba Ranks — Epic
5. **When I'm Good And Ready** — Sybil — PWL International
6. **Show Me Love** — Robin S — Champion
7. **Fever** — Madonna — Maverick/Sire
8. **No Limit** — 2 Unlimited — PWL Continental
9. **Don't Walk Away** — Jade — Giant
10. **Ain't No Love (Ain't No Use)** — Sub Sub Featuring Melanie Williams — Rob's

us singles

1. **Informer** — Snow — Eastwest
2. **Freak Me** — Silk — Keia
3. **Nuthin' But A "G" Thang** — Dr. Dre — Death Row
4. **I Have Nothing** — Whitney Houston — Arista
5. **Don't Walk Away** — Jade — Giant
6. **Cat's In The Cradle** — Ugly Kid Joe — Stardog
7. **Two Princes** — Spin Doctors — Epic Associated
8. **Love Is** — Vanessa Williams/Brian McKnight — Giant
9. **Mr Wendal** — Arrested Development — Chrysalis
10. **Bed Of Roses** — Bon Jovi — Jambco

indy albums

1. **Songs Of Faith And Devotion** — Depeche Mode — Mute
2. **Westing (By Musket And...)** — Pavement — Big Cat
3. **Frank Black** — Frank Black — 4AD
4. **Feels Like Rain** — Buddy Guy — Silvertone
5. **So Tough** — Saint Etienne — Heavenly

dance singles

1. **Ain't No Love (Ain't No Use)** — Sub Sub/Melanie Williams — Rob's
2. **Show Me Love** — Robin S — Champion
3. **U Got 2 Know** — Cappella — Internal
4. **Looks Like I'm In Love Again** — Key West featuring Erik — PWL Sanctuary
5. **Don't Walk Away** — Jade — Giant

uk albums

1. **Suede** — Suede — Nude
2. **Songs Of Faith And Devotion** — Depeche Mode — Mute
3. **Their Greatest Hits** — Hot Chocolate — EMI
4. **Are You Gonna Go My Way?** — Lenny Kravitz — Virgin America
5. **Unplugged** — Eric Clapton — Duck
6. **Cover Shot** — David Essex — Polygram TV
7. **Diva** — Annie Lennox — RCA
8. **Automatic For The People** — R.E.M. — Warner Bros
9. **So Close** — Dina Carroll — A&M
10. **The Very Best Of Randy Crawford** — Randy Crawford — Dino
11. **Ingenue** — kd lang — Sire
12. **Taxi** — Bryan Ferry — Virgin
13. **Ten Summoner's Tales** — Sting — A&M
14. **The Greatest Hits** — Boney M — Telstar
15. **The Air That I Breathe** — The Hollies — EMI
16. **3 Years, 5 Months & 2 Days In The Life** — Arrested Development — Cooltempo
17. **A Real Live One** — Iron Maiden — EMI
18. **Coverdale Page** — Coverdale Page — EMI
19. **The Bliss Album?...(Vibrations Of Love...)** — PM Dawn — Gee Street
20. **Dangerous** — Michael Jackson — Epic

Apr'93:4th-10th

159

uk albums

1	**Black Tie, White Noise** David Bowie	Arista
2	**Suede** Suede	Nude
3	**Beaster** Sugar	Creation
4	**Cover Shot** David Essex	Polygram TV
5	**Powertrippin'** The Almighty	Polydor
6	**Diva** Annie Lennox	RCA
7	**Automatic For The People** R.E.M.	Warner Bros
8	**Unplugged** Eric Clapton	Duck
9	**3 Years, 5 Months & 2 Days In The Life** Arrested Development	Cooltempo
10	**So Close** Dina Carroll	A&M
11	**Are You Gonna Go My Way?** Lenny Kravitz	Virgin America
12	**Their Greatest Hits** Hot Chocolate	EMI
13	**Songs Of Faith And Devotion** Depeche Mode	Mute
14	**Ten Summoner's Tales** Sting	A&M
15	**Take That & Party** Take That	RCA
16	**The Air That I Breathe** The Hollies	EMI
17	**The Greatest Hits** Boney M	Telstar
18	**Gorecki Symphony 3** Zinman/Upshaw/London Sinfonietta	Elektra Nonesuch
19	**The Very Best Of Randy Crawford** Randy Crawford	Dino
20	**Ingenue** kd lang	Sire

us albums

1	**The Bodyguard** Soundtrack	Arista
2	**Breathless** Kenny G	Arista
3	**Unplugged** Eric Clapton	Duck/Reprise
4	**Pocket Full Of Kryptonite** Spin Doctors	Epic Associated
5	**14 Shots To The Dome** L.L. Cool J	Def Jam
6	**Songs Of Faith And Devotion** Depeche Mode	Sire/Reprise
7	**Ten Summoner's Tales** Sting	A&M
8	**12 Inches Of Snow** Snow	Eastwest
9	**The Chronic** Dr. Dre	Death Row
10	**Lose Control** Silk	Keia
11	**Some Gave All** Billy Ray Cyrus	Mercury
12	**Aladdin** Soundtrack	Walt Disney
13	**Coverdale/Page** Coverdale/Page	Geffen
14	**Love Deluxe** Sade	Epic
15	**19 Naughty III** Naughty By Nature	Tommy Boy
16	**Ten** Pearl Jam	Epic Associated
17	**It's Your Call** Reba McEntire	MCA
18	**Hard Workin' Man** Brooks & Dunn	Arista
19	**3 Years 5 Months & 2 Days In The Life** Arrested Development	Chrysalis
20	**Dangerous** Michael Jackson	Epic

uk singles

1	**Young At Heart** The Bluebells	London
2	**Informer** Snow	Atlantic
3	**Oh Carolina** Shaggy	Greensleeves
4	**Ain't No Love (Ain't No Use)** Sub Sub Featuring Melanie Williams	Rob's
5	**When I'm Good And Ready** Sybil	PWL International
6	**Show Me Love** Robin S	Champion
7	**Mr Loverman** Shabba Ranks	Epic
8	**Don't Walk Away** Jade	Giant
9	**U Got 2 Know** Cappella	Internal Dance
10	**No Limit** 2 Unlimited	PWL Continental

us singles

1	**Informer** Snow	Eastwest
2	**Freak Me** Silk	Keia
3	**Nuthin' But A "G" Thang** Dr. Dre	Death Row
4	**I Have Nothing** Whitney Houston	Arista
5	**Don't Walk Away** Jade	Giant
6	**Love Is** Vanessa Williams/Brian McKnight)	Giant
7	**Cat's In The Cradle** Ugly Kid Joe	Stardog
8	**Two Princes** Spin Doctors	Epic Associated
9	**I'm So Into You** SWV	RCA
10	**Comforter** Shai	Gasoline Alley

indy albums

1	**Suede** Suede	Nude
2	**Songs Of Faith And Devotion** Depeche Mode	Mute
3	**Westing (By Musket And...)** Pavement	Big Cat
4	**Star** Belly	4AD
5	**Frank Black** Frank Black	4AD

dance singles

1	**Ain't No Love (Ain't No Use)** Sub Sub/Melanie Williams	Rob's
2	**U Got 2 Know** Cappella	Internal
3	**Sweet Freedom** Positive Gang	PWL Continental
4	**Show Me Love** Robin S	Champion
5	**Regret** New Order	London

uk albums

1	**Automatic For The People** R.E.M.	Warner Bros
2	**Black Tie, White Noise** David Bowie	Arista
3	**Cover Shot** David Essex	Polygram TV
4	**In Concert: MTV Plugged** Bruce Springsteen	Columbia
5	**Suede** Suede	Nude
6	**So Close** Dina Carroll	A&M
7	**3 Years, 5 Months & 2 Days In The Life** Arrested Development	Cooltempo
8	**Diva** Annie Lennox	RCA
9	**Walthamstow** East 17	London
10	**Wrestlemania – The Album** WWF Superstars	Arista
11	**Unplugged** Eric Clapton	Duck
12	**San Francisco Days** Chris Isaak	Reprise
13	**Take That & Party** Take That	RCA
14	**Duran Duran (The Wedding Album)** Duran Duran	Parlophone
15	**The Singles Collection** Connie Francis	Polydor/Polygram TV
16	**Are You Gonna Go My Way?** Lenny Kravitz	Virgin America
17	**Greatest Hits** Gloria Estefan	Epic
18	**Ingenue** kd lang	Sire
19	**Ten Summoner's Tales** Sting	A&M
20	**Beaster** Sugar	Creation

us albums

1	**The Bodyguard** Soundtrack	Arista
2	**Breathless** Kenny G	Arista
3	**Pocket Full Of Kryptonite** Spin Doctors	Epic Associated
4	**Unplugged** Eric Clapton	Duck/Reprise
5	**12 Inches Of Snow** Snow	Eastwest
6	**Ten Summoner's Tales** Sting	A&M
7	**The Chronic** Dr. Dre	Death Row
8	**Lose Control** Silk	Keia
9	**Songs Of Faith And Devotion** Depeche Mode	Sire/Reprise
10	**Aladdin** Soundtrack	Walt Disney
11	**14 Shots To The Dome** L.L. Cool J	Def Jam
12	**Love Deluxe** Sade	Epic
13	**Coverdale/Page** Coverdale/Page	Geffen
14	**Some Gave All** Billy Ray Cyrus	Mercury
15	**19 Naughty III** Naughty By Nature	Tommy Boy
16	**Ten** Pearl Jam	Epic Associated
17	**Dangerous** Michael Jackson	Epic
18	**It's Your Call** Reba McEntire	MCA
19	**3 Years 5 Months & 2 Days In The Life** Arrested Development	Chrysalis
20	**Jon Secada** Jon Secada	SBK

uk singles

1	**Young At Heart** The Bluebells	London
2	**Informer** Snow	Atlantic
3	**Ain't No Love (Ain't No Use)** Sub Sub Featuring Melanie Williams	Rob's
4	**Regret** New Order	Centredate Co.
5	**When I'm Good And Ready** Sybil	PWL International
6	**U Got 2 Know** Cappella	Internal Dance
7	**Don't Walk Away** Jade	Giant
8	**Oh Carolina** Shaggy	Greensleeves
9	**I Have Nothing** Whitney Houston	Arista
10	**Show Me Love** Robin S	Champion

us singles

1	**Informer** Snow	Eastwest
2	**Freak Me** Silk	Keia
3	**Nuthin' But A "G" Thang** Dr. Dre	Death Row
4	**I Have Nothing** Whitney Houston	Arista
5	**Don't Walk Away** Jade	Giant
6	**Love Is** Vanessa Williams/Brian McKnight)	Giant
7	**I'm So Into You** SWV	RCA
8	**Two Princes** Spin Doctors	Epic Associated
9	**Cat's In The Cradle** Ugly Kid Joe	Stardog
10	**Ditty** Paperboy	Next Plateau

indy albums

1	**Suede** Suede	Nude
2	**Beaster** Sugar	Nude
3	**Songs Of Faith And Devotion** Depeche Mode	Mute
4	**Wake Up Call** John Mayall	Silvertone
5	**Star** Belly	4AD

dance singles

1	**U R The Best Thing** Dream	Magnet
2	**Do You Love Me Like You Say?** Terence Trent D'arby	Columbia
3	**P.ower Of A.merican N.atives** Dance 2 Trance	Logic
4	**Ain't No Love (Ain't No Use)** Sub Sub/Melanie Williams	Rob's
5	**Regret** New Order	London

indy albums

1	**Suede** Suede	Nude
2	**Beaster** Sugar	Nude
3	**Songs Of Faith And Devotion** Depeche Mode	Mute
4	**Star** Belly	4AD
5	**Wake Up Call** John Mayall	Silvertone

dance singles

1	**I'm So Into You** SWW	RCA
2	**Hell's Party** Glam	Six By 6
3	**U R The Best Thing** Dream	Magnet
4	**P.ower Of A.merican N.atives** Dance 2 Trance	Logic
5	**Ain't No Love (Ain't No Use)** Sub Sub/Melanie Williams	Rob's

Suede and David Bowie spend much of May jostling for a place at the top of the charts – rather ironic, considering the heavy influence Bowie's Ziggy Stardust made on the starstruck Suede. While both artists vie for attention – NME featured them together on their front cover – that other great British institution crept to the top virtually unnoticed. Cliff – we salute you.

uk singles

1	**Five Live (EP)** George Michael/Queen	Parlophone
2	**Young At Heart** The Bluebells	London
3	**I Have Nothing** Whitney Houston	Arista
4	**Ain't No Love (Ain't No Use)** Sub Sub Featuring Melanie Williams	Rob's
5	**Informer** Snow	Atlantic
6	**U Got 2 Know** Cappella	Internal Dance
7	**When I'm Good And Ready** Sybil	PWL International
8	**Regret** New Order	Centredate Co.
9	**Everybody Hurts** REM	Warner Brothers
10	**Show Me Love** Robin S	Champion

us singles

1	**Freak Me** Silk	Keia
2	**Informer** Snow	Eastwest
3	**Nuthin' But A "G" Thang** Dr. Dre	Death Row
4	**I Have Nothing** Whitney Houston	Arista
5	**Love Is** Vanessa Williams/Brian McKnight	
6	**Don't Walk Away** Jade	Giant
7	**I'm So Into You** SWV	RCA
8	**Two Princes** Spin Doctors	Epic
9	**Looking Through Patient Eyes** P.M. Dawn	Gee Street
10	**Ditty** Paperboy	Next Plateau

1	**The Bodyguard** Soundtrack	Arista
2	**Breathless** Kenny G	Arista
3	**Pocket Full Of Kryptonite** Spin Doctors	Epic Associated
4	**Unplugged** Eric Clapton	Duck/Reprise
5	**12 Inches Of Snow** Snow	Eastwest
6	**The Chronic** Dr. Dre	Death Row
7	**Lose Control** Silk	Keia
8	**Ten Summoner's Tales** Sting	A&M
9	**Love Deluxe** Sade	Epic
10	**Songs Of Faith And Devotion** Depeche Mode	Sire/Reprise
11	**14 Shots To The Dome** L.L. Cool J	Def Jam
12	**Are You Gonna Go My Way?** Lenny Kravitz	Virgin
13	**It's About Time** SWV	RCA
14	**Some Gave All** Billy Ray Cyrus	Mercury
15	**Ten** Pearl Jam	Epic Associated
16	**19 Naughty III** Naughty By Nature	Tommy Boy
17	**Hard Workin' Man** Brooks & Dunn	Arista
18	**It's Your Call** Reba McEntire	MCA
19	**Coverdale/Page** Coverdale/Page	Geffen
20	**Dangerous** Michael Jackson	Epic

uk albums

1	**Cliff Richard – The Album** Cliff Richard	EMI
2	**Get A Grip** Aerosmith	Geffen
3	**Automatic For The People** R.E.M.	Warner Bros
4	**Ten Summoner's Tales** Sting	A&M
5	**Duran Duran (The Wedding Album)** Duran Duran	Parlophone
6	**So Close** Dina Carroll	A&M
7	**Cover Shot** David Essex	Polygram TV
8	**Black Tie, White Noise** David Bowie	Arista
9	**3 Years, 5 Months & 2 Days In The Life** Arrested Development	Cooltempo
10	**Suede** Suede	Nude
11	**Jurassic Shift** Ozric Tentacles	Dovetail
12	**The Singles Collection** Connie Francis	Polydor/Polygram TV
13	**Unplugged** Eric Clapton	Duck
14	**In Concert: MTV Plugged** Bruce Springsteen	Columbia
15	**Diva** Annie Lennox	RCA
16	**Walthamstow** East 17	London
17	**Greatest Hits** Gloria Estefan	Epic
18	**Are You Gonna Go My Way?** Lenny Kravitz	Virgin America
19	**San Francisco Days** Chris Isaak	Reprise
20	**Ingenue** kd lang	Sire

uk singles

1	**Five Live (EP)** George Michael/Queen	Parlophone
2	**That's The Way Love Goes** Janet Jackson	Virgin
3	**I Have Nothing** Whitney Houston	Arista
4	**Tribal Dance** 2 Unlimited	PWL Continental
5	**All That She Wants** Ace Of Base	London
6	**Sweat (a La La La La Long)** Inner Circle	WEA
7	**Ain't No Love (Ain't No Use)** Sub Sub Featuring Melanie Williams	Rob's
8	**Young At Heart** The Bluebells	London
9	**Everybody Hurts** REM	Warner Brothers
10	**Informer** Snow	Atlantic

us singles

1	**Freak Me** Silk	Keia
2	**That's The Way Love Goes** Janet Jackson	Virgin
3	**Informer** Snow	Eastwest
4	**Love Is** Vanessa Williams/Brian McKnight	Giant
5	**I Have Nothing** Whitney Houston	Arista
6	**Nuthin' But A "G" Thang** Dr. Dre	Death Row
7	**Don't Walk Away** Jade	Giant
8	**I'm So Into You** SWV	RCA
9	**Looking Through Patient Eyes** P.M. Dawn	Gee Street
10	**Ditty** Paperboy	Next Plateau

indy albums

1	**Jurassic Shift** Ozric Tentacles	Dovetail
2	**Suede** Suede	Nude
3	**Songs Of Faith And Devotion** Depeche Mode	Mute
4	**Beaster** Sugar	Nude
5	**Wake Up Call** John Mayall	Silvertone

dance singles

1	**That's The Way Love Goes** Janet Jackson	Virgin
2	**Packet of Peace** Lionrock	DeConstruction
3	**I'm Going All The Way** Sounds of Blackness	A & M
4	**Slumberland** Solitaire Gee	Warp
5	**Believe In Me** Utah Saints	ffrr

1	**Get A Grip** Aerosmith	Geffen
2	**The Bodyguard** Soundtrack	Arista
3	**Breathless** Kenny G	Arista
4	**Pocket Full Of Kryptonite** Spin Doctors	Epic Associated
5	**Unplugged** Eric Clapton	Duck/Reprise
6	**The Chronic** Dr. Dre	Death Row
7	**Pork Soda** Primus	Interscope
8	**12 Inches Of Snow** Snow	Eastwest
9	**Losc Control** Silk	Keia
10	**Love Deluxe** Sade	Epic
11	**Ten Summoner's Tales** Sting	A&M
12	**Are You Gonna Go My Way?** Lenny Kravitz	Virgin
13	**It's About Time** SWV	RCA
14	**Songs Of Faith And Devotion** Depeche Mode	Sire/Reprise
15	**Ten** Pearl Jam	Epic Associated
16	**19 Naughty III** Naughty By Nature	Tommy Boy
17	**Some Gave All** Billy Ray Cyrus	Mercury
18	**14 Shots To The Dome** L.L. Cool J	Def Jam
19	**It's Your Call** Reba McEntire	MCA
20	**Hard Workin' Man** Brooks & Dunn	Arista

uk albums

1	**Automatic For The People** R.E.M.	Warner Bros
2	**Bang!** World Party	Ensign
3	**Rid Of Me** PJ Harvey	Island
4	**Cliff Richard – The Album** Cliff Richard	EMI
5	**Ten Summoner's Tales** Sting	A&M
6	**Duran Duran (The Wedding Album)** Duran Duran	Parlophone
7	**Get A Grip** Aerosmith	Geffen
8	**So Close** Dina Carroll	A&M
9	**The Infotainment Scan** The Fall	Permanent
10	**Cover Shot** David Essex	Polygram TV
11	**Unplugged** Eric Clapton	Duck
12	**3 Years, 5 Months & 2 Days In The Life** Arrested Development	Cooltempo
13	**Porno For Pyros** Porno For Pyros	Warner Bros
14	**In Concert: MTV Plugged** Bruce Springsteen	Columbia
15	**Walthamstow** East 17	London
16	**Black Tie, White Noise** David Bowie	Arista
17	**Diva** Annie Lennox	RCA
18	**Ingenue** kd lang	Sire
19	**Suede** Suede	Nude
20	**Are You Gonna Go My Way?** Lenny Kravitz	Virgin America

indy albums

1	**Suede** Suede	Nude
2	**Jurassic Shift** Ozric Tentacles	Dovetail
3	**Songs Of Faith And Devotion** Depeche Mode	Mute
4	**Forever** The Cranes	Dedicated
5	**Beaster** Sugar	Nude

dance singles

1	**That's The Way Love Goes** Janet Jackson	Virgin
2	**Packet of Peace** Lionrock	DeConstruction
3	**Express** Dina Carroll	A&M
4	**I'm Going All The Way** Sounds of Blackness	A&M
5	**Housecall (Remix)** Shabba Ranks featuring Maxi Priest	Epic

uk singles

1	**Five Live (EP)** George Michael/Queen	Parlophone
2	**All That She Wants** Ace Of Base	London
3	**That's The Way Love Goes** Janet Jackson	Virgin
4	**Tribal Dance** 2 Unlimited	PWL Continental
5	**Sweat (a La La La La Long)** Inner Circle	WEA
6	**I Have Nothing** Whitney Houston	Arista
7	**Everybody Hurts** REM	Warner Brothers
8	**Believe In Me** Utah Saints	Ffrr
9	**Ain't No Love (Ain't No Use)** Sub Sub Featuring Melanie Williams	Rob's
10	**Informer** Snow	Atlantic

us singles

1	**That's The Way Love Goes** Janet Jackson	Virgin
2	**Freak Me** Silk	Keia
3	**Love Is** Vanessa Williams/Brian McKnight)	Giant
4	**Informer** Snow	Eastwest
5	**I Have Nothing** Whitney Houston	Arista
6	**Nuthin' But A "G" Thang** Dr. Dre	Death Row
7	**Knockin' Da Boots** H-Town	Luke
8	**I'm So Into You** SWV	RCA
9	**Looking Through Patient Eyes** P.M. Dawn	Gee Street
10	**Don't Walk Away** Jade	Giant

us albums

1	**The Bodyguard** Soundtrack	Arista
2	**Get A Grip** Aerosmith	Geffen
3	**Porno For Pyros** Porno For Pyros	Warner Bros.
4	**Breathless** Kenny G	Arista
5	**Pocket Full Of Kryptonite** Spin Doctors	Epic Associated
6	**Unplugged** Eric Clapton	Duck/Reprise
7	**The Chronic** Dr. Dre	Death Row
8	**12 Inches Of Snow** Snow	Eastwest
9	**It's About Time** SWV	RCA
10	**Lose Control** Silk	Keia
11	**Love Deluxe** Sade	Epic
12	**Ten Summoner's Tales** Sting	A&M
13	**Exposed** Vince Neil	Warner Bros.
14	**Are You Gonna Go My Way?** Lenny Kravitz	Virgin
15	**Core** Stone Temple Pilots	Atlantic
16	**Some Gave All** Billy Ray Cyrus	Mercury
17	**Ten** Pearl Jam	Epic Associated
18	**Pork Soda** Primus	Interscope
19	**Jon Secada** Jon Secada	SBK
20	**It's Your Call** Reba McEntire	MCA

uk albums

1	**Republic** New Order	Centredate Co
2	**Automatic For The People** R.E.M.	Warner Bros
3	**Ten Summoner's Tales** Sting	A&M
4	**Symphony Or Damn** Terence Trent D'Arby	Columbia
5	**Banba** Clannad	RCA
6	**Bang!** World Party	Ensign
7	**Duran Duran (The Wedding Album)** Duran Duran	Parlophone
8	**Cliff Richard – The Album** Cliff Richard	EMI
9	**So Close** Dina Carroll	A&M
10	**Breathless** Kenny G	Arista
11	**Rid Of Me** PJ Harvey	Island
12	**Unplugged** Eric Clapton	Duck
13	**Get A Grip** Aerosmith	Geffen
14	**Diva** Annie Lennox	RCA
15	**Take That & Party** Take That	RCA
16	**Are You Gonna Go My Way?** Lenny Kravitz	Virgin America
17	**Rage Against The Machine** Rage Against The Machine	Epic
18	**In Concert: MTV Plugged** Bruce Springsteen	Columbia
19	**3 Years, 5 Months & 2 Days In The Life** Arrested Development	Cooltempo
20	**Songs Of Faith And Devotion** Depeche Mode	Mute

REM's Automatic For The People goes back to Number One and wins a triple platinum award for selling over 900,000 copies in the UK. Their fourth single from the album, Everybody Hurts, is their first to reach the UK Top 10. It's their second biggest of 13 hits in all. Ace of Base become first Swedish act to hit the number one UK single spot since... Abba. Neneh Cherry came close, as did Roxette.

indy albums

1	**Songs Of Faith And Devotion** Depeche Mode	Mute
2	**...More Unchartered Heights...** Dogs D'Amour	China
3	**Suede** Suede	Nude
4	**Jurassic Shift** Ozric Tentacles	Dovetail
5	**Down With The King** Run-DMC	Profile

dance singles

1	**Jump Around/Top O' The...** House Of Pain	Ruffness
2	**Happiness** Serious Rope/Sharon Dee Clarke	Rumour
3	**That's The Way Love Goes** Janet Jackson	Virgin
4	**Express** Dina Carroll	A&M
5	**Stars** Felix	Deconstruction

uk singles

1	**All That She Wants** Ace Of Base	London
2	**Five Live (EP)** George Michael/Queen	Parlophone
3	**Sweat (a La La La La Long)** Inner Circle	WEA
4	**Can't Help Falling In Love** UB40	Dep International
5	**Tribal Dance** 2 Unlimited	PWL Continental
6	**That's The Way Love Goes** Janet Jackson	Virgin
7	**Everybody Hurts** REM	Warner Brothers
8	**Housecall** Shabba Ranks Featuring Maxi Priest	Epic
9	**In These Arms** Bon Jovi	Jambco
10	**Believe In Me** Utah Saints	Ffrr

us singles

1	**That's The Way Love Goes** Janet Jackson	Virgin
2	**Freak Me** Silk	Keia
3	**Knockin' Da Boots** H-Town	Luke
4	**Love Is** Vanessa Williams/Brian McKnight	Giant
5	**Nuthin' But A "G" Thang** Dr. Dre	Death Row
6	**I'm So Into You** SWV	RCA
7	**Looking Through Patient Eyes** P.M. Dawn	Gee Street
8	**Weak** SWV	RCA
9	**I Have Nothing** Whitney Houston	Arista
10	**Informer** Snow	Eastwest

us albums

1	**The Bodyguard** Soundtrack	Arista
2	**Breathless** Kenny G	Arista
3	**Get A Grip** Aerosmith	Geffen
4	**Pocket Full Of Kryptonite** Spin Doctors	Epic Associated
5	**The Chronic** Dr. Dre	Death Row
6	**Unplugged** Eric Clapton	Duck/Reprise
7	**Down With The King** Run-D.M.C.	Profile
8	**It's About Time** SWV	RCA
9	**Love Deluxe** Sade	Epic
10	**12 Inches Of Snow** Snow	Eastwest
11	**Ten Summoner's Tales** Sting	A&M
12	**Lose Control** Silk	Keia
13	**Porno For Pyros** Porno For Pyros	Warner Bros.
14	**Are You Gonna Go My Way?** Lenny Kravitz	Virgin
15	**Core** Stone Temple Pilots	Atlantic
16	**Fever For Da Flavor** H-Town	Luke
17	**Jon Secada** Jon Secada	SBK
18	**It's Your Call** Reba McEntire	MCA
19	**Some Gave All** Billy Ray Cyrus	Mercury
20	**Duran Duran** Duran Duran	Capitol

uk albums

1	**Automatic For The People** R.E.M.	Warner Bros
2	**No Limits** 2 Unlimited	PWL Continental
3	**Republic** New Order	Centredate Co.
4	**On The Night** Dire Straits	Vertigo
5	**Home Movies** Everything But The Girl	Blanco Y Negro
6	**Ten Summoner's Tales** Sting	A&M
7	**Banba** Clannad	RCA
8	**Blues Alive** Gary Moore	Pointblank
9	**Breathless** Kenny G	Arista
10	**So Close** Dina Carroll	A&M
11	**Duran Duran (The Wedding Album)** Duran Duran	Parlophone
12	**Symphony Or Damn** Terence Trent D'Arby	Columbia
13	**Beethoven Was Deaf** Morrissey	HMV
14	**Bang!** World Party	Ensign
15	**Modern Life Is Rubbish** Blur	Food
16	**Keep The Faith** Bon Jovi	Mercury
17	**Cliff Richard – The Album** Cliff Richard	EMI
18	**Unplugged** Eric Clapton	Duck
19	**Rage Against The Machine** Rage Against The Machine	Epic
20	**Jim Diamond** Jim Diamond	Polygram TV

us albums

1	**The Bodyguard** Soundtrack	Arista
2	**Get A Grip** Aerosmith	Geffen
3	**Breathless** Kenny G	Arista
4	**Pocket Full Of Kryptonite** Spin Doctors	Epic Associated
5	**Tell Me Why** Wynonna	Curb
6	**The Chronic** Dr. Dre	Death Row
7	**Unplugged** Eric Clapton	Duck/Reprise
8	**It's About Time** SWV	RCA
9	**Love Deluxe** Sade	Epic
10	**Ten Summoner's Tales** Sting	A&M
11	**Republic** New Order	Qwest
12	**Core** Stone Temple Pilots	Atlantic
13	**12 Inches Of Snow** Snow	Eastwest
14	**Are You Gonna Go My Way?** Lenny Kravitz	Virgin
15	**Down With The King** Run-D.M.C.	Profile
16	**Lose Control** Silk	Keia
17	**It's Your Call** Reba McEntire	MCA
18	**Hard Workin' Man** Brooks & Dunn	Arista
19	**Fever For Da Flavor** H-Town	Luke
20	**Porno For Pyros** Porno For Pyros	Warner Bros.

uk singles

1	**All That She Wants** Ace Of Base	London
2	**Can't Help Falling In Love** UB40	Dep International
3	**Sweat (a La La La La Long)** Inner Circle	WEA
4	**Five Live (EP)** George Michael/Queen	Parlophone
5	**Tribal Dance** 2 Unlimited	PWL Continental
6	**That's The Way Love Goes** Janet Jackson	Virgin
7	**I Don't Wanna Fight** Tina Turner	Parlophone
8	**Jump Around** House Of Pain	XI Recordings
9	**In These Arms** Bon Jovi	Jambco
10	**Everybody Hurts** REM	Warner Brothers

us singles

1	**That's The Way Love Goes** Janet Jackson	Virgin
2	**Freak Me** Silk	Keia
3	**Knockin' Da Boots** H-Town	Luke
4	**Weak** SWV	RCA
5	**Love Is** Vanessa Williams/Brian McKnight	Giant
6	**Looking Through Patient Eyes** P.M. Dawn	Gee Street
7	**I'm So Into You** SWV	RCA
8	**Nuthin' But A "G" Thang** Dr. Dre	Death Row
9	**I Have Nothing** Whitney Houston	Arista
10	**Don't Walk Away** Jade	Giant

indy albums

1	**Suede** Suede	Nude
2	**Songs Of Faith And Devotion** Depeche Mode	Mute
3	**06:21:03:11 Up Evil** Front 242	RRE
4	**Magic Bullets** Mega City Four	Big Life
5	**Jurassic Shift** Ozric Tentacles	Dovetail

dance singles

1	**Jump Around/Top O' The...** House Of Pain	Ruffness
2	**Rockin' To The Rhythm** Convert	A&M
3	**Creation** Stereo MCs	4th+B'way
4	**Shout** Louchie Lou & Michie One	ffrr
5	**Daydreaming** Penny Ford	Columbia

Donald Fagen's laid-back car opus, Kamakiriad, cruises in at Number Three – higher than his previous decade's outing, The Nightfly, and all of the entire Steely Dan output!

uk albums

1	**Janet** Janet Jackson	Virgin
2	**Automatic For The People** R.E.M.	Warner Bros
3	**No Limits** 2 Unlimited	PWL Continental
4	**Breathless** Kenny G	Arista
5	**Republic** New Order	Centredate Co.
6	**So Close** Dina Carroll	A&M
7	**On The Night** Dire Straits	Vertigo
8	**Home Movies** Everything But The Girl	Blanco Y Negro
9	**Keep The Faith** Bon Jovi	Mercury
10	**Live At The Royal Albert Hall With The Wren Orch.** Wet Wet Wet	Precious
11	**Blues Alive** Gary Moore	Pointblank
12	**Banba** Clannad	RCA
13	**Ten Summoner's Tales** Sting	A&M
14	**Sound Of White Noise** Anthrax	Elektra
15	**Sleepwalking** Kingmaker	Chrysalis
16	**Jim Diamond** Jim Diamond	Polygram TV
17	**Duran Duran (The Wedding Album)** Duran Duran	Parlophone
18	**Pocket Full Of Kryptonite** The Spin Doctors	Epic
19	**Unplugged** Eric Clapton	Duck
20	**Are You Gonna Go My Way?** Lenny Kravitz	Virgin America

us albums

1	**Janet** Janet Jackson	Virgin
2	**The Bodyguard** Soundtrack	Arista
3	**Get A Grip** Aerosmith	Geffen
4	**Pocket Full Of Kryptonite** Spin Doctors	Epic Associated
5	**Breathless** Kenny G	Arista
6	**Tell Me Why** Wynonna	Curb
7	**The Chronic** Dr. Dre	Death Row
8	**It's About Time** SWV	RCA
9	**Alive III** Kiss	Mercury
10	**Ten Summoner's Tales** Sting	A&M
11	**Unplugged** Eric Clapton	Duck/Reprise
12	**Core** Stone Temple Pilots	Atlantic
13	**Love Deluxe** Sade	Epic
14	**Are You Gonna Go My Way?** Lenny Kravitz	Virgin
15	**12 Inches Of Snow** Snow	Eastwest
16	**Fever For Da Flavor** H-Town	Luke
17	**Hard Workin' Man** Brooks & Dunn	Arista
18	**Lose Control** Silk	Keia
19	**Duran Duran** Duran Duran	Capitol
20	**Some Gave All** Billy Ray Cyrus	Mercury

uk singles

1	**All That She Wants** Ace Of Base	London
2	**Can't Help Falling In Love** UB40	Dep International
3	**Sweat (a La La La La Long)** Inner Circle	WEA
4	**Two Princes** Spin Doctors	Epic
5	**Three Little Pigs** Green Jelly	Zoo
6	**Five Live (EP)** George Michael/Queen	Parlophone
7	**Shout** Louchie Lou And Michie One	Ffrr
8	**Tribal Dance** 2 Unlimited	PWL Continental
9	**I Don't Wanna Fight** Tina Turner	Parlophone
10	**That's The Way Love Goes** Janet Jackson	Virgin

us singles

1	**That's The Way Love Goes** Janet Jackson	Virgin
2	**Freak Me** Silk	Keia
3	**Knockin' Da Boots** H-Town	Luke
4	**Weak** SWV	RCA
5	**Love Is** Vanessa Williams/Brian McKnight	Giant
6	**I'm So Into You** SWV	RCA
7	**Looking Through Patient Eyes** P.M. Dawn	Gee Street
8	**Show Me Love** Robin S.	Big Beat
9	**Have Told You Lately** Rod Stewart	Warner Bros.
10	**Bad Boys** Inner Circle	Big Beat

indy albums

1	**Suede** Suede	Nude
2	**Songs Of Faith And Devotion** Depeche Mode	Mute
3	**06:21:03:11 Up Evil** Front 242	RRE
4	**Jurassic Shift** Ozric Tentacles	Dovetail
5	**Down With The King** Run-DMC	Profile

dance singles

1	**London X-press** X-press 2	Junior Boys Own
2	**Blow Your Mind** Janiroquai	Sony
3	**Rushing** Loni Clark	A&M
4	**What Is Love** Haddaway	Logic
5	**I Wanna Hold On To You** Mica Paris	4th+B'way

uk albums

1	**Janet** Janet Jackson	Virgin
2	**Automatic For The People** R.E.M.	Warner Bros
3	**Kamakiriad** Donald Fagen	Warner Bros
4	**No Limits** 2 Unlimited	PWL Continental
5	**Dream Harder** The Waterboys	Geffen
6	**Fate Of Nations** Robert Plant	Fontana/Es Paranza
7	**Unplugged...and Seated** Rod Stewart	Warner Bros
8	**Breathless** Kenny G	Arista
9	**Pocket Full Of Kryptonite** The Spin Doctors	Epic
10	**Utah Saints** Utah Saints	Ffrr
11	**Chronologie** Jean Michel Jarre	Polydor/Dreyfus
12	**Keep The Faith** Bon Jovi	Mercury
13	**So Close** Dina Carroll	A&M
14	**More Abba Gold** Abba	Polydor
15	**Republic** New Order	Centredate Co.
16	**Home Movies** Everything But The Girl	Blanco Y Negro
17	**Ten Summoner's Tales** Sting	A&M
18	**Are You Gonna Go My Way?** Lenny Kravitz	Virgin America
19	**Banba** Clannad	RCA
20	**On The Night** Dire Straits	Vertigo

uk albums

#	Title	Artist	Label
1	No Limits	2 Unlimited	PWL Continental
2	Automatic For The People	R.E.M.	Warner Bros
3	Janet	Janet Jackson	Virgin
4	Too Long In Exile	Van Morrison	Polydor/Exile
5	Unplugged...and Seated	Rod Stewart	Warner Bros
6	So Close	Dina Carroll	A&M
7	Pocket Full Of Kryptonite	The Spin Doctors	Epic
8	Kamakiriad	Donald Fagen	Warner Bros
9	Dream Harder	The Waterboys	Geffen
10	Connected	Stereo MC's	4th+b'Way
11	Never Let Me Go	Luther Vandross	Epic
12	Breathless	Kenny G	Arista
13	Good 'n' Ready	Sybil	PWL International
14	More Abba Gold	Abba	Polydor
15	Keep The Faith	Bon Jovi	Mercury
16	Fate Of Nations	Robert Plant	Fontana/Es Paranza
17	Ten Summoner's Tales	Sting	A&M
18	Utah Saints	Utah Saints	Ffrr
19	Are You Gonna Go My Way?	Lenny Kravitz	Virgin America
20	Unplugged	Eric Clapton	Duck

us albums

#	Title	Artist	Label
1	Janet	Janet Jackson	Virgin
2	UnPlugged... And Seated	Rod Stewart	Warner Bros.
3	The Bodyguard	Soundtrack	Arista
4	Breathless	Kenny G	Arista
5	Pocket Full Of Kryptonite	Spin Doctors	Epic Associated
6	Get A Grip	Aerosmith	Geffen
7	Sound Of White Noise	Anthrax	Elektra
8	The Chronic	Dr. Dre	Death Row
9	It's About Time	SWV	RCA
10	Kamakiriad	Donald Fagen	Reprise
11	Tell Me Why	Wynonna	Curb
12	Core	Stone Temple Pilots	Atlantic
13	Ten Summoner's Tales	Sting	A&M
14	Unplugged	Eric Clapton	Duck/Reprise
15	Love Deluxe	Sade	Epic
16	Are You Gonna Go My Way?	Lenny Kravitz	Virgin
17	12 Inches Of Snow	Snow	Eastwest
18	Fever For Da Flavor	H-Town	Luke
19	Lose Control	Silk	Keia
20	Duran Duran	Duran Duran	Capitol

uk singles

#	Title	Artist	Label
1	Can't Help Falling In Love	UB40	Dep International
2	All That She Wants	Ace Of Base	London
3	Two Princes	Spin Doctors	Epic
4	Sweat (a La La La La Long)	Inner Circle	WEA
5	Three Little Pigs	Green Jelly	Zoo
6	What Is Love	Haddaway	Logic
7	Can You Forgive Her?	Pet Shop Boys	Parlophone
8	Shout	Louchie Lou And Michie One	Ffrr
9	In All The Right Places	Lisa Stansfield	MCA
10	Do You See The Light (Looking For)	Snap	Logic

us singles

#	Title	Artist	Label
1	That's The Way Love Goes	Janet Jackson	Virgin
2	Freak Me	Silk	Keia
3	Knockin' Da Boots	H-Town	Luke
4	Weak	SWV	RCA
5	Show Me Love	Robin S.	Big Beat
6	Looking Through Patient Eyes	P.M. Dawn	Gee Street
7	I'm So Into You	SWV	RCA
8	Bad Boys	Inner Circle	Big Beat
9	Have Told You Lately	Rod Stewart	Warner Bros.
10	Come Undone	Duran Duran	Capitol

indy albums

#	Title	Artist	Label
1	Orbital	Orbital	Internal
2	Suede	Suede	Nudo
3	Red House Painters	Red House Painters	4AD
4	Songs Of Faith And Devotion	Depeche Mode	Mute
5	Jurassic Shift	Ozric Tentacles	Dovetail

dance singles

#	Title	Artist	Label
1	All Funked Up	Mother	Bosting
2	Thinking Of You ('93 Mixes)	Sister Sledge	Atlantic
3	Blow Your Mind	Janiroquai	Sony
4	Do You See The Light (Looking For)	Snap	Logic
5	What Is Love	Haddaway	Logic

Dina Carroll's debut album, So Close, became the first album by a UK artist to go platinum in 1993. It did so without the benefit of any Top Ten singles. Twenty-four-year-old Trinidadian Haddaway continues the poptastic run for the German-based Logic label (aka Snap, Dr Alban, Dance 2 Trance) by debuting at Number 19 with What Is Love?

uk albums

#	Title	Artist	Label
1	What's Love Got To Do With It	Tina Turner	Capitol
2	Automatic For The People	R.E.M.	Warner Bros
3	No Limits	2 Unlimited	PWL Continental
4	Pocket Full Of Kryptonite	The Spin Doctors	Epic
5	Elemental	Tears For Fears	Mercury
6	Unplugged...and Seated	Rod Stewart	Warner Bros
7	Janet	Janet Jackson	Virgin
8	Connected	Stereo MC's	4th+b'Way
9	So Close	Dina Carroll	A&M
10	Too Long In Exile	Van Morrison	Polydor/Exile
11	Kamakiriad	Donald Fagen	Warner Bros
12	Breathless	Kenny G	Arista
13	Good 'n' Ready	Sybil	PWL International
14	Ten Summoner's Tales	Sting	A&M
15	Keep The Faith	Bon Jovi	Mercury
16	Never Let Me Go	Luther Vandross	Epic
17	More Abba Gold	Abba	Polydor
18	Dream Harder	The Waterboys	Geffen
19	Utah Saints	Utah Saints	Ffrr
20	Unplugged	Eric Clapton	Duck

us albums

#	Title	Artist	Label
1	Janet	Janet Jackson	Virgin
2	UnPlugged... And Seated	Rod Stewart	Warner Bros.
3	The Chronic	Dr. Dre	Death Row
4	The Bodyguard	Soundtrack	Arista
5	Breathless	Kenny G	Arista
6	Get A Grip	Aerosmith	Geffen
7	Pocket Full Of Kryptonite	Spin Doctors	Epic Associated
8	Never Let Me Go	Luther Vandross	Epic
9	It's About Time	SWV	RCA
10	Core	Stone Temple Pilots	Atlantic
11	Menace II Society	Soundtrack	Jive
12	Ten Summoner's Tales	Sting	A&M
13	Unplugged	Eric Clapton	Duck/Reprise
14	Kamakiriad	Donald Fagen	Reprise
15	Are You Gonna Go My Way?	Lenny Kravitz	Virgin
16	Sound Of White Noise	Anthrax	Elektra
17	Fever For Da Flavor	H-Town	Luke
18	Love Deluxe	Sade	Epic
19	12 Inches Of Snow	Snow	Eastwest
20	Tell Me Why	Wynonna	Curb

uk singles

#	Title	Artist	Label
1	Can't Help Falling In Love	UB40	Dep International
2	Dreams	Gabrielle	Go! Beat
3	What Is Love	Haddaway	Logic
4	All That She Wants	Ace Of Base	London
5	Two Princes	Spin Doctors	Epic
6	Tease Me	Chaka Demus & Pliers	Island
7	Can You Forgive Her?	Pet Shop Boys	Parlophone
8	Sweat (a La La La La Long)	Inner Circle	WEA
9	Three Little Pigs	Green Jelly	Zoo
10	In All The Right Places	Lisa Stansfield	MCA

us singles

#	Title	Artist	Label
1	That's The Way Love Goes	Janet Jackson	Virgin
2	Weak	SWV	RCA
3	Knockin' Da Boots	H-Town	Luke
4	Freak Me	Silk	Keia
5	Have I Told You Lately	Rod Stewart	Warner Bros.
6	Show Me Love	Robin S.	Big Beat
7	Come Undone	Duran Duran	Capitol
8	Bad Boys	Inner Circle	Big Beat
9	Looking Through Patient Eyes	P.M. Dawn	Gee Street
10	I'm So Into You	SWV	RCA

indy albums

#	Title	Artist	Label
1	Suede	Suede	Nude
2	Boces	Mercury Rev	Beggars Banquet
3	Souvlaki	Slowdrive	Creation
4	Orbital	Orbital	Internal
5	Songs Of Faith And Devotion	Depeche Mode	Mute

dance singles

#	Title	Artist	Label
1	Dreams	Gabrielle	Go! Discs
2	Tease Me	Chaka Demus & Pliers	Mango
3	What Is Love	Haddaway	Logic
4	All Funked Up	Mother	Bosting
5	Thinking Of You ('93 Mixes)	Sister Sledge	Atlantic

indy albums

1	**In On The Killtaker**	
	Fugazi	Dischord
2	**Suede**	
	Suede	Nude
3	**Patriot Games**	
	Gunshot	Vinyl Solution
4	**Dimension Intrusion**	
	Fuse	Warp
5	**Burning Blue Soul**	
	The The	4AD

dance singles

1	**Dreams**	
	Gabrielle	Go! Discs
2	**One Night In Heaven**	
	M People	Deconstruction
3	**I Will Survive (Phel Kelsey Remix)**	
	Gloria Gaynor	Polydor
4	**What Is Love**	
	Haddaway	Logic
5	**Baby Be Mine**	
	Blackstreet feat Teddy Riley	MCA

indy albums

1	**Suede**	
	Suede	Nude
2	**So Tough**	
	Saint Etienne	Heavenly
3	**In On The Killtaker**	
	Fugazi	Dischord
4	**Tuber**	
	Bivouac	Elemental
5	**Burning Blue Soul**	
	The The	4AD

dance singles

1	**Everybody Dance**	
	Evolution	Deconstruction
2	**Dreams**	
	Gabrielle	Go! Discs
3	**One Night In Heaven**	
	M People	Deconstruction
4	**Can't Get Enough Of Your Love**	
	Taylor Dayne	Arista
5	**I Can See Clearly**	
	Deborah Harry	Chrysalis

uk singles

1	**Dreams**	
	Gabrielle	Go! Beat
2	**Can't Help Falling In Love**	
	UB40	Dep International
3	**What Is Love**	
	Haddaway	Logic
4	**All That She Wants**	
	Ace Of Base	London
5	**Two Princes**	
	Spin Doctors	Epic
6	**Tease Me**	
	Chaka Demus & Pliers	Island
7	**Have I Told You Lately**	
	Rod Stewart	Warner Bros
8	**In All The Right Places**	
	Lisa Stansfield	MCA
9	**One Night In Heaven**	
	M People	Deconstruction
10	**Sweat (a La La La La Long)**	
	Inner Circle	WEA

us singles

1	**That's The Way Love Goes**	
	Janet Jackson	Virgin
2	**Weak**	
	SWV	RCA
3	**Knockin' Da Boots**	
	H-Town	Luke
4	**Freak Me**	
	Silk	Keia
5	**Have I Told You Lately**	
	Rod Stewart	Warner Bros.
6	**Show Me Love**	
	Robin S.	Big Beat
7	**Come Undone**	
	Duran Duran	Capitol
8	**Whoomp! (There It Is)**	
	Tag Team	Life
9	**Dre Day**	
	Dr. Dre	Death Row
10	**Bad Boys**	
	Inner Circle	Big Beat

uk singles

1	**Dreams**	
	Gabrielle	Go! Beat
2	**What Is Love**	
	Haddaway	Logic
3	**Can't Help Falling In Love**	
	UB40	Dep International
4	**Tease Me**	
	Chaka Demus & Pliers	Island
5	**Have I Told You Lately**	
	Rod Stewart	Warner Bros
6	**I Will Survive (Phil Kelsey Remix)**	
	Gloria Gaynor	Polydor
7	**One Night In Heaven**	
	M People	Deconstruction
8	**Two Princes**	
	Spin Doctors	Epic
9	**All That She Wants**	
	Ace Of Base	London
10	**In All The Right Places**	
	Lisa Stansfield	MCA

us singles

1	**That's The Way Love Goes**	
	Janet Jackson	Virgin
2	**Weak**	
	SWV	RCA
3	**Knockin' Da Boots**	
	H-Town	Luke
4	**Whoomp! (There It Is)**	
	Tag Team	Life
5	**Have I Told You Lately**	
	Rod Stewart	Warner Bros.
6	**Show Me Love**	
	Robin S.	Big Beat
7	**Can't Help Falling In Love**	
	UB40	Virgin
8	**Dre Day**	
	Dr. Dre	Death Row
9	**Come Undone**	
	Duran Duran	Capitol
10	**I'll Never Get Over You**	
	Expose	Arista

us albums

1	**Janet**	
	Janet Jackson	Virgin
2	**UnPlugged... And Seated**	
	Rod Stewart	Warner Bros.
3	**The Chronic**	
	Dr. Dre	Death Row
4	**The Bodyguard**	
	Soundtrack	Arista
5	**Core**	
	Stone Temple Pilots	Atlantic
6	**Breathless**	
	Kenny G	Arista
7	**Pocket Full Of Kryptonite**	
	Spin Doctors	Epic Associated
8	**Get A Grip**	
	Aerosmith	Geffen
9	**Never Let Me Go**	
	Luther Vandross	Epic
10	**It's About Time**	
	SWV	RCA
11	**Menace II Society**	
	Soundtrack	Jive
12	**Last Action Hero**	
	Soundtrack	Columbia
13	**Ten Summoner's Tales**	
	Sting	A&M
14	**Provocative**	
	Johnny Gill	Motown
15	**Unplugged**	
	Eric Clapton	Duck/Reprise
16	**12 Inches Of Snow**	
	Snow	Eastwest
17	**Duran Duran**	
	Duran Duran	Capitol
18	**Kamakiriad**	
	Donald Fagen	Reprise
19	**Are You Gonna Go My Way?**	
	Lenny Kravitz	Virgin
20	**Fever For Da Flavor**	
	H-Town	Luke

us albums

1	**Janet**	
	Janet Jackson	Virgin
2	**UnPlugged... And Seated**	
	Rod Stewart	Warner Bros.
3	**Core**	
	Stone Temple Pilots	Atlantic
4	**The Chronic**	
	Dr. Dre	Death Row
5	**Breathless**	
	Kenny G	Arista
6	**Never Let Me Go**	
	Luther Vandross	Epic
7	**The Bodyguard**	
	Soundtrack	Arista
8	**Pocket Full Of Kryptonite**	
	Spin Doctors	Epic Associated
9	**Last Action Hero**	
	Soundtrack	Columbia
10	**It's About Time**	
	SWV	RCA
11	**Get A Grip**	
	Aerosmith	Geffen
12	**Menace II Society**	
	Soundtrack	Jive
13	**Ten Summoner's Tales**	
	Sting	A&M
14	**Unplugged**	
	Eric Clapton	Duck/Reprise
15	**Duran Duran**	
	Duran Duran	Capitol
16	**Bigger, Better, Faster, More!**	
	4 Non Blondes	Interscope
17	**Provocative**	
	Johnny Gill	Motown
18	**Kamakiriad**	
	Donald Fagen	Reprise
19	**Are You Gonna Go My Way?**	
	Lenny Kravitz	Virgin
20	**Bacdafucup**	
	Onyx	JMJ/Chaos

uk albums

1	**Emergency On Planet Earth**	
	Jamiroquai	Sony Soho Square
2	**What's Love Got To Do With It**	
	Tina Turner	Capitol
3	**Unplugged...and Seated**	
	Rod Stewart	Warner Bros
4	**Unplugged**	
	Neil Young	Reprise
5	**Automatic For The People**	
	R.E.M.	Warner Bros
6	**Pocket Full Of Kryptonite**	
	The Spin Doctors	Epic
7	**No Limits**	
	2 Unlimited	PWL Continental
8	**Ten Summoner's Tales**	
	Sting	A&M
9	**Janet**	
	Janet Jackson	Virgin
10	**Connected**	
	Stereo MC's	4th+b'Way
11	**Too Long In Exile**	
	Van Morrison	Polydor/Exile
12	**Elemental**	
	Tears For Fears	Mercury
13	**So Close**	
	Dina Carroll	A&M
14	**Liberator**	
	OMD	Virgin
15	**Unplugged**	
	Eric Clapton	Duck
16	**Take A Look**	
	Natalie Cole	Elektra
17	**Memorial Beach**	
	A-ha	Warner Bros
18	**Breathless**	
	Kenny G	Arista
19	**Kamakiriad**	
	Donald Fagen	Warner Bros
20	**Whisper A Prayer**	
	Mica Paris	4th+b'Way

uk albums

1	**Emergency On Planet Earth**	
	Jamiroquai	Sony Soho Square
2	**Unplugged...and Seated**	
	Rod Stewart	Warner Bros
3	**Pocket Full Of Kryptonite**	
	The Spin Doctors	Epic
4	**Automatic For The People**	
	R.E.M.	Warner Bros
5	**What's Love Got To Do With It**	
	Tina Turner	Capitol
6	**Unplugged**	
	Neil Young	Reprise
7	**Ten Summoner's Tales**	
	Sting	A&M
8	**Gold Against The Soul**	
	Manic Street Preachers	Columbia
9	**Muddy Water Blues**	
	Paul Rodgers	Victory
10	**No Limits**	
	2 Unlimited	PWL Continental
11	**Janet**	
	Janet Jackson	Virgin
12	**So Close**	
	Dina Carroll	A&M
13	**Connected**	
	Stereo MC's	4th+b'Way
14	**Keep The Faith**	
	Bon Jovi	Mercury
15	**Too Long In Exile**	
	Van Morrison	Polydor/Exile
16	**Elemental**	
	Tears For Fears	Mercury
17	**Kamakiriad**	
	Donald Fagen	Warner Bros
18	**Breathless**	
	Kenny G	Arista
19	**Cereal Killer**	
	Green Jelly	Zoo
20	**Unplugged**	
	Eric Clapton	Duck

indy albums

1	**A Storm In Heaven** Verve	Hut
2	**Painkillers** Babes In Toyland	Southern
3	**Suede** Suede	Nude
4	**So Tough** Saint Etienne	Heavenly
5	**In On The Killtaker** Fugazi	Dischord

dance singles

1	**The Key The Secret** Urban Cookie Collective	Pulse 8
2	**Gimme Luv** David Morales/Bad Yard Club	MERX
3	**Everybody Dance** Evolution	Deconstruction
4	**Can't Get Enough Of Your Love** Taylor Dayne	Arista
5	**Runaround/Carry On** Martha Wash	RCA

Zooropa becomes U2's fifth Number One album, shipping platinum (or 300,000 copies) and anticipated to sell 100,000 in the first week(s). Rattle & Hum actually sold 320,000 in its first week – the second fastest-selling UK album ever – but that was before the recession and SuperMario Bros. The UK's fastest selling album ever? MJ's Bad. Globally, Zooropa hits Number One in Austria, Denmark, Ireland, France, Germany, Holland, Iceland, Italy, Norway, Sweden, Switzerland and the UK. Not to mention Australia, New Zealand, Japan, and the USA.

indy albums

1	**A Storm In Heaven** Verve	Hut
2	**Ginger** Speedy J	Warp
3	**Suede** Suede	Nude
4	**Painkillers** Babes In Toyland	Southern
5	**So Tough** Saint Etienne	Heavenly

dance singles

1	**The Key The Secret** Urban Cookie Collective	Pulse 8
2	**Rez** Underworld	Junior Boy's Own
3	**Break From The Old Routine** Oui 3	MCA
4	**Do You Really Want Me** Jon Secada	SBK
5	**Zeroes & Ones** Jesus Jones	Food

uk singles

1	**Dreams** Gabrielle	Go! Beat
2	**What Is Love** Haddaway	Logic
3	**Tease Me** Chaka Demus & Pliers	Island
4	**Can't Help Falling In Love** UB40	Dep International
5	**I Will Survive (Phil Kelsey Remix)** Gloria Gaynor	Polydor
6	**Have I Told You Lately** Rod Stewart	Warner Bros
7	**One Night In Heaven** M People	Deconstruction
8	**What's Up** 4 Non Blondes	Interscope
9	**Two Princes** Spin Doctors	Epic
10	**All That She Wants** Ace Of Base	London

us singles

1	**Weak** SWV	RCA
2	**That's The Way Love Goes** Janet Jackson	Virgin
3	**Whoomp! (There It Is)** Tag Team	Life
4	**Can't Help Falling In Love** UB40	Virgin
5	**Knockin' Da Boots** H-Town	Luke
6	**Show Me Love** Robin S.	Big Beat
7	**Have I Told You Lately** Rod Stewart	Warner Bros.
8	**Dre Day** Dr. Dre	Death Row
9	**I'll Never Get Over You** Expose	Arista
10	**Come Undone** Duran Duran	Capitol

uk singles

1	**Pray** Take That	RCA
2	**Dreams** Gabrielle	Go! Beat
3	**What Is Love** Haddaway	Logic
4	**Tease Me** Chaka Demus & Pliers	Island
5	**What'S Up** 4 Non Blondes	Interscope
6	**One Night In Heaven** M People	Deconstruction
7	**I Will Survive (Phil Kelsey Remix)** Gloria Gaynor	Polydor
8	**Can't Help Falling In Love** UB40	Dep International
9	**Will You Be There** Michael Jackson	Epic
10	**Have I Told You Lately** Rod Stewart	Warner Bros

us singles

1	**Weak** SWV	RCA
2	**Can't Help Falling In Love** UB40	Virgin
3	**Whoomp! (There It Is)** Tag Team	Life
4	**That's The Way Love Goes** Janet Jackson	Virgin
5	**Knockin' Da Boots** H-Town	Luke
6	**Have I Told You Lately** Rod Stewart	Warner Bros.
7	**Show Me Love** Robin S.	Big Beat
8	**I'll Never Get Over You** Expose	Arista
9	**I'm Gonna Be (500 Miles)** The Proclaimers	Chrysalis
10	**Dre Day** Dr. Dre	Death Row

us albums

1	**Janet** Janet Jackson	Virgin
2	**UnPlugged... And Seated** Rod Stewart	Warner Bros.
3	**Core** Stone Temple Pilots	Atlantic
4	**Breathless** Kenny G	Arista
5	**The Chronic** Dr. Dre	Death Row
6	**It Won't Be The Last** Billy Ray Cyrus	Mercury
7	**Last Action Hero** Soundtrack	Columbia
8	**The Bodyguard** Soundtrack	Arista
9	**Pocket Full Of Kryptonite** Spin Doctors	Epic Associated
10	**It's About Time** SWV	RCA
11	**Get A Grip** Aerosmith	Geffen
12	**Menace II Society** Soundtrack	Jive
13	**Never Let Me Go** Luther Vandross	Epic
14	**Ten Summoner's Tales** Sting	A&M
15	**Bigger, Better, Faster, More!** 4 Non Blondes	Interscope
16	**Unplugged** Eric Clapton	Duck/Reprise
17	**Bacdafucup** Onyx	JMJ/Chaos
18	**Duran Duran** Duran Duran	Capitol
19	**Hootie Mack** Bell Biv Devoe	MCA
20	**Are You Gonna Go My Way?** Lenny Kravitz	Virgin

us albums

1	**Back To Broadway** Barbra Streisand	Columbia
2	**Janet** Janet Jackson	Virgin
3	**It Won't Be The Last** Billy Ray Cyrus	Mercury
4	**Core** Stone Temple Pilots	Atlantic
5	**UnPlugged... And Seated** Rod Stewart	Warner Bros.
6	**The Chronic** Dr. Dre	Death Row
7	**Breathless** Kenny G	Arista
8	**Last Action Hero** Soundtrack	Columbia
9	**Sleepless In Seattle** Soundtrack	Epic Soundtrax
10	**It's About Time** SWV	RCA
11	**The Bodyguard** Soundtrack	Arista
12	**Menace II Society** Soundtrack	Jive
13	**Pocket Full Of Kryptonite** Spin Doctors	Epic Associated
14	**Get A Grip** Aerosmith	Geffen
15	**Ten Summoner's Tales** Sting	A&M
16	**Bigger, Better, Faster, More!** 4 Non Blondes	Interscope
17	**What's Love Got To Do With It** Tina Turner	Virgin
18	**Never Let Me Go** Luther Vandross	Epic
19	**Bacdafucup** Onyx	JMJ/Chaos
20	**Duran Duran** Duran Duran	Capitol

uk albums

1	**Emergency On Planet Earth** Jamiroquai	Sony Soho Square
2	**Unplugged...and Seated** Rod Stewart	Warner Bros
3	**Pocket Full Of Kryptonite** The Spin Doctors	Epic
4	**Back To Broadway** Barbra Streisand	Columbia
5	**Ten Summoner's Tales** Sting	A&M
6	**Automatic For The People** R.E.M.	Warner Bros
7	**What's Love Got To Do With It** Tina Turner	Capitol
8	**Unplugged** Neil Young	Reprise
9	**No Limits** 2 Unlimited	PWL Continental
10	**Connected** Stereo MC's	4th+b'Way
11	**Mi Tierra** Gloria Estefan	Epic
12	**Muddy Water Blues** Paul Rodgers	Victory
13	**Janet** Janet Jackson	Virgin
14	**Gold Against The Soul** Manic Street Preachers	Columbia
15	**So Close** Dina Carroll	A&M
16	**Keep The Faith** Bon Jovi	Mercury
17	**Are You Gonna Go My Way?** Lenny Kravitz	Virgin America
18	**Cereal Killer** Green Jelly	Zoo
19	**Unplugged** Eric Clapton	Duck
20	**Cyberpunk** Billy Idol	Chrysalis

uk albums

1	**Zooropa** U2	Island
2	**Emergency On Planet Earth** Jamiroquai	Sony Soho Square
3	**Debut** Bjork	One Little Indian
4	**Unplugged...and Seated** Rod Stewart	Warner Bros
5	**Pocket Full Of Kryptonite** The Spin Doctors	Epic
6	**Automatic For The People** R.E.M.	Warner Bros
7	**Always** Michael Ball	Polydor
8	**Ten Summoner's Tales** Sting	A&M
9	**Back To Broadway** Barbra Streisand	Columbia
10	**Bigger Better Faster More** 4 Non Blondes	Interscope
11	**What's Love Got To Do With It** Tina Turner	Capitol
12	**Mi Tierra** Gloria Estefan	Epic
13	**Unplugged** Neil Young	Reprise
14	**No Limits** 2 Unlimited	PWL Continental
15	**Keep The Faith** Bon Jovi	Mercury
16	**Connected** Stereo MC's	4th+b'Way
17	**Walthamstow** East 17	London
18	**Unplugged** Eric Clapton	Duck
19	**Janet** Janet Jackson	Virgin
20	**So Close** Dina Carroll	A&M

us albums

1	**Zooropa** U2	Island
2	**Back To Broadway** Barbra Streisand	. Columbia
3	**Janet** Janet Jackson	Virgin
4	**Sleepless In Seattle** Soundtrack	Epic Soundtrax
5	**It Won't Be The Last** Billy Ray Cyrus	Mercury
6	**Core** Stone Temple Pilots	Atlantic
7	**UnPlugged... And Seated** Rod Stewart	Warner Bros.
8	**The Chronic** Dr. Dre	Death Row
9	**Last Action Hero** Soundtrack	Columbia
10	**Breathless** Kenny G	Arista
11	**It's About Time** SWV	RCA
12	**The Bodyguard** Soundtrack	Arista
13	**Pocket Full Of Kryptonite** Spin Doctors	Epic Associated
14	**Menace II Society** Soundtrack	Jive
15	**Get A Grip** Aerosmith	Geffen
16	**Bigger, Better, Faster, More!** 4 Non Blondes	Interscope
17	**What's Love Got To Do With It** Tina Turner	Virgin
18	**Ten Summoner's Tales** Sting	A&M
19	**Bacdafucup** Onyx	JMJ/Chaos
20	**Grave Dancers Union** Soul Asylum	Columbia

uk singles

1	**Pray** Take That	RCA
2	**What's Up** 4 Non Blondes	Interscope
3	**Dreams** Gabrielle	Go! Beat
4	**Tease Me** Chaka Demus & Pliers	Island
5	**What Is Love** Haddaway	Logic
6	**One Night In Heaven** M People	Deconstruction
7	**Almost Unreal** Roxette	Capitol
8	**I Will Survive (Phil Kelsey Remix)** Gloria Gaynor	Polydor
9	**Will You Be There** Michael Jackson	Epic
10	**Can't Help Falling In Love** UB40	Dep International

us singles

1	**Can't Help Falling In Love** UB40	Virgin
2	**Weak** SWV	RCA
3	**Whoomp! (There It Is)** Tag Team	Life
4	**That's The Way Love Goes** Janet Jackson	Virgin
5	**Knockin' Da Boots** H-Town	Luke
6	**Show Me Love** Robin S.	Big Beat
7	**Slam** Onyx	JMJ/Ral
8	**I'll Never Get Over You** Expose	Arista
9	**I'm Gonna Be (500 Miles)** The Proclaimers	Chrysalis
10	**Have I Told You Lately** Rod Stewart	Warner Bros.

indy albums

1	**Debut** Bjork	One Little Indian
2	**Suede** Suede	Nude
3	**Tales Of Ephidrina** Amorphous Androgynous	EBV
4	**Everything Is Now** Drum Club	Butterfly/Big Life
5	**Levelling The Land** The Levellers	China

dance singles

1	**Reconnection (EP)** Zero B	Internal
2	**The Key The Secret** Urban Cookie Collective	Pulse 8
3	**Down That Road** Shara Nelson	Cooltempo
4	**Break From The Old Routine** Oui 3	MCA
5	**Do You Really Want Me** Jon Secada	SBK

uk albums

1	**Promises And Lies** UB40	Dep International
2	**Zooropa** U2	Island
3	**Always** Michael Ball	Polydor
4	**Unplugged...and Seated** Rod Stewart	Warner Bros
5	**Pocket Full Of Kryptonite** The Spin Doctors	Epic
6	**Emergency On Planet Earth** Jamiroquai	Sony Soho Square
7	**Bigger Better Faster More** 4 Non Blondes	Interscope
8	**Automatic For The People** R.E.M.	Warner Bros
9	**Ten Summoner's Tales** Sting	A&M
10	**Back To Broadway** Barbra Streisand	Columbia
11	**Debut** Bjork	One Little Indian
12	**Unplugged** Neil Young	Reprise
13	**Take That & Party** Take That	RCA
14	**What's Love Got To Do With It** Tina Turner	Capitol
15	**The Sound Of Speed** Jesus & Mary Chain	Blanco Y Negro
16	**Unplugged** Eric Clapton	Duck
17	**Keep The Faith** Bon Jovi	Mercury
18	**No Limits** 2 Unlimited	PWL Continental
19	**Connected** Stereo MC's	4th+b'Way
20	**Mi Tierra** Gloria Estefan	Epic

us albums

1	**Zooropa** U2	Island
2	**Sleepless In Seattle** Soundtrack	Epic Soundtrax
3	**Back To Broadway** Barbra Streisand	Columbia
4	**Janet** Janet Jackson	Virgin
5	**Core** Stone Temple Pilots	Atlantic
6	**UnPlugged... And Seated** Rod Stewart	Warner Bros.
7	**It Won't Be The Last** Billy Ray Cyrus	Mercury
8	**The Chronic** Dr. Dre	Death Row
9	**It's About Time** SWV	RCA
10	**Breathless** Kenny G	Arista
11	**The Bodyguard** Soundtrack	Arista
12	**Last Action Hero** Soundtrack	Columbia
13	**Bigger, Better, Faster, More!** 4 Non Blondes	Interscope
14	**No Time To Kill** Clint Black	RCA
15	**Pocket Full Of Kryptonite** Spin Doctors	Epic Associated
16	**Grave Dancers Union** Soul Asylum	Columbia
17	**Menace II Society** Soundtrack	Jive
18	**Bacdafucup** Onyx	JMJ/Chaos
19	**What's Love Got To Do With It** Tina Turner	Virgin
20	**Get A Grip** Aerosmith	Geffen

uk singles

1	**Pray** Take That	RCA
2	**What's Up?** 4 Non Blondes	Interscope
3	**Dreams** Gabrielle	Go!Beat
4	**Tease Me** Chaka Demus & Pliers	Mango
5	**Living On My Own** Freddie Mercury	Parlophone
6	**What Is Love** Haddaway	Logic/Arista
7	**Rain** Madonna	Maverick/Sire
8	**Almost Unreal** Roxette	EMI
9	**One Night In Heaven** M People	Deconstruction
10	**This Is It** Dannii Minogue	MCA

us singles

1	**Can't Help Falling In Love** UB40	Virgin
2	**Whoomp! (There It Is)** Tag Team	Life
3	**Weak** SWV	RCA
4	**I'm Gonna Be (500 Miles)** The Proclaimers	Chrysalis
5	**Slam** Onyx	JMJ/Ral
6	**That's The Way Love Goes** Janet Jackson	Virgin
7	**Lately** Jodeci	Uptown
8	**Show Me Love** Robin S.	Big Beat
9	**Knockin' Da Boots** H-Town	Luke
10	**I'll Never Get Over You** Expose	Arista

indy albums

1	**Debut** Bjork	One Little Indian
2	**Levelling The Land** The Levellers	China
3	**Suede** Suede	Nude
4	**A Storm In Heaven** Verve	Hut
5	**Tales Of Ephidrina** Amorphous Androgynous	EBV

dance singles

1	**Caught In The Middle** Juliet Roberts	Cooltempo
2	**Luv 4 Luv** Robin S	Champion
3	**Never Let Go** Hyper Go-Go	Positiva
4	**Unforgiven** Dream	Magnet
5	**Insane In The Brain** Cypress Hill	Ruffhouse

uk albums

1	**Promises And Lies** UB40	DEP
2	**Zooropa** U2	Island
3	**Always** Michael Ball	Polydor
4	**Siamese Dream** Smashing Pumpkins	Hut
5	**Pocket Full Of Kryptonite** Spin Doctors	Epic
6	**Bigger, Better, Faster, More!** 4 Non Blondes	Interscope
7	**Automatic For The People** REM	Warner Bros
8	**Gold-Greatest Hits** Abba	Polydor
9	**Unplugged...And Seated** Rod Stewart	Warner Bros
10	**Emergency On Planet Earth** Jamiroquai	Sony
11	**Ten Summoner's Tales** Sting	A & M
12	**Take That And Party** Take That	RCA
13	**Debut** Bjork	One Little Indian
14	**Back To Broadway** Barbra Streissand	Columbia
15	**Dangerous** Michael Jackson	Epic
16	**More Abba Gold – More Abba Hits** Abba	Polydor
17	**Keep The Faith** Bon Jovi	Jambco
18	**Connected** The Stereo MC's	4th+Broadway
19	**No Limits** 2 Unlimited	PWL
20	**Unplugged** Eric Clapton	Duck

uk albums

1	**Promises And Lies** UB40	DEP
2	**Zooropa** U2	Island
3	**Automatic For The People** REM	Warner Bros
4	**Bigger, Better, Faster, More!** 4 Non Blondes	Interscope
5	**Pocket Full Of Kryptonite** Spin Doctors	Epic
6	**Always** Michael Ball	Polydor
7	**Take That And Party** Take That	RCA
8	**Emergency On Planet Earth** Jamiroquai	Sony
9	**Unplugged...And Seated** Rod Stewart	Warner Bros
10	**Evolution** Oleta Adams	Fontana
11	**Siamese Dream** Smashing Pumpkins	Hut
12	**Ten Summoner's Tales** Sting	A & M
13	**Black Sunday** Cypress Hill	Ruffhouse
14	**Gold – Greatest Hits** Abba	Polydor
15	**Debut** Bjork	One Little Indian
16	**Dangerous** Michael Jackson	Epic
17	**Sex & Religion** Vai	Relativity
18	**What's Love Got To Do With It** Tina Turner	Parlophone
19	**Back To Broadway** Barbra Streisand	Columbia
20	**Janet** Janet Jackson	Virgin

us albums

1	**Black Sunday** Cypress Hill	Ruffhouse
2	**Zooropa** U2	Island
3	**Sleepless In Seattle** Soundtrack	Epic Soundtrax
4	**Janet** Janet Jackson	Virgin
5	**Back To Broadway** Barbra Streisand	Columbia
6	**Core** Stone Temple Pilots	Atlantic
7	**UnPlugged... And Seated** Rod Stewart	Warner Bros.
8	**The Bodyguard** Soundtrack	Arista
9	**The Chronic** Dr. Dre	Death Row
10	**It Won't Be The Last** Billy Ray Cyrus	Mercury
11	**It's About Time** SWV	RCA
12	**Breathless** Kenny G	Arista
13	**Grave Dancers Union** Soul Asylum	Columbia
14	**Bigger, Better, Faster, More!** 4 Non Blondes	Interscope
15	**Last Action Hero** Soundtrack	Columbia
16	**Pocket Full Of Kryptonite** Spin Doctors	Epic Associated
17	**No Time To Kill** Clint Black	RCA
18	**Bacdafucup** Onyx	JMJ/Chaos
19	**Get A Grip** Aerosmith	Geffen
20	**Menace II Society** Soundtrack	Jive

uk singles

1	**Pray** Take That	RCA
2	**Living On My Own** Freddie Mercury	Parlophone
3	**What's Up?** 4 Non Blondes	Interscope
4	**Tease Me** Chaka Demus & Pliers	Mango
5	**Dreams** Gabrielle	Go!Beat
6	**The Key Is The Secret** Urban Cookie Collective	Pulse 8
7	**Rain** Madonna	Maverick/Sire
8	**Almost Unreal** Roxette	EMI
9	**What Is Love** Haddaway	Logic/Arista
10	**This Is It** Dannii Minogue	MCA

us singles

1	**Can't Help Falling In Love** UB40	Virgin
2	**Whoomp! (There It Is)** Tag Team	Life
3	**Weak** SWV	RCA
4	**I'm Gonna Be (500 Miles)** The Proclaimers	Chrysalis
5	**Slam** Onyx	JMJ/Ral
6	**Lately** Jodeci	Uptown
7	**If I Had No Loot** Tony! Toni! Tone!	Wing
8	**That's The Way Love Goes** Janet Jackson	Virgin
9	**Show Me Love** Robin S.	Big Beat
10	**I Don't Wanna Fight** Tina Turner	Virgin

indy albums

1	**Siamese Dream** Smashing Pumpkins	Hut
2	**Debut** Bjork	One Little Indian
3	**Levelling The Land** The Levellers	China
4	**Suede** Suede	Nude
5	**Songs Of Faith And Devotion** Depeche Mode	Mute

dance singles

1	**Give It Up** The Goodman	Fresh Fruit
2	**Caught In The Middle** Juliet Roberts	Cooltempo
3	**If** Janet Jackson	Virgin
4	**Mr Vain** Culture Beat	Epic
5	**Luv 4 Luv** Robin S	Champion

Earth to Houston: soundtrack album The Bodyguard ricochets sales of over 22 million copies worldwide. Only Travolta with The Bee Gees has topped that. It remains in the UK and US Top Ten charts... Meanwhile, Freddie Mercury makes a posthumous return to the singles chart with Living On My Own, while UB40 continue their fantastic year by hogging the Number One album spot with Promises and Lies.

uk albums

1	**Promises And Lies** UB40	DEP
2	**Zooropa** U2	Island
3	**Automatic For The People** REM	Warner Bros
4	**River Of Dreams** Billy Joel	Columbia
5	**Pocket Full Of Kryptonite** Spin Doctors	Epic
6	**Bigger, Better, Faster, More!** 4 Non Blondes	Interscope
7	**Always** Michael Ball	Polydor
8	**Emergency On Planet Earth** Jamiroquai	Sony
9	**Take That And Party** Take That	RCA
10	**Unplugged...And Seated** Rod Stewart	Warner Bros
11	**Gold – Greatest Hits** Abba	Polydor
12	**Ten Summoner's Tales** Sting	A & M
13	**Keep The Faith** Bon Jovi	Jambco
14	**Black Sunday** Cypress Hill	Ruffhouse
15	**Dangerous** Michael Jackson	Epic
16	**Siamese Dream** Smashing Pumpkins	Hut
17	**Janet** Janet Jackson	Virgin
18	**Back To Broadway** Barbra Streisand	Columbia
19	**Evolution** Oleta Adams	Fontana
20	**What's Love Got To Do With It** Tina Turner	Parlophone

us albums

1	**Black Sunday** Cypress Hill	Ruffhouse
2	**Sleepless In Seattle** Soundtrack	Epic Soundtrax
3	**Zooropa** U2	Island
4	**Janet** Janet Jackson	Virgin
5	**Core** Stone Temple Pilots	Atlantic
6	**Back To Broadway** Barbra Streisand	Columbia
7	**Promises And Lies** UB40	Virgin
8	**The Bodyguard** Soundtrack	Arista
9	**UnPlugged... And Seated** Rod Stewart	Warner Bros.
10	**Siamese Dream** Smashing Pumpkins	Virgin
11	**Grave Dancers Union** Soul Asylum	Columbia
12	**It's About Time** SWV	RCA
13	**Get A Grip** Aerosmith	Geffen
14	**Breathless** Kenny G	Arista
15	**The Chronic** Dr. Dre	Death Row
16	**Bigger, Better, Faster, More!** 4 Non Blondes	Interscope
17	**Pocket Full Of Kryptonite** Spin Doctors	Epic Associated
18	**Bacdafucup** Onyx	JMJ/Chaos
19	**A Lot About Livin'** Alan Jackson	Arista
20	**It Won't Be The Last** Billy Ray Cyrus	Mercury

uk singles

1	**Living On My Own** Freddie Mercury	Parlophone
2	**The Key Is The Secret** Urban Cookie Collective	Pulse 8
3	**Pray** Take That	RCA
4	**What's Up?** 4 Non Blondes	Interscope
5	**It Keeps Rainin' (Tears)** Bitty McLean	Brilliant
6	**The River Of Dreams** Billy Joel	Columbia
7	**Tease Me** Chaka Demus & Pliers	Mango
8	**Nuff Vibes (EP)** Apache Indian	Island
9	**Dreams** Gabrielle	Go!Beat
10	**Rain** Madonna	Maverick/Sire

us singles

1	**Can't Help Falling In Love** UB40	Virgin
2	**Whoomp! (There It Is)** Tag Team	Life
3	**Weak** SWV	RCA
4	**I'm Gonna Be (500 Miles)** The Proclaimers	Chrysalis
5	**Slam** Onyx	JMJ/Ral
6	**Lately** Jodeci	Uptown
7	**If I Had No Loot** Tony! Toni! Tone!	Wing
8	**Runaway Train** Soul Asylum	Columbia
9	**I Don't Wanna Fight** Tina Turner	Virgin
10	**If** Janet Jackson	Virgin

indy albums

1	**Siamese Dream** Smashing Pumpkins	Hut
2	**Debut** Bjork	One Little Indian
3	**Levelling The Land** The Levellers	China
4	**Songs Of Faith And Devotion** Depeche Mode	Mute
5	**Suede** Suede	Nude

dance singles

1	**Mr Vain** Culture Beat	Epic
2	**Caught In The Middle** Juliet Roberts	Cooltempo
3	**Give It Up** The Goodman	Fresh Fruit
4	**Looking Up** Michelle Gayle	RCA
5	**The Key Is The Secret** Urban Cookie Collective	Pulse 8

indy albums

1	**Siamese Dream** Smashing Pumpkins	Hut
2	**Debut** Bjork	One Little Indian
3	**The Story So Far** Moby	Equator
4	**Levelling The Land** The Levellers	China
5	**Songs Of Faith And Devotion** Depeche Mode	Mute

dance singles

1	**Slave To The Vibe** Aftershock	Virgin
2	**Mr Vain** Culture Beat	Epic
3	**Afro Sleaze/Transatlantic** Roach Motel	Junior Boy's Own
4	**Ain't No Casanova** Sinclair	Dome
5	**Give It Up** The Goodman	Fresh Fruit

uk singles

1	**Living On My Own** Freddie Mercury	Parlophone
2	**The Key Is The Secret** Urban Cookie Collective	Pulse 8
3	**It Keeps Rainin' (Tears)** Bitty McLean	Brilliant
4	**The River Of Dreams** Billy Joel	Columbia
5	**Nuff Vibes (EP)** Apache Indian	Island
6	**Mr Vain** Culture Beat	Epic
7	**What's Up?** 4 Non Blondes	Interscope
8	**Higher Ground** UB40	DEP
9	**Pray** Take That	RCA
10	**Tease Me** Chaka Demus & Pliers	Mango

us singles

1	**Can't Help Falling In Love** UB40	Virgin
2	**Whoomp! (There It Is)** Tag Team	Life
3	**I'm Gonna Be (500 Miles)** The Proclaimers	Chrysalis
4	**Slam** Onyx	JMJ/Ral
5	**Lately** Jodeci	Uptown
6	**Weak** SWV	RCA
7	**If I Had No Loot** Tony! Toni! Tone!	Wing
8	**Runaway Train** Soul Asylum	Columbia
9	**Dreamlover** Mariah Carey	Columbia
10	**If** Janet Jackson	Virgin

us albums

1	**Sleepless In Seattle** Soundtrack	Epic Soundtrax
2	**Black Sunday** Cypress Hill	Ruffhouse
3	**Janet** Janet Jackson	Virgin
4	**Zooropa** U2	Island
5	**Core** Stone Temple Pilots	Atlantic
6	**Promises And Lies** UB40	Virgin
7	**The Bodyguard** Soundtrack	Arista
8	**UnPlugged... And Seated** Rod Stewart	Warner Bros.
9	**Get A Grip** Aerosmith	Geffen
10	**Blind Melon** Blind Melon	Capitol
11	**Back To Broadway** Barbra Streisand	Columbia
12	**Grave Dancers Union** Soul Asylum	Columbia
13	**Da Bomb** Kris Kross	Ruffhouse
14	**It's About Time** SWV	RCA
15	**Bigger, Better, Faster, More!** 4 Non Blondes	Interscope
16	**Breathless** Kenny G	Arista
17	**The Chronic** Dr. Dre	Death Row
18	**A Lot About Livin'** Alan Jackson	Arista
19	**Bacdafucup** Onyx	JMJ/Chaos
20	**Siamese Dream** Smashing Pumpkins	Virgin

uk albums

1	**Promises And Lies** UB40	DEP
2	**Zooropa** U2	Island
3	**River Of Dreams** Billy Joel	Columbia
4	**Pocket Full Of Kryptonite** Spin Doctors	Epic
5	**Automatic For The People** REM	Warner Bros
6	**Bigger, Better, Faster, More!** 4 Non Blondes	Interscope
7	**Always** Michael Ball	Polydor
8	**Emergency On Planet Earth** Jamiroquai	Sony
9	**Unplugged...And Seated** Rod Stewart	Warner Bros
10	**What's Love Got To Do With It** Tina Turner	Parlophone
11	**Take That And Party** Take That	RCA
12	**Ten Summoner's Tales** Sting	A & M
13	**Debut** Bjork	One Little Indian
14	**Keep The Faith** Bon Jovi	Jambco
15	**The Freddie Mercury Album** Freddie Mercury	Parlophone
16	**Gold – Greatest Hits** Abba	Polydor
17	**Achtung Baby** U2	Island
18	**Janet** Janet Jackson	Virgin
19	**Black Sunday** Cypress Hill	Ruffhouse
20	**Siamese Dream** Smashing Pumpkins	Hut

uk singles

1	**Mr Vain** Culture Beat	Epic
2	**Living On My Own** Freddie Mercury	Parlophone
3	**It Keeps Rainin' (Tears)** Bitty McLean	Brilliant
4	**The Key Is The Secret** Urban Cookie Collective	Pulse 8
5	**The River Of Dreams** Billy Joel	Columbia
6	**Nuff Vibes (EP)** Apache Indian	Island
7	**Right Here** SWV	RCA
8	**Higher Ground** UB40	DEP
9	**What's Up?** 4 Non Blondes	Interscope
10	**Dreamlover** Mariah Carey	Columbia

us singles

1	**Can't Help Falling In Love** UB40	Virgin
2	**Whoomp! (There It Is)** Tag Team	Life
3	**Dreamlover** Mariah Carey	Columbia
4	**Lately** Jodeci	Uptown
5	**Runaway Train** Soul Asylum	Columbia
6	**I'm Gonna Be (500 Miles)** The Proclaimers	Chrysalis
7	**If** Janet Jackson	Virgin
8	**Slam** Onyx	JMJ/Ral
9	**If I Had No Loot** Tony! Toni! Tone!	Wing
10	**Weak** SWV	RCA

indy albums

1	**Debut** Bjork	One Little Indian
2	**Siamese Dream** Smashing Pumpkins	Hut
3	**The Story So Far** Moby	Equator
4	**Levelling The Land** The Levellers	China
5	**Holy Bandits** The Oyster Band	Cooking Vinyl

dance singles

1	**Right Here** SWV	RCA
2	**Slave To The Vibe** Aftershock	Virgin
3	**Mr Vain** Culture Beat	Epic
4	**Ain't No Casanova** Sinclair	Dome
5	**Slam** Onyx	Columbia

us albums

1	**River Of Dreams** Billy Joel	Columbia
2	**Sleepless In Seattle** Soundtrack	Epic Soundtrax
3	**Black Sunday** Cypress Hill	Ruffhouse
4	**Janet** Janet Jackson	Virgin
5	**Core** Stone Temple Pilots	Atlantic
6	**Zooropa** U2	Island
7	**Blind Melon** Blind Melon	Capitol
8	**Promises And Lies** UB40	Virgin
9	**Get A Grip** Aerosmith	Geffen
10	**The Bodyguard** Soundtrack	Arista
11	**UnPlugged... And Seated** Rod Stewart	Warner Bros.
12	**It's About Time** SWV	RCA
13	**Back To Broadway** Barbra Streisand	Columbia
14	**Grave Dancers Union** Soul Asylum	Columbia
15	**Da Bomb** Kris Kross	Ruffhouse
16	**Breathless** Kenny G	Arista
17	**A Lot About Livin'** Alan Jackson	Arista
18	**Bigger, Better, Faster, More!** 4 Non Blondes	Interscope
19	**Pocket Full Of Kryptonite** Spin Doctors	Epic
20	**Live** James Taylor	Columbia

uk albums

1	**Promises And Lies** UB40	DEP
2	**Pocket Full Of Kryptonite** Spin Doctors	Epic
3	**Zooropa** U2	Island
4	**River Of Dreams** Billy Joel	Columbia
5	**Keep The Faith** Bon Jovi	Jambco
6	**Automatic For The People** REM	Warner Bros
7	**Antmusic – The Very Best Of Adam Ant** Adam Ant	Arcade
8	**Bigger, Better, Faster, More!** 4 Non Blondes	Interscope
9	**Emergency On Planet Earth** Jamiroquai	Sony
10	**Unplugged...And Seated** Rod Stewart	Warner Bros
11	**What's Love Got To Do With It** Tina Turner	Parlophone
12	**Always** Michael Ball	Polydor
13	**The Freddie Mercury Album** Freddie Mercury	Parlophone
14	**Ten Summoner's Tales** Sting	A & M
15	**Debut** Bjork	One Little Indian
16	**Take That And Party** Take That	RCA
17	**Giant Step** Boo Radleys	Creation
18	**Gold – Greatest Hits** Abba	Polydor
19	**Achtung Baby** U2	Island
20	**Janet** Janet Jackson	Virgin

What's it all Labatt then?

"Live on Virgin 1215 this is ..."

intones mild-mannered, handsomely-quiffed I'm-a-DJ-not-a-clairvoyant **Russ Williams,** as he gives the rundown on **... the Virgin Labatt's Album Chart.**

"There's a surprise lurking in this week's chart" I announce from Virgin 1215's Studio 1. The place is bright and airy, bathed in evening light, with a view over Golden Square that most office workers would kill for. "There's a brand new number one, which is quite out of the blue."

Yes, I am definitely enjoying myself, working at six o'clock on a Sunday evening when most people are probably flaked out, contemplating the awful prospect of Monday gloom. I'm slightly hyper underneath my habitual laid-back on-air persona, because I'm slap bang in the middle of presenting another Virgin Labatt's Album Chart.

Although it's not always quite so idyllic, this particular part of my job – presenting the first ever album rock chart on national commercial radio (catchy, that) – has got to be the most fun I've ever had, but I don't suppose you can call it working, not really. Here I am on the still new radio station, playing music I personally love, and all the planning's done over an orange juice down the pub at lunchtime or the odd curry. Mike on. "Live on Virgin 1215, this is the Virgin Labatt's Album Chart." I flick a fader, doff my earphones and glance at Roger Pusey, producer extraordinaire, who is sitting completely motionless in front of a large sheet of white paper which contains the timings for the chart rundown. Another Sunday evening's work is well under way.

I have three very clear memories of the first chart we ever broadcast: I remember being nervous, excited and relieved. Nervous, because it was our maiden outing, and although between us Roger and I had perfected a failsafe, idiot-proof system for collating the charts and getting them ready in time, we still didn't know whether the theory would actually hold up in practice and under pressure. Excited, simply because of the real buzz of being on the air with the very first Virgin Labatt's Album Chart (and being part of the infant station). And relieved because it was my first time on air since the launch the Friday before. Suffice to say that the company commode was in constant use that afternoon!

I was highly aware too that we were making a small, but perfectly formed, fragment of radio and music history with the first official rock chart for the UK music industry. This show was about to have a significant impact on all the people out there in the nation who wanted something substantially more sustaining than the average hit parade pap.

Since that first broadcast, I've grown used to the adrenalin rush of pulling the chart together at high speed, and have also had the time to observe how it reflects the true ebb and flow of buying. Often there's no simple curve going up and returning back down, but a more erratic route: REM's *Automatic for the People*, Sade's *Promises* and Simply Red's *Stars* are three that oscillated up and down in the first few months of the show, as buying patterns changed across the nation.

Another strength that has emerged about the station is that while we can evoke some kind of nostalgia for thirtysomethings whose faculties are not yet shot to pieces and can still tell good rock music from indifferent, a high percentage of the overall output is new stuff. We've managed to avoid creating a golden oldie graveyard and I think the chart has reflected this too.

I was first told that I would be fronting the chart show within a couple of weeks of agreeing to join the station – and it felt good to know that I would be presenting one of Virgin 1215's flagship shows – but this flicker of pride was instantly quashed by the need to sort out the more practical considerations involved.

The trick, I learnt quickly, is to be ruthlessly disciplined. The wild abandon of the zoo radio approach is something I reserve for trying to get a drink in the pub afterwards. Everything is extremely ordered, and based on very tight timings. All of the 40 tracks we play, selected by a combination of myself, Roger and Richard Skinner as executive producer, plus the links, news and commercials must add up to precisely 180 minutes, not a second more, not a second less (must write a book called that one day). I've found myself becoming more and more engrossed in the time slots and the statistics. Excuse me while I just slip this anorak off.

However, you won't find any sign of a script in the studio. I need to leave an area for improvisation amidst this manic military organisation. It's all in my brain. But you have to be flexible. If someone rushes in with a surprise shift from number 32 up to number 3, then I have to hoof it ...

The smooth and seamless organisation was also under a little stress when we did the show live from Toronto with Labatt's. That was hairy, if not hirsute. We only just got the chart through in time, and were winging the timing calculations as we went along.

The chart comes in from Gallup on fax just

before the show. It's as accurate as possible, compiled that very day from the sales records of 1550 shop computers countrywide. If you buy a record at 11.59 on Saturday night, I'll know about it. The data is collected until the end of Saturday for processing, something whirrs and there it is, in my hands.

Beforehand I do some background research and arrive at Virgin about 1.30 so that Roger and I can discuss the show, possible problems, collate the running order and bingo – at four 'o clock we're flying. After the show we disappear to the local to sink a couple of pints (Labatt's of course).

It's as easy as that. Allegedly.

One of the statistics I like to spout (I'll just pop that anorak back on) is that CD albums now outsell singles by a hefty 3 to 1, so that the chart is a genuinely accurate reflection of current musical tastes. To my mind singles still influence the rival charts and radio station playlists, whereas the Virgin Labatt's chart is true to by far the greater proportion of sales. From my own point of view, I think that singles have simply become too expensive, when for not much over £5 more you can get another 6 or 7 tracks.

It's a trend I'm not about to discourage! As someone who would be an ideal target listener if I wasn't inside the studio, it all makes perfect sense to me. ***Now can I keep my job?***

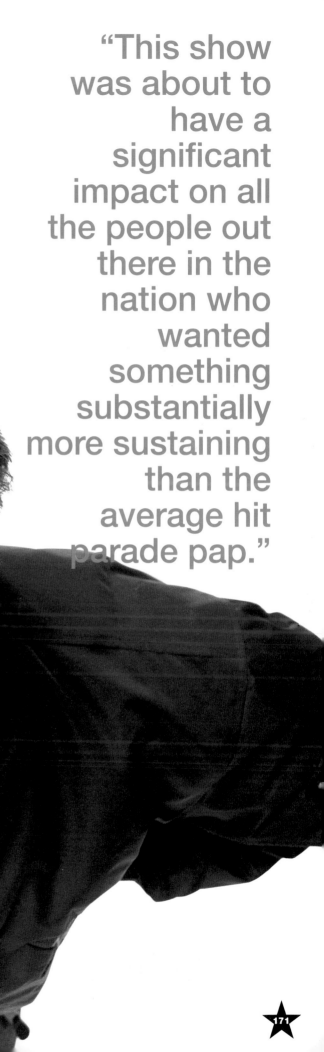

"This show was about to have a significant impact on all the people out there in the nation who wanted something substantially more sustaining than the average hit parade pap."

The end of innocence

In the wake of U2's success, Irish rock was in danger of becoming a safe career option. *Things are changing though,* writes

Dave Fanning.

Irish rock, now in its adolescence, is finally losing its innocence. In the 80s, we stumbled blindly and naively into the international spotlight, emboldened by the success of U2 and ignorant of the pitfalls potholes and plunging chasms of the rock industry. Some of us soared past these obstacles on a rush of youthful exuberance, but most others simply fell into oblivion.

The casual visitor to Ireland will be forgiven for thinking that we are obsessed with rock'n'roll. Bands like The Stunning, The Four Of Us, An Emotional Fish, The Saw Doctors and Something Happens permeate the airwaves with the regularity of 2 Unlimited or East 17. There's a rock school in Ballyfermot where budding bands can learn how to set up their drumkit or package their demo, and these things are taught with all the po-faced seriousness of Mathematics or Latin. Dublin even has a tourist trail called Rock 'N' Stroll, which features landmarks of Irish Rock, including Phil Lynott's house and the Windmill Lane Wall.

In fact, Irish Rock is in serious danger of becoming a Government-sponsored safe alternative to being an accountant or a plumber. With so many official cooks sticking their authoritative fingers into the Irish rock broth, the whole thing may get spoiled. Rock'n'Roll, once the symbol of rebellion and teenage angst, is growing up into a smug, self-satisfied young adult with a ponytail, and its mentors pat it on the back for doing a good job, and reward it with prizes like record deals, musical equipment and 100 hours of free recording time. In Ireland, you've more chance of winning money in a sponsored band competition than earning it from gigs and record sales.

The buzzing Irish rock industry is a great thing for bands working within the country, boosting their self-esteem and giving them rock god status at home. But all too often the confidence turns to arrogance, and bands believe they can actually conquer the world after a few rehearsals and a showcase gig. The big-fish-in-a-little-pond syndrome has never rung so true as it does in Ireland. When a band that feels safe and secure in its own neighbourhood is suddenly thrust into the rat race of international rock, the outward smugness is soon stripped away, and only those with the right stuff will prevail. When Irish bands sign to a major UK or American label, they may suddenly find themselves under pressure to sell records in figures far exceeding

their home sales. Until their recent signing with Geffen Records, Kilkenny band My Little Funhouse had only to fill small venues like Dublin's Rock Garden or Cork's Sir Henry's to justify their existence. Now they may have to do no less than equal the worldwide success of label-mates Guns N' Roses in order to survive. This could just be too much to ask for a bunch of wide-eyed small-town boys.

Another Kilkenny band, Engine Alley, are taking a different, more clued-in route to worldwide recognition. Having already won hearts and minds at home with a couple of superb singles (*Infamy*, *Mrs Winder*) and an excellent debut album, this gaggle of glammed-up Bowie-clones have relocated themselves to London and are starting off from scratch, using only their wits and their excellent songwriting and absurd sense of theatrics. If they don't make it big, at least they won't have to pay back their advance to the record label.

A House have already crashed the UK indie charts with their third album *I Am The Greatest* and the classic *Endless Art* single, but they only did this after a major label slap in the face. Originally beneficiaries of the signing frenzy that followed U2's *Joshua Tree* financial harvest, A House were forced to re-assess their motives for making music, and realized that there was more to it than 'getting a deal'. In the period between getting dropped and picking up unprecedented acclaim in the music press, A House grew up, and it shows in every glorious note of their current album.

The list of casualties grows as quickly as rock music changes direction. A whole generation of bands, once clutching their precious passports into the promised land of rock stardom, now find themselves being deported to the ghettos of might-have-beens. Something Happens, once the chirpy, psychedelic foursome of *Been There, Seen That, Done That* and *Stuck Together With God's Glue*, became the angry, venomous guitar-grinding quartet of *Bedlam A-Go Go*. Perhaps their sudden severance with Virgin gave them grist to add to the mill, or perhaps they've simply learnt that nice guys always finish last.

Power Of Dreams with their *Second Son* EP, The Pale with their *Light Up My World* EP and Something Happens with their paean to supermodel sex *C.C. Incidentally* (guess who C.C. stands for), all have crawled back into the boxing ring, bloody but unbowed, and all the stronger after their knockout blows. And it looks like the new crop of bands are learning

> *"The big-fish-in-a-little-pond syndrome has never rung so true as it does in Ireland."*

"In fact, Irish Rock is in serious danger of becoming a Government-sponsored safe alternative to being an accountant or a plumber."

from the mistakes of their predecessors. Bands like Pet Lamb, The Castanedas, The Idiots and Puppy Love Bomb are avoiding the rush to sign record deals, preferring instead to craft their own styles outside the pigeonholing and patronizing of the Irish music industry. In a business where 'radio-friendly' is actually taken as a compliment, these bands are retaining the subversive power of rock and avoiding the respectability that too many others have striven to gain.

It's not easy to share a nationality with the world's biggest band and settle for second best, but until Irish bands learn to lose their U2 envy, they'll always be dogged by disappointment. Therapy?, Sultans of Ping and Frank & Walters have all hit the Top 40 without having to stare into the desert distance, and if more Irish bands remain true to themselves, instead of adapting to a false idea of how Irish rock is perceived internationally, then the very term 'Irish Rock', restrictive in itself, may soon cease to be a relevant tag.

RECORD COMPANIES

● **4AD LTD,**
15 Alma Road, London
SW18 1AA.
081-870-9724

A&M RECORDS,
136-144 New Kings Road, London
SW6 4LZ.
071-736-3311

ACE RECORDS LTD,
46-50 Steele Road, London
NW10 7AS.
081-453-1311

ACID JAZZ RECORDS,
1st Floor, 21 Denmark Street,
London WC2H 8NE.
021-379-9808

ALLEGRO,
Pickwick House, The Waterfront,
Elstree Road, Elstree,
Hertfordshire WD6 3BS.
081-207-6207

ALTERNATIVE TENTACLES,
64 Mountgrove Road, London
N5 2LT.
071-354-5455

ALVA RECORDS,
17 West Nicolson Street,
Edinburgh EH8 9DA.
031-668-2374

ANXIOUS RECORDS,
Devonshire House, 2-4 The
Broadway, London N8 9SN.
081-341-4322

APPLE CORPS LTD,
6 Stratton Street, London
W1X 5FD.
071-499-1543

ARIOLA,
Cavendish House, 423 New Kings
Road, London SW6 4RN.
071-973-8040

ARTLOS RECORDS,
P O Box 132, London W3 8XQ.
081-887-0321

ATLANTIC RECORDS,
83 Baker Street, London
W1M 1AJ.
071-486-6271

AWESOME RECORDS LTD,
59 Moore Park Road, London
SW6 2HH.
071-731-0022

● **BBC RECORDS,**
Woodlands, 80 Wood Lane,
London W12 0TT.
081-743-5588

**BMG ARISTA RECORDS (UK)
LTD,**
Cavendish House, 423 New Kings
Road, London SW6 4RN.
071-973-8040

BMG RECORDS UK LTD,
Bedford House, 69-79 Fulham
High Street, London SW6 3JW.
071-973-0011

BACKS RECORDING CO LTD,
St Mary's Works, St Mary's Plain,
Norwich, Norfolk NR3 3AF.
0603-626221

BAD GIRL,
4th Floor, 40 Thurlow Park Road,
London SE21 8JA.
081-761-7107

**BEGGARS BANQUET
RECORDS,**
17-19 Alma Road, London
SW18 1AA.
081-870-9912

BIG CAT,
P O Box 1561, London NW6 4SW.
081-960-0228

BIG LIFE RECORDS,
15 Little Portland Street, London
W1N 5DE.
071-323-2888

BLAST FIRST,
21 Wren Street, London WC1 0HX.
071-278-0916

● **CASTLE COMMUNICATIONS
PLC,**
A29 Barwell Business Park,
Leatherhead Road, Chessington,
Surrey KT9 2NY.
081-974-1021

CHAPTER 22,
Unit 17, Newhall Place, 16-17
Newhall Hill, Birmingham B13 JH.
021-236-8422

CHARLY RECORDS LTD,
156-166 Ilderton Road, London
SE15 1NT.
071-639-8603

CHEREE RECORDS,
16b Hermon Hill, London E11 2AP.
081-530-8381

CHERRY RED RECORDS,
3rd Floor, Bishop's Park House,
25-29 Fulham High Street, London
SW6 3JH.
071-371-5844

CHINA RECORDS LTD,
27 Queensdale Place, London
W11 4SQ.
071-602-5031

CHRYSALIS GROUP,
The Chrysalis Building, Bramley
Road, London W10 6SP.
071-221-2213

CIRCA,
Kendal House, 553-579 Harrow
Road, London W10 4RH.
081-968-6688

CLAWFIST,
231 Portobello Road, London
W11 1LT.
071-792-3566

COOKING VINYL,
Unit 2 Park Mews, 213 Kilburn
Lane, London W10 4BQ.
081-960-6000

COOLTEMPO RECORDS,
The Chrysalis Building, Bramley
Road, London W10 6SP.
071-221-2213

CREATION RECORDS LTD,
2nd Floor, 8 Westgate Street,
London E8 3RN.
081-986-7145

● **DJM RECORDS LTD,**
P O Box 1420, 1 Sussex Place,
London W6 9XS.
081-846-8515

DAMAGED GOODS,
P O Box 671, London E17 6NF.
081-807-0618

DEAD DEAD GOOD RECORDS,
2 Witton Walk, Northwich,
Cheshire CW9 5AT.
0606-44559

DECONSTRUCTION RECORDS,
Bedford House, 69-79 Fulham
High Street,
London SW6 3JW.
071-384-2298

DEDICATED RECORDS,
37 Uxbridge Street, London
W8 7TQ.
071-221-6677

DEF AMERICAN RECORDS,
Chancellor's House, 72
Chancellor's Road, Hammersmith,
London W6 9RS.
081-741-1212

DEMON RECORDS LTD,
Canal House, Stars Estate,
Transport Avenue, Brentford,
Middlesex TW8 0QP.
081-847-2481

DEVA RECORDS,
P O Box 174, London WC1X 9XN.
071-713-7734

DOVETAIL RECORDS,
2 York Parade, Great West Road,
Brentford, Middlesex TW8 9AA.
081-568-6565

● **EMI RECORDS,**
20 Manchester Square, London
W1A 1ES.
071-486-4488

EARACHE,
P O Box 144, Nottingham
NG3 4GE.
0602-506400

EAST WEST RECORDS,
The Electric Lighting Station,
46 Kensington Court, London
W8 5DP.
071-938-2181

ELEMENTAL,
64 Mountgrove Road, London
N5 2LT.
071-354-5455

ENSIGN RECORDS LTD,
3 Monmouth Place, London
W2 5SH.
071-727-0527

ESSENTIAL,
A29 Barwell Business Park,
Leatherhead Road, Chessington,
Surrey KT2 9NY.
081-974-1021

EVE RECORDINGS,
P O Box 2637, London
N16 7DZ.
071-275-8126

● **FFRR RECORDS,**
P O Box 1422, Chancellor's
House, Chancellor's Road,
London W6 9SG.
081-741-1234

F-BEAT,
Canal House, Stars Estate,
Transport Avenue, Brentford,
Middlesex TW8 0QP.
081-847-2481

FICTION RECORDS LTD,
97 Charlotte Street, London
W1P 1LB.
071-323-5555

FIRE RECORDS,
21a Maury Road, London
N16 7BP
081-806-9922

FLUTE,
Shepperton International Studios,
Studios Road, Shepperton
TW17 0QD.
0932-562611

FOOD RECORDS,
172a Arlington Road, Camden,
London NW1 7HL.
071-284-2554

FOURTH & BROADWAY,
22 St Peter's Square, London
W6 9NW.
081-741-1511

● **GEE STREET,**
22 St Peter's Square, London
W6 9NW.
081-741-1511

GO! DISCS,
72 Black Lion Lane,
Hammersmith, London W6 9BE.
081-748-7973

GIFT RECORDS,
Studio 2, 1 Brown Street, Sheffield
S1 2BS.
0742-757856

GREENSLEAVES RECORDS LTD,
Unit 14 Metro Centre, St John's
Road, Isleworth, Middlesex
TW7 6NJ.
081-758-0564

GUERNICA,
15 Alma Road, London SW18 1AA.
081-870-9724

● **HEAVENLY RECORDS,**
50-52 Monmouth Street, London
WC2H 9EP.
071-240-2474

HIT LABEL,
Chrysalis Group Plc, The Chrysalis
Building, Bramley Road, London
W10 6SP.
071-221-2213

HUT,
Kendal House, 553-579 Harrow
Road, London W10 4RH.
081-968-6688

● **IRS RECORDS LTD,**
20 Manchester Square, London
W1A 1ES.
071-486-4488

ICE RINK,
2nd Floor, 8 Westgate Street,
London E8 3RN.
081-986-7145

IMAGO RECORDING CO LTD,
1 Adam & Eve Mews, London
W8 6UG.
071-938-3000

INFONET,
2nd Floor, 8 Westgate Street,
London E8 3RN.
081-986-7145

ISLAND RECORDS LTD,
22 St Peter's Square, London
W6 9NW.
081-741-1511

● **JIVE RECORDS,**
Zomba House, 165-167 Willesden
High Road, London NW10 2SG.
081-459-8899

JUNGLE RECORDS,
Old Dairy Mews, 62 Chalk Farm
Road, London NW1 8AN.
071-267-0171

● **KITCHENWARE RECORDS,**
St Thomas Street Stables, St
Thomas Street, Newcastle Upon
Tyne, Tyne & Wear NE1 4LE.
091-232-4895

● **LEMON RECORDS,**
17 Dorset Square, London
NW1 6QB.
071-724-6490

& RECORD LABELS

LONDON RECORDS,
P O Box 1422, Chancellors House,
Chancellor's Road, London
W6 9SG.
081-741-1234

● **M&G RECORDS LTD,**
Queens Studios,
121 Salusbury Road, London
NW6 6BG.
071-625-7993

MCA RECORDS LTD,
139 Piccadilly, London W1V 0AS.
071-957-8600

MAGNET,
Electric Lighting Station, 46
Kensington Court, London
W8 5DP.
071-938-2181

MUSIC FOR NATIONS,
102 Belsize Lane, London
NW3 5BB.
071-794-0283

MUSIDISC UK,
32 Queensdale Road, London
W11 4SB.
071-602-1124

MUTE RECORDS,
425 Harrow Road, London
W10 4RE.
081-969-8866

● **NATION RECORDS LTD,**
1st Floor, 19 All Saints Road,
London W11 1HE.
071-792-8167

NUDE RECORDS,
38 Langham Street, London
W1N 5RH.
071-636-5822

● **OLD GOLD RECORDS,**
Hyde Industrial Estate, The Hyde,
London NW9 6JU.
081-200-5335

ON U SOUND,
P O Box 59, London N22 1AR.
081-888-8949

ONE LITTLE INDIAN RECORDS,
250 York Road, London
SW11 3SJ.
071-924-1661

OVAL RECORDS,
326 Brixton Road, London
SW4 0DG.
071-326-4907

● **PAISLEY PARK RECORDS,**
The Warner Building, 28a
Kensington Church Street, London
W8 4EP.
071-937-8844

PAPERHOUSE RECORDS,
21a Maury Road, London
N16 7BP.
081-806-9922

PERFECTO RECORDS LTD,
32 Holmes Road, London
NW5 3AB.
071-482-4535

PHONOGRAM,
P O Box 1425, Chancellor's
House, Chancellor's Road,
London W6 9QB.
081-741-1212

PICKWICK GROUP PLC,
Pickwick House, The Waterfront,
Elstree Road, Elstree,
Hertfordshire WD6 3BS.
081-207-6207

PINNACLE RECORDS,
Electron House, Cray Avenue,
St Mary Cray, Orpington, Kent
BR5 3NP.
0689-870622

POLYDOR RECORDS,
P O Box 1420, 1 Sussex Place,
London W6 9XS.
081-846-8090

POLYGRAM UK LTD,
P O Box 1420, 1 Sussex Place,
London W6 9XS.
081-846-8515

PULSE 8 RECORDS LTD,
31 Norfolk Place, London
W2 1QH.
071-224-9405

PWL INTERNATIONAL LTD,
The Borough, 4-7 The Vineyard,
Sanctuary Street, London SE1 1QL.
071-403-0007

● **RCA,**
Cavendish House, 423 New
Kings Road, London SW6 4RN.
071-973-0011

RPO,
Pickwick House, The Waterfront,
Elstree Road, Elstree,
Hertfordshire WD6 3BS.
081-207-6207

RTM,
98 St Pancras Way, London
NW1 9NF.
071-284-1155

RAK RECORDING STUDIOS,
42-48 Charlbert Street, London
NW8 7BU.
071-586-2012

RAPTURE RECORDINGS,
98 St Pancras Way, London
NW1 9NF.
071-267-6222

REVOLVER MUSIC LTD,
152 Goldthorne Hill, Penn,
Wolverhampton, West Mids
WV2 3BA.
0902-345345

RHINO RECORDS LTD,
The Chilterns, France Hill Drive,
Camberley, Surrey GU15 3QA.
0276-686077

RHYTHM KING RECORDS,
Queens Studios, 117-121
Salusbury Road, London
NW6 6RG.
071-372-3959

ROADRUNNER RECORDS,
15 Great Western Road, London
W9 3NW.
071-289-1021

ROBS RECORDS,
11 Whitworth Street West,
Manchester M1 5WG.
061-237-5957

ROCKET RECORD CO LTD,
32 Galena Road, Hammersmith,
London W6 0LT.
081-741-9933

ROO ART,
22a Lamboole Place, London
NW3 4HP.
071-483-4020

ROUGH TRADE RECORDINGS,
66 Golbourne Road, London
W10 5PS.
081-960-9888

**ROUGHNECK RECORDING
COMPANY,**
21a Maury Road, London
N16 7BP.
081-806-9922

SBK RECORDS,
127 Charing Cross Road, London
WC2H 0EA.
071-434-2131

● **SETANTA,**
123 Shakespeare Road, London
SE24 0PY.
071-703-0971

SHUT UP AND DANCE,
53 Belgrade Road, London
N16 8DH.
071-254-2943

SILVERTONE RECORDS,
Zomba House, 165-167 Willesden
High Road, London NW10 2SG.
081-459-8899

SNAP RECORDS,
Unit 401-404, Brixton Road,
London SW9 8EJ.
071-978-8611

SOME BIZARRE,
166 New Cavendish Street,
London W1M 7FJ.
071-631-3140

SONY MUSIC ENTERTAINMENT,
17-19 Soho Square, London
W1V 6HE.
071-734-8181

SOUTHERN RECORDS,
P O Box 59, London N22 1AR.
081-888-8949

SUBURBAN BASE RECORDS,
3 Old Mill Parade, Victoria Road,
Romford, Essex RM1 2HU.
0708-727029

SURVIVAL RECORDS LTD,
P O Box 888, Maidenhead,
Berkshire SL6 2YQ.
0628-788700

SWANYARD RECORDS,
12-27 Swan Yard, London N1 1SD.
071-354-3737

● **TALKIN' LOUD RECORDS,**
Chancellor's House, 72
Chancellor's Road, Hammersmith,
London W6 9RS.
081-741-1212

TELSTAR RECORDS PLC,
Prospect Studio, Barnes High
Street, London SW13 9LE.
081-878-7888

TEN RECORDS,
Kendal House, 553-579 Harrow
Road, London W10 4RH.
081-968-6688

**THAT'S ENTERTAINMENT
RECORDS,**
107 Kentish Town Road, London
NW1 8PD.
071-485-9593

THIRD MIND RECORDS,
15 Great Western Road, London
W9 3NW.
071-266-3454

THIS WAY UP,
10 Kendrick Mews, London
SW7 3HG.
071-584-9944

TOO PURE,
P O Box 1944, London NW10 5PJ.
071-609-2415

TOPIC RECORDS,
50 Stroud Green Road, London
N4 3EF.
071-263-6403

**TRANSATLANTIC RECORDS
LTD,**
52 Red Lion Street, London
WC1R 4PF.
071-242-9397

TRIBAL BASS,
21 Denmark Street, London
WC2H 8NA.
071-379-0038

TROJAN RECORDINGS LTD,
Twyman House, 31-39 Camden
Road, London NW1 9LF.
071-267-6899

● **ULTIMATE,**
271 Royal College Street, London
NW1 9LU.
071-482-0115

UNION CITY,
Kendal House, 553-579 Harrow
Road, London W10 4RH.
081-968-6688

● **VINYL SOLUTION,**
231 Portobello Road, London
W11.
071-792-9791

VIRGIN RECORDS LTD,
Kensal House, 553-579 Harrow
Road, London W10 4RH.
081-968-6688

● **WEA RECORDS LTD,**
The Warner Building, 28a
Kensington Church Street, London
W8 4EP.
071-937-8844

WAU! MR MODO,
P O Box 483, Sheffield, Yorkshire
S1 2BY.
0742-725804

WARNER MUSIC (UK) LTD,
The Warner Building, 28a
Kensington Church Street, London
W8 4EP.
071-937-8844

WARP RECORDS,
Studio 2, 1 Brown Street,
Sheffield, Yorkshire S1 2BS.
0742-757586

WIIIJA,
130 Talbot Road, London
W11 1JA.
071-229-8541

WORKERS PLAYTIME,
64 Mountgrove Road, London
N5 2LT.
071-354-5455

● **XL RECORDING,**
17-19 Alma Road, London
SW18 1AA.
081-870-9912

● **ZTT RECORDS LTD,**
The Blue Building, 42-46 St Lukes
Mews, London W11 1DG.
071-221-5101

ZOMBA RECORDS LTD,
Zomba House, 165-167 Willesden
High Road, London NW10 2SG.
081-459-8899

Music Publishers

● **ALL BOYS MUSIC,**
4-7 The Vineyard, Sanctuary
Street, London SE1 1QL.
071-403-0007

ANXIOUS MUSIC,
Devonshire House, 2-4 The
Broadway, Crouch End, London
N8 9SN.
081-341-4322

ARIWA SOUNDS,
34 Whitehorse Lane, London
SE25 6RE.
081-653-7744

ATMOSPHERE MUSIC LTD,
65 Maltings Place, Bagleys Lane,
London SW6 3AR.
071-371-5888

ATOMIC SONGS,
32 Neal Street, London
WC2H 9PS.
071-240-0616

AUDIO NAMES,
4 Auckland Court, London
SE27 9PE.
081-761-0178

● **BBC ENTERPRISES LTD,**
Woodlands, 80 Wood Lane,
London W12 0TT.
081-743-5588

BMG MUSIC PUBLISHING LTD,
Bedford House, 69-79 Fulham
High Street, London
SW6 3JW.
071-973-0980

BTW MUSIC,
125 Myddleton Road, Wood
Green, London N22 4NG.
081-888-6655

BASEHEAD MUSIC,
1st Floor, 21 Denmark Street,
London WC2H 8NE.
071-379-9808

BELSIZE MUSIC LTD,
29 Manor House, Marylebone
Road, London NW1 5NP.
071-723-7177

BIG LIFE MUSIC LTD,
15 Little Portland Street, London
W1N 5DE.
071-323-2888

BOCU MUSIC LTD,
1 Wyndham Place, London
W1H 1AR.
071-402-7433

**BOOSEY & HAWKES MUSIC
PUBLISHERS LTD,**
295 Regent Street, London
W1R 8JH.
071-580-2060

BROTHERS ORGANISATION,
Falcon Mews, Oakmead Road,
London SW12 9SJ.
081-675-5584

● **CAMBELL CONNELLY & CO
LTD,**
8-9 Frith Street, London
W1V 5TZ.
071-434-0066

CARLIN MUSIC CORPORATION,
Iron Bridge House, 3 Bridge
Approach, Chalk Farm, London
NW1 8BD.
071-734-3251

**CATALYST (MUSIC
PUBLISHING) LTD,**
171 Southgate Road, London
N1 3LE.
071-359-2974

CATHEDRAL MUSIC,
Maudlin House, Westhampnett,
Chichester, Sussex
PO18 0PB.
0243-776325

CAVELL MUSIC LTD,
26 Goodge Street, London
W1P 1FG.
071-580-4740

CAVENDISH MUSIC CO LTD,
295 Regent Street, London
W1R 8JH.
071-580-2060

CELTIC MUSIC,
24 Mercer Row, Louth,
Lincolnshire LN11 9JJ.
0507-606371

**CHARISMA MUSIC
PUBLISHING,**
24 Ives Street, London NW3 2ND.
071-581-0261

CHARLY PUBLISHING LTD,
156-166 Ilderton Road, London
SE15 1NT.
071-732-5647

CHARMING MUSIC LTD,
56-60 Islington Park Street,
London N1 1PX.
071-354-3414

**CHELSEA MUSIC PUBLISHING
CO LTD,**
70 Gloucester Place, London
W1H 4AJ.
071-224-0066

CHILDISH RECORDS,
130 London Road, London
SE1 6LF.
071-620-1383

CHRYSALIS MUSIC LTD,
The Chrysalis Building, Bramley
Road, London W10 6SP.
071-221-2213

CITYBEAT,
17-19 Alma Road, London
SW18 1AA.
081-870-9912

COOKING VINYL,
Unit 2, Park Mews, 213 Kilburn
Lane, London W10 4BQ.
081-960-6000

CORNUCOPIA MUSIC LTD,
29 North End Road, Golders
Green, London NW11 7RJ.
081-455-4707

CRAMER MUSIC LTD,
23 Garrick Street, London
WC2E 9AX.
071-240-1612

● **DE WOLFE MUSIC LTD,**
80-88 Wardour Street, London
W1V 3LF.
071-439-8481

DEAD DEAD GOOD MUSIC LTD,
2 Witton Walk, Northwich,
Cheshire CW9 5AT.
0606-44559

DEJAMUS LTD,
Suite 11, Accurist House, 44 Baker
Street, London W1M 1DH.
071-486-5838

DEMON MUSIC LTD,
Canal House, Stars Estate,
Transport Avenue, Brentford,
Middlesex TW8 9HF.
081-847-2481

● **EG MUSIC PUBLISHERS LTD,**
63a Kings Road, London SW3 4NT.
071-730-2162

EMI MUSIC PUBLISHING LTD,
127 Charing Cross Road, London
WC2H 0EA.
071-434-2131

EATON MUSIC LTD,
8 West Eaton Place, Belgravia,
London SW1X 8LS.
071-235-9046

EDWARD KASSNER MUSIC LTD,
Exmouth House, 11 Pine Street,
London EC1R 0JH.
071-837-5020

EMPIRE MUSIC LTD,
27 Queensdale Place, London
W11 4SQ.
071-602-5031

● **FFRR RECORDS,**
P O Box 1422, Chancellors House,
Chancellors Road, London
W6 9SG.
081-741-1234

FABER MUSIC LTD,
3 Queen Square, London
WC1N 3AU.
071-278-7436

FRESH AIR LTD,
3rd Floor, 9 Carnaby Street,
London W1V 1PG.
071-437-1958

● **GLOBAL MUSIC LTD,**
171 Southgate Road, London
N1 3LE.
071-359-2974

GO! DISCS MUSIC LTD,
72 Black Lion Lane,
Hammersmith, London W6 9BE.
071-748-7973

GREENSLEAVES RECORDS LTD,
Unit 14, Metro Centre, St Johns
Road, Isleworth, Middlesex
TW7 6NJ.
081-758-0564

● **HALLIN MUSIC LTD,**
8 Wendall Road, London W12 9RT.
081-746-1727

HALYCON MUSIC LTD,
11 Howitt Road, London NW3 4LT.
071-586-0288

**HANDLE GROUP OF
COMPANIES LTD,**
Handle House, 1 Albion Place,
Galena Road, Hammersmith,
London W6 0QT.
081-846-9111

HANDYMAN MUSIC LTD,
8 Seymour Place, London
W1H 5WF.
071-724-4648

HEART & SOUL MUSIC,
41 Blackhorse Road, London
E17 7AS.
081-521-2040

HEAVEN MUSIC,
P O Box 92, Gloucester,
Gloucestershire GL4 8HW.
0452-812442

HELM MUSIC PUBLISHING,
Helm House, Broadhurst Gardens,
London NW6 3QX.
071-328-0440

● IZM PUBLISHING & MANAGEMENT,
56 Beethoven Street, London W10 4LG.
081-960-1088

ISLAND MUSIC LTD,
334-336 King Street, London W6 0RA.
081-846-9141

● JOSEF WEINBERGER LTD,
12-14 Mortimer Street, London W1N 7RD.
071-580-2827

● KPM MUSIC LTD,
127 Charing Cross Road, London WC2H 0EA.
071-412-9111

KITCHENWARE RECORDS,
St Thomas Street Stables, St Thomas Street, Newcastle Upon Tyne, Tyne & Wear NE1 4LE.
091-232-4895

● LANSDOWNE RECORDING STUDIOS,
Lansdowne House, Lansdowne Road, London W11 3LP.
071-727-0041

LANTERN MUSIC PUBLISHING LTD,
32 Stafford Mansions, Stafford Place, London SW1E 6NL.
071-828-4595

LONDON MUSIC,
P O Box 1422, Chancellors House, Chancellors Road, London W6 9SG.
081-741-1234

● MCA MUSIC LTD,
Unit 9 Elsinore House, 77 Fulham Palace Road, Hammersmith, London W6 8JA.
081-741-8686

MPL COMMUNCATIONS,
1 Soho Square, London W1V 6BQ.
081-439-6621

MAD HAT MUSIC,
16 Hyde Park Place, Bayswater Road, London W2 2LP.
071-402-5083

MASTERSONG MUSIC (UK),
47 Kelburn Close, Chandlers Ford, Eastleigh, Hampshire SO5 2PW.
0703-267449

MAWSON & WAREHAM MUSIC LTD,
Midgy Hall, Sharperton, Morpeth, Northumberland NE65 7AS.
0669-40252

MEADOWMAN MUSIC,
Unit 3, 7 Chalcot Road, London NW1 8LH.
071-586-9433

MEMORY LAND MUSIC LTD,
22 Denmark Street, London WC2H 8NA.
071-240-5439

MINDER MUSIC LTD,
22 Bristol Gardens, London W9 2JQ.
071-289-7281

MIX MUSIC,
27 Newton Street, Holborn, London WC2B 5EL.
071-242-0415

MOMENTUM MUSIC LTD,
17-19 Alma Road, London SW18 1AA.
081-871-2121

MORRISON LEAHY MUSIC LTD,
1 Star Street, London W2 1QD.
071-258-0093

MULTIMEDIA MUSIC COMPANY LTD,
7 The Woodlands, Hither Green, London SE13 6TZ.
081-698-0534

● NEGUS-FANCY CO LTD,
8 Sunderland Terrace, London W2 5PA.
071-727-2063

NERVOUS MUSIC PUBLISHING,
7-11 Minerva Road, London NW10 6HJ.
081-963-0352

NEW AGE MUSIC,
100 Chalk Farm Road, London NW1 8EH.
071-485-0133

NOEL GAY ARTISTS,
6th Floor, 76 Oxford Street, London W1N 0AT.
071-836-3941

NOVELLO & CO LTD,
8 Lower James Street, London W1R 3PL.
071-287-5060

● OASIS MUSIC,
81 Wallingford Road, Goring, Reading, Berkshire RG8 0HL.
0491-873612

OBELISK MUSIC,
32 Ellerdale Road, London NW3 6BB.
071-435-5255

OPAL MUSIC,
330 Harrow Road, London W9 2HP.
071-286-9532

● PASSION RECORDS,
81 Crabtree Lane, London SW6 6LW.
071-381-8315

PEERMUSIC (UK) LTD,
8 Denmark Street, London WC2H 8LT.
071-836-4524

PERFECT SONGS,
The Blue Building, 42-46 St Luke's Mews, London W11 1DG.
071-221-5101

PERFECTO MUSIC LTD,
52 Chagford Street, London NW1 6EE.
071-224-8252

POLAR UNION LTD,
119-121 Freston Road, London W11 4BD.
071-243-0011

POLYGRAM INTERNATIONAL,
30 Berkeley Square London W1X 5HA.
071-493-8800

● RAK RECORDING STUDIOS,
42-48 Charlbert Street, London NW8 7BU.
071-586-2012

REALLY USEFUL GROUP LTD,
22 Tower Street, London WC2H 9NS.
071-240-0880

RED BUS MUSIC INTERNATIONAL,
34 Salisbury Street, London NW8 8QE.
071-402-9111

RHYTHM KING MUSIC,
Queens Studios, 121 Salusbury Road, Queens Park, London NW6 6RG.
071-372-5474

ROCKMASTERS MANAGEMENT LTD,
Brunswick Studios, 7 Westbourne Grove Mews, London W11 2RU.
071-727-8636

ROCKSONG MUSIC PUBLISHING LTD,
152 Goldthorn Hill, Penn, Wolverhampton, West Mids WV2 3JA.
0902-345345

RONDOR MUSIC (LONDON) LTD,
Rondor House, 10a Parsons Green, London SW6 4TW.
071-731-4161

ROUGH TRADE PUBLISHING,
81 Wallingford Road, Goring, Reading, Berkshire RG8 0HL.
0491-873612

RYKOMUSIC LTD,
Unit 3, The Linen House, 253 Kilburn Lane, London W10 4BQ.
081-964-3031

● S&J MUSIC LTD,
5 Paddington Street, London W1M 3LA.
071-935-1588

SBK SONGS,
127 Charing Cross Road, London WC2H 0EA.
071-434-2131

SCHAUER & MAY LTD,
67 Belsize Lane, Hampstead, London NW3 5AX.
071-794-8038

SCHOTT & CO LTD,
48 Great Marlborough Street, London W1V 2BN.
071-437-1246

SHAPIRO BERNSTEIN & CO LTD,
8-9 Frith Street, London W1V 5TZ.
071-434-0066

SONET RECORDS LTD,
78 Stanley Gardens, London W3 7SN.
081-746-1234

SONY MUSIC PUBLISHING,
17-19 Soho Square, London W1V 6HE.
071-734-8181

SOUTHERN MUSIC PUBLISHING CO LTD,
8 Denmark Street, London WC2H 8LT.
071-836-4524

SURVIVAL RECORDS,
P O Box 888, Maidenhead, Berkshire SL6 2YQ.
0628-788700

● TKO PUBLISHING LTD,
P O Box 130, Hove, Sussex BN3 6QU.
0273-550088

TELSTAR RECORDS PLC,
Prospect Studio, Barnes High Street, London SW13 9LE.
081-878-7888

TONY HALL GROUP OF COMPANIES,
3rd Floor, 9 Carnaby Street, London W1V 1PG.
071-437-1958

● UNITED MUSIC PUBLISHERS LTD,
42 Rivington Street, London EC2A 3BN.
071-729-4700

UNIVERSAL EDITION (LONDON) LTD,
Warwick House, 9 Warwick Street, London W1R 5RA.
071-437-5203

● VALENTINE MUSIC GROUP,
7 Garrick Street, London WC2E 9AR.
071-240-1628

VIRGIN MUSIC (PUBLISHERS) LTD,
EMI Music Publishing Ltd, 127 Charing Cross Road, London WC2H 0EA.
071-434-2131

● WARNER CHAPPELL MUSIC LTD,
129 Park Street, London W1Y 3FA.
071-629-7600

WOLF MUSIC,
83 Brixton Water Lane, London SW2 1PH.
071-733-8088

● ZOMBA MUSIC PUBLISHERS LTD,
Zomba House, 165-167 Willesden High Road, London NW10 3SG.
081-459-8899

● **AIR LTD,**
AIR House, Spennymoor, County
Durham DL16 7SE.
0388-814632

ACHIEVEMENT MANAGEMENT,
Unit 3, 9-12 St Anne's Court,
Soho, London W1V 3AX.
071-515-2951

ADDICTIVE MANAGEMENT,
4 Birchfields Road, Manchester
M13 0XR.
061-225-5140

ADRIAN BOSS PROMOTIONS,
363-365 Harrow Road, London
W9 3NA.
081-964-0112

ALAN JAMES,
130 London Road, London
SE1 6LF.
071-620-1383

**ALAN ROBINSON
MANAGEMENT,**
Suite 3 Foundry Studios, 207
Putney Bridge Road, London
SW15 2WY.
081-870-5425

**ALL ROUND MUSIC
MANAGEMENT,**
30 Ives Street, London SE3 2ND.
071-581-0261

ALL TIME MANAGEMENT LTD,
The Basement, 754 Fulham Road,
London SW6 5SH.
071-731-5287

ALLIED MANAGEMENT,
76 Tottenham Court Road, London
W1P 9PA.
071-636-1174

**ARTIST MANAGEMENT
SERVICES,**
363-365 Harrow Road, London
W9 3NA.
081-968-5354

ASGARD,
125 Parkway, London NW1 7PS.
071-387-5090

AVALON PROMOTIONS,
25 Litchfield Street, London
WC2H 9NJ.
071-497-2656

● **BIG LIFE MANAGEMENT LTD,**
15 Little Portland Street, London
W1N 5DE.
071-323-3888

BIG ROCK TALENT,
28 Rosemont Road, Hampstead,
London NW3 6NE.
071-435-0101

BIGTIME MANAGEMENT,
42 Effingham Road, London
SE12 8NU.
071-403-0007

BLACK MAGIC MANAGEMENT,
296 Earls Court Road, London
SW5 9BA.
071-373-3849

BRIGHT MUSIC LTD,
Chelsea Walk, 2 Harwood Terrace,
London SW6 2AB.
071-384-1599

BRILLIANT MANAGEMENT,
20 Stamford Brook Avenue,
London W6 0YD.
081-846-9469

● **CMO MANAGEMENT
(INTERNATIONAL) LTD,**
Unit 32, Ransomes Dock, 35-37
Park Gate Road, London
SW11 4NP.
071-228-4000

CSA MANAGEMENT,
101 Chamberlayne Road, London
NW10 3ND.
081-960-8466

CHAKRA,
Avondale Coach House, London
Road East, Bathford, Bath
BA1 7RB.
0225-858028

CHILDISH MANAGEMENT,
130 London Road, London
SE1 6LF.
071-620-1383

CLUB CULTURE,
Unit 134-136 Holmes Buildings,
Wood Street, Liverpool,
Merseyside L1 4AQ.
051-709-7938

● **DAG PROMOTIONS CO LTD,**
126 Ashleigh Road, Mortlake,
London SW14 8PX.
081-876-4433

DBM,
172a Arlington Road, Camden,
London NW1 7HL.
071-284-2554

DAMAGE MANAGEMENT,
16 Lambton Place, London
W11 2SH.
071-229-2992

DANGEROUS MANAGEMENT,
438 Poole Road, Branksome,
Poole, Dorset BH12 1DG.
0202-768766

**DAVID JAYMES ASSOCIATES
LTD,**
P O Box 2902, London W11 2NF.
071-727-0576

**DECONSTRUCTION
MANAGEMENT,**
4th Floor, Bedford House, 69-79
Fulham High Street, London
SW6 3JW.
071-384-2298

DIVINE MANAGEMENT,
37 Bowness Crescent, London
SW15 3QN.
081-546-4590

ECCENTRIC DIRECTIONS,
294 Holloway Road, London
N7 4AH.
071-609-1575

**ECLIPSE ARTIST
MANAGEMENT,**
3 Armstrong Avenue, Stoke,
Coventry, West Mids.
0203-451231

● **EG MANAGEMENT LTD,**
63a King's Road, London
SW3 5XS.
071-730-2162

ELYSIAN MANAGEMENT LTD,
3rd Floor, Leeder House, 6 Erkine
Road, London NW3 3AJ.
071-722-7511

EMKAY ENTERTAINMENTS,
3-5 Slateford Road, Edinburgh,
Scotland EH11 1PA.
031-337-1707

**ENTERTAINMENT SERVICES &
MANAGEMENT,**
Empress Buildings, 380 Chester
Road, Manchester M16 9EA.
061-877-5579

ETERNAL MANAGEMENT,
55 Lark Lane, Liverpool,
Merseyside L17 8UW.
051-728-8400

● **FAR NORTH MUSIC,**
Cheapside Chambers, 43
Cheapside, Bradford, Yorkshire
BD1 4HP.
0274-306361

FICTION RECORDS LTD,
97 Charlotte Street, London
W1P 1LB.
071-323-5555

FORWARD MANAGEMENT,
Unit 2 Park Mews, 213 Kilburn
Lane, London W10 4BQ.
081-960-6000

● **GAILFORCE MANAGEMENT,**
30 Ives Street, London SW3 2ND.
071-581-0261

GORGEOUS MANAGEMENT,
1st Floor, 48 Princess Street,
Manchester M1 6HR.
061-228-1256

● **HALL OR NOTHING,**
8 Poplar Mews, Uxbridge Road,
London W12 7JS.
081-740-6288

**HANDLE GROUP OF
COMPANIES,**
Handle House, 1 Albion Place,
Galena Road, Hammersmith,
London W6 0QT.
081-846-9111

HEAVENLY RECORDS,
50-52 Monmouth Street, London
WC2H 9EP.
071-240-2474

HIT & RUN MANAGEMENT,
30 Ives Street, London SW3 2ND.
071-581-0261

HUGE & JOLLY MANAGEMENT,
56-60 Islington Park Street,
London N1 1PX.
071-354-3414

● **ICM ARTISTS (LONDON) LTD,**
Oxford House, 76 Oxford Street,
London W1R 1RB.
071-323-3223

INVASION GROUP,
17 Gosfield Street, London
W1P 7HE.
071-631-5221

● **JLP CONCERTS AND
MANAGEMENT,**
32 Holmes Road, London
NW5 3AB.
071-482-4535

JDF BLOWES ASSOCIATES,
P O Box 174, London WC1X 9XN.
071-713-7734

JACK BRUCE,
Mayfield, Alphamstone, Bures,
Suffolk CO8 5HW.
0787-269402

JEFF HANLON MANAGEMENT,
1 York Street, London W1H 1PZ.
071-487-2558

JOHN HENRY ENTERPRISES,
The John Henry Building, 16-24
Brewery Road, London N7 9NH.
071-609-9181

JOHN REID ENTERPRISES LTD,
32 Galena Road, Hammersmith,
London W6 0LT.
081-741-9933

● **KITCHENWARE RECORDS,**
St Thomas Street Stables, St
Thomas Street, Newcastle Upon
Tyne, Tyne & Wear NE1 4LE.
091-232-4895

● **LEGENDARY ARTISTS LTD,**
6 Pembridge Road, London
W11 3HL.
071-221-1522

**LEIGHTON-POPE
ORGANISATION,**
8 Glenthorne Mews, 115a
Glenthorne Road, Hammersmith,
London W6 0LJ.
081-741-4453

LIFETIME MANAGEMENT,
18 St George's Road, St
Margaret's, Twickenham,
Middlesex TW1 1QR.
081-892-4810

LONDON ARTISTS,
P O Box 1077, Slough, Berkshire
SL2 4DB.
0753-655432

LONDON MANAGEMENT LTD,
London Management House, 2-4
Noel Street, London W1V 3RB.
071-287-9000

LYSTER, PRYOR & TODD LTD,
Mews House, 33 Knox Street,
London W1H 1FS.
071-723-3271

● **MAD HAT MUSIC,**
16 Hyde Park Place, Bayswater
Road, London W2 2LP.
071-402-5803

Management

MANAGEMENT WORKS,
32 Galena Road, London
W6 0LT.
081-741-9933

**MANNA ENTERTAINMENTS &
MANAGEMENT LTD,**
3rd Floor, 9 Carnaby Street,
London W1V 1PG.
071-437-1958

MARSHALL ARTS LTD,
Leeder House, 6 Erkskine Road,
London SW3 3AJ.
071-586-3831

MATRIX MANAGEMENT,
37 Inglis Road, Ealing, London
W5 3RL.
081-992-0775

**MEL BUSH ORGANISATION
LTD,**
2-3 Petersham Place, London
SW7 5PX.
071-225-3722

METRO MANAGEMENT,
155d Holland Park Avenue,
London W11 4AU.
071-371-6211

**MIKE MALLEY
ENTERTAINMENTS,**
10 Holly Park Gardens, Finchley,
London N3 3NJ.
081-346-4109

MISMANAGEMENT,
754 Fulham Road, London
SW6 5SH.
071-731-7074

MIX MANAGEMENT,
27 Newton Street, Holborn,
London WC2B 5EL.
071-242-0415

MOJO RECORDS,
Flat 5, 69 St Quentin Avenue,
London W10 6NZ.
081-696-5322

**MUSIC FACTORY
MASTERMIXES,**
Hawthorne House, 5-7 Fitzwilliam
Street, Parkgate, Rotherham,
Yorkshire S62 6EP.
0709-710022

● **NEW CRAZY GANG,**
The Parson's Nose, 11
Archbishops Place, London
SW2 2AH.
081-671-5926

NO WAY REF!,
1026-1028 Harrow Road, London
NW10 5NN.
081-960-2225

NOEL GAY ARTISTS,
6th Floor, 76 Oxford Street,
London W1N 0AT.
071-836-3941

● **ON,**
19 All Saints Road, London
W11 1HE.
071-229-7661

OUR MANAGEMENT,
14a Longbeach Road, Battersea,
London SW11 5ST.
071-350-1195

● **PAN,**
21a Noel Street, London
W1V 3PD.
071-434-2345

PWL MANAGEMENT LTD,
The Borough, 4-7 The Vineyard,
Sanctuary Street, London
SE1 1QL.
071-403-0007

**PET SHOP BOYS
PARTNERSHIP,**
Studio 8, 27a Pembridge Villas,
London W11 3EP.
071-221-3355

PETE ZAK (MANAGEMENT),
P O Box 133, Malmesbury,
Wiltshire SN16 9SZ.
0666-577725

PINK POP RECORDS,
1 Hesketh Street, Liverpool,
Merseyside L17 8XJ.
051-727-7557

PIT BULL MANAGEMENT,
156-158 Gray's Inn Road, London
WC1X 8ED.
071-813-1386

POLAR UNION LTD,
119-121 Freston Road, London
W11 4BD.
071-243-0011

PRO-BANG MANAGEMENT,
148 Cavendish Mansions, London
EC1R 5EQ.
071-278-7292

PROTOCOL MANAGEMENT,
23a Benwell Road, Islington,
London N7 7BW.
071-607-9495

PURE MANAGEMENT,
9 Pembroke Mews, London
W8 6ER.
071-938-3555

● **RAW POWER MANAGEMENT,**
Unit 11, Grand Union Centre, West
Row, Ladbrook Grove, London
W10 5AX.
081-964-1777

**REAL LIFE LTD AND PAUL
LILLY LTD,**
122 Holland Park Avenue, London
W11 4UA.
071-221-3077

REALLY ORIGINAL GROUP,
118a Asken Road, Stamford
Brook, London W12 9BL.
081-740-1288

ROBERT REED ORGANISATION,
17 Greenacres, Duxford,
Cambridgeshire CB2 4RB.
0223-833894

ROCK HARD MANAGEMENT,
19d Pinfold Road, London
SW16 2SL.
081-677-8466

**ROCKMASTERS MANAGEMENT
LTD,**
Brunswick Studios, 7 Westbourne
Grove Mews, London
W11 2RU.
071-727-8636

**ROGER DAVIES MANAGEMENT
UK,**
37 Limerston Street, London
SW10 0BQ.
071-352-9607

**RUNNING DOG MANAGEMENT
LTD,**
Minka, Lower Hampton Road,
Sunbury, Middlesex TW16 5PR.
081-941-8180

● **SCAM LTD,**
120 Curtain Road, London
EC2A 3PJ.
071-739-0061

SDM LTD,
2nd Floor, 5 Paddington Street,
London W1M 3LA.
071-935-1588

SOS MANAGEMENT,
81 Harley House, Marylebone
Road, London NW1 5HF.
071-486-8794

SANCTUARY GROUP PLC,
The Colonnades, 82 Bishop's
Bridge Road, London W2 6BB.
071-243-0640

SELECT MANAGEMENT,
8 Woodnook Way, Ashgate,
Chesterfield, Derbyshire S42 7PZ.
0246-569873

SERIOUS SPEAKOUT,
42 Old Compton Street, London
W1V 5PB.
071-439-0807

SINCERE MANAGEMENT,
421 Harrow Road, London
W10 4RD.
081-960-4438

SINCLAIR MANAGEMENT,
St Peters House, Hewitt Street,
Manchester M15 4GB.
061-228-3555

SOLID BOND PRODUCTION LTD,
45-53 Sinclair Road, London
W14 0NS.
071-602-6351

SOLO MANAGEMENT,
55 Fulham High Street, London
SW6 3JJ.
071-736-5925

SOME BIZARRE,
166 New Cavendish Street,
London W1M 7FJ.
071-631-3140

SOUTHERN STUDIOS,
P O Box 59, London
N22 1AR.
081-888-8949

STARGARD ORGANISATION,
Conisgold House, 302-304
Wellingborough Road,
Northampton, Northamptonshire
NN1 4EP.
0604-34105

STEVE BLACKWELL,
145c Crouch Hill, London
N8 9QH.
081-348-4465

SWANYARD MANAGEMENT,
12-27 Swan Yard, London
N1 1SD.
071-354-3737

● **TALENT ARTISTS LTD,**
4 Mews House, Princes Lane,
London N10 3LU.
081-444-4088

TONY BEARD MANAGEMENT,
145a Ladbroke Grove, London
W10 6HJ.
071-221-8353

**TONY HALL GROUP OF
COMPANIES,**
3rd Floor, 9 Carnaby Street,
London W1V 1PG.
071-437-1958

● **UP LATE MANAGEMENT,**
212 Dalling Road, London
W6 0ER.
081-748-5331

● **VAGUE MANAGEMENT,**
Top Floor, 940 Sauchiehall Street,
Glasgow, Scotland G3 7TH.
041-339-2263

VALUE ADDED TALENT,
1-2 Purley Place, London N1 1QA.
071-704-9720

**VERY DAB MANAGEMENT
COMPANY,**
147 Crouch Hill, London N8 9QH.
081-340-6004

● **WAU! MR MODO,**
P O Box 483, Sheffield, S1 2BY.
0742-725804

WAR ZONES,
33 Kersley Road, London
N16 0NT.
071-249-2894

WILD! MANAGEMENT,
Brunswick Studios, 7 Westbourne
Grove Mews, London W11 2RU.
071-727-0608

● **XL TALENT,**
Studio 7, 27a Pembridge Villas,
London W11 3EP.
071-938-1917

● **ZOMBA PRODUCTIONS,**
Zomba House, 165-167 Willesden
High Road, Willesden, London
NW10 2SG.
081-459-8899

● **ALAN JAMES PR,**
1st Floor, 130 London Road,
London SE1 6LF.
071-620-1383

ANGLO PLUGGING,
72 Black Lion Lane,
Hammersmith, London W6 9BE.
081-748-3297

**APPEARING MEDIA
PROMOTIONS,**
61-71 Collier Street, London
N1 9BE.
071-833-2841

● **BAD MOON,**
19 All Saints Road, London
W11 1HE.
071-221-9612

BCR PLUGGING,
95 Spencer Street, Birmingham,
West Mids B18 6DA

BEER DAVIS,
50 Margaret Street, London
W1N 7FD.
071-323-3003

BRASSNECK,
Warehouse D, 6th Floor,
Metropolitan Wharf, Wapping Wall,
London E1 9SS.
071-481-2172

● **CHRIS CARR PR,**
34-5 D'Arblay Street, London
W1V 3FE.
071-734-2712

● **DISC CONNECT,**
43 Stafford Street, Norwich
NR2 3BD.
0603-250020

● **EXCESS PRESS,**
83 Clerkenwell Road, London
EC1R 5AR.
071-430-9060

● **FRONTIER PROMOTION,**
115 Old Lodge Lane, Purley,
Surrey. CR2 4DP.
081-668-3457

● **HALL OR NOTHING PR,**
8 Poplar Mews, Uxbridge Road,
London W12 7JS.
081-740-6288

● **JUDY TOTTON,**
6 Archway Street, London
SW13 0AR.
071-371-8159

● **LOWE PROFILE PUBLICITY,**
Studio 406, Panther House, 38
Mount Pleasant, London
WC1X 0AP.
071-837-2655

● **MAGGI FARRAN PR,**
110 Canalot Studios, 222 Kensal
Road, London W10 5BN.
081-960-6309

● **NEWS PR AGENCY,**
14-15 D'Arblay Street, London
W1V 3FP.
071-437- 3588

NTT MEDIA,
P O Box 132, London W3 8XQ.
081-877-0321

● **POOLE EDWARDS,**
2nd Floor, 44 Charlotte Street,
London W1P 1HA.
071-436-3633

POWER PROMOTIONS,
32 Holmes Road, Kentish Town,
London NW5 3AB.
071-482-0728

PRESS COUNSEL,
1st Floor, 21 Denmark Street,
London WC2H 8NE.
071-379-9805

● **RAPTURE PROMOTIONS
(RTMP),**
98 St Pancras Way, London
NW1 9NF.
071-267-6222

REAL TIME PROMOTIONS,
69 Wells Street, London W1P 2RB.
071-436-7469

REVOLUTION PROMOTIONS,
17 Dorset Square, London
NW1 6QB.
071-724-6490

ROCK HARD PR,
19d Pinfold Road, London
SW16 2SL.
081-677-8466

RUSH RELEASE LTD,
Falcon Mews, Oakmead Road,
London SW12 9SJ.
081-675-4916

● **SAVIDGE AND BEST,**
172 Arlington Road, London
NW1 7HL.
071-284-1922

SINGLE MINDED PROMOTIONS,
32 Queensdale Road, Holland
Park, London W11 4SB.
071-602-5200

STATION II STATION,
322 Kentish Town Road, London
NW5 2TH.
071-482-5272

STONE IMMACULATE,
Studio 2, 8 Nursery Road, London
SW9 8BP.
071-738-7707

SUBSTANCE,
Devonshire House, 12 Barley Mow
Passage, London W4 4PH.
081-995-2325

● **TONY BEARD PRESS,**
145a Ladbroke Grove, London
W10 6HJ.
071-221-8353

TYGER,
621 Green Lanes, London N8 1AA.
081-348-1716

● **WAYWARD,**
Unit 401-444, Brixton Road,
London SW9 8EJ.
071-978-8611

WOODSTOCK PROMOTIONS,
40 Brightling Road, Crofton Park,
London SE4 1SQ.
081-690-6777

● **X-RAY AIR PLAY
PROMOTIONS,**
12 Vale Court, South Vale,
Sudbury Hill, Harrow, Middlesex
HA1 3PJ.
081-423-2569

● **AIR LTD,**
Air House, Spennymoor, County
Durham DL16 7SE.
0388-814632

ABS AGENCY,
363-365 Harrow Road, London
W9 3NA.
081-968-5354

ACORN ENTERTAINMENTS,
Winterfold House, 46 Woodfield
Road, Kings Heath, Birmingham,
West Mids B13 9UJ.
021-444-7258

AGENCY,
370 City Road, London EC1V 2QA.
071-278-3331

ALLIED MANAGEMENT,
76 Tottenham Court Road, London
W1P 9PA.
071-636-1174

ASGARD,
125 Parkway, London NW1 7PS.
071-387-5090

AVENUE ARTISTES LTD,
47 The Polygon, Southampton,
Hampshire SO1 2BP.
0703-227077

● **BARRY CLAYMAN
CONCERTS,**
144 Wigmore Street, London
W1H 9FF.
071-486-1222

BIG CITY ARTISTES,
Kerrison Hall, 28 Kerrison Road,
London W5 5NW.
081-579-2748

BIG ROCK TALENT,
28 Rosemont Road, Hampstead,
London NW3 6NE.
071-435-0101

● **CENTRAL AGENCY,**
112 Gunnersbury Avenue, Ealing,
London W5 4HB.
081-993-7441

CHALMERS WOOD LTD,
79 West Regent Street, Glasgow,
Scotland G2 2AW.
041-332-4262

CLARION AND SEVEN MUSES,
47 Whitehall Park, London
N19 3TW.
071-272-4413

**CONCORDE INTERNATIONAL
ARTISTS LTD,**
Concorde House, 101 Shepherd's
Bush Road, London W6 7LP.
071-602-8822

● **EMKAY ENTERTAINMENTS,**
3-5 Slateford Road, Edinburgh,
Scotland EH11 1PA.
031-337-1707

● **FLYING MUSIC COMPANY
LTD,**
110 Clarendon Road, London
W11 2HR.
071-221-7799

FOX LTD,
Concorde House, 101 Shepherds
Bush Road, London W6 7LP.
071-602-8822

● **HAL CARTER
ORGANISATION,**
101 Hazelwood Lane , Palmers
Green, London N13 5HQ.
081-886-2801

**HELM INTERNATIONAL
BOOKINGS,**
Helm House, Broadhurst Gardens,
London NW6 3QX.
071-328-0440

● **ICM AND FAIR WARNING,**
The Plaza, 535 King's Road,
London NW10 0SZ.
071-376-8501

IAIN HILL PRESENTS,
P O Box 964, London N5 1XY.
071-254-3168

IMPACT TALENT,
3rd Floor, 145 Oxford Street,
London W1A 1TB.
071-439-4439

**INTERNATIONAL TALENT
BOOKING,**
Third Floor, 27a Floral Street,
Covent Garden, London
WC2E 9DQ.
071-379-1313

● **JOHN MARTIN PROMOTIONS,**
29 Hartfield Road, Wimbledon,
London SW19 3SG.
081-543-4457

● **LJD4 PRESENTATIONS,**
53 Keyes House, Dolphin Square,
London SW1V 3NA.
071-828-7132

● **LEIGHTON-POPE
ORGANISATION,**
8 Glenthorne Mews, 115a
Glenthorne Road, Hammersmith,
London W6 0LJ.
081-741-4453

● **MPI,**
Miracle Prestige International Ltd,
Bugle House, 21a Noel Street,
London W1V 3PD.
071-434-2345

**MISSION CONTROL ARTIST
AGENCY,**
63 Lant Street, London SE1 1QN.
071-417-7022

● **NOEL GAY ARTISTS,**
6th Floor, 76 Oxford Street,
London W1N 0AT.
071-836-3941

● **ONE ENTERTAINMENT
AGENCY,**
The Rowans, Hill Top, Baddesley
Ensor, Nr Atherstone,
Warwickshire CV9 2BG.
0827-713113

● **PERMANENT ARTISTS,**
32 Holmes Road, London
NW5 3AB.
071-482-4535

**PRIMARY TALENT
INTERNATIONAL,**
251-256 Upper Street, London
N1 1RY.
071-359-9000

PURPLE PALACE,
34a Flower Lane, Mill Hill, London
NW7 2JE.
081-959-2825

● **ROBERTO GERMAINS**
AGENCY, 19 Denmark Street,
London WC2H 8NJ.
071-836-3941

● **SESSION CONNECTION,**
110-112 Disraeli Road, London
SW15 2DX.
081-871-1212

● **SOLO AGENCY,**
55 Fulham High Street, London
SW6 3JJ.
071-736-5925

STAGE 2 (THE AGENCY),
Unit G, 44 St Pauls Crescent,
Camden, London NW1 9TN.
071-284-1868

● **UNIVERSAL BOOKING
AGENCY,**
141 Railton Road, London
SE24 0LT.
071-733-3181

● **VALUE ADDED TALENT,**
1-2 Purley Place, London N1 1QA.
071-704-9720

● **WALLY DENT
ENTERTAINMENTS,**
121a Woodlands Avenue, West
Byfleet, Surrey KT14 6AS.
0932-347885

**WASTED TALENT ARTISTS
AGENCY LTD,**
321 Fulham Road, London
SW10 9QL.
071-351-7421

WILLIAM MORRIS AGENCY,
31-32 Soho Square, London
W1V 5DG.
071-434-2191

Booking Agents

● **APT DISTRIBUTION LTD,**
The Grain Store, 74 Eldon Street, York, Yorkshire YO3 7NE.
0904-611656

● **BMG OPERATIONS,**
Lyng Lane, West Bromwich, West Mids B70 7ST.
021-500-5545

BACKS RECORDING CO LTD,
St Mary's Works, St Mary's Plain, Norwich, Norfolk NR3 3AF.
0603-626221

● **CM DISTRIBUTION,**
2-4 High Street, Starbeck, Harrowgate, Yorkshire HG1 7HY.
0423-888979

CADILLAC RECORDS,
61-71 Collier Street, London N1 9DF.
071-278-7391

CHARLY RECORDS LTD,
156-166 Ilderton Road, London SE15 1NT.
071-639-8603

CONIFER RECORDS LTD,
Horton Road, West Drayton, Middlesex UB7 8JL.
0895-447707

● **DIRECT DISTRIBUTION,**
50 Stroud Green Road, London N4 3EF.
071-281-3465

● **FOLK SHOP & FOLK MAIL,**
Cecil Sharp House, 2 Regent's Park Road, London NW1 7AY.
071-485-2206

● **GREYHOUND RECORDS LTD,**
130a Plough Road, Battersea, London SW11 2AA.
071-924-1166

● **HARMONIA MUNDI UK LTD,**
19-21 Nile Street, London N1 7LR.
071-253-0863

● **JAZZ MUSIC,**
Glenview, Moylegrove, Cardigan, Dyfed, Wales SA43 3BW.
0923-86278

JETSTAR LTD,
155 Acton Lane, Park Royal, London NW10 7NJ.
081-961-5818

JUNGLE RECORDS,
Old Dairy Mews, 62 Chalk Farm Road, London NW1 8AN.
071-267-0171

● **MUSIC COLLECTION INTERNATIONAL,**
Strand VC1 House, 36-38 Caxton Way, Watford Business Park, Hertfordshire WD1 8UF.
0923-255558

MUSIC MASTERS LTD,
The End House, Gurnells Road, Seer Green, Buckinghamshire HP9 2XJ.
0494-672803

● **NERVOUS RECORDS,**
Unit 6, 7-11 Minerva Road, London NW10 6HJ.
081-963-0352

● **OLDIES UNLIMITED,**
Halesfield 10, Telford, Shropshire TF7 4LQ.
0952-684578

● **PANTHER MUSIC LTD,**
Unit 4, Chapmans Park Estate, 378-388 High Road, Willesden, London NW10 2DY.
081-459-1212

PICKWICK GROUP PLC,
Pickwick House, The Waterfront, Elstree Road, Elstree, Hertfordshire WD6 3BS.
081-207-6207

PINNACLE RECORDS,
Electron House, Cray Avenue, St Mary Cray, Orpington, Kent BG5 3NP.
0689-870622

POLYGRAM RECORD OPERATIONS,
Clyde Works, Grove Road, Chadwell Heath, Romford, Essex RM6 4QR.
081-590-6088

PRESIDENT RECORDS LTD,
Exmouth House, 11 Pine Street, London EC1R 0JH.
071-837-5020

● **RARE RECORDS LTD,**
13 Bank Square, Wilmslow, Cheshire SK9 1AN.
0625-522017

REVOLVER APT,
The Mezzanine, Portland House, 22-24 Portland Square, Bristol, Avon.
0272-446777

REVOLVER DISTRIBUTION LTD,
3 Dove Lane, Bristol, Avon BS2 9HP.
0272-540004

RIO COMMUNICATIONS LTD,
P O Box 36, Clyde Works, Grove Road, Chadwell Heath, Romford, Essex RM6 4QR.
081-983-8633

ROSS RECORDS,
29 Main Street, Turrif, Aberdeenshire, Scotland AB53 7AB.
0888-62403

RTM,
98 St Pancras Way, London NW1.
071-284-1155

● **SONY MUSIC OPERATIONS,**
Rabans Lane, Aylesbury, Buckinghamshire HP19 3BX.
0926-26151

SRD,
70 Lawrence Road, London N15 4EJ.
081-802-3000

● **TBD (TERRY BLOOD DISTRIBUTION),**
Unit 1, Rosevale Business Park, Newcastle Under Lyme, Staffordshire ST5 7QT.
0782-566566

TARGET RECORDS SALES LTD,
23 Gardner Industrial Estate, Kent House Lane, Beckenham, Kent BR3 1QZ.
081-778-4040

TOPIC DISTRIBUTION,
50 Stroud Green Road, London N4 3EF.
071-263-1240

THE TOTAL RECORD COMPANY LTD,
7 Pepys Court, 96 The Chase, London SW4 0NF.
071-978-2300

● **WEA RECORDS,**
P O Box 59, Alperton Lane, Wembley, Middlesex HA0 1FJ.
081-998-8844

WORK (UK) LTD,
9 Holdom Avenue, Bletchley, Milton Keynes, Buckinghamshire MK1 1QR.
0908-648440

● **ABBEY ROAD STUDIOS,**
3 Abbey Road, London NW8 9AY.
071-286-1161

● **BACKYARD STUDIO,**
Units 4 & 5 Willow Brook, Crickhowell Road, St Mellons, Cardiff, Wales CF3 0EF.
0222-777739

BANDWAGON STUDIOS,
Westfield Lane, Mansfield, Nottinghamshire NG18 1TL.
0623-422962

● **CHOP 'EM OUT,**
Trinity Mews, Cambridge Gardens, London W10 6JA.
081-960-8128

COPYMASTERS,
13 The Talina Centre, Bagley's Lane, London SW6 2BW.
071-731-5758

● **DUPLITAPE RECORDING SERVICES,**
37 Shaw Road, Heaton Moor, Stockport, Cheshire SK4 4AG.
061-442-6910

● **FAIRVIEW MUSIC,**
Great Gutter Lane, Willerby, Hull, Humberside, HU10 6DP.
0482-653116

● **GWBB AUDIOVISION,**
42 Lancaster Gate, London W2 3NA.
071-723-5190

GOLDDUST STUDIOS,
14 Cromwell Avenue, Bromley, Kent BR2 9AQ.
081-466-735

● **HIT FACTORY,**
31-37 Whitfield Street, London W1P 5RE.
071-636-3434

● **MAGNETIC DREAMS,**
3-4 Prospect Terrace, Farsley, Leeds, Yorkshire LS28 5ES.
0532-567961

MASTER ROOM CO LTD,
59-61 Ridinghouse Street, London W1P 7PP.
071-637-2223

MAX SOUND (LEEDS) LTD,
6 Stainbeck Lane, Leeds, Yorkshire LS7 3QY.
0532-370441

MIRROR CASSETTES,
346 North End Road, London SW6 1NB.
071-385-1751

MIRRORIMAGE,
474 Manchester Road, Heaton Chapel, Stockport, Cheshire SK4 5DL.
061-442-9045

● **NOTTINGHAM MUSICAL SERVICES,**
103 Radford Boulevard, Radford, Nottinghamshire NG7 3BS.
0602-706502

● **OCTAGON RECORDS & TAPES,**
PRE Complex, Roper Street, Pallion Industrial Estate, Sunderland, Tyne & Wear SR4 6SN.
091-565-8577

● **PRERECORD LTD,**
The Heritage Complex, Fleck Way, Stockton, Cleveland TS19 9JZ.
0642-762600

● **RMS STUDIOS,**
43-45 Clifton Road, London SE25 6PX.
081-653-4965

RTS LTD,
Units M1 & M2, Prescot Trade Centre, Albany Road, Prescot, Merseyside L34 2SH.
051-430-9001

REAL RECORDINGS LTD,
The Works, Unit 1, Britannia Road, Sale, Cheshire M33 2AA.
061-973-1884

REFLEX AUDIO SYSTEMS,
Unit 5, Cirrus Court, Glebe Road, Huntingdon, Cambridgeshire PE18 7DX.
0480-434333

● **SVS TAPE DISTRIBUTORS (UK) LTD,**
Shentonfield Road, Sharston Industrial Estate, Manchester M22 4RW.
061-491-6660

SELECTA SOUND,
5 Margaret Road, Romford, Essex RM2 5SH.
0708-453424

SILVERWORD LTD,
Crickhowell, Powys, Wales NP8 1LB.
0873-810142

SOUND CELLAR,
2-4 Trinity Mews, Cambridge Gardens, London W10 6JA.
081-969-9488

● **TAPE DUPLICATION CO,**
77 Barlow Road, Stannington, Sheffield, Yorkshire S6 5HR.
0742-330033

THE EXCHANGE,
42 Bruges Place, Randolph Street, London NW1 0TX.
071-485-0530

TOUCHSTONE,
Units 1-15, Southend Road Industrial Estate, Bungay, Suffolk NR35 1DP.
0986 892349

TOWNHOUSE TAPE COPYING,
150 Goldhawk Road, London W12 8HH.
081-743-9313

TRANSFERMATION,
63 Lant Street, London SE1 1QN.
071-417-7021

● **WHITE HOUSE SOUND,**
24a Brookfield Street, Syston, Leicestershire LE7 2AD.
0533-609401

● **ZELLA RECORDS (BIRMINGHAM) LTD,**
Walker Hall, Ampton Road, Edgbaston, West Mids BV15 2UJ.
021-455-0645

AIR LTD,
AIR House, Spennymoore, County
Durham DL16 7SE.
0388-814632

ACORN ENTERTAINMENTS,
Winterfold House, 40 Woodfield
Road, Kings Heath, Birmingham,
West Mids B13 9UJ.
021-444-7258

**ALLIED ENTERTAINMENTS
GROUP PLC,**
The Glassworks, 3-4 Ashland
Place, London W1M 3JH.
071-224-1992

ALTERNATIVE ARTS,
49-51 Carnaby Street, London
W1V 1PF.
071-287-0907

ANDREW MILLER CONCERTS,
55 Fulham High Street, London
SW6 3JJ.
071-736-5500

ANOTHER PLANET,
39 Pall Mall Deposit, 124-128
Barlby Road, London W10 6BL.
081-960-1811

ASGARD,
125 Parkway, London NW1 7PS.
071-387-5090

AVALON PROMOTIONS,
25 Litchfield Street, London
WC2H 9NJ.
071-497-2656

● BRIAN RIX & ASSOCIATES,
P O Box 100, Ashford, Kent
TN24 8AR.
0223-633652

● CLUB CULTURE,
Unit 134-136 Holmes Buildings,
Wood Street, Liverpool,
Merseyside L1 4AQ.
051-709-7938

**COSMOS AGENCY &
PROMOTIONS,**
26a Bellevue Crescent, Edinburgh,
Scotland EH3 6NF.
031-558-3146

● DANCE FACTORY,
20 Dunhead Of Gray, Dundee,
Scotland DD2 5JX.
0382-561166

**DEREK BLOCK
INTERNATIONAL ARTISTS,**
9-11 Richmond Buildings, London
W1V 5AF.
071-434-2100

● EEC LTD,
1-2 Munro Terrace, London
SW10 0DL.
071-351-3355

● FEEDBACK PROMOTIONS,
9a Well Street, Great Torrington,
Devon EX38 7DP.
0805-22730

FLYING MUSIC COMPANY LTD,
110 Clarendon Road, London
W11 2HR.
071-221-7799

● GLOBALDALE,
20 Ascham Street, Kentish Town,
London NW5 2PD.
071-482-0878

GRANT JAMES MUSIC LTD,
67 Old Kent Road, London
SE1 4RF.
071-252-2002

● HARVEY GOLDSMITH,
The Glassworks, 3-4 Ashland
Place, London W1M 3JH.
071-224-1992

HETHERINGTON SEELIG,
35 Little Russell Street, London
WC1A 2HA.
071-637-5661

● IAIN HILL PRESENTS,
P O Box 964, London N5 1XY.
071-254-3168

**INTERNATIONAL TALENT
BOOKING,**
3rd Floor, 27a Floral Street,
Covent Garden, London
WC2E 9DQ.
071-379-1313

**● JLP CONCERTS AND
MANAGEMENT,**
32 Holmes Road, London
NW5 3AB.
071-482-4535

JOHN BURROWS,
Capital Radio Ltd, Euston Tower,
London NW1 3DR.
071-608-6277

JOHN MARTIN PROMOTIONS,
29 Hartfield Road, Wimbledon,
London SW19 3SG.
081-543-4457

**● KITCHENWARE
INDEPENDENT RECORDINGS,**
St Thomas Street Stables, St
Thomas Street, Newcastle Upon
Tyne, Tyne & Wear NE1 4LE.
091-232-4895

**● LIVEWIRE GROUP OF
COMPANIES,**
P O Box 244, Barnet, Hertfordshire
EN4 0PN.
081-364-1212

● MCP LTD,
16 Birmingham Road, Walsall,
West Mids WS1 2NA.
0922-20123

MALCOLM FELD AGENCY,
7 The Old Quarry, Quarry Street,
Woolton, Liverpool, Merseyside
L25.
051-421-1441

MARSHALL ARTS LTD,
Leeder House, 6 Erskine Road,
London NW3 3AJ.
071-586-3831

MEL BUSH ORGANISATION LTD,
2-3 Petersham Place, London
SW7 5PX.
071-225-3722

METROPOLIS MUSIC,
491a Holloway Road, London
N19 4DD.
071-272-2442

● ORANGE MUSIC LTD,
3 North End Crescent, North End
Road, West Kensington, London
W14 8TG.
071-371-4317

**● PAUL CROCKFORD
MANAGEMENT,**
56-60 Islington Park Street,
London N1 1PX.
071-354-3414

● RIVERMAN,
91 Finborough Road, London
SW10 9DU.
071-244-6660

● SGB ENTERTAINMENTS,
12 Rutland Street, Hanley, Stoke
on Trent, Staffordshire ST1 5JG.
0782-279309

**SCOUNDREL MUSIC
CONCERNS,**
36 Upland Crescent, Leeds,
Yorkshire LS8 2TB.
0532-400285

SERIOUS SPEAKOUT,
42 Old Compton Street, London
W1V 5PB.
071-439-0807

SHOW ME PROMOTIONS,
Block C, Imperial Works, Perren
Street, Kentish Town, London
NW5 3ED.
071-267-4555

SOLO PROMOTIONS,
55 Fulham High Street, London
SW6 3JJ.
071-736-5925

● TKO PROMOTIONS LTD,
P O Box 130, Hove, Sussex
BN3 6QU.
0273-550088

TOTAL MUSIC CO LTD,
42 Swaby Road, London
SW18 3RA.
081-947-9978

TRYCLOPS,
115 New Barn Lane, Cheltenham,
Gloucestershire GL52 3LQ.
0242-234045

● WORKERS BEER CO LTD,
177 Lavender Hill, London
SW7 5TE.
071-228-5169

FIRSTCALL,
73-75 Endell Street, London
WC2H 9AJ.
071-836-9001

PREMIER BOX OFFICE,
188 Shaftesbury Avenue, London
WC2H 8JN.
071-240-2245

STAR GREEN BOX OFFICE LTD,
20-21a Argyll Street, London
W1V 1AA.
071-734-8932

T&C STATION LTD,
9-17 Highgate Road, Kentish
Rown, London NW5 1JY.
071-284-1221

TICKETMASTER LTD,
48 Leicester Square, London
WC2H 7LR.
071-344-4000

● BURLEY & CO,
6 Portugal Street, London
WC2A 2HH.
071-404-4002

● CLINTONS,
Wellington House, 6-9 Upper St
Martin's Lane, London WC2H 9DF.
071-379-6080

● DAVENPORT LYONS,
1 Old Burlington Street, London
W1X 1LA.
071-287-5353

● EATONS,
22 Blades Court, Deodar Road,
Putney, London SW15 2NU.
081-877-9727

● FRERE CHOLMELEY,
4 John Carpenter Street, London
EC4Y 0NH.
071-615-8000

● HARBOTTLE & LEWIS,
Hanover House, 14 Hanover
Square, London W1R 0BE.
071-629-7633

HART-JACKSON & HALL,
3a Ridley Place, Newcastle Upon
Tyne, Tyne & Wear NE1 8JQ.
091-232-1987

HEPBURN,
Blenheim House, Blenheim Grove,
Peckham, London SE15 4QX.
071-639-9991

HILLS SEARLE,
322 King Street, Hammersmith,
London W6 0RR.
081-563-0222

HOLMAN, FENWICK & WILLAN,
Marlow House, Lloyd's Avenue,
London EC3N 3AL.
071-488-2300

● KELLY MUSIC LTD,
West Wing House, Beacon Hill
Park, Churt Road, Hindhead,
Surrey GU26 6HU.
0428-605771

**● LEE & THOMPSON
SOLICITORS,**
Green Garden House, St

Christopher's Place, London
W1M 5HD.
071-935-4665

● RUSSELLS,
Regency House, 1-4 Warwick
Street, London W1R 5WB.
071-439-8692

● SALAMONS,
5-8 Lower John Street, Golden
Square, London W1R 3PE.
071-439-0388

SIMKINS PARTNERSHIP,
45-51 Whitfield Street, London
W1P 5RJ.
071-631-1050

**STARGARD ORGANISATION
(BAILIFFS),**
Conisgold House, 302-304
Wellingborough Road,
Northampton, Northamptonshire
NN1 4EP.
0604-34105

● WILLIAMS & PHILLIPS,
216 Tower Bridge Road, London
SE1 2UP.
071-378-7779

WOOLF SEDDON,
5 Portman Square, London
W1H 9PS.
071-486-9681

● **AUDIO MEDIA,**
Media House, Burrell Road, St
Ives, Cambridgeshire PE17 4LE.
0480-61244

● **BILLBOARD,**
23 Ridgemount Street, London
WC1E 7AH.
071-323-6686

BLUES & SOUL,
153 Praed Street, London W2 1RL.
071-402-6869

● **CD REVIEW,**
Media House, Boxwell Road,
Berkhamstead, Hertfordshire
HP4 3ET.
0442-876191

COSMOPOLITAN,
National Magazine House, 72
Broadwick Street, London
W1V 2BP.
071-439-7144

● **DAILY EXPRESS,**
Ludgate House, 245 Blackfriars
Road, London SE1 9UX.
071-928-8000

DAILY MAIL,
Northcliffe House, 2 Derry Street,
Kensington, London W8 5TT.
071-938-6000

DAILY MIRROR,
Holborn Circus, London
EC1P 1DQ.
071-353-0246

DAILY STAR,
Ludgate House, 245 Blackfriars
Road, London SE1 9UX.
071-928-8000

DAILY TELEGRAPH,
Peterborough Court, South Quay,
181 Marsh Wall, London E14 9SR.
071-538-5000

DEADLINE, 36
Leroy Street, London SE1 4SS.
071-232-2840

DJ,
4th Floor, Centro House, Mandela
Street, Camden, London
NW1 0DU.
071-387-3848

● **ECHOES,**
15-16 Newman Street, London
W1P 3HD.
071-436-4540

● **THE FACE,**
3rd Floor, Block A, Exmouth
House, Pine Street, London
EC1R 0JL.
071-837-7270

FOR THE RECORD,
57-63 Brownfields, Welwyn
Garden City, Hertfordhire AL7 1AN.
0707-375167

● **THE GUARDIAN,**
119 Farringdon Road, London
EC1R 3ER.
071-278-2332

GUITARIST,
Alexander House, Forehill, Ely,
Cambridgeshire CB7 4AF.
0353-665577

THE GUITAR,
4 Selsdon Way, London E14 9GL.
071-712-0550

● **HI-FI,**
Link House, Dingwall Avenue,
Croydon, Surrey CR9 2TA.
081-686-2599

HIP HOP CONNECTIONS,
Alexander House, Forehill, Ely,
Cambridgeshire CB7 4AX.
0353-665577

HIT THE DECKS,
Studio 4, 222 Kensal Road,
London W10 5BN.
081-960-2739

HOME & STUDIO RECORDING,
Alexander House, Forehill, Ely,
Cambridgeshire CB7 4AF.
0353-665577

● **I-D,**
5th Floor, Seven Dials Warehouse,
44 Earlham Street, London
WC2H 9LA.
071-240-3282

THE INDEPENDENT,
40 City Road, London EC1Y 2DV.
071-253-1222

● **JAZZ RAG,**
P O Box 944, Birmingham, West
Mids B16 8UT.
021-454-7020

● **KERRANG,**
51-55 Carnaby Street, London
W1V 1PF.
071-437-8050

KEYBOARD,
330 Hertford Road, London N19 7HB.
081-443-3690

● **LIGHTING & SOUND
INTERNATIONAL,**
7 Highlight House, St Leonards
Road, Eastbourne, Sussex
BN21 3UH.
0323-642639

LIME LIZARD,
Unit 2b, Aberdeen Studios, 22
Highbury Grove, London N5 3EA.
071-704-9767

LIVE!,
35 High Street, Sandridge, St
Albans, Hertfordshire AL4 9DD.
0727-843995

● **MAKING MUSIC,**
20 Bowling Green Lane, London
EC1R 0BD.
071-251-1900

MEDIA WEEK,
20-22 Wellington Street, London
WC2E 7DD.
071-379-5155

MELODY MAKER,
26th Floor, King's Reach Tower,
Stamford Street, London SE1 9LS.
071-261-6229

METAL CD,
P O Box 3205, London E14 9ZR.
071-712-0550

METAL HAMMER,
134b King Street, Hammersmith,
London W6 0RQ.
081-748-1200

MUSIC TECHNOLOGY,
Alexander House, Forehill, Ely,
Cambridgeshire CB7 4AX.
0353-665577

MUSIC WEEK,
245 Blackfriars Road, London
SE1 9UR.
071-620-3636

● **NEWS OF THE WORLD,**
1 Pennington Street, London E1 9BD.
071-782-5000

NEW MUSICAL EXPRESS,
25th Floor, King's Reach Tower,
Stamford Street, London SE1 9LS.
071-261-6472

NUMBER ONE,
35 Marylebone High Street,
London W1N 4AA.
071-927-5949

● **THE OBSERVER,**
Chelsea Bridge House,
Queenstown Road, London SW8 4NN.
071-627-0700

● **Q,**
Mappin House, 4 Winsley Street,
London W1N 7AR.
071-436-1515

● **RADIO TIMES,**
Woodlands, 80 Wood Lane,
London W12 0TT.
081-576-2000

RAW,
52-55 Carnaby Street, London
W1V 1PS.
071-437-8050

RIFF RAFF,
19 Islington Park Street, London
N1 1QB.
071-226-4695

ROCK CD,
P O Box 3205, London E14 9ZR.
071-712-0550.

ROCK POWER,
193 St John Street, London EC1 1EN.
071-253-4478

● **SELECT,**
Mappin House, 4 Winsley Street,
London W1N 7AR.
071-436-1515

SKY,
Mappin House, 4 Winsley Street,
London W1N 7AR.
071-436-1515

SMASH HITS,
52-55 Carnaby Street, London
W1V 1PF.
071-437-8050

SOUL CD,
P O Box 3205, London E14 9ZR.
071-712-0550

SOUND ON SOUND,
P O Box 30, St Ives,
Cambridgeshire PE17 4XQ.
0480-61244

STUDIO SOUND,
8th Floor, Ludgate House, 245
Blackfriars Road, London SE1 9UR.
071-620-3636

THE SUN,
1 Pennington Street, Wapping,
London E1 9BD.
071-782-4031

● **THE TELEGRAPH,**
181 Marsh Wall, South Quay,
London E14 9SR.
071-538-6492

THE TIMES,
1 Virginia Street, London E1 9XN.
081-782-5000

TIME OUT,
Tower House, Southampton
Street, London WC2 7HD.
071-836-4411

TV TIMES,
10th Floor, King's Reach Tower,
Stamford Street, London SE1 9LS.
071-261-7000

● **VOLUME,**
P O Box 699, London SW10 0LS.
071-351-4060

VOX,
25th Floor, King's Reach Tower,
Stamford Street, London SE1 9LS.
071-261-6312

● **APRS,**
2 Windsor Square, Silver Street,
Reading, Berkshire RG1 2TH.
0734-756218

ASCAP,
Suite 10-11, 52 Haymarket,
London SW1Y 4RP.
071-973-0069

● **BEA (BRITISH
ENTERTAINMENT AGENCIES),**
240 Tolworth Rise South,
Surbiton, Surrey TK5 9NB.
081-330-3070

BPI,
273-287 Regent Street, London
W1R 7PB.
071-629-8642

**BLACK MUSIC INDUSTRY
ASSOCIATION,**
146 Manor Park Road, Harlesden,
London NW10 4LT.
081-961-4857

**BRITISH ACADEMY OF
SONGWRITERS COMPOSERS &
AUTHORS (BASCA),**
34 Hanway Street, London
W1P 9DE.
071-436-2261

**BRITISH MUSIC INFORMATION
CENTRE,**
10 Stratford Place, London
W1N 9AE.
071-499-8567

● **IEAM (INSTITUTE OF
ENTERTAINMENT & ARTS
MANAGEMENT),**
3 Trinity Road, Scarborough,
Yorkshire YO11 2TD.
0723-367449

**INCORPORATED SOCIETY OF
MUSICIANS,**
10 Stratford Place, London
W1N 9AE.
071-629-4413

● **MCPS,**
Elgar House, 41 Streatham High
Road, London SW16 1ER.
081-769-4400

**MUSIC PUBLISHERS
ASSOCAION,**
3rd Floor, Strandgate, 18-20 York
Buildings, London WC2B 6QX.
071-839-7779

**MUSIC RETAILERS
ASSOCIATION,**
P O Box 249, London W4 5EX.
081-994-7592

**MUSICIANS BENEVOLENT
FUND,**
16 Ogle Street, London W1P 7LG.
071-636-4481

MUSICIANS UNION,
60-62 Clapham Road, London
SW9 0JJ.
071-582-5566

● **PERFORMING RIGHTS
SOCIETY LTD,**
29-33 Berners Street, London
W1P 4AA.
071-580-5544

**PHONOGRAPHIC
PERFORMANCE LTD,**
Ganton House, 14-22 Ganton
Street, London W1V 1LB.
071-437-0311

● **REGGAE MUSIC
ASSOCIATION UK,**
Suite B, 2 Tunstall Road, London
SW9 8DA.
071-738-7950

● BATH MOLES,
14 George Street, Avon BA1 2EN.
0225-333423

BIRMINGHAM ASTON UNIVERSITY,
Aston Street, Gosta Green, West Mids B4 7SH.
021-359-6531

BIRMINGHAM EDWARDS
No.8, Lower Severn Street, West Mids B1 1LR.
021-643-5835

BIRMINGHAM HUMMINGBIRD,
52 Dale End, City Centre, West Mids B4 7LS.
021-236-4236

BIRMINGHAM NEC,
Bickenhill, West Mids B40 1NT.
021-780-4133

BOURNEMOUTH INTERNATIONAL CENTRE.
Exeter Road, Dorset BH2 5BH.
0202-552122

BRADFORD ST GEORGE'S HALL,
Bridge Street, Yorkshire BD1 1JS.
0274-752000

BRIGHTON CENTRE,
Kings Road, East Sussex BN1 2GR.
0273-203131

BRIGHTON DOME COMPLEX,
29 New Road, East Sussex BN1 1UG.
0273-685097

BRIGHTON THE EVENT,
Kings West Centre, West Street, East Sussex BN1 2RE.
0273-732627

BRIGHTON UNIVERSITY OF SUSSEX,
Mandela Hall, Falmer House, Falmer, East Sussex BN1 9QF.
0273-698111

BRISTOL BIERKELLER,
The Pithay, All Saints Street, Avon BS1 2NA.
0272-268514

BRISTOL COLSTON HALL,
Colston Street, Avon BS1 5AR.
0272-223693

BRISTOL FLEECE & FIRKIN,
12 St Thomas Street, Avon BS1 6JJ.
0272-277150

BUCKLEY TIVOLI,
Brunswick Road, Clywdd, North Wales CH7 2EF.
0244-550782

● CAMBRIDGE ARTS THEATRE,
6 St Edward's Passage, Cambridgeshire CB2 3PL.
0223-355246

CAMBRIDGE CORN EXCHANGE,
3 Parson's Court, Wheeler Street, Cambridgeshire CB2 3QB.
0223-463204

CAMBRIDGE JUNCTION,
Clifton Road, Cambridgeshire CB1 4GX.
0223-412600

CARDIFF ST DAVID'S HALL,
The Hayes, South Glamorgan, Wales CF1 2SH.
0222-342611

CARDIFF UNIVERSITY,
Main Hall, Park Place, South Glamorgan, Wales CF1 3QN.
0222-396421

CARLISLE SANDS CENTRE,
The Sands, Cumbria CA1 1JQ.
0228-810208

CHELMSFORD ARMY & NAVY,
Army & Navy Roundabout, Parkway, Essex CM2 7PU.
0245-262424

COLCHESTER ARTS CENTRE,
Church Street, Essex CO1 1NF.
0206-577301

COLCHESTER ESSEX UNIVERSITY,
Wivenhoe Park, Essex CO4 3SQ.
0206-863211

CORNWALL COLISEUM,
Cornish Leisure World, Carlyon Bay, St Austell, Cornwall PL25 3RG.
0726-814261

COVENTRY TIC TOC,
Primrose Hill Street, Hillfields, West Mids CV1 5LY.
0203-632462

COVENTRY UNIVERSITY,
Priory Street, West Mids CV1 5FB.
0203-838445

COVENTRY WARWICK UNIVERSITY,
Arts Centre Hall, Gibbet Hill Road, West Mids CV4 7AL.
0203-524524

CRAWLEY THE HAWTH,
Hawth Avenue, West Sussex RH10 6YZ.
0293-552941

● DERBY ASSEMBLY ROOMS,
Market Place, Derbyshire DE1 3AH.
0332-369311

DERBY THE WHEREHOUSE,
110a Friargate, Derbyshire DE1 1EX.
0332-381169

DUNDEE FAT SAM'S,
31 South Ward Road, Tayside, Scotland DD1 1PU.
0382-26836

DUDLEY JB'S,
King Street, West Mids DY2 8PN.
0384-253597

● EAST GRINSTEAD DORSET ARMS,
101 Club, 58 High Street, West Sussex RH19 3DE.
0342-316363

EDINBURGH ASSEMBLY ROOMS,
54 George Street, Lothian, Scotland EH2 2LR.
031-220-4348

EXETER CAVERN CLUB,
83-84 Queen Street, Devon.
0392-495370

● FOLKESTONE LEAS CLIFF HALL,
The Leas, Kent CT20 2DZ.
0303-254695

● GLASGOW BARROWLANDS,
244 Gallow Gate, Glasgow, Strathclyde, Scotland G4 OTS.
041-552-4601

GLASGOW KING TUT'S WAH WAH HUT,
272a St Vincent Street, Strathclyde, Scotland G2 5RL.
041-248-5158

GLASGOW MAYFAIR BALLROOM AND VENUE,
490 Sauchiehall Street, Strathclyde, Scotland G2 3LW.
041-332-3872

GUILFORD CIVIC HALL,
London Road, Surrey GU1 2AA.
0483-444720

● HARLOW SQUARE,
4th Avenue, Harlow, Essex CN20 1DW.
0279-417029

HATFIELD FORUM,
Lemsford Road, Hertfordshire AL10 0EB.
0707-263117

HULL ADELPHI,
89 De Grey Street, Beverley Road, Humberside HU5 2RU.
0482-48216

HULL CITY HALL,
Queen Victoria Square, Humberside HU1 3NA.
0482-20123

● LEEDS DUCHESS OF YORK,
Vicar Lane, Yorkshire LS1 6QA.
0532-453929

LEEDS METROPOLITAN UNIVERSITY,
Caverley Street, Yorkshire LS1 3HE.
0532-430171

LEEDS TOWN & COUNTRY CLUB,
55 Cookridge Street, Yorkshire LS2 3AW.
0532-800100

LEICESTER DE MONTFORT HALL.
Granville Road, Leicestershire LE1 7RU.
0533-544444

LEICESTER PRINCESS CHARLOTTE,
8 Oxford Street, Leicestershire LE1 5XZ.
0533-553956.

LICHFIELD ARTS CENTRE,
Bird Street, Staffordshire WS13 6PR.
0543-262223

LIVERPOOL KRAZY HOUSE,
Wood Street, Merseyside.
051-708-5016

LIVERPOOL THE PICKET,
24 Hardman Street, Merseyside L1 9AX.
051-709-3995

LIVERPOOL ROYAL COURT,
Roe Street, Merseyside L1 1HH.
051-709-1808

● MANCHESTER ACADEMY,
Oxford Road, Greater Manchester M13 9PR.
061-275-2959

MANCHESTER APOLLO,
Stockport Road, Ardwick Green, Greater Manchester M12 6AP.
061-273-6921

MANCHESTER BAND ON THE WALL,
25 Swan Street, Greater Manchester M4 5JQ.
061-834-1786

MANCHESTER BOARDWALK,
Little Peter Street, Greater Manchester M15 4PS.
061-228-3555

MANCHESTER HACIENDA,
11-13 Whitworth Street West, Greater Manchester M1 5WG.
061-236-5051

MANCHESTER UNDERGROUND, UMIST UNION,
Sackville Street, Greater Manchester M60 1QD.
061-200-3270

MANCHESTER UNIVERSITY UNION,
Oxford Road, Greater Manchester M13 9PR.
061-275-2959

MANCHESTER WITCHWOOD,
152 Old Street, Ashton-Under-Lyne, Thameside, Greater Manchester OL6 7SJ.
061-344-0321

MIDDLESBROUGH TOWN HALL,
Albert Road, Cleveland TS1 1EL.
0642 263040

MILTON KEYNES NATIONAL BOWL,
Watling Street, Buckinghamshire.
0908-666520

● NEWCASTLE MAYFAIR SUITE,
Newgate Street, Tyne & Wear NE1 5XA.
091-232-3109

NEWCASTLE RIVERSIDE,
57-59 Melbourne Street, Tyne & Wear NE1 2JQ.
091-261-4386

NEWCASTLE UNIVERSITY,
Kings Walk, Tyne & Wear WE1 8AB.
091-232-8402

NEWPORT CENTRE,
Kingsway, Gwent, Wales NP9 1UH.
0633-841522

NORTHAMPTON ROADMENDER CENTRE,
1 Lady's Lane, Northamptonshire NN1 3AH.
0604-604222

NORWICH OVAL ROCKHOUSE,
Dereham Road, Norfolk NR5 8TD.
0603-748244

NORWICH UNIVERSITY OF EAST ANGLIA (UEA),
University Complex, Norfolk NR4 7TG.
0603-56161

NOTTINGHAM ROCK CITY,
8 Talbot Street, Nottinghamshire NG1 5GG.
0602-412544

NOTTINGHAM ROYAL CONCERT HALL.
South Sherwood Street, Nottinghamshire NG1 5ND.
0602-483505

NOTTINGHAM UNIVERSITY,
Social Committee, Portland Building, University Park, Nottinghamshire NG7 2RD.
0602-505912

● OXFORD APOLLO THEATRE,
George Street, Oxfordshire OX1 2AG.
0865-243041

OXFORD JERICHO TAVERN,
56 Walton Street, Oxfordshire OX2 6AE.
0865-54502

● POOLE ARTS CENTRE,
Wessex Hall, Kingland Road, Dorset BH15 1UG.
0202-670521

PORTSMOUTH PYRAMIDS CENTRE,
Clarence Esplanade, Southsea, Hampshire PO5 3ST.
0705-877895

PORTSMOUTH WEDGEWOOD ROOMS,
147b Albert Road, Southsea, Hampshire PO4 0JW.
0705-863911

● **READING UNIVERSITY,**
Whiteknights Park, Reading, Berkshire RG6 2AZ.
0734-860222

● **SALISBURY ARTS CENTRE,**
Bedwin Street, Wiltshire SP1 3UT.
0722-321744

SHEFFIELD ARENA,
Broughton Lane, South Yorkshire S9 2DS.
0742-562002

SHEFFIELD CITY HALL,
Bakers Pool, South Yorkshire S1 2JA.
0742-722885

SHEFFIELD LEADMILL,
6-7 Leadmill Road, South Yorkshire S1 4SF.
0742-754500

SHEFFIELD UNIVERSITY AND OCTAGON,
Western Bank, South Yorkshire S10 2TG.
0742-753300

SOUTHAMPTON JOINERS ARMS,
St Mary's Street, Hampshire SO1 1NS.
0703-225612

SOUTHAMPTON MAYFLOWER THEATRE,
Commercial Road, Hampshire SO1 0GE.
0703-330083

ST HELEN'S CITADEL,
Waterloo Street, Merseyside WA10 1PX.
0744-35436

STOKE WHEATSHEAF,
Church Street, Stoke On Trent, Staffordshire ST4 IBU.
0782-44438

● **TUNBRIDGE WELLS ASSEMBLY HALL,**
Crescent Road, Kent TN1 1RS.
0892-526121

TUNBRIDGE WELLS THE FORUM,
The Common, Kent.
0892-530411

● **UXBRIDGE BRUNEL UNIVERSITY,**
Kingston Lane, Middlesex UB8 3PH.
0895-239125

● **WHITLEY BAY ICE RINK,**
Hill Heads Road, Hill Heads, Tyne & Wear NE25 8HP.
091-252-6240

WINDSOR OLD TROUT,
River Street, Berkshire SL4 1HL.
0753-869897

WOLVERHAMPTON CIVIC HALL AND WULFREN HALL,
North Street, West Mids WV1 1RQ.
0902-312029

● **100 CLUB,**
100 Oxford Street, W1N 9FB.
071-636-0933

● **ACADEMY,**
211 Stockwell Road, Brixton, SW9 9SL.
071-326-1022

ALBANY EMPIRE,
Douglas Way, Deptford, SE8 4AG.
081-691-8016

ALEXANDRA PALACE,
Alexandra Park, Wood Green, N22 4AY.
081-365-2121

AMERSHAM ARMS,
The Gig, 388 New Cross Road, New Cross, SE14 6TY.
081-694-8992

ARENA,
Limeharbour, Isle Of Dogs, E14 9TH.
071-538-8880

ASTORIA,
157 Charing Cross Road, WC2H 0EN.
071-434-0403

● **BARBICAN CENTRE,**
Barbican Complex, EC2Y 8DS.
071-638-4141

BASS CLEF,
35 Coronet Street, N1 6NU.
071-729-2476

BLOOMSBURY THEATRE,
15 Gordon Street, Euston, WC1 0AH.
071-383-5876

BORDERLINE,
Orange Yard, Manette Street, W1V 5LB.
071-734-2095

BULL & GATE,
389 Kentish Town Road, Kentish Town, NW5 2TG.
071-485-5358

● **CAMDEN PALACE,**
1a Camden Road, Camden, NW1.
071-387-0428

CRICKETERS,
Kennington, Oval, SE11 5SG.
071-735-0718

● **DOME,**
178 Junction Road, Tufnell Park, N19 5QQ.
071-281-2195

DOMINION THEATRE,
Tottenham Court Road, W1P 0AG.
071-580-1889

DUBLIN CASTLE,
94 Parkway, Camden, NW1 7AN.
071-485-1773

● **EARLS COURT EXHIBITION CENTRE,**
Warwick Road, SW5 9TA.
071-385-1200

ELECTRIC BALLROOM,
184 Camden High Street, NW1 8QP.
071-485-9006

THE EMPIRE THEATRE,
291 Mare Street, Hackney, E8 1EJ.
071-986-0171

EQUINOX,
Leicester Square, WC2H 7NH.
071-437-1446

● **THE FALCON,**
234 Royal College Street, NW1 9LT.
071-485-3834

THE FORUM,
9-17 Highgate Road, Kentish Town, NW5 1JY.
071-284-2200

THE FRIDGE,
Town Hall Parade, Brixton Hill, SW2 1RJ.
071-326-5100

● **THE GARAGE,**
20-22 Highbury Corner, N5 1RD.
071-607-1818

THE GRAND,
St John's Hill, Clapham Junction, SW11 2RS.
071-738-9000

● **HALF MOON,**
13 Half Moon Lane, Herne Hill, SE24 9HU.
071-274-2733

THE HIPPODROME,
Hippodrome Corner, Leicester Square, WC2 7JH.
071-437-4837

● **INSTITUTE OF CONTEMPORARY ART (ICA),**
The Mall, SW1Y 5AH.
071-930-0493

● **JAZZ CAFE,**
5 Parkway, Camden, NW1 7PG.
071-916-6000

● **KING'S HEAD,**
4 Fulham High Street, SW6 3LQ.
071-736-1413

● **LABATT'S APOLLO,**
Queen Caroline Street, Hammersmith, W6 9QH.
081-741-4868

LE PALAIS,
242 Shepherd's Bush Road, W6 7NL.
081-748-2812

● **MARQUEE,**
105 Charing Cross Road, WC2H 0DT.
071-437-6603

MEAN FIDDLER AND ACOUSTIC ROOM,
24-28a High Street, Harlesden, NW10 4LX.
081-961-5490

● **THE ORANGE,**
North End Crescent, North End Road, West Kensington, W14 8TG.
071-371-4317

● **POWERHAUS,**
1 Liverpool Road, Islington, N1 0RP.
071-837-3218

● **QUEEN MARY COLLEGE,**
Mile End Road, London E1 4NS.
071-975-5555

● **RAILS,**
Zombie Club, Unit 3, Block D, Euston Station Concourse, NW1.
071-388-2221

THE ROBEY,
240 Seven Sisters Road, Finsbury Park, N4 2HX.
071-263-4581

ROCK GARDEN,
The Piazza, Covent Garden, WC2E 8HA.
071-240-3961

RONNIE SCOTT'S,
47 Frith Street, W1V 6HT.
071-439-0747

ROYAL ALBERT HALL,
Kensington Gore, SW7 2AP.
071-589-3203

ROYAL FESTIVAL HALL,
Belvedere Road, SE1 8XX.
071-928-0601

ROYAL STANDARD,
1 Blackhorse Lane, Walthamstow, E17 6DS.
081-527-1966

● **SAMUEL BECKETT,**
175 High Street, Stoke Newington, N16 0LH.
071-254-2266

SUBTERANIA,
12 Acklam Road, Ladbroke Grove, W10.
081-960-4590

THE SWAN,
1 Fulham Broadway, SW6 1AA.
071-385-1840

THE TORRINGTON,
4 Lodge Lane, North Finchley, N12 8JR.
081-445-4710

● **UNIVERSITY OF GREENWICH,**
Thomas Street, SE18 6HU.
081-855-0618

UNIVERSITY OF LONDON UNION (ULU),
Malet Street, WC1H 7DY.
071-580-9551

UNIVERSITY OF NORTH LONDON,
Holloway Road, N7 8DB.
071-607-2789

UNIVERSITY OF WESTMINSTER,
104-108 Bolsover Street, W1P 7HF.
071-636-6271

UNDERWORLD,
174 Camden High Street, Camden, NW1 0NE.
071-482-1932

● **THE VENUE,**
2a Clifton Rise, New Cross, SE14 6JP.
081-692-4077

VOX CLUB,
9 Brighton Terrace, Brixton, SW9 8DJ.
071-737-2095

● **WATER RATS,**
Splash Club, 328 Gray's Inn Road, King's Cross, WC1X 8BZ.
071-837-7269

THE WEAVERS,
98 Newington Green Road, N1 4RG.
071-226-6911

WEMBLEY STADIUM AND ARENA,
Empire Way, Middlesex HA9 0DW.
081-902-8833

RECORDING

● **145,**
145 Wardour Street, London
W1V 3TB.
071-734-5784

2001,
19 Ash Street, Ash, Surrey
GU12 6LA.
0252-336505

● **ABBEY ROAD STUDIOS,**
3 Abbey Road, London NW8 9AY.
071-286-1161

ADDIS ABABA,
389 Harrow Road, London
W9 3QA.
081-960-7141

ADVISION STUDIOS,
1 Montague Place, Kemptown,
Brighton, Sussex BN2 1JE.
0273-677375

**AIR STUDIOS (LYNDHURST)
LTD,**
Lyndhurst Hall, Lyndhurst Road,
Hampstead, London NW3 5NG.
071-794-0660

ALASKA STREET STUDIOS,
127-129 Alaska Street, Waterloo,
London SES1 8XE.
071-928-7440

**AMAZON RECORDING
STUDIOS,**
33-45 Parr Street, Liverpool,
Merseyside L1 4JN.
051-707-1050

ANGEL RECORDING STUDIOS,
311 Upper Street, London N1 2TU.
071-354-2525

ARIWA SOUND STUDIO,
34 Whitehorse Lane, London
SE25 6RE.
081-653-7744

AXIS RECORDING STUDIO,
3 Brown Street, Sheffield,
Yorkshire S1 2BS.
0742-750283

● **BBC TRANSCRIPTION
RECORDING UNIT,**
Kensington House, Richmond
Way, London W14 0AX.
081-895-6903

BTW RECORDING STUTDIOS,
125 Myddleton Road, Wood
Green, London N22 4NG.
081-888-6655

BACKTRACK PRODUCTIONS,
Acacia Cottage, Princess Road,
Thornton Heath, Croydon, Surrey
CR0 2QS.
081-683-2492

BACKYARD STUDIO,
Units 4 & 5, Willow Brook,
Crickhowell Road, St Mellons,
Cardiff, Wales CF3 0EF.
0222-777739

BATTERY STUDIOS,
1 Maybury Garens, London
NW10 2SG.
081-459-8899

BEAT FACTORY, 1
Christopher Place, Chalton Street,
London NW1 1JF.
071-388-7826

BEST SOUND,
114 North View Road, London
N8 7LP.
081-292-4266

**BILLIARD ROOM RECORDING
STUDIO,**
4 Welburn Drive, West Park,
Leeds, Yorkshire LS16 5QD.
0532-786671

BLACK BARN STUDIOS,
3 Dunsborough Cottages, The
Green, Ripley, Surrey GU23 6AL.
0483-222600

**BLACKWING RECORDING
STUDIOS,**
All Hallows Church, 1 Pepper
Street, London SE1 0EP.
071-261-0118

**BLOWINGHOUSE RESIDENTIAL
RECORDING STUDIO,**
Higher Penwartha Farm,
Blowinghouse, Perranporth, Truro,
Cornwall TR6 0BA.
0872-571575

BONE IDOL,
9 Denmark Street, London
WC2H 8LS.
071-497-8239

BRITANNIA ROW STUDIOS,
35 Britannia Row, Islington,
London N1 8QH.
071-226-3377

● **CABIN STUDIOS,**
84 London Road, Coventry,
Warwickshire CV1 2JT.
0203-220749

CASTLE SOUND STUDIOS LTD,
The Old School Park View,
Pencaitland, Scotland EH34 5DT.
0875-340143

CAVA EAST,
Albion Business Centre, 78 Albion
Road, Edinburgh, Scotland
EH7 5QZ.
031-659-6673

CHANNEL 1 RECORDING,
6 Jubilee Road, Reading,
Berkshire RG6 1NX.
0734-267362

CHARLOTTE STREET STUDIOS,
63 Charlotte Street, London W1P 1LA.
071-636-4840

CHISWICK REACH RECORDING,
Lamb House, Church Street,
Chiswick, London W4 2PD.
081-995-6504

CHURCH STUDIOS,
145h Crouch Hill, London N8 9QH.
081-340-9779

CLOCK HOUSE STUDIOS,
The Clock House, Keele,
Staffordshire ST5 5BG.
0782-583301

**COACH HOUSE RECORDING
STUDIOS,**
7 Richmond Hill Avenue, Clifton,
Bristol, Avon BS8 1BG.
0272-238444

CUTTING ROOMS,
Abraham Moss Centre, Crescent
Road, Manchester M8 6UF.
061-740-9438

CYBERZONE DIGITAL,
14 Wenlock Court, New North
Road, London N1 7QR.
071-253-8865

● **DAYLIGHT STUDIO,**
The Old Bakehouse, 150 High
Street, Honiton, Devon EX14 8JX.
0404-42234

DE WOLFE MUSIC LTD,
80-88 Wardour Street, London
W1V 3LF.
071-439-8481

● **E-ZEE STUDIOS,**
14-18 Market Road, London N7 9PW.
071-609-0246

EARTH,
163 Gerrard Street, Birmingham,
West Mids B19 2AP.
021-554-7424

EASY STREET STUDIOS,
45 Blythe Street, Bethnal Green,
London E2 7AW.
071-739-8887

EDEN STUDIOS LTD,
20-24 Beaumont Road, Chiswick,
London W4 5AP.
081-995-5432

**ELEPHANT RECORDING
STUDIOS,**
Basement N, Metropolitan Wharf,
Wapping Wall, London E1.
071-481-8615

● **FX STUDIOS,**
Chantry Mews, Upper High Street,
Sevenoaks, Kent TN13 1NZ.
0732-460515

FAB RECORDING STUDIOS,
15 Knoll Street, Salford,
Manchester M7 9EQ.
061-792-0203

**FAIR DEAL RECORDING
STUDIOS,**
1 Gledwood Drive, Hayes,
Middlesex UB4 0AG.
081-573-8744

FALCONER STUDIOS,
17 Ferdinand Street, London
NW1 8EU.
071-227-7777

FALLOVER STUDIO LTD,
Fallover House, Harlech Close,
Hulme, Manchester M15 6PF.
061-226-6128

FON STUDIOS LTD,
3 Brown Street, Sheffield,
Yorkshire S1 2BS.
0742-754644

● **GLASS TRAP,**
1 Priory Way, Southall, Middlesex
UB2 5EH.
081-571-4679

GOLDDUST STUDIOS,
14 Cromwell Avenue, Bromley,
Kent BR2 9AQ.
081-466-7435

GRANNYS LTD,
Basement, 346 North End Road,
London NW6.
071-385-1816

GRAPEVINE STUDIOS,
25 Vine Street, Brighton, Sussex
BN1 4AG.
0273-698555

**GREENHOUSE RECORDING
STUDIOS,**
34-38 Provost Street, London
N1 7NJ.
071-253-7101

● **HEAR NO EVIL,**
17 Baron's Court Road, West
Kensington, London W14 9DP.
071-385-8244

HI-LEVEL RECORDING,
Level Four, British India House,
Carliol Square, Newcastle, Tyne &
Wear NE1 6UF.
091-261-5869

HIT FACTORY LONDON,
31-37 Whitfield Streeet, London
W1P 5RE.
071-636-3434

HOME GROWN,
140 Brightwell Avenue, Westcliff
On Sea, Essex SS0 9EH.
0702-348894

HUMAN LEAGUE STUDIO,
50 Shoreham Street, Sheffield,
Yorkshire S1 4SQ.
0742-730300

● **ISLAND STUDIO - THE
FALLOUT SHELTER,**
47 British Grove, London W4.
081-741-1511

**ISLINGTON MUSIC WORKSHOP
LTD,**
44 Peartree Street, London
EC1V 3SB.
071-608-0231

● **JACOBS STUDIOS,**
Ridgway House, Runwick Lane,
Near Farnham, Surrey GU10 5EE.
0252-715546

JAYMAR STUDIOS,
25 Barrett Crescent, Wokingham,
Berkshire RG11 2JJ.
0734-788340

JIGSAW STUDIOS,
115 Old Lodge Lane, Purley,
Surrey CR8 4DP.
081-668-3457

JOHN MOUNTFORD STUDIOS LTD,
Park Farm, Hethersett, Norwich,
Norfolk NR9 3DL.
0603-811855

● **KING BEE RECORDING,**
76-80 Bridport Place, London
N1 5DS.
071-729-1595

KOH-SAN,
Avondale Coach House, London
Road, East Bathford, Bath, Avon
BA1 7RB.
0225-858028

KOLD SWEAT STUDIO,
The Basement, 127 Askew Road,
Shepherds Bush, London
W12 9AU.
081-746-2118

KONK STUDIOS,
84-86 Tottenham Lane, Hornsey,
London N8 7EE.
081-340-7873

● **LAZY MOON STUDIOS,**
Upper Brailes, Banbury,
Oxfordshire OX15 5BA.
0608-85360

LILLIE YARD STUDIOS,
6 Lillie Yard, 19 Lillie Road,
London SW6 1UB.
071-385-9299

STUDIOS

MCP RECORDING CO,
13 Davidgor Road, Brighton,
Sussex BN3 1QB.
0273-774621

MPF,
Bon Marche Buiding, Ferndale
Road, London SW9 8EJ.
071-737-7152

MAISON ROUGE STUDIOS,
2 Wansdown Place, Fulham
Broadway, London SW6 1DN.
071-381-2001

MANOR STUDIOS,
The Manor, Shipton On Cherwell,
Oxfordshire OX5 1JL.
0867-577551

MATRIX STUDIOS,
35 Little Russell Streeet, London
WC1A 2HH.
071-580-9956

METROPOLIS STUDIOS,
The Power House, 70 Chiswick
High Road, London W4 1SY.
081-742-1111

MILL RECORDING STUDIOS,
Mill Lane, Cookham, Berkshire
SL6 9QT.
0628-810788

MOLES STUDIO,
14 George Street, Bath, Avon
BA1 2EN.
0225-333448

MOLINAIRE,
34 Foubert's Place, London
W1V 2BH.
071-439-2244

**MUSHROOM RECORDING
STUDIOS,**
18 West Mall, Clifton, Bristol, Avon
BS8 2BQ.
0272-735994

NARK MIDI SUITE,
Flat 20, Whiteoak Court, Whiteoak
Road, Fallowfield, Manchester
B14 6UA.
061-225-0633

NETWORK MUSIC & MEDIA,
22a Forest Road West,
Nottingham NG7 4EQ.
0602-784714

NOMIS STUDIOS,
45-53 Sinclair Road, London
W14 0NS.
071-602-6351

NOVA STUDIOS,
27-31 Bryanston Street, London
W1H 7AB.
071-493-7403

OLYMPIC STUDIOS,
117 Church Road, Barnes, London
SW13 9HL.
081-748-7961

PWL,
The Borough, 4-7 The Vineyard,
Sanctuary Street, London SE1 1QL.
071-403-0007

PACE RECORDING STUDIOS,
1 Portland Drive, Willen, Milton
Keynes, Buckinghamshire
MK15 9JW.
0908-663848

PINK MUSEUM,
1 Hesketh Street, Liverpool,
Merseyside L17 8XJ.
051-727-7557

PRIORITY,
246 West Streeet, Sheffield,
Yorkshire S1 4EU.
0742-761117

PROTOCOL STUDIOS,
23a Benwell Road, London
N7 7BW.
071-607-9495

PULP RECORDING STUDIOS,
Oak View Stud Farm, Lombard
Street, Horton Kirby, Kent.
0689-836817

Q STUDIOS,
1487 Melton Road, Queniborough,
Leicestershire LE7 8FP.
0533-608813

RAK RECORDING STUDIOS,
42-48 Charlbert Street, London
NW8 7BU.
071-586-2012

RAVEN RECORDING,
Swaysland, Tanner's Green,
Garvestone, Norwich, Norfolk
NR9 4QR.
0362-850326

**RED BUS RECORDING
STUDIOS LTD,**
34 Salisbury Street, London
NW8 8QE.
071-402-9111

REVIVAL STUDIOS,
17-19 Motherwell Road, Carfin,
Scotland ML1 4EE.
0698-275581

REVOLUTION STUDIOS,
11 Church Road, Cheadle,
Cheshire SK8 7JD.
061-485-8942

REVOLVER STUDIOS,
152 Goldthorn Hill, Penn, West
Mids WV2 3JA.
0902-345345

RICH BITCH STUDIOPLEX,
505 Bristol Road, Selly Oak,
Birmingham, West Mids
B29 6AU.
021-471-1339

RIDGE FARM STUDIOS,
Ridge Farm, Capel, Surrey
RH5 5HG.
0306-711202

RIVERSIDE STUDIO COMPLEX,
7 Lower Mill Road, Clarkston,
Glasgow, Scotland
G76 8BJ.
041-644-5572

ROCKFIELD STUDIOS,
Amberley Court, Rockfield Road,
Monmouth, Gwent, Wales
NP5 4ET.
0600-712449

**ROOSTER RECORDING
STUDIOS,**
117 Sinclair Road, London
W14 0NP.
071-602-2881

**ROUNDHOUSE RECORDING
STUDIOS,**
100 Chalk Farm Road, London
NW1 8EH.
071-485-0131

SARM EAST,
9-13 Osborn Street, London
E1 6TD.
071-247-1311

SARM WEST,
8-10 Basing Street, London
W11 1ET.
071-229-1229

SELECT SOUND,
Big M House, 1 Stevenage Road,
Knebworth, Hertfordshire
SG3 6AN.
0438-814433

SONET STUDIO,
78 Church Path, Fletcher Road,
London W4 5BJ.
081-994-3142

SONICA RECORDING STUDIO,
100a Clapham Park Road, London
SW4 7BZ.
071-498-2990

SOUND ADVICE,
Unit C104, Faircharm Trading
Estate, 8-12 Creekside, London
SE8 3DX.
081-694-9484

SOUND BUREAU,
38 Datchet Road, London
SE6 4BX.
081-291-5914

SOUND HOUSE,
Forth House, Forth Street,
Edinburgh, Scotland.
031-557-1557

**SOUNDSPACE STUDIO
COMPEX,**
West Wharf Road, Cardiff, Wales
CF1 5DD.
0222-373707

SOUTHERN STUDIOS,
10 Myddleton Road, London
N22 4NS.
081-888-8949

SPIRIT RECORDING STUDIOS,
10 Tariff Street, Manchester
M1 2FF.
061-228-3072

**SQUARE ONE RECORDING
STUDIOS,**
Alexander House, Phoenix Street,
Bury, Lancashire BL9 0HS.
061-797-2908

STEAMROOM,
Poplar Baths, East India Dock
Road, London E14 0EH.
071-987-2738

STRAWBERRY HILLS STUDIOS,
47 Kings Road, East Sheen,
London SW14 8PF.
081-876-6445

STRONGROOM,
120 Curtain Road, London
EC2A 3PJ.
071-726-6165

STUDIO 125,
125 Junction Road, Burgess Hill,
Sussex RH15 0JL.
0444-871818

SUITE 16,
16 Kenion Street, Rochdale,
Lancashire OL16 1SN.
0706-353789

SULTAN SOUND,
51 Loveridge Road, London
NW6 2DU.
071-624-1816

SURREY SOUND STUDIOS,
70 Kingston Road, Leatherhead,
Surrey, KT22 7BW.
0372-379444

SWALLOW STUDIOS,
Congleton Road, Smallwood,
Sandbach, Cheshire CW11 0UT.
0477-500201

**SWANYARD RECORDINGS
STUDIOS,**
12-27 Swan Yard, London
N1 1SD.
071-354-3737

TARAN STUDIOS,
Unit F35, Cardiff Workshops,
Lewis Road, Cardiff, Wales
CF1 5EH.
0222-484298

**TEESBEAT RECORDING
STUDIOS,**
Castlegate Mill, Castlegate Quay,
Riverside, Stockton On Tees,
Cleveland TS18 1BZ.
0642-602839

TONE DEAF LTD,
The Lane, Gangsdown Hill,
Ewelme, Wallingford, Oxfordshire
OX9 6QE.
0491-641942

**TOUCHWOOD AUDIO
PRODUCTIONS,**
6 Hyde Park Terrace, Leeds,
Yorkshire LS6 1BJ.
0532-787180

TOWNHOUSE STUDIOS,
150 Goldhawk Road, London
W12 8HH.
081-743-9313

TOWNHOUSE THREE,
115 Thessally Road, Battersea,
London SW8 4EJ.
071-720-5066

VON'S RECORDING STUDIOS,
505-507 Liverpool Road, London
N7 8NS.
071-609-9450

**WALNUT BANK RECORDING
STUDIOS LTD,**
Walnut Bank, Lower Claverham,
Yatton, Near Bristol, Avon
BS19 4PU.
0934-834864

WOOL HALL STUDIOS,
Castle Corner, Beckington, Near
Bath, Somerset BA3 6TA.
0373-830731

YMCA RECORDING STUDIO,
East Street, Leicester,
Leicestershire LE1 6EY.
0533-556507

**ZIPPER NEW AGE
PRODUCTIONS,**
7 Oakleigh Park South, London
N20 9JS.
081-446-3098

REHEARSAL STUDIOS

● **A&R STUDIOS,**
Unit 1 Horseshoe Close,
Off Oxgate Lane, Cricklewood,
London NW2 7JJ.
081-450-0869

AP PRODUCTIONS AND PORKY PIG PA HIRE,
Fiddington Farm Estate,
Fiddington, Tewkesbury,
Gloucestershire GL20 7DJ.
0684-290181

ALASKA STREET STUDIOS,
127-129 Alaska Street, Waterloo,
London SE1 8XE.
071-928-7440

● **BACKSTREET REHEARSAL STUDIOS,**
313 Holloway Road, London
N7 9SU.
071-609-1313

BAK 2 BAK MUSIC,
Unit 4b, 11-13 Benwell Road,
Holloway, London N7 7BL.
071-607-4347

BANDWAGON STUDIOS,
Westfield Lane, Mansfield,
Nottingham NG18 1TL.
0623-422962

BASEMENT STUDIOS,
15-19 Park House, Greenhill
Crescent, Watford, Hertfordshire
WD1 8QU.
0923-220169

BERKELEY 2,
54 Washington Street, Glasgow,
Scotland G3 8AZ.
041-248-7290

BLOWINGHOUSE RESIDENTIAL REHEARSALS,
Higher Penwortha Farm,
Blowinghouse, Perranporth,
Cornwall TR6 0BA.
0872-571575

BLUESTONE STUDIOS,
Whitland, Pembrokeshire, Dyfed,
Wales SA34 0YP.
0994-419425

BOB MARLEY RECORDING STUDIO,
48 The Wicker, Sheffield,
Yorkshire S3 8JB.
0742-769676

● **CHANNEL STUDIOS,**
Channel C Business Park, Canning
Road, Stratford, London E15 3ND.
081-503-1665

CHRISTOFORI STUDIOS,
29 Marylebone Lane, London
W1M 5FH.
071-486-0025

COURTYARD RECORDING STUDIOS,
Unit 2, Gorsey Mount Street,
Stockport, Cheshire SK1 3BU.
061-477-6531

CRASH REHEARSAL STUDIOS,
Imperial Warehouse, 11 Davies
Street, Liverpool, Merseyside
L1 6HB.
051-236-0989

● **DAMAJIVE STUDIOS,**
Unit 5b Station Approach, Hitchin,
Hertfordshire SG4 9UW.
0462-457264

THE DEPOT,
Unit L, Albion Yard, Balfe Street,
King's Cross, London N1.
071-226-1356

● **E-ZEE STUDIOS,**
14-18 Market Road, London
N7 9PW.
071-609-0246

ENGLISH FOLK DANCE & SONG SOCIETY,
Cecil Sharp House, 2 Regents
Park Road, London NW1 7AY.
071-485-2206

● **FALLOVER STUDIO LTD,**
Fallover House, Harlech Close,
Hulme, Manchester M15 6PF.
061-226-6128

● **THE GREENHOUSE,**
Unit 16, Brighton Road Industrial
Estate, Heaton Norris, Stockport,
Cheshire SK4 2BE.
061-431-4127

GUITAR CENTRE,
126 Meadfield Road, Langley,
Slough, Berkshire SL3 8JF.
0753-542720

● **HI-FASHION MUSIC CO-OP,**
45-53 Brewery Road, London
N7 9QH.
071-607-9271

● **JOHN HENTRY ENTERPRISES,**
16-24 Brewery Road, London
N7 9NH.
071-609-9181

JUMBO STUDIOS,
387-389 Chapter Road, Willesden,
London NW2 5NQ.
081-459-7256

● **KING BEE REHEARSAL & RECORDING STUDIOS,**
76-80 Bridport Place, London
N1 5DS.
071-729-1595

KOH-SAN RECORDING STUDIOS,
Avondale Coach House, London
Road, East Bathford, Bath, Avon
BA1 7RB.
0225-858028

● **LA ROCKA,**
Cross Lane, Hornsey, London
N8 7SA.
081-348-2822

● **MAPLE STUDIOS,**
Unit 39-45, Grainger Road
Industrial Estate, Southend-on-
Sea, Essex S2 5DD.
0702-613066

MUSIC BOX REHEARSAL STUDIOS,
Unit 15, 98 Victoria Road, Acton,
London NW10 6NB.
081-965-0155

MUSIC CITY,
22 New Cross Road, London
SE14 5BA.
071-277-9657

MUSIC COMPLEX LTD,
Unit 5, Bessemer Park Trading
Estate, 250 Milkwood Road,
London SE24 0HG.
071-924-0166

THE MUSIC ROOM,
26 Monson Road, New Cross
Gate, London SE41 5EH.
071-252-8271

● **NOMIS STUUDIOS,**
45-53 Sinclair Road, London
W14 0NS.
071-602-6351

● **THE PLAYGROUND,**
Unit J, 44 St Paul's Crescent,
Camden, London NW1 9TN.
071-485-7412

THE PREMISES,
201-203 Hackney Road, London
E2 8JL.
071-729-7593

● **QUAY SOUND STUDIOS,**
11-15 High Bridge Wharf, Eastney
Street, London SE10.
081-853-2950

● **RED TAPE STUDIOS,**
50 Shoreham Street, Sheffield,
Yorkshire S1 4SP.
0742-761151

RICH BITCH STUDIOPLEX,
505 Bristol Road, Bournbrook,
Birmingham, West Mids B29 6AU.
021-414-1139

RITZ REHEARSAL STUDIOS,
101-112 Disraeli Road, London
SW15 3DX.
081-870-1335

RIVERSIDE STUDIO COMPLEX,
7 Lower Mill Road, Clarkston,
Glasgow, Scotland G76 8BJ.
041-644-5572

ROGUE STUDIOS,
Arch 4, Bermondsey Trading
Estate, Rotherhithe New Road,
London SE16 3LL.
071-231-3257

● **THE SCOUNDREL ROOMS,**
Beehive Mill, Jersey Street,
Manchester M4 6JG.
061-228-0357

SHOW ME STUDIOS,
Block C, Imperial Works, Perran
Street, Kentish Town, London
NW5 3ED.
071-267-4555

SOUND ADVICE,
Unit C102, Faircharm Trading
Estate, 8-12 Creekside, London
SE8 3DX.
081-694-9484

SOUNDSPACE STUDIO COMPLEX,
West Wharf Road, Cardiff, Wales
CF1 5DD.
0222-373707

SPLASH STUDIOS,
Pepper Mill Basement, Darlington
Street, Wigan Lancashire
WN1 1DL.
0942-322822

ST CLAIR TRADING LTD,
Kings Court, 7 Oxborne Street,
Glasgow, Scotland G1 5QQ.
041-552-6677

STANBRIDGE STUDIOS,
A23 Brighton Road, Near
Handcross, Sussex RH17 6BB.
0444-400432

SUNDAY SCHOOL STUDIOS,
Rotary Street, London SE1 6LG.
071-928-1960

SURVIVAL STUDIOS,
Unit B18, Acton Business Centre,
School Road, Acton, London
NW10 6TD.
081-961-1977

SWALLOW STUDIOS,
Congleton Road, Smallwood,
Sandbach, Cheshire CW11 0UT.
0477-500201

SYNC CITY,
Millmead Business Centre, Mill
Mead Road, Tottenham, London
N17 0QU.
081-808-0472

● **TERMINAL STUDIOS,**
4-10 Lamb Walk, London
SE1 3TT.
071-703-0347

TRACKSIDE,
24 Wallis Avenue, Southend,
Essex SS2 6HS.
0702-333453

● **THE VENUE REHEARSAL STUDIOS,**
37 Commercial Street,
Birmingham, West Mids B1 1RS.
021-643-5952

● **WAREHOUSE STUDIOS,**
Unit A01, Tower Bridge Business
Complex, Clements Road, London
SE16 4DG.
071-237-9570

THE WARREN,
Warren Road, Orpington, Kent
BR1 0BS.
0689-836817

WATERSHED STUDIOS,
Unit F4, Cumberland Business
Centre, Northumberland Road,
Portsmouth, Hampshire PO5 1DP.
0705-839224

WEEMEENIT MUSIC,
62 High Street, Barnet,
Hertfordshire EN5 5SJ.
081-449-5907

WESTAR STUDIOS,
1 Priory Way, Southall, Middlesex
UB2 5EH.
081-571-4679

WOOD WHARF REHEARSAL STUDIOS,
28-30 Horseferry Place,
Greenwich, London SE10 9BT.
081-853-4766

PA Hire

● **AB ACOUSTICS,**
Unit 10, Ely Industrial Estate,
Williamstown, Mid Glamorgan,
Wales CF40 1RA.
0443-440404

AP PRODUCTIONS AND PORKY PIG PA HIRE,
Fiddington Farm Estate,
Fiddington, Tewkesbury,
Gloucestershire GL20 7DJ.
0684-290181

ACE PA HIRE & SALES,
Park House, Bassano Street, East
Dulwich, London SE22 8RY.
081-693-1734

AUDIO & ACOUSTICS LTD,
United House, North Road,
London N7 9DP.
071-700-2900

AUDIO CONTROL,
26 Church Lane, Dore, Sheffield,
Yorkshire S17 3GS.
0742-369772

AUDIOTECH,
54 St James Road, Bridlington,
Yorkshire YO15 3PQ.
0262-672780

● **COMPOST PA,**
11 Page Moss Parade, Huyton,
Merseyside L36 2PA.
051-489-3384

CONCERT SOUND LTD,
Unit 4, Shakespear Industrial
Estate, Shakespear Street,
Watford, Hertfordshire WD2 5HD.
0923-240854

● **ESS PA HIRE,**
Unit 14 Bleak Hill Way, Hermitage
Lane Industrial Estate, Mansfield,
Nottinghamshire NG18 5EZ.
0623-647291

ENCORE GROUP,
Audio House, Penny Road, Park
Royal, London NW10 7RW.
081-965-2044

ENTEC SOUND & LIGHT,
517 Yeading Lane, Northolt,
Middlesex UB5 6LN.
081-842-4004

● **GEARHOUSE LTD,**
17 Penn Street, Birmingham,
West Mids B4 7RJ.
021-333-3390

● **HARDWARE HOUSE,**
West Works, Chalgrove Road,
London E9 6PB.
081-986-6111

● **JHE AUDIO,**
16-24 Brewery Road, London
N7 9NH.
071-609-9181

● **OASIS PA HIRE,**
61 Belmonth Road, St Andrews,
Bristol, Avon BS6 5AP.
0272-246221

● **PW ENTERPRISES LTD,**
Unit 11, Chelsea Fields Industrial
Estate, 278 Western Road,
Merton, London SW19 2QA.
081-646-6131

PANDORA PRODUCTIONS,
Unit 3, Impress House, Vale
Grove, London W3 7QF.
081-743-3984

PINK NOISE,
247 Upper Richmond Road,
London SW15 6SW.
081-780-9231

PRO AUDIO SYSTEMS LTD,
Unit M7, Enterprise 5, Five Lane
Ends, Idle, Bradford, Yorkshire
BD20 8BW.
0274-621242

● **SOUND COMPANY,**
2-4 Foulden Terrace, Foulden
Road, London N16 7UT.
071-923-4121

STAGE & AUDIO PA HIRE,
P O Box 133, Malmesbury,
Wiltshire SN16 9SZ.
0666-577725

STAGE AUDIO SERVICES,
Unit 4, Talbot Street, Brierley Hill,
West Mids DY5 3EA.
0384-263629

STAGE NORTH,
Unit 5 Woodham Road, Aycliffe
Industrial Estate, County Durham
DL5 6HT.
0325-314946

STAGE TWO LTD,
Unit J, Penfold Trading Estate,
Imperial Way, Watford,
Hertfordshire WD2 4YY.
0923-230789

STAR HIRE,
Milton Road, Thurleigh,
Bedfordshire MK44 2DG.
0234-772233

● **TASCO COMMUNICATIONS LTD,**
138-142 Nathan Way, Woolwich,
London SE28 0AU.
081-311-8800

TEN OUT OF TEN PRODUCTIONS LTD,
Unit 14, Forest Hill Business
Centre, Clyde Vale, London
SE23 3JF.
081-291-6885

TERMINAL STUDIO HIRE,
4-10 Lamb Walk, London
SE1 3TT.
071-703-0347

TOURCO CONCERT PRODUCTIONS,
Unit 4, Kent House, Kent Street,
Birmingham, West Mids B5 6QF.
021-622-1894

TOURTECH,
75 Kettering Road, Northampton,
Northamptonshire NN1 4AW.
0604-30322

● **WANGO RILEY'S TRAVELLING STAGE,**
"The Factory", Rear of 125 Leigh
Road, Leigh on Sea, Essex
SS9 2PX.
0702-480070

THE WAREHOUSE SOUND SERVICES LTD,
Unit 14, 50 West Harbour Road,
Edinburgh, Scotland EH5 1PU.
031-552-8194

WILLPOWER PA SYSTEMS LTD,
Unit 4, Acorn Production Centre,
105 Blundell Street, London
N7 9BN.
071-609-9870

WING SOUND & LIGHT,
354-356 Purley Way, Croydon,
Surrey CR0 4NY.
081-688-0440

● **YORKSHIRE AUDIO,**
537 Dewsbury Road, Leeds,
Yorkshire LS11 5LE.
0532-770952

Instrument Hire

● **ADVANCED SOUNDS LTD,**
259 Queensway, West Wickham,
Kent BR4 9DX.
081-462-6261

AP PRODUCTIONS AND PORKY PIG PA HIRE,
Fiddington Farm Estate,
Fiddington, Tewkesbury,
Gloucestershire GL20 7DJ.
0684-290181

ASTRA MUSIC,
Fairview Farm, Fiddling Lane,
Monks Horton, Ashford, Kent
TN25 6AP.
0303-812715

ATLANTIC HIRE SERVICES,
4 The Limes, North End Way,
London NW3 7HG.
081-209-1385

AUDIO HIRE,
2 Langler Road, Kensal Rise,
London NW10 5TL.
081-960-4466

● **BABEL SYSTEMS,**
7 Goldhawk Mews, London
W12 8PA.
081-749-8222

BLUE WEAVER,
12 South Parade, London W4 1JU.
081-994-1284

● **CHANDLER GUITARS,**
300-302 Sandycombe Road,
Richmond, Surrey TW9 3NG.
081-940-5874

CHILTERN PIANO COMPANY,
127 Station Road, Amersham,
Buckinghamshire HP7 0AH.
0494-727077

CHRISTOFORI PIANOFORTE LTD,
29 Marylebone Lane, London
W1M 5FH.
071-486-0025

● **DRUMHIRE,**
Unit 14, Triangle Business Centre,
Enterprise Way, Salter Street,
London NW10 6UE.
081-960-0221

● **EMPIRE DRUMS,**
Arch 64, Ewer Street, London
SE1 0NR.
071-928-1286

● **FX RENTALS LTD,**
Unit 3, Park Mews, 213 Kilburn
Lane, London W10 4BQ.
081-964-2288

● **GP PA CO,**
Unit D, 51 Brunswick Road,
Edinburgh, Scotland EH7 5PD.
031-661-0022

GIGSOUNDS LTD,
20 Rushey Green, London
SE6 4JF.
081-690-8622

GUITAR CENTRE,
126 Meadfield Road, Langley,
Slough, Berkshire SL3 8JF.
0753-542720

● **IMPACT PERCUSSION,**
120-122 Bermondsey Street,
London SE1 3TX.
071-403-5900

● **JOHN HENRY ENTERPRISES,**
The John Henry Building, 16-24
Brewery Road, London N7 9NH.
071-609-9181

● **LOUDMOUTH SOUND SERVICES,**
14-18 Station Street, Mansfield,
Woodhouse, Nottingham
NG19 8AB.
0623-653000

● **ML EXECUTIVES,**
138-140 Nathan Way, London
SE28 0AU.
081-311-8800

MX HIRE,
Old Snow Hill, Birmingham, West
Mids B4 6HX.
021-236-7544

MAPLE EQUIPMENT HIRE,
Unit 39-43, Grainger Road
Industrial Estate, Southend On
Sea, Essex SS2 5DD.
0702-613066

MUSIC BOX REHEARSAL STUDIOS,
Unit 15, 98 Victoria Road, Acton,
London NW10 6NB.
081-965-0155

MUSIC CONTROL,
Crofton, 8 Wilbrahams Walk,
Audley, Staffordshire ST7 8HL.
0782-723101

MUSIC LAB LTD,
72-74 Eversholt Street, London
NW1 1BY.
071-388-5392

● **OCTAVE CLASSICS,**
414 Essex Road, London N1 3PJ.
071-226-5759

● **PETER WEBBER HIRE,**
110-112 Disraeli Road, London
SW15 2DX.
081-870-1335

PIANO PLUS,
2-4 Ashdon Road, London
NW10 4EH.
081-749-2994

● **SAM THERAPY,**
222 Kensal Road, London
W10 5BN.
081-969-9394

SENSIBLE MUSIC LTD,
Unit 10, Acorn Production Centre,
105 Bludell Street, London
N7 9BN.
071-700-6655

STRAWBERRY RENTAL SERVICES,
3 Waterloo Road, Stockport,
Cheshire SK1 3BD.
061-577-6270

STUDIO HIRE,
8 Daleham Mews, London
NW3 5DB.
071-431-0212

● **TERMINAL STUDIO HIRE,**
4-10 Lamb Walk, London
SE1 3TT.
071-703-0347

● **VINTAGE & RARE CLASSICS,**
68 Kenway Road, London
SW5 0RA.
071-370-7835

● **WORLD OF SOUND SYSETMS,**
144 Fleet Road, Hampstead,
London NW3 2QX.
071-482-4090

Professional Audio Dealers & Distributors

● **AES,**
North Lodge, Stonehill Road, Ottershaw, Surrey KT16 0AQ.
0932-872672

AP PRODUCTIONS AND PORKY PIG PA HIRE,
Fiddington Farm Estate, Fidding, Tewkesbury, Gloucestershire Gl20 7DJ.
0684-290181

AGM DIGITAL ARTS LTD,
14-16 Deacons Lane, Ely, Cambridgeshire CB7 4PS.
0353-665588

AMI (AIRWAVE MARKETING INTERNATIONAL),
Northgate Place, Crawley, Sussex RH10 2BB.
0293-523441

ACE USED MUSICAL & STUDIO EQUIPMENT SALES,
259 Queensway, West Wickham, Kent BR4 9DX.
081-462-6261

AMPSOUND,
153a Victoria Street, St Albans, Hertfordshire AL1 3TA.
0727-50075

ANNOUNCEMENT AUDIO SERVICES,
45 Sturcombe Avenue, Paignton, Devon TQ4 7EB.
0803-527811

ARRAY SOUND TECHNOLOGY,
41 Upper Headland Park Road, Preston, Paignton, Devon TQ3 1JG.
0803-550957

AXIS AUDIO SYSTEMS,
3 Waterloo Road, Stockport, Cheshire SK1 3BD.
061-474-7626

● **BABEL SYSTEMS,**
7 Goldhawk Mews, Hammersmith, London W12 8PA.
081-749-8222

BONZA SOUND SERVICES,
Alfriston House, Guildford Road, Normandy, Surrey GU3 2AR.
081-749-8222

BOOMERANG SOUNDS,
43a Elsinore Road, Old Trafford, Manchester M16 0WG.
061-873-7770

● **CAV (CONTRACT AUDIO VISUAL),**
Unit F2, Bath Road Trading Estate, Lightpill, Stroud, Gloucestershire GL5 3QF.
0453-751865

CONCERT SYSTEMS,
Unit 4d, Stag Industrial Estate, Atlantic Street, Altrincham, Cheshire WA14 5DW.
061-927-7700

● **DYER AUDIO SYSTEMS,**
13 Molesworth, Hoddesdon, Hertfordshire EN11 9PT.
0992-468674

● **ESS PA HIRE,**
Unit 14, Bleak Hill Way, Hermitage Lane Industrial Estate, Mansfield, Nottingham NG18 5EZ.
0623-647291

ELECTRACOUSTIC LTD,
1 Hoxton Square, London N1 6NU.
071-613-0111

THE EUROPEAN OFFICE,
56 Albion Road, Pitstone, Near Leighton Buzzard, Bedfordshire LU7 9AY.
0296-661748

● **FENDER A&R CENTRE,**
Nomis Studios, 45-53 Sinclair Road, London W14 0NS.
071-602-6351

● **GB PA CO,**
Unit D, 51 Brunswick Road, Edinburgh, Scotland EH7 5PD.
031-661-0022

GO DIGITAL,
The Reading Room, The Street, Stowlangtoft, Bury St Edmunds, Suffolk IP31 3JX.
0359-31023

● **HHB COMMUNICATIONS LTD,**
75 Scrubs Lane, London NW10 6QU.
081-960-2144

HW AUDIO LTD,
174-176 St Georges Road, Bolton, Lancashire BL1 2NZ.
0204-385199

HARDWARE HOUSE,
West Works, Chalgrove Road, London E9 6PD.
081-986-6111

HARMAN AUDIO LTD,
Mill Street, Slough, Berkshire SL2 5DD.
0753-576911

HAYDEN PRO AUDIO,
Hayden House, Chiltern Hill, Chalfont St Peter, Buckinghamshire SL9 9UG.
0753-888447

THE HOME SERVICE (UK) LTD,
178 High Street, Teddington, Middlesex TW11 8HU.
081-943-4949

● **JOHN HENRY ENTERPRISES,**
The John Henry Building, 16-24 Brewery Road, London N7 9NH.
071-609-9181

JOHN HORNBY SKEWES & CO LTD,
Salem House, Garforth, Leeds, Yorkshire LS25 2HR.
0532-865381

● **KGM STUDIO SPECIALIST,**
18-42 Charlotte Street, Wakefield, Yorkshire WF1 1UH.
0924-371766

KGM STUDIO SPECIALISTS (WEST),
Unit 18, Kansas Avenue, Salford, Manchester M5 2GL.
061-876-0625

KELSEY ACOUSTICS LTD,
28 Powis Terrace, London W11 1JH.
071-727-1046

KEY AUDIO SYSTEMS,
Unit C, 37 Robjohns Road, Chelmsford, Essex CM1 3AG.
0245-344001

● **LMC (AUDIO SYSTEMS),**
Unit 10, Acton Vale Industrial Park, Cowley Road, London W3 7QE.
081-743-4680

LABTEK,
Unit 7, Denton Drive Industrial Estate, Northwich, Cheshire CW9 7LU.
0606-40447

LONDON STUDIO EXCHANGE LTD,
The Studio, Rickmansworth, Hertfordshire WD3 2XD.
0923-772351

● **MARQUEE AUDIO LTD,**
Shepperton Film Studios, Studios Road, Shepperton, Middlesex TW17 0QD.
0923-566777

MARQUEE AUDIO SCOTLAND LTD,
30 Erksine Square, Hillington, Glasgow, Scotland G52 4BJ.
041-810-3375

MERIDIEN COMMUNCATION INDUSTRIES LTD,
33 Greenwich Market, London SE10 9HZ.
081-293-0909

MIDLAND MUSICAL SERVICES,
11 Hayes Road, Wigston, Leicester, Leicestershire LE8 1RH.
0533-882108

THE MUSIC COMPANY,
Unit 3e, Hillam Road Industrial Estate, Canal Road, Bradford, Yorkshire BD2 1QN.
0274-370966

MUSIC CONTROL,
Crofton, 8 Wilbrahams Walk, Audley, Staffordshire ST7 8HL.
0782-723101

MUSIC LAB LTD,
72-74 Eversholt Street, London NW1 1BY.
071-388-5392

THE MUSIC ROOM,
26 Monson Road, New Cross Gate, London SE14 5EH.
071-252-8271

● **NETWORK,**
Unit 2, 12-48 Northumberland Park, London N17 0TX.
081-885-5858

NORTHERN AUDIO,
Greylands Studios, Mereside Road, Mere, Knutsford, Cheshire WA16 6QQ.
0565-830005

● **PD AUDIO,**
15 Stockton Drive, Chinley, Stockport, Cheshire SK12 6DG.
0663-750948

PF MAGNETS,
Unit 14, 11 South Avenue, Simpson Court, Clydebank Business Park, Clydebank, Scotland G81 2NR.
041-952-8626

PSP ELECTRONICS LTD,
Unit 22b, Abbey Manufacturing Estate, Mount Pleasant, Wembley, Middlesex HA0 1NR.
081-903-9061

PRO AUDIO SYSTEMS LTD,
Unit M7, Enterprise 5, Five Lane Ends, Idle, Bradford, Yorkshire BD10 8BW.
0274-621242

PRO MUSIC,
152 St Michaels Hill, Kingsdown, Bristol, Avon BS2 3DA.
0272-273765

● **Q-LOGIC,**
Parkmill, 95 Douglas Street, Dundee, Scotland DD1 5AT.
0796-472001

● **RMPA (WORCESTER),**
42 Lower Ferry Lane, Callow End, Worcestershire WR2 4UN.
0905-831877

RS COMPONENTS LTD,
P O Box 99, Corby, Northamptonshire NN17 9RS.
0536-201234

RAPER & WAYMAN,
Unit 3, Crusader Industrial Estate, 167 Hermitage Road, London N4 1LZ.
081-800-8288

ROWAT AUDIO,
864a Harrow Road, London NW10 5JU.
081-964-1588

● **SDL (UK) LTD,**
Unit 10, Ruxley Corner Industrial Estate, Edgington Way, Sidcup, Kent DA14 5SS.
081-309-5000

SSE MARKETING LTD,
Unit 2, 10 William Road, London NW1 3EN.
071-387-1262

SENSIBLE MUSIC LTD,
Unit 10, Acorn Production Centre, 105 Blundell Street, London N7 9BN.
071-700-6655

SHUTTLESOUND LTD,
4 The Willows Centre, Willow Lane, Mitcham, Surrey CR4 4NX.
081-640-9600

SILICA SYSTEMS,
52 Tottenham Court Road, London W1P 0BA.
071-580-4000

SOUND & VIDEO SERVICES (UK) LTD,
Shentonfield Road, Sharston Industrial Estate, Manchester M22 4RW.
061-491-6660

SOUND COMPANY,
2-4 Foulden Terrace, Foulden Road, London N16 7UT.
071-923-4121

SOUND CONTROL PRO AUDIO,
61 Jamaica Street, Glasgow, Scotland G1 4NN.
041-204-2774

SOUND DEPARTMENT LIMITED,
Unit 6, Murdock Road, Bicester,
Oxfordshire OX6 7PP.
0869-322666

SOUND TECHNOLOGY PLC,
17 Letchworth Point, Letchworth,
Hertfordshire SG6 1ND.
0462-480000

SQUARE DANCE STUDIO (2),
The Square Centre, 389-394 Alfred
Street North, Nottingham
NG3 1AA.
0602-414488

STACK ELECTRONICS,
17 Jubilee Close, Isleham, Ely,
Cambridgeshire CB7 5RW.
0638-780518

STIRLING AUDIO SYSTEMS LTD,
Kimberley Road, London NW6 7SF.
071-624-6000

**STRAWBERRY RENTAL
SERVICES,**
3 Waterloo Road, Stockport,
Cheshire SK1 3BD.
061-477-6270

STUDER REVOX UK LTD,
Studer Division, Foster House,
Maxwell Road, Elstree Way,
Borehamwood, Hertfordshire
WD6 1JH.
081-953-3533

STUDIO SPARES,
61-63 Rochester Place, Camden
Town, London NW1 9JU.
071-485-4908

SUNSET HIRE,
201-215 Jesmond Road,
Newcastle, Tyne & Wear
NE2 1LA.
091-281-4248

SYNTHESIZER CO,
9 Hatton Street, London
NW8 8PR.
071-258-3454

SYSTEMS WORKSHOP,
24 Church Street, Oswestry,
Shropshire SY11 2SP.
0691-658550

● **TS PROFESSIONAL AUDIO,**
7 Hove Park Villas, Hove,
Sussex BN3 6HP.
0273-822485

THATCHED COTTAGE AUDIO,
North Road, Wendy, Nr Royston,
Hertfordshire SG8 0AB.
0223-208110

● **VW MARKETING,**
13 Yew Tree Gardens, Epsom,
Surrey KT18 7HH.
0372-728481

VILLA AUDIO LTD,
Baileys Farm, Chatham Green,
Little Waltham, Essex CM3 3LE.
0245-361694

● **WASHBURN (UK) LTD,**
Amor Way, Letchworth,
Hertfordshire SG6 1UG.
0462-482466

**WEST LONDON ELECTRIC
(ACTON) LTD,**
9-11 High Street, Acton, London
W3 6NQ.
081-992-2155

WIGWAM ACOUSTICS LTD,
St Annes House, Ryecroft Avenue,
Heywood, Lancashire PL10 1QB.
0706-624547

WING SOUND & LIGHT,
354-356 Purley Way, Croydon,
Surrey CR0 4NY.
081-688-0440

● **ZONE DISTRIBUTION,**
Unit 6-7, 49 Effra Road, London
SW2 1BZ.
071-738-5444

Merchandisers & T-Shirt Manufacturers

● **ACME,**
66 Buntin Road, Northampton,
Northamptonshire NN2 6EE.
0604-720805

ACME,
11 Poland Street, London
W1V 3DE.
071-287-2472

**ADRIAN HOPKINS
PROMOTIONS LTD,**
24 Fulham Palace Road,
Hammersmith, London W6 9PH.
081-741-9910

ALBA MERCHANDISE,
7 Osborne Street, Glasgow,
Scotland G1 5QQ.
041-552-6677

ALEXCO,
94 Guildford Road, Croydon,
Surrey CR0 2HJ.
081-683-0546

● **B&M PRODUCTIONS,**
2 Lionel Street, Birmingham,
West Mids B3 1AG.
021-233-1573

BCL MERCHANDISING LTD,
78 Harley House, Marylebone
Road, London NW1 5HN.
071-487-4782

BRAVADO,
12 Deer Park Road, London
SW19 3TU.
081-540-8211

BRILLIANT MERCHANDISING,
130 London Road, London
SE1 6LF.
071-620-1383

● **CONCESSIONS LTD,**
6th Floor, Bedford House, 69-79
Fulham High Street, London
SW6 3JW.
071-973-8673

COOL MILLION LTD,
Unit 16a, 149 Roman Way,
Islington, London N7 8XH.
071-609-9191

● **DIRECT MERCHANDISING,**
167 Clapham Road, London
SW9 0PU.
071-735-2442

● **EVENT MERCHANDISING,**
199 Queens Crescent, London
NW5 4DS.
071-485-3333

FLOCKS PROMOTIONS,
The Old Piggery, Diss Business
Centre, Frenze, Scole, Diss,
Suffolk IP21 4EY.
0379-650707

● **GIANT,**
Glenthorne Mews, Hammersmith,
London W6 0DW.
081-741-7100

● **JMB TOUR SERVICES,**
38 Parkstone Avenue, Hornchurch,
Essex RM11 3LW.
0708-442042

● **MAP,**
46 Grafton Road, London NW5.
071-916-0545

**MUSIC MERCHANDISING
MANAGEMENT LTD,**
The Depot, Curtis Road, Dorking,
Surrey RH4 1EJ.
0306-742226

**MUSIC MERCHANDISING
SERVICES LTD,**
The Warehouse, 60 Queen Street,
Desborough, Northamptonshire
NN14 2RE.
0536-763600

● **NICEMAN,**
Ground Floor, Bedford House,
69-79 Fulham High Street, London
SW6 3JW.
071-973-8585

● **PARK MERCHANDISE,**
20 Raleigh Park Road, North
Hinksey, Oxfordshire OX2 9AZ.
0865-248493

POPWORLD PROMOTIONS,
94 Guildford Road, Croydon,
Surrey CR0 1HJ.
081-683-2585

● **SCORPIO MUSIC SERVICES,**
Basement, 18a Pepys Road, New
Cross, London SE14 5SB.
071-277-6712

● **WINTERLAND PRODS,**
37 Soho Square, London
W1V 5DG.
071-434-4503

**All facts in this reference section were correct at
time of going to press. If you wish to amend, add
or delete, please write to:
Virgin 1215 Rock Yearbook, P.O Box 1870,
London, W10 5ZJ.**

the year in... contributors

TH

CR

TD

HP

GK

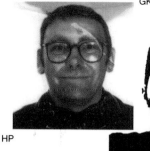

PT

Clockwise

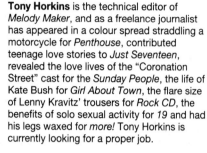

Tony Horkins is the technical editor of *Melody Maker*, and as a freelance journalist has appeared in a colour spread straddling a motorcycle for *Penthouse*, contributed teenage love stories to *Just Seventeen*, revealed the love lives of the "Coronation Street" cast for the *Sunday People*, the life of Kate Bush for *Girl About Town*, the flare size of Lenny Kravitz' trousers for *Rock CD*, the benefits of solo sexual activity for *19* and had his legs waxed for *more!* Tony Horkins is currently looking for a proper job.

Chris Roberts has written for love, money, *Melody Maker*, a host of other publications, and the hell of it. His twin sister cats are now 7½ years old and he sings for the band Catwalk, who he swears blind are huge in Germany, Italy and Holland. He is currently recording a "romantically machiavellian" solo LP.

Tom Doyle won his first Virgin Yearbook in the Scottish finals of the TSB Rock School competition at the age of 13 while drumming with heavy metal group Spearhead. They have subsequently split up due to "musical differences".

Three things about **Hannah Platten**: gin, chocolate and hot sunny countries. That's all.

Graeme Kay is a 38-year-old freelance journalist who has contributed to *Q, Select, Smash Hits, Empire, more!, The Sunday People* and *Hot Metal*. He lives in south London with his girlfriend, her son and a dog named Blade. Graeme's hobbies are painting and motorcycling, his favourite colour is cadmium yellow, his favourite pop star is Julian Cope and the historical person with whom he most identifies is Balou The Bear. As a boy somebody once told him, "there are special schools for people like you Kay."

Nick Duerden likes his music, so writes about it. A lot. A budding travel writer also, he lives in London with a cat called Chelsea (don't ask).

Zane was born in the East End of London in the late 60s. He has worked at *Melody Maker* for the past three years and is currently organising a glowing musical career. His favourite bands are Ramones, Kraftwerk and The Drum Club, and his hobbies include world domination, shopping and bazooki baiting.

RSP

PA

Caitlin Moran is 18 years old, *The Times'* pop 'n' rock critic, and presenter of Channel 4's music programme, "The Naked City". She would like everyone to send her kittens for her birthday, which is the 5th of April. That's the 5th of April.

Cliff Jones was conceived in the Summer Of Love and weaned on obscure jazz albums, The Beach Boys, The Beatles and Tiny Tim. His love and knowledge of obscure psychedelic and progressive music is legendary, as is his banjo playing. Currently putting the finishing touches to his first album – The Psychedelic Banjo Of Cliff Jones – he earns a crust writing for *The Face, RCD, The Observer, Melody Maker* and *The Earl Scruggs Country Banjo Review*.

David Davies is editor of *Mixmag*, Britain's best-selling dance music and club culture magazine. His idea of a good time is going to the Dorian Gray club underneath Frankfurt airport at six in the morning to hear a guy called Dag play records.

David Hutcheon, a regular *Time Out* contributor, has managed loss-making tours by artists from every continent and once accidentally married a Cambodian demi-goddess in a Chinese restaurant in Newcastle.

Glyn Brown is a freelance journalist who has also had short stories published in a number of collections. She has just completed her first novel, and lives in a dream world just off the Lea Bridge roundabout.

The son of a Welsh coal-mining poet, **Jon Wilde** was a Swansea City apprentice in his youth. Forced to give up football due to a painful toe injury, he has since divided his time between journalism, screenwriting, breeding and collecting glass animals.

Paul Lester used to teach Spanish to glamorous young northerners in a Sheffield Comprehensive School. Today, he is the Features Editor of *Melody Maker*, travels the world, stays in hotels and interviews pop stars. His ambition is to go back to teaching.

Lloyd Bradley compiles Mastercuts' best-selling Classic Funk series; writes for *The Independent, The Independent On Sunday, Empire* and *Q*; is humiliated by his children at Nintendo; is old enough to remember the last

glorious season when Arsenal won two cups; believes letting your dog foul the footpath should be punished by drive-by shooting; is metamorphosing into a cartoon.

Mal Peachey was the features editor of *Vox* magazine from November 1990 to August 1993. He is currently the rock critic of the *Mail On Sunday* newspaper and contributes to a number of other prestigious publications.

Phil Alexander is the editor of the world's biggest heavy metal magazine *Kerrang!* He has previously written interesting articles on barometers and turned down work in a pizza parlour. His ambition is to launch a magazine called *Loser* which would feature sections on car boot sales and kitchen decay. He currently lives in south London surrounded by a 12-year-old stereo and vinyl. He is the world's only known Heavy Metal mod.

Author of Carlton Books' The Blues Story, **Roger St Pierre** has contributed to *Blues & Soul* magazine since 1966, and handled press promotion in the UK for James Brown, Marvin Gaye and The Jacksons. His writings have appeared in *NME, Record Mirror* and *The Times*.

Simon Williams is a reviews editor at *New Musical Express*. He DJs regularly at the groovy and popular Smashed club and has been seen on television typing whilst drunk. While he balks at the phrase 'Indie Guru', his energy and enthusiasm are legendary. Except when he's a bit tired.

Sylvia Patterson is a freelance music journalist specialising in pop. Jon Bon Jovi once called her "a kooky chic". Marti Pellow from Wet Wet Wet once called her "a fucking bitch". Neneh Cherry once called her "the voice of sanity". She drinks vodka.

Paul Trynka is editor of *Rock CD* magazine, was founding editor of *The Guitar Magazine*, and has also written for *Melody Maker, Elle, The Face* and *Wire*. He is editor of the Virgin/Design Museum book The Electric Guitar, and is curator of The Design Museum's forthcoming exhibition on the sound and history of the electric guitar. And it's all thanks to that wonderful man Tony Horkins.

Z

CM

CJ

DD

DH

GK

MP

LB

PL

JW

GB